THE Revolutionary Mystique AND Terrorism IN Contemporary Italy

THE Revolutionary Mystique AND Terrorism IN Contemporary Italy

SECOND EDITION

Richard Drake

INDIANA UNIVERSITY PRESS

This book is a publication of

Indiana University Press
Office of Scholarly Publishing
Herman B Wells Library 350
1320 East 10th Street
Bloomington, Indiana 47405 USA

iupress.indiana.org

Manufactured in the United States of America

First printing 2021

Library of Congress Cataloging-in-Publication Data

Names: Drake, Richard, 1942- author.
Title: The revolutionary mystique and terrorism in contemporary Italy /
    Richard Drake.
Description: Second edition. | Bloomington, Indiana : Indiana University
    Press, [2021] | Includes bibliographical references and index.
Identifiers: LCCN 2020050359 (print) | LCCN 2020050360 (ebook) |
    ISBN 9780253057129 (hardback) | ISBN 9780253057136 (paperback) |
    ISBN 9780253057150 (ebook)
Subjects: LCSH: Terrorism—Italy—History—20th century.
Classification: LCC HV6433.I8 D73 2021 (print) | LCC HV6433.I8
    (ebook) | DDC 363.3250945/09045—dc23
LC record available at https://lccn.loc.gov/2020050359
LC ebook record available at https://lccn.loc.gov/2020050360

In homage to Gaetano Mosca, whose
Elementi di Scienza Politica was the one treatise of political theory
I had to read all the way through in order to write this book.

Every age and every society has a cherished lore and will draw on it in season and out of season.

L. B. Namier

Contents

Illustrations are on pages 59–62

Introduction for the Second Edition

Between 1969 and 1988, the so-called years of lead in Italy, the country suffered from the worst outbreak of terrorist violence in the industrialized world. According to the Italian Association for Victims of Terrorism website (www.vittimeterrorismo.it/memorie/memorie .htm), terrorists killed 428 people and wounded some 2,000 more in 14,615 attacks. This same source notes, however, that a precise and reliable accounting for all the victims is still not to be had. Indeed, statistics for the terror in Italy vary from source to source. Not all acts of violence in this period were claimed by the groups that perpetrated them, making it impossible to determine the responsibility for every case or whether the involvement of political motives associated with terrorist violence could be presumed. It is unlikely that a definitive tally ever will be forthcoming.

Yet numbers alone do not convey the true significance of the years of lead. Day after day, newspaper headlines and television news reports related shocking accounts of kidnappings, mutilations, assassinations, and mass terror bombings. Among the killed and wounded were judges, politicians, factory executives, union officials, journalists, policemen, military officers, prison guards, and university professors. For twenty years, Italy presented a unique spectacle to the world: an advanced Western nation unable to maintain even a semblance of public order by the usual democratic methods employed by other capitalist societies. To tens of thousands of Italian activists and sympathizers, the mystique of revolution justified the bombing and shooting spree against a democratic establishment that to them had no moral legitimacy at all. The government and financial scandals of the 1990s known as *Tangentopoli* (Kickback City) would reveal that the country's power structure did reek of corruption. For revolutionaries of the Right and Left, however, the primordial fault of the system lay not in ethical irregularities but in its intrinsic nature. The system could not be reformed. Violence alone would suffice as the means of liberating the Italian people from their enslavement by the most exploitative and destructive ruling class in all history.

In writing this book, I wanted to explain why it had been Italy's fate to set such a gruesome record in the years of lead. As always in the writing of history, the first question was where to begin. I found in newspaper accounts, court records, and parliamentary commission reports the basic outlines of the sanguinary story. For people who think of Italy as the eternally pleasing and carefree land of *dolce far niente*, the prolonged spate of terrorist attacks seemed utterly out of place. Those with a deeper sense of Italian history would have been less surprised by the violence.

The book's epigraph, L. B. Namier's "Every age and every society has a cherished lore and will draw on it in season and out of season," provided me with the governing conception for the work that I wanted to do. The terrorists came from the communist left and the neo-fascist right. A cherished lore of revolution long had existed in both these Italian political traditions. Fascism was conceived in Italy and carried to triumph there in that ideology's pioneering regime. Radically anti-liberal and anti-socialist, fascism had a long history of violent episodes in its acquisition and retention of political power. When the regime of Benito Mussolini fell, fascism did not disappear. It survived in a postwar neo-fascist movement that sought to maintain his legacy and to adapt it as an instrument of struggle against both the pro-American Christian Democratic establishment and the Soviet-aligned Communist Party. The neo-fascist movement included moderates and radicals. Among the latter were to be found fanatics eager for violence.

The Marxist revolutionary tradition went back even farther in Italian history. It began with a group of nineteenth-century intellectuals and activists who imported their ideology from Marx himself and his political heirs in Russia. I related their story in a subsequent book, *Apostles and Agitators: Italy's Marxist Revolutionary Tradition* (2003). Most of them were southerners, and the desperate poverty of that region figured prominently in the radical political choices they made. As one of them asked at the time, who in Italy with a heart and a mind could be other than a revolutionary. By the time of the First World War, revolutionary Marxism had become a national phenomenon. The epochal success of the Bolshevik Revolution in 1917 led to the creation of the Italian Communist Party, which defined itself in opposition to the Socialists as the country's authentic party of revolution. Throughout its history, the Communist Party would have an umbilical relationship with the Soviet Union.

When I wrote this book in the late 1980s, I had no more idea than the Central Intelligence Agency (CIA) did that the Soviet Union and its entourage of communist client states and parties stood on the verge of oblivion. Only two years after the book's 1989 publication, the Soviet Union went out of existence, leaving the United States with its entourage of client states and parties as the world's lone superpower. Communism, which throughout the Cold War loomed as the chief alternative to the American consumer capitalist way of life, suddenly had become an exhibit for the museum. For the Cold War's victors, the end of history seemed to be at hand, with the American political and economic model triumphant as the way, the truth, and the life for all mankind.

The post–Cold War period proved to be politically disorienting for the Italians. The Communist Party, the largest such organization in Europe outside the Iron Curtain, disappeared almost overnight. The Italian left has been in a state of suspended animation ever since. With the propulsive ideological force of Marxism almost entirely missing now in Italian political life, the left has struggled in vain to define itself anew. The faction-ridden and ideologically rudderless Democratic Party, an heir many times removed from the old Communist Party, is the chief example in Italian politics today of the left's identity crisis. Communism's other political heirs barely register in polling data.

For the moment, the revolutionary mystique of communism that I sought to portray in this book has subsided into politically impotent nostalgia for diehards on the radical left. Virtually everyone else in Italian public life today looks elsewhere for political and intellectual inspiration. At the time of the events in this book, though, "living the revolution" had much broader support in Italian society than appearances today would indicate. Then vast numbers of radical students and factory workers joined or supported militant extra-parliamentary left groups, such as Lotta Continua, which was far to the left of the official Communist Party and fiercely calling for revolutionary violence. The extra-parliamentary left claimed to be carrying on the revolutionary tradition that had been abandoned by the increasingly moderate Communists. That tradition called for the violent overthrow of corporate capitalism and the military support structure for it supplied mainly by the United States. To Marxist-Leninist radicals, American-style democratic freedom was verbal camouflage for a vampire-like economic system in which the rich slaked their thirst for profits with the lifeblood of the poor. The Red Brigades and Prima Linea, the two most famous and active terrorist groups, filled their communications with just this kind of extra-parliamentary left rhetoric and imagery, as did the Collettivi Politici Veneti per il Potere Operaio, Azione Rivoluzionaria, Nuclei Armati Proletari, and more than a dozen other major organizations on the left calling for the revolutionary destruction of the capitalist order in Italy. Many smaller armed bands with the same ideological goals contributed to the mayhem.

In thinking about the ways in which radical ideologies fueled Italian terrorism, I benefited from Eric Hoffer's reminder in *The True Believer* about the role played by men of words who influence men of action. He had observed connections throughout history between intellectual theorists and revolutionary movements. Individuals who articulated grievances against the prevailing order of things and inspired alternative visions of society and the world had been catalysts for the true believers of every age. A rich theoretical literature, which I discuss in the book, added some necessary refinements to Hoffer's method of understanding radical politics. He had formulated a shorthand way of noting relationships expressed with magisterial authority and amplitude by Alexis de Tocqueville in *The Old Régime and the French Revolution*. For Tocqueville, "the vapourings of the littèrateurs" had created the essential precondition of 1789 by furnishing the men of action who led the French Revolution with the "abstract words, gaudy flowers of speech, sonorous clichés, and literary turns of phrase" that led straight to the storming of the Bastille and the carnage of the Terror. The original introduction traces the line of historical descent from Tocqueville to the other theorists who guided my approach in understanding Italian terrorism, most importantly Karl Mannheim, the *Annales* historians, and Max Weber.

I found in Raniero Panzieri and Toni Negri two proponents of the Marxist-Leninist revolutionary tradition who exerted a pervasive influence on the radical left in Italy. In opposition to the stated commitment of the Communist Party to a completely legal non-revolutionary political strategy, Panzieri, who would die at the age of forty-three in 1964, called for a return to authentic Marxist-Leninism by which he meant the revolutionary termination of the capitalist system and its replacement by communism. Negri entered Panzieri's *Quaderni rossi* orbit and then, as the chief theorist and leader of Potere Operaio and Autonomia Operaia Organizzata, surpassed him for ideological fervor against the capitalist status quo. In the memoir literature written by former communist terrorists and in court testimony involving terrorism cases, these two names came up repeatedly. Writers cannot be held responsible for the ways in which readers interpret their arguments, but the history of Italian terrorism in the years of lead would be unknowable without understanding the political culture from which it sprang. Panzieri and Negri are representative men of that culture.

It would be premature to rule out the possibility of a revolutionary communist revival. Indeed, one revival of Red Brigadism already has occurred. In 1999, after more than a decade with little sign of revolutionary left-wing terrorism, a group claiming to identify with the strategy and tactics of the Red Brigades murdered an economist, Massimo D'Alema. In 2002, they killed another economist, Marco Biagi, and the following year, during a routine check of documents on a train, Emanuele Petri, a policeman. Authorities swiftly apprehended the policeman's killers, Mario Galesi and Nadia Desdemona, who later professed to be acting in the name of the "Marxist conception of the historically necessary Communist Revolution" and "the Leninist conception of the imperialism of the State." Specifically, they condemned the globalized economy as the ultimate solution adopted by capitalism for the disposal of its labor problem. D'Antona and Biagi had been prominently involved in reforms seen by the radical left as conducive to the requirements of the globalized labor market. By 2003, however, the new Red Brigades had been defeated and its leaders imprisoned.

The crisis conditions in Italy today normally would constitute an ideal setting for another revival of the revolutionary left. The economic meltdown of 2008 produced problems that landed Italy in the worst-case category of crisis-ridden European nations, along with Portugal, Ireland, Greece, and Spain—denominated in the press as the PIIGS. With varying degrees of success, Portugal, Ireland, and Spain overcame the crisis. Italy never overcame it. The Greek situation continues to be the worst of these cases. Italy's extant plight, however, poses the greatest European challenge to the economic stability of the world. Alone among the PIIGS, Italy is a G7 country. The failure of an advanced industrial economy like Italy's would introduce unimaginably severe distortions into the international system.

The foremost concern for Italians today remains the economic crisis involving a national unemployment rate that has hovered in recent years between 10 and 12 percent, with young people the hardest hit, especially in the chronically depressed south. Under the auspices of economic globalization, much of the country's manufacturing base has been outsourced. Hatred of the economic and political institutions responsible for the finance-driven economic order has fueled the internationally active Black Bloc anarchist movement. In Italy, violent protests by anarchists against the World Bank, the International Monetary Fund, the European Union, and G7 conference meetings are commonplace. A group called the Federazione Anarchica Informale has mailed package bombs to banks and politicians. Claiming inspiration from a father of violent anarchism Mikhail Bakunin, they have as mottoes, "War on the Europe of bankers, death to the bloodsuckers who govern us" and "Eat the rich." Sympathy for their opposition to economic globalization, if not for their methods, links them to a broad spectrum of dissident political opinion, left and right.

Not only the machinations of high finance but also developments in technology contribute to convictions prevalent on the far left that working people are being prepared for their liquidation. Advances in the computerization of the workplace and robotics have eliminated many jobs. The replacement of workers by machines has only begun, making future prospects for working-class people seem hopeless, in keeping with Marxist predictions about the sinister end game of corporate capitalism. One of sociologist Domenico De Masi's consultant authorities in *Lavoro 2025: Il futuro dell'occupazione (e della disoccupazione)* fears that with the structural decline of agriculture and industry, coupled with the likely erosion of even service economy jobs, Italy's fate is to be that of "a theme park for rich foreigners." The question of how a democratic society can be maintained without the secure economic foundation provided by stable and decently remunerated employment does not find an answer in this deeply troubling compilation of interviews with leading Italian experts. The *reddito di cittadinanza* policy of a guaranteed income proposed by many Italian politicians possesses at most stopgap possibilities. It does not address either the psychological need for meaningful work underscored by Thorstein Veblen in *The Work Instinct* or the abiding dilemmas in capitalism of wealth inequality, now at the runaway stage described by Thomas Piketty in *Capital in the Twenty First-Century*.

The Five Star Movement (M5S), the biggest winner in the March 4, 2018, election and the foremost proponent in Italian politics of the guaranteed income idea, commissioned De Masi's 2017 study of Italian employment and unemployment when it still appeared that this ideologically eclectic group possessed considerable left-wing potential. Pro-environmentalist and opposed to the economics of globalization, M5S leaders had a long record of objecting to American military interventions as a source of instability in the world. They had expressed admiration for the Hugo Chavez and Rafael Correa governments in Latin America. After the elevation in September 2017 of Luigi Di Maio as its leader, however, the movement veered steadily toward the center, issuing an unbroken series of reassuring notifications about its reliability as a steadfast ally of the United States and the Italian financial community. The 2018 election produced many marvels, but the resuscitation of the Italian left was not among them. For the past two-and-one-half years, M5S has shared power with other parties in forming the government. Now internally divided and uncertain of its political direction, the *cinquestellati* have blended into the morass of the status quo party system.

Political developments in Italy, as in Europe generally today, are much more promising for the right than for the left. The rise of nativist movements and parties now defines European politics. By comparison, the left has an exiguous hold on public attention. Virtually every one of the rising anti-establishment personalities stands for one version or another of the right-wing populism that fueled Donald Trump's victorious 2016 presidential campaign in the United States. For a few years, Labour's Jeremy Corbyn in the United Kingdom commanded interest as the main exception to the rule of contemporary European anti-establishment politics, but the party's crushing defeat in the 2019 general election drove him from power. Matteo Salvini, leader of the anti-immigrant Lega Party, has used the slogan, in English, "Go, Donald." The United Kingdom Independence Party's Nigel Farage took to the campaign trail for Trump in the United States for the 2016 presidential election. Marine Le Pen of the National Front wrote to him after his victory, "Congratulations to the new president of the United States Donald Trump and to the free American people!"—as if to say that they had not been free before. Germany's anti-immigrant Alternative für Deutschland also celebrated Trump's victory, as did numerous other similarly minded parties in Europe. Still adhering to its leftist positions on the environment and globalization, M5S is not such a party. Nevertheless, in its anti-immigrant and anti-European Union fervor the movement shares some of the convictions of the populist right. Beppe Grillo, the founding father of M5S and long its public face, expressed his preference for Trump over Hillary Clinton, viewed by him as a paramount human symbol of the degraded transnational oligarchy that with the utmost woe for mankind rules the world.

In 2014, at a conference in the Vatican, the then relatively little-known executive chair of the far-right Breitbart News, Steve Bannon, cited Julius Evola as an important catalyst for certain traditionalist principles that he admired and wanted to promote. Evola had been an important figure in *The Revolutionary Mystique and Terrorism in Contemporary Italy*. Like Panzieri and Negri, he had served as a man of words during the years of lead, only on the right. I found the same kind of intellectual connections between Evola and the extra-parliamentary right that had existed between Panzieri and Negri and the extra-parliamentary left. As the *maestro segreto* of post–World War II neo-fascism, he had been a cult figure first in Italy and then for like-minded groups across Europe. His many books were required reading for the "children of the sun" who aspired to rise from the ruins of contemporary Western society, as they saw it. Some Evola-inspired radicals in Ordine Nuovo surfaced as protagonists in the so-called strategy of tension that included the horrific right-wing terror bombings of the 1960s, 1970s, and 1980s.

Although Bannon's and Trump's politics have almost nothing in common with Evola's, the mere mention of his notorious name and its repetition two years later in the *New York Times* achieved what I had failed to do with my book: introduce the foremost intellectual figure in neo-fascism to the mainstream American audience. In 2016, Bannon took over as the chief executive of the Trump presidential campaign. After the election, he was made chief strategist and senior counselor to the President-elect. The reference to Evola took on added significance in the public mind with the dawning awareness of Bannon's proximity to power. For an understanding of Bannon's world view and, possibly, its influence on Trump, people would be best advised to watch his 2010 film, *Generation Zero*. It is a paean to the mystique of American exceptionalism. For Bannon, America once had been great because of its dedication to free-market economics and its devotion to Judeo-Christian values. The country could be great again, provided it overcame its progressive liberal aberrations and returned to the twin pillars of its true national creed.

As a self-described Nietzschean super-fascist, Evola might not be an author one would expect Bannon to cite. Evola attacked American culture precisely because it was the supreme embodiment of the worst elements in free-market capitalism and Judeo-Christian values. He could scarcely imagine a worse destiny for Europe than an imperial regime of American corporations and military bases, other than the Italian Communist Party's dream of a continent-wide expansion of Soviet-controlled people's democracies. To him, Italy's democracy merely constituted the external shell covering the country's real power structure, which derived its ultimate authority from Washington, DC, and New York City. At their extremes, the right and the left find common ground in a shared belief about the unparalleled evil of the American empire, while retaining antithetical ideas for replacement polities.

As Evola saw it, the American hegemony in Italy operated at levels high and low. He did not live to see the opening of a McDonald's restaurant right across the way from the Pantheon in the heart of historic Rome. Nevertheless, he would have understood the historical lesson that the placement of this hamburger establishment proclaimed as a conspicuous symbol of Italy's immersion into the mainstream of American consumer society culture. Early on, Evola had developed a sardonic view of the American cultural imperialism that had absorbed Italy and had transformed the Italians into a reliable customer base for Madison Avenue and Hollywood. The cultural crisis arising from Italy's transformation during the post–World War II period from a largely traditional agricultural society into a G7 country of Americanized high-consumption habits formed the historical context for both left-wing and right-wing radicalism. In addition to the importance of Evola's influence in stimulating extremist political attitudes among some of his followers, he merits study as a social critic, particularly for his withering examination of American culture, in *L'arco e la clava* (1968).

Evola's evocative writing about the imminent collapse of Western civilization is the one part of his legacy that does mesh with the world view of men like Bannon. In such neo-fascist classics as *Men Among the Ruins: Postwar Reflections of a Radical Traditionalist* and *Ride the Tiger: A Survival Manual for Aristocrats of the Soul*, he wrote as a latter-day Edward Gibbon, the eighteenth-century author whose *Decline and Fall of the Roman Empire* furnished a historical paradigm for understanding the current history of Europe. Just as a fatal poison had seeped into the vitals of the Roman Empire, so were death-dealing energies at work in contemporary Europe. When in *Generation Zero* Bannon depicts the dangers threatening the United States, there is a Gibbon-like tone in the film's commentary. He connects the evils emanating from Woodstock in 1969 with the educational and institutional failures that produced the economic collapse of 2008. Complete destruction will follow unless there is an all-American renewal. Evola's crisis rhetoric lends itself to Bannon's way of describing the plight of America today, even though the two men could not be more different in their proposed solutions.

Thanks to Bannon, Evola became news in America, and the Amazon.com sales of his books soared. In 1989, Evolianism was more of an acquired taste for people with arcane right-wing sensibilities than a subject liable to be featured in the *New York Times*. People in Europe knew of Evola's work, but few outside his cult cared about it. None of his books had been translated into English yet. His ideas had been consigned to the ghetto set aside for neo-fascist kooks who lacked the grace even to try to mouth the platitudes of democracy. Neo-fascist moderates did make such an attempt but always wanly. No one believed them. The entire neo-fascist legacy seemed fated to take a place in the landfill for historical rejects. Evidently, however, ideas seemingly out of circulation once and for all have a strange way of coming back in new forms.

The same historical process conceivably might unfold for the moribund Marxist-Leninist legacy. Negri remains an important intellectual, though no longer as a Marxist-Leninist. After his arrest in 1979, he went to prison, gaining release only in 1983 after winning a seat in Parliament as a Radical Party candidate. He soon fled the country for Paris and stayed there for the next fourteen years. This Paris period became a time of ideological change for him. Inspired by Michel Foucault and Jacques Derrida and in close association with Gilles Deleuze and Félix Guattari, he abandoned his Marxist-Leninist strategy and vocabulary in favor of a postmodernist approach to revolution. A Marxist hatred of capitalism continued to animate Negri's thought, but he now superimposed on the fundamental communist theory of dialectical materialism philosophical circumlocutions emanating from Paris. As Derrida would explain in *Specters of Marx: The State of the Debt, the Work of Mourning, and the New International* (1994), postmodernist deconstruction only could be understood *"in the tradition of a certain Marxism, in a certain spirit of Marxism."* At the same time, it can be guaranteed that Marx would not accept the theoretical addenda of postmodernism as improvements on his system.

Returning to Italy in the hope of becoming politically active in a renascent anti-capitalist movement and in promoting the cause of amnesty for his fellow political exiles, Negri served several more years of his prison sentence, which had been reduced through a plea bargain. While still in prison, he produced a series of neo-Marxist books, in the postmodernist manner, against global capitalism. He also wrote plays about the evils of capitalist power and the duty to resist it. These recent books, however, belong to a phase much different from the one that dominated his thinking during the years of lead when he thrilled the extra-parliamentary left nationwide with a call to revolutionary action echoing the rhetoric in Lenin's *The State and Revolution*.

Regardless of the capacity for both the left and the right to mount comeback efforts, the most important element in radical politics concerns not the radicals themselves but the status quo they face. Governments with the wit to maintain reasonable levels of employment, to avoid misconceived wars that end in disaster, and to foster in their citizens a sense of promise for the future generally do not have to worry about revolutions. Where that wit is lacking, revolutionaries might find a politically significant audience. Italy's current leaders, President Sergio Mattarella and Prime Minister Giuseppe Conte, receive high public approval ratings for their effective handling of the country's severe and ongoing COVID 19 crisis, but the far larger long-term issues of unemployment, income inequality, and immigration—the main constituent elements of what the Italians refer to as their *disagio sociale* (social distress)—await resolution.

The Italian status quo contains a prominent foreign element as well. For the past seventy years, the Italians have belonged in the orbit of American military and economic power. In addition to suffering from the domestic blunders of their own government, particularly regarding the globalized economy, they are vulnerable as citizens of a NATO country to blowback from the consequences of America's failed wars in the Middle East and Afghanistan. One of those consequences for Italy is a politically explosive influx of Muslim refugees, coming now in huge numbers from Libya where in 2011 an allegedly humanitarian bombing campaign by US-dominated NATO against Muammar Gadhafi's regime succeeded mainly in producing the current conditions of anarchy and squalor from which Libyans desperately seek refuge in Europe.

The chief political response thus far to unwanted Muslim immigrants has been the right-wing populist xenophobia that has reintroduced to Italian politics certain fascist concerns about the capacity of any liberal status quo to protect the racial and cultural integrity of the collective or to have any real concerns about it. Evola certainly did think in the fascist manner about liberalism as a wanton oligarchic form of government that would leave Europe defenseless and prey to American melting-pot delusions about race, but he hated populism in all its forms. Evola could not be bothered about the masses other than to think of them in the way Nietzsche did in "The Use and Abuse of History," the philosopher's caustic analysis of malpractice by historians: "first as faded copies of great men printed on poor paper with worn-out plates; second, as resistance to the great, and, finally, as tools of the great." Nevertheless, Evola's locutions of contempt for the capitalist status quo translate very well into the idiom of contemporary politics, even if his aristocratic policy ideas belong to a world entirely removed from populism, left or right.

Evola's increased public visibility in the English-speaking world comes at a time when Mussolini admirer Ezra Pound is receiving far more press in accounts of the radical right in Italy. CasaPound, a movement inspired by the American poet's pro-fascist thought, boasts more than twenty thousand members in a network of some hundred sections spread throughout Italy. Though successful in some local elections, CasaPound remains far down in national polls. With the sharp decline of the liberal left and the virtual disappearance of the radical left, however, fascist-style movements like CasaPound stand to gain momentum in a political context characterized by economic crisis, poverty, and unemployment, as well as by a backlash against European Union policies regarding open borders, massive non-European immigration, and human rights involving a perceived condemnation of traditional mores. CasaPound denigrates this human rights rhetoric as an open sesame for homosexuality and feminism, ever from a fascist perspective the paramount threats to the family and now to the last chance of white people to stave off the demographic catastrophe awaiting them in a world controlled by the banks and the corporations. Whatever may be said against this movement, its leaders have read their Pound.

The Marxist critique of capitalism has not even managed to produce a remotely approximate political version of itself with any standing at all today in Italy. One of the reasons for this failure stems from the Marxist-Leninist reign of terror that not long ago disfigured Italian life for more than two decades. Horrific as the neo-fascist terror bombings and murders were, they occurred infrequently over a long period of time. The Red Brigades, on the other hand, maintained during those years an almost daily presence in the news media. Their nearly two-month-long kidnapping of the nation's foremost political leader, Aldo Moro, culminating in their murder of him, traumatized the country as no other single act of Italian terrorism did. The Moro murder case continues to be a national obsession, with no end of conspiracy theory books and films dedicated to it.

In my own book, *The Aldo Moro Murder Case* (1995), I concluded, based on the evidence produced up till then, that he died because of the plot against him by the Marxist-Leninist Red Brigades, not by the treachery of the Italian government or the CIA, as conspiracy theorists variously have claimed. In several update articles that I have written about the case, I have found no reason to change my original conclusions, although the University of Padova's Angelo Ventura, a historian of great standing in Italy, has written about the need to keep the turbid world of Italy's *poteri occulti* in mind as pervasive forces in Italian life. He mainly had in mind deviant deep-state elements of Italy's secret services, right-wing Masonic lodges, organized crime, and the clandestine operations of outside powers. He acknowledged, however, that such shifting and ambiguous themes lacked a foundation in verifiable evidence for explaining with a historian's precision specific acts of terrorism in Italy. In my writing about Italian terrorism, I have tried to stay as close as possible to the evidence base in the findings and revelations in court records, judicial investigations, parliamentary inquiries, and memoirs.

Some defeats are irreparable in life and in history. It seems to have taken the full Red Brigade experience, including the complete fiasco of the New Red Brigades from 1999 to 2003, to uproot the revolutionary culture in Italy that for so long had proliferated in a luxuriant growth. To read the communications of the original Red Brigades was to receive a refresher course on the revolutionary principles of Marxist-Leninism. They presented themselves as the true guardians in Italy of that tradition and made a propaganda specialty of embarrassing the official Communist Party over its lapse of memory about what Lenin unmistakably meant in *The State and Revolution*. Red Brigade documents profusely quoted the passages in that book about smashing the state and breaking it up if one were sincere about wanting to overthrow the vile capitalist order. Election campaigns, parliamentary resolutions, and even the most democratically earnest lectures in the classroom and articles in the newspaper would not be sufficient for the task. The Red Brigades during the years of lead and then their successors twenty years ago succeeded in binding Lenin to their cause. He appears to have gone down in flames with them. It may be a long while before politically significant numbers of Italians invoke his legacy again.

Even before they met their decisive defeat in the 1980s, the heart had gone out of the Red Brigades. How many of their members would testify in court and in memoirs about the embarrassment and shame they felt for killing people in the name of revolutionary daydreams. It was a complete waste of time that left the status quo strengthened and, as events have proved, almost completely invulnerable to attacks from the Marxist left. The failure of Marxist-Leninism to resurface in Italian political life owes much to the desolating record of the Red Brigades old and new. Evola-quoting neo-fascist radicals do not have any kind of political momentum either, tied as they are in the public mind to the monstrous terror bombings of that period. Still, people forget, and if government policies scale the heights of criminal stupidity, the revolutionary mystique in one form or another will have its encore.

Richard Drake
10 September 2020

Acknowledgments

I could not have written this book without the cooperation and assistance of numerous institutions and individuals. The American Philosophical Society, the American Council of Learned Societies, Wellesley College, Princeton University, and the University of Montana provided financial support. The students and colleagues that I had in those schools gave me the opportunity to test my ideas on terrorism. It is impossible to thank all of these people by name, but I have special reason to mention Princeton's Arno Mayer, who gave me encouragement at an early stage of the project. For a strenuous and enlightening seminar on one of my book's chapters, I am indebted to Lawrence Stone of Princeton's Davis Center. Mario Miegge, a very youthful participant in some of the events I write about, was present at that seminar and helped to clarify my thinking about the extraparliamentary Left in Italy. I had a similarly rewarding experience in the University of Montana's Philosophy Forum, directed by Albert Borgmann, where I presented a paper summarizing my work.

Felix Gilbert, of the Institute for Advanced Study in Princeton, read the entire manuscript and gave me some excellent criticism. Performing the same deeply appreciated service for me were Alexander J. De Grand of North Carolina State University Raleigh, Charles F. Delzell of Vanderbilt University, Jack Reece of the University of Pennsylvania, and Roland Sarti of the University of Massachusetts at Amherst. The following scholars read individual chapters of this book: Marion Miller of the University of Illinois at Chicago, Alan J. Reinerman of Boston College, Clara M. Lovett of George Washington University, Thomas Sheehan of Loyola University in Chicago, Franco Ferrarotti of the University of Rome, Ronald Perrin and Linda Frey of the University of Montana. From their criticism, too, I derived much profit. I found gifted editors in Lauren J. Bryant and Kenneth Goodall. They made many useful suggestions to me.

From the experience of delivering scholarly papers I discovered much about the approach I ultimately took in this book. Some of these papers have been published as articles. They reappear here in either a completely different form or a substantially different one, but I want to express my thanks to all those individuals who took an interest in my work and published portions of it as I went along. "The Red Brigades and the Italian Political Tradition," based on a paper I gave in Washington before the Council for European Studies in October 1980, appeared in *Terrorism in Europe* (London: Croom Helm; New York: St. Martin's Press, 1982), edited by Yonah Alexander and Kenneth A. Myers. "The Red and the Black: Terrorism in Contemporary Italy" came out in a special issue of the *International Political Science Review*, edited by Mattei Dogan (vol. 5, no. 3, July 1984) and was republished in Frank J. Coppa (ed.), *Studies in Modern Italian History: From the Risorgimento to the Republic* (New York, Berne, Frankfurt am Main: Peter Lang, 1986); this article originated in a September 1983 paper that I gave at a Columbia University conference in honor of A. William Salomone. "Julius Evola and the Ideological Origins of the Radical Right in Contemporary Italy" was a chapter in *Political Violence and Terror: Motifs and Motivations* (Berkeley: University of California Press, 1986), edited by Peter H. Merkl. The University of California Press has given me permission to reproduce portions of the Evola essay here. It was based on two papers that I gave in 1982, before the Council for European Studies and the Department of State in Washington, D.C. A paper that I gave in 1986 before an international academic conference at the University of Aberdeen, "Contemporary Terrorism and the Intellectuals: The Case of Italy," was published by Paul Wilkinson and Alasdair M. Stewart (eds.), *Contemporary Research on Terrorism* (Aberdeen: University Press, 1987).

Librarians and archivists facilitated my work, beginning with the staff at Princeton's Firestone Library. I am especially indebted to Carol Tobin of that institution. Assunta Pisani, of Harvard's Widener Library, was another extremely valuable human resource for me. I can say the same thing about Clara M. Lovett during her tenure at the Library of Congress. The University of Montana's Marianne Farr expedited my interlibrary loan requests with impressive efficiency. I appreciate her efforts very deeply. No less generous and helpful were the Italian professionals I encountered in the magnificent libraries of Rome, especially the Biblioteca Nazionale, the Biblioteca Universitaria Alessandrina, the Biblioteca dell' Istituto di Storia Moderna e Contemporanea, and the Biblioteca dell' Istituto Gramsci. In this last library Bruna Conti deserves special mention.

Massimo Faraglia, the archivist of *La Repubblica* in Rome, gave unstintingly of his time and advice. The value of his contribution to my work would be impossible to overestimate. Professor Sabino Acquaviva, of the University of Padua, allowed me to examine his precious archive, and I benefited enormously from lengthy discussions with him during the summer of 1983. Professor Ferrarotti in Rome also proved to be agreeably patient with a foreign historian's questions regarding political violence in contemporary Italy, and my discussions with him during the same period confirmed some of my earlier intuitions about the subject. I wish to thank Professor Renato del Ponte, the director of the Centro Studi Evoliani in Pontremoli (La Spezia) for a most illuminating discussion in his home, on 13 June 1983, regarding the influence of Julius Evola on right-wing Italian culture. He very generously allowed me to peruse and to copy documents that were of the utmost value to me in understanding Evola's mental development. In the same vein, Mr. Renato Annibali of the Fondazione Julius Evola—located in the author's former residence, Corso Vittorio Emanuele 197, Rome—took time to acquaint me with the difficult ideas of a figure quite unlike anyone to be found within an American's ken.

In the writing of every book there is a category of benefactors difficult to label. These are the loved ones and friends who sustain a writer in his work. There are many people I should cite here, but I can only do justice to a few. I am thankful for the esteem and support given me by my colleagues in the Department of History at the University of Montana. Reverend John Baptist Frisoli, O. F. M., the pride of the Padri Penitenzieri Lateranensi at San Giovanni in Laterano, rounded up books and other research materials for me when I could no longer remain in Rome. My debt to him goes very far beyond this, however, as I hope he knows. Joseph Blacker, an American teacher in Bari, kept me well supplied with Italian newspapers and magazines. He managed to perform this service over a period of years, and I am forever grateful to him for his kind and efficacious concern. My stalwart friends Terry McGuire of Chicago and Phil Freshman of Los Angeles combined their passion for history with an affectionate interest in me and my book. I received as much from Robert Wohl, my mentor at UCLA. His example as a teacher and writer remains uppermost in my mind.

The assistance and inspiration of all the individuals and institutions cited here would have been wasted without the support of my family. My wife, Megen, and our son, Richard, Jr., have lived this book with me. I am sure that there were times when they wished to be spared such a trying association. I dedicate the book to them, for their patience and love.

Contemporary Italian Terrorism and the Limits of History

In the immediate aftermath of Aldo Moro's death, in May 1978, I began to think about writing a book on Italian terrorism. Until then I had been content to labor in the major field of my graduate training, nineteenth-century Italian intellectual and political history. Moro's violent end at the hands of the Red Brigades struck me, however, as an event of such profound significance for the people of Italy that I resolved to investigate it. This resolve was inspired by personal considerations as well. Several years earlier I had been honored to receive the first Aldo Moro fellowship for study in Italy, and that connection heightened my interest in his fate.

I wanted to know why he had been killed—a seemingly straightforward question. But the path of knowledge in this case led into a wilderness of political and historical riddles. To solve them it became necessary to recount the history of the terror that claimed Moro's life. More than this, at a very early stage of my research I realized that to understand the Moro tragedy it would have to be placed in a meaningful relationship with the historical themes of which terrorism, the distinctive scourge in Italian life during the past two decades, is a culmination. This realization changed the form of my study from an investigation of a particular episode to a more general inquiry. What began as the source of my interest in Italian terrorism became an element in a much larger story. Lacking the presumption to instruct the Italians on a phenomenon into which they possess a privileged insight derived from firsthand experience, I offer this work to English-speaking readers whose knowledge of the subject will be limited mainly to their recollections of occasional media reports on discrete events.

Contemporary Italian terrorism had its concrete beginnings in December 1969 with the Piazza Fontana bombing in Milan. After initially blaming the anarchist Left for this crime, the public perceived terrorism as primarily the work of right-wing bombers. That view began to change only in the mid-1970s when such left-wing terrorist groups as the Red Brigades and Front Line asserted themselves. The Bologna train station massacre of August 1980 signaled yet a third phase, characterized by a resurgence of right-wing terrorism. For the past several years both left-wing and right-wing extremists have contributed to Italy's toll of political violence. After 1982 there was a sharp statistical decline in terrorist acts as a whole, but Italy has not yet entered the post-terrorist era of her history.

My chronicle of Italian terrorism is incomplete. Not every death, injury, and kidnapping have been recorded, nor could they have been, for the same reasons of space and reader tolerance that keep the historian from chronicling all the bloody vicissitudes of any war. Yet fragmentary though the account by necessity is, it should be clear from what follows that since 1969 Italy has suffered a devastating terrorist assault on her political, social, and educational institutions. My aim is to show what actually happened during these years by analyzing the salient facts, dates, names, and ideas in historical order.

The story of how some twelve hundred Italians were either injured or killed through terrorism might not make a deep impression on the average citizen of the United States, a country that has a vastly larger problem with violence in general than Italy does. American society is, by far, the most murderous in the Western world, a distinction that makes a pair with our unexcelled record for rape.[1] Nevertheless, this American violence, grotesque as it is, does not possess a notably political character, and its implications for the survival of the United States government appear to be distinctly less menacing and immediate than Italy's revolutionary violence was for that country's government. To be sure, the American people have been victimized by political violence as well. With the Kennedy and King murders of the 1960s, political assassinations and assassination attempts became a regular feature of American life. In none of these deeds has it been possible, however, to uncover decisive evidence that would prove the existence of any conspiracies to overthrow the country's institutions. As far as we can tell, these desolating events were the work of isolated madmen and fanatics.

It is just the opposite in Italy. The terrorist casualties since 1969 have been the front-line victims of a revolutionary struggle—really of two such struggles, distinct yet convergent. Reacting to the fortunes of these conflicts, Italian leaders more than once in the late 1970s trembled for the future of their country. Except in the wake of the most spectacular terrorist episodes, the general public did not share this anxiety. Many Italians today recall how normal life seemed even during the worst terrorist violence. One wonders how normal life could have been, though, when in the fall of 1981, at a Washington conference on contemporary European politics, a distinguished Italian historian declined to comment on a paper dealing with the Red Brigades. He told me that it would have been too dangerous for him to do so. Moreover, to men such as Moro, the danger was real enough. Long before his own direct encounter with terrorism, Moro, ever the realist, thought that on the whole the people of Italy were much more serene about their situation than they should have been. He was aware, as the historian must be, that public opinion reflects public perceptions of reality, which are not always faithful to reality itself.

Taking Moro's deeper view in this particular matter, many Italian political scientists, historians, and sociologists have busied themselves in efforts to uncover the causes and the perpetrators of Italian terrorism. Nevertheless, even on the factual level terrorism in Italy remains a fundamentally mysterious phenomenon. The facts of the Piazza Fontana massacre are still uncertain nearly twenty years after the event, with the Left and the Right accusing each other of conspiracy. The same assessment holds true for most of the terrorist events in the 1970s and 1980s. We do not yet know all the particulars of the Moro murder or the Bologna train station massacre. What was the role of right-wing conspiratorial groups in these years, or of the Italian secret-service agencies, or of foreign secret-service agencies, or of the Camorra and the Mafia? The debate over the complicity of certain notorious intellectuals in left-wing terrorism is far from over. For a while it was hoped that the testimony of the repentant terrorists, the *pentiti*, would make the job of reconstructing these events easier, but the validity of their testimony has been subjected to serious doubt in Italy. Critics of the pentiti have asked, with undeniable logic, how much faith can be placed in the testimony of self-confessed kidnappers and murderers who may only be trying to avoid punishment. That extremely difficult question can only be answered on a case-by-case basis. It is likely that many years will pass before anyone will be able to write a complete history of Italian terrorism.

In fact, to follow these stories in the newspapers and to read the findings of the various parliamentary commissions on terrorism is to discover the limits of history. Unfortunately, history is not very useful in explaining its own raw materials while they are being formed. That is because history means synthesis—the interpretation of events in context. An historical context necessarily implies a concrete situation, a specific background, a definite environment in time, the limits of which are demonstrable. This necessary implication makes contemporary history, in a strict sense, a contradiction in terms, for the present is open-ended. The most intelligent and carefully considered thesis regarding a current event is apt to be invalidated and even made to look preposterous by a totally unforeseen and unforeseeable development.

Situated where we are in time, we still cannot be absolutely certain that we know the end of this story. That is an exceptionally important piece of information to be missing, and its absence condemns all interpretations of Italian terrorism to a highly tentative, provisional status. Until we know the sum we cannot assign a definitive value to any of the parts. Conceivably, we could be in a position analogous to that of analysts observing events in Russia during the late winter of 1917. To these analysts the February Revolution and its aftermath must have seemed the most momentous events in Russian history—and they were. Only the improbable appearance of Lenin in April followed by the completely unexpected Bolshevik triumph in October pointed toward the true character of post-tsarist Russia. Completely unexpected developments are not a peculiarity of Russian history.

Beginning in 1980–81 when the number of terrorist episodes went into sharp decline— a downward movement that has been accelerating ever since—many in Italy welcomed the approaching defeat of terrorism. More recently this defeat has been described as an accomplished fact. Nevertheless, the climactic act of eliminating terrorism continues to elude the country's law-enforcement officials. It is true that numerous terrorist organizations of the Left and the Right have suffered decisive military defeats, and the threat of terrorism to Italy's institutions, so real and immediate in the late 1970s, has clearly abated. There are three additional points to be made about these defeats, however.

First, as George Orwell noted, the most common mistake of political analysts is to assume that the momentum of the hour will be perpetual. But the assumption of perpetual motion is no more valid in politics than it is in physics. Another resurgence of terrorism in Italy cannot automatically be ruled out. It is to be hoped that right-wing terror bombings are over, but the most recent one at this writing occurred just three years ago. Given the history of previous lulls between such bombings, it would be premature for Italy to breathe a collective sigh of relief on this score. Moreover, for a full two years after the officially proclaimed defeat of left-wing terrorism in 1982, the government and the pentiti continued to issue dire warnings about the likelihood of new Red Brigade campaigns. These campaigns never materialized in anything like their predicted form, but it is well to remember that as late as March 1987 people were being shot to death in the streets of Italy by *brigatisti rossi*, the members of the Red Brigades. As with terrorists of the Right, it seems sensible to conclude that terrorists of the Left are not a vanished species in Italy.

Second, and an even greater source of danger than a resurgence of terrorism in the forms we have seen, is terrorist activity in new forms. For instance, since 1984 the involvement of left-wing terrorist groups with international terrorism in general and Middle Eastern politics in particular has intensified. During the late 1985 Palestinian terror attacks in Rome, culminating in the Christmas slaughter at Leonardo da Vinci Airport, the police thought that surviving Red Brigadists might have been involved. Certainly Red Brigade propaganda statements about the Middle East suggested the possibility and even the likelihood of an alliance with the perpetrators. The 20 March 1987 terrorist murder of General Licio Giorgieri in Rome encouraged further speculation along these lines. It now appears that the Red Brigades have joined forces with such Euroterrorist groups as the Red Army Faction, Direct Action, and the Fighting Communist Cells, all of which have established links with Middle Eastern terrorists.

Third, the well-documented connections between the Red Brigades and the underworld point to a united front of terrorist and criminal activity as an eerie twentieth-century mutation of the anarchist theories in the *Revolutionary Catechism* of Mikhai Bakunin and Sergei Nechayev. Moreover, right-wing terror groups have also formed alliances with Italy's criminal organizations. Terrorists on both fringes and criminals have a shared interest in ridding the country of efficient policemen, fearless judges, and capable political leaders. It is difficult to foresee what all the consequences of this contact will be—whether we will witness the politicization of criminals or, more likely, the criminalization of terrorists—but this difficulty is in keeping with the inadequacy of the means at our disposal to predict the course that terrorism will take in Italy.

Apart from our inability even to write a completely satisfying chronicle of Italy's recent political violence, the definition of terrorism is itself a subject of deep controversy. This conceptual problem is the crowning difficulty for those scholars and analysts who have come to be known as terrorologists. No definiton of terrorism can possibly cover all the various forms of state and individual or group violence that have appeared throughout history. That is because our understanding of terrorism is bound to be biased by our own cultural, political, and moral values. Obviously, any government establishment under physical attack from within is going to call its enemies terrorists, that is, individuals who employ violence illegitimately. These so-called terrorists will always view themselves as patriots forced to use violence to strike down a greater evil, which they will call state terrorism. The subjective character of terrorism is its chief trait. Terrorism, therefore, is much like pornography; everyone develops a personal understanding of what these two terms mean, but no one can offer a universal definition.

At issue on the subject of terrorism is a fundamental moral question: who has the right to launch a violent attack against an established order or a dissident group? There is no clear answer to this question. For example, most of us presumably would agree that the violent actions of the Red Brigades are morally wrong. Yet their rationale for terrorism is not different in principle from the rationale of the partisans in World War II or, for that matter, of the patriots in the American Revolution—that the so-called legally constituted authority is in fact a ruinous tyranny and therefore a legitimate object of subversion. Both the partisans and the patriots were denounced as terrorists or worse by the established authorities of their day, in keeping with a time-honored tradition in politics. Governments have always been only too eager to pin the most pejorative labels at hand on their violent opponents.

Certainly the brigatisti rossi see themselves as a new generation of partisans. They claim to be at war with democratic capitalism in the moral sense exemplified by the partisans during World War II. Expressly calling themselves the heirs of the Resistance, the Red Brigadists describe Italy as an occupied country under the effective control of capitalists, with Christian Democratic puppets performing the same role for their American masters that the Italian Fascist government eventually performed for Hitler. In their minds the historical parallel, despite superficial differences, is exact in almost all of its essential points. According to the Red Brigadists the only serious difference between these two struggles is that democratic capitalism remains a more insidious enemy than capitalism in its gross Nazi form. The democratic insistence that governments in countries such as Italy and the United States come to power through the will of the people and therefore should be granted a special dispensation from revolutionary overthrow is for the Red Brigadists a pathetic, self-serving fiction, which any Marxist worthy of the name should be eager to denounce and destroy.

Does this mean that the Italian terrorists of today who kidnap politicians and kill police officers should be compared with George Washington or Roberto Rossellini's protagonists in his classic celebration of the Resistance, *Rome Open City*? Of course not, although it would have been miraculous if either the American Revolution or the Italian Resistance had been entirely free of terrorist episodes, that is, of illegitimate or excessive or inappropriate violence. What war is ever without its terror on both sides? The question for each individual is whether or not this terror arises as a tragic consequence of a morally defensible cause. For anyone but the radical pacifist, violence itself is not intrinsically evil. In certain circumstances violence may be necessary and good to the extent that it challenges a greater evil, such as a regime of remorseless inhumanity or physical attacks on loved ones. The circumstances of the case should inform our judgment of it. Each episode of political violence must be studied on its own terms, neither dismissed with a moralizing wave of the hand as an act of terrorism—a word that by itself, given human nature and human history, is often misleading in a blatant political sense—nor draped in the flag as an obvious example of legitimate counterterrorism. Terrorists may be and often are monsters of psychopathic violence, devoid of all reason and mercy, but not everyone in history who has been called a terrorist suffers from these defects, any more than do the large nation states that wage conventional war, the morally privileged manifestation of human violence that established governments reserve to themselves.

Our judgment of the Red Brigadists, the partisans, and the American patriots should not then be predicated on their use of violence alone, but on the rationale for which they struck their blows. Precisely at this point our own religious, ethical, and political values will make us either sympathetic or not to these violent groups. Whatever judgment we reach about them will not obtain universal approbation for reasons of human subjectivity. Third-world revolutionaries such as Frantz Fanon in *The Wretched of the Earth* are right to draw the attention of Westerners to our strong tendency toward hypocrisy on the subject of terrorism. As one of Gillo Pontecorvo's revolutionary characters conveys in the film *The Battle of Algiers*, the West is outraged by the news of women surreptitiously setting off explosives in crowded civilian areas but has little difficulty accepting the propriety of jet pilots raining death down on terrorists, who are more often than not killed alongside innocent women and children. This example may help us to see how, as a rule, terrorism is the name we give to the violence of people we do not like or support; for the violence of people we do like or support, we find other names.

A prudent historian might want to keep away from the vexed topic of Italian terrorism. Semantic difficulties and uncertainty about many crucial facts remain formidable obstacles in his way. Nevertheless, this terrible crisis in Italy has a prehistory on which he can bring his skills to bear. If the concluding act of terrorism in Italy and many of its details are unknown and in some instances unknowable, the same cannot be said about all of its details or its origins. I seek to explain these known facts.

I begin with the events of 1969. Thereafter, no other comparable country in the West endured anything like Italy's experience with terrorism. To find out why that should have been so, I examined as much of the evidence as I could find in newspaper accounts of the violence, memoirs of both victims and perpetrators, documents of the leading terrorist groups and their government antagonist, books and articles by Italian experts on various aspects of terrorism, discussions with individuals in Italy who had acquired a first-hand knowledge of the subject, and information taken from parliamentary reports and judicial proceedings. I base my interpretation of Italian terrorism on these sources.

The same sources make plain the crucial role played by intellectuals in the history of this violence, and my book is in large part about the difficult question of terrorism's ideological origins in the mystique of revolution on both the left and the right, that is, the long-standing intellectual traditions in Italy of making violence "photogenic" by justifying and beautifying it.[2] The culture of violence, so alive and important in Italian intellectual and political life, cannot be avoided in our analysis of Italy's problems with terrorism. Karl Mannheim addressed this point in terms that are certainly applicable to Italy. He held that the intellectual and political life of an age—and Italian terrorism is about both—will be influenced not only by the socioeconomic factors and by the peculiar problems or experiences of a given generation, but also by the ideological possibilities that are feasibly open to a country's intellectuals and political leaders—what he calls the "cake of custom" and the "historical milieu" in a society.[3] The spirit and character of a people are formed by a unique historical environment outside of which their value structures, belief systems, and cultural norms as well as their particular patterns of interaction would remain unintelligible.

Mannheim's approach to history is augmented by the *Annales* historians, who have made distinguished contributions to our understanding of *mentalités*—the long-term cultural forms and categories—and how such forces condition the temper of society. We learn from them that each society has its own mental inventory of words, symbols, and concepts that are formed and preserved through long periods of time. These cultural schemes and principles become internalized and are held almost unconsciously by the members of a culture, providing coherence and meaning for certain ways of thinking. Every society is characterized by such habit-forming idea forces, which become categories of fundamental thought for its citizens. Their specific attitudes and actions are inevitably colored by some aspect of the collective mentality, which orders the past in a way that is comprehensible to the present without having to make these fundamental values explicit.

Thus, while a large complexity of factors bears on the situation of intellectual and political elites, the history of each country tends to foreclose some ideological possibilities and to sanction others. These distinctive modes of thinking that we ascribe, for the sake of convenience, to national character, Machiavelli conceived in terms of *necessità*, or the limitations placed on human choice by the society in which political decisions are made.

Modern societies of the West inherit several competing visions of the world, only one of which is dominant. Spurred on by these visions intellectuals engage in a range of activities, from debating to murder. In this way, discontinuity may be as important in the history of a culture as continuity. Some societies, however, are more fully integrated from an ideological point of view than others, with relatively little disagreement over fundamental values. In such historically favored societies the citizens can get on with the routine business of politics, family, and work no matter how turbulent life may be for other reasons. Acts of violently deviant behavior will be identified as criminal and lunatic, even though the actors may think of themselves as the revolutionary vanguard of one ideological cause or another. For Italy this degree of integration has not been achieved. Unusually potent revolutionary traditions exist on both the left and the right, each with a more glamorous history than that of Italian liberalism and each possessing both the potential for and a record of terrorist action.

The endemic weakness of liberalism in Italy has been an essential ideological precondition for that country's highly volatile, comparatively extremist political and intellectual life. This situation has resulted in vigorous socialist, communist, Catholic, and fascist traditions. They all offer channels for career advancement in the forms of party jobs, teaching and editorial positions, and networks of literary publications. Unlike the United States, whose political system is beset by difficulties peculiar to itself, the radical parties in Italy offer extremists practical incentives. To explain why that is so would necessitate writing a history of the country—and not just for the modern period.[4] A chronic imbalance in Italy between people, land, and resources, together with a long, tragic history of foreign exploitation and, after the Risorgimento, the failure of native elites to develop a hegemony by consensus, produced a culture in which the radical Right and the radical Left have been constant and, despite their shared antiliberalism, essentially distinct and antagonistic forces. They have produced highly influential ideological traditions, each with a hotheaded fringe liable to erupt in violence during crises.

It is notoriously hazardous to draw connections between political ideas and activities of different centuries. Obviously, as society changes, its values, ideologies, and habits change, too, but Mannheim persuades us that no country can ever fully escape its own historical character. While conceding the enormous differences between contemporary and nineteenth-century Italy, it remains true that there are historical precedents for Red Brigade-style terrorism in the extreme left-wing tradition of violently resisting the bourgeois status quo, just as the antidemocratic violence of such neofascist groups as the Black Order is a familiar theme in Italian history. Old tactics and modes of expression yield to new, but the chiliastic visions of the utopian Left and Right have been remarkably constant. The scholar Nando Dalla Chiesa noted in 1981 that Italian culture is marked by "the exceptional diffusion and abuse of the term revolution."[5] That is nothing new in Italy, where belief in revolution as the most efficacious way of adjusting society to desirable change has been invincible.

Perhaps the journalist Giorgio Bocca went too far a few years ago when, in writing about the Red Brigades, he argued that "terrorism does not invent but rediscovers, recycles, and readapts that which is already in the womb of the nation."[6] In fact, the phenomenon of Red Brigadism contains much that is without precedent in the history of Italian terrorism, principally a remarkable efficiency over a long period and skillful manipulation of the mass media. On the other hand, while virtually every segment of political opinion in Italy is anxious to dissociate itself from any responsibility for terrorism—even the residual responsibility of intellectual influence—it is difficult to believe that a phenomenon of such violent, bitter, and prolonged animosity could have arisen in an historical vacuum. Certainly, no historian writing today can afford to ignore Michel Foucault's cautionary statements in *The Archaeology of Knowledge* on the misrepresentation of history as the teleological unfolding of a grand theme.[7] History, we are told in this powerful, imaginative, and convincing book, is difference, not unity. And yet Foucault also asserts that within the endlessly varied patterns of history "continuities, returns, and repetitions" do manifest themselves.[8]

Indeed, throughout her modern history Italy has been the promised land of revolutionary thinkers and activists. It was not an accident that Bakunin, Marx, Sorel, and Lenin found vast stretches of fertile ground in Italy for their theories of class hatred and class war, any more than it was purely fortuitous for fascism to be invented and carried to triumph in Italy. The historical juxtaposition of desperately poor and exploited people on the one hand and constantly insecure elites on the other severely impedes centrist politics, as the annals of the Italian people convincingly illustrate.

Above all, it was Marx who set the tone for revolutionary left-wing politics in Italy. The idea that force is the midwife of history is not the whole of Marxism, but some people of action have appropriated this element of Marx's thought to rationalize their revolutionary deeds. Although Marx vociferously condemned anarchist terrorism, he had no illusions about the need for violence in realizing his own communist schemes: the revolutionary overthrow of capitalism, the estabblishment of a proletarian dictatorship, and the forcible expropriation of all private property. Revolutionary violence was the preferred Marxist means of freeing humanity from the unspeakable evils of capitalism. Nowhere is the explicitness of his revolutionary conviction more in evidence than in *The Civil War in France*, where he enlarged on the moral economy of Marxism: violence by the state warranted a violent response from the people, always provided that the revolutionary cause of the proletariat would be advanced by such a response.[9] Such violence is not terrorism, according to Marx. Lenin in *State and Revolution* (1917) and Trotsky in *Terrorism and Communism: A Reply to Karl Kautsky* (1920) made the same argument in even stronger terms. In particular, Lenin's recommendations for a violent attack upon the state possessed a canonical authority for Red Brigade leaders.[10] Precisely on this argument the Red Brigades and ideologically related groups in Italy claim to be acting as heirs of Marxism-Leninism.

The protean variousness of Marxism is reflected in the history of Italian communism. While many Marxists today minimize the importance of the revolutionary project, the repeated assertions in the classic texts of Marxism-Leninism regarding the necessity of a violent anticapitalist revolution have always been highly suggestive to a certain type of fanatical left-wing mind, of which the Red Brigades are the latest and most ferocious expression in Italy. Between Marxism-Leninism and contemporary Italian terrorism there does exist a group of mediating intellectuals, of self-proclaimed Marxist-Leninist provenance, who themselves cannot always be shown to have direct links with the terrorists but whose ideas and preachments have reinforced and glamorized the mystique of proletarian revolution—precisely the kind of revolution that the Red Brigades claim to be sponsoring. The actual relationship between these intellectuals and Italian terrorists remains the subject of one of the country's major controversies. I hope to shed some light on this problem.

On the radical right, Nietzsche has been the dominant ideological inspiration. With the creation of the liberal state in 1860, substantial enclaves of traditionally minded Italians began to experience the kind of desperation long familiar to those on the radical left. For these alienated conservative elites who became the core troops of reaction, Nietzsche's ideas, which Gabriele D'Annunzio popularized in Italy with his fin de siècle novels, offered a brilliant intellectual defense of aristocratic principles and a most welcome refutation of democracy, socialism, and communism.[11]

The vital principle of Nietzsche's social and political thought is to be found in his withering critique of what he called the slave morality. According to this son of a Lutheran minister, the world could thank Christianity for a moral value system, long regnant in Europe, of weakness, humility, and pity that had resulted in the ruination of all the instincts proper to the highest, strongest, and most successful men. He believed that modern-day socialism was simply secularized Christianity and therefore a miserably degenerate phenomenon, signaling an even more severe stage than Christianity in the disintegration of Western civilization. Nietzsche claimed that, despite the loud insistence of sundry progressive thinkers speaking for the uncreative conformists and the complacent hedonists, there was, contra Marx and Darwin, no such thing as progress. To the misfortune of the modern world, Nietzsche lamented, the progressive mentality, which was based not on anything real in nature but on the dreams of weaklings and knaves, had become dominant in Europe, with the result that European man had lost all contact with reality and indeed had become an almost ludicrous species.

He countered that life as it actually was could only be understood as a cycle of eternal return by the movement of which conscious mankind, in every period of history represented by a handful of superior human beings who were recognizable through their total self-mastery, comes back again and again to its point of origin in nature. Therefore, the goal of humanity lay not in the wholly fictitious destination of socialist mythology but rather in the nurturing of overmen such as Michelangelo and Goethe. Every age produced a few such individuals while the masses below these mobile zones of superiority always remained inert, for men were not equal and never could become so. In his view this precious minority had achieved all that was noble and beautiful in the history of the world. Modern Europe was by definition for Nietzsche a place where conditions favored mediocrity and worse at the expense of heroes who in these entirely corrupted times had to be solitary, concealed, and divergent—men "beyond good and evil."[12]

The parallel between Nietzsche and the radical Right and Marx and the radical Left is of limited utility because in Marx we find both a diagnosis and a prescription, whereas Nietzsche offered only a diagnosis. Nevertheless, Nietzschean ideas have served as an intellectual starting point for generations of radical right-wing zealots in Europe. In vain did he supplicate his readers and posterity in *Ecce Homo*: "Above all, do not misunderstand me." His books, easier to read than to understand, have been misused on behalf of movements with which he would have had nothing to do. Certainly, the integrity of his thought was wantonly violated by Nazi ideologues who annexed his illustrious name to their intellectually disabled cause. Still, that Nietzsche's name continues to be invoked by neofascist extremists today draws attention to the affinity between elements of his thought and the world view of the radical Right.[13] I attempt to show in what ways Nietzsche's bellicose critique of modernity is a driving intellectual force in the neofascist mystique of revolution and serves as a rationale for exponents of right-wing violence. Like Marx, Nietzsche has not always been faithfully served by his admirers, but radicals of both extremes claim to have found the nourishment they crave in these thinkers.

A history of Italian terrorism must take a modest form at this point, and yet it should be inclusive enough to account for the social, economic, political, and ideological origins of Italy's crisis. In this history of Italian terrorism I have put a special emphasis on the ideological origins because that is where the evidence led me. The red and the black are real forces in history. Quite independently of each other, though with a collateral effect, the unreconstructed elements within these forces have declared war on Italy's liberal political institutions and culture.[14] To make sense of Italian terrorism we need to know what motivates the terrorists—Left and Right—and how they perceive the modern world as a monstrosity to be pulverized, not reformed.

The Italian terror of our time cannot be explained by the biographies and intellectual itineraries of certain radical ideologists alone. It would be fruitless to try to make generalizations about a social phenomenon of so vast an extent as Italian terrorism on the basis of a few individual portraits. It seems reasonable, however, to proceed from Max Weber's assertion that social phenomena involve the action of agents who themselves attach a sense to what they are trying to do. Therefore, I felt obliged to determine what the sense of terrorist action is, what the intentions of those involved in terrorism are. In other words, Weber's task in *The Protestant Ethic and the Spirit of Capitalism*, to identify the historical sources of bourgeois consciousness, became for me a matter of identifying the historical sources of revolutionary consciousness on the right and the left.

The precise political function of radical intellectuals can never be stated with absolute certainty. Questions such as which terrorists read or followed a particular theorist do not lend themselves to clear-cut answers, as the Italian courts have been in the process of discovering. While the difficulties in trying to establish the relationship between thought and action are daunting, Antonio Gramsci was surely correct in his assertion that intellectuals are "the specialized representatives and standard-bearers of society," articulating the political and cultural aspirations of certain groups in society and, to some extent, influencing them.[15] This principle is emphatically not a Marxist discovery. Alexis de Tocqueville illustrated it in *The Old Régime and the French Revolution*: "the vapourings of the littérateurs," he noted, had created one of the essential preconditions for the events of 1789 by undermining respect for traditional values and customs—or, in the idiom of Gramsci, by furnishing the shock troops for an assault of an enlightened counterhegemony against the Bourbon hegemony of Crown and Altar.[16] Nevertheless, Marxists succeeded brilliantly, with Gramsci at the head of the class, in fully developing a convincing theory that touched on the unbreakable links between the mental work of nonrevolutionary intellectuals and the hegemony of a capitalist society.

At the same time, what is true theoretically about nonrevolutionary intellectuals and the capitalist hegemony is equally true about revolutionary intellectuals and the counterhegemonies of the Left and the Right. Of an historic necessity made evident by Marxist theory, revolutionary intellectuals are involved in revolutionary activity, if not in specific acts of revolution, in the same dialectical sense that their establishment counterparts are involved on the other side of the political fence. Distinctions must be made with painstaking care. It is only in theory that most people confront revolution as an either/or proposition. Nevertheless, Marxist principles of historical analysis permit us to grasp how the revolutionary preachments of radical intellectuals might influence the mental world in which the revolutionary Marxist projects of such groups as the Red Brigades are formed. The same historical process is at work on the radical right, and, as on the radical left, the process is sometimes ambiguous and sometimes not.

Radical political programs do not necessarily remain limited to the exact specifications of their original designers. Revolutionary energy, once unleashed or made conscious of itself, may eventually assume a form strikingly unlike its first incarnation. These differences must be noted, but in noting them the entire historical record needs to be examined. We cannot understand the history of revolutionary movements if, like lawyers arguing on behalf of their clients, we confine our analysis to the movements' final stages. Italy's recent trials for subversion have been filled with this kind of rhetoric, and it has worked, properly so upon occasion. In a liberal state revolutionary intellectuals cannot be held legally responsible for acts they may have inspired through words on a printed page. Nonetheless, they may be responsible in other ways deserving of the historian's notice.

As with all important events in history, human consciousness had to be prepared for the coming terrorism before it appeared as a fact in contemporary Italy. Theoretical considerations always precede and prepare the way for revolutionary movements. Historically, intellectuals help to create a state of mind for revolutionary violence, and it is from the mental world of radical utopianism that Italian terrorists took their bearings. This is a realm that we can explore now and thereby understand what the terrorists were trying to accomplish. The terror itself—on the level of what Fernand Braudel called "the history of events: surface disturbances, crests of foam that the tides of history carry on their strong backs"—was not the product of abstractions alone.[17] Abstractions can only herald a protracted campaign of revolutionary violence if society has already created an expectant audience for them. For radical intellectuals to be effective, the minimal requirement is that a politically significant portion of the population must be suffering from varying degrees of disequilibrium, as in the Italy of our time. I propose to examine the nature and the violent consequences of this disequilibrium.

THE Revolutionary Mystique AND Terrorism IN Contemporary Italy

ONE

▄▄▄▄▄

The Two Faces
of Italian Terrorism

1969–1974

The terror that disfigured public life in Italy during the 1970s and 1980s did not suddenly manifest itself on 12 December 1969 with the Piazza Fontana bombing in Milan. It is true that this particular terrorist act went so far beyond all previous standards for subversive activity that a new epoch of Italian terrorism did begin then. Nevertheless, the incidence of political violence had been rising sharply in Italy during the mid-1960s as the most obvious feature of the country's widespread economic decline after the phenomenal boom of the previous decade. With public expectations still soaring in the early 1960s, progress had slowed and then stopped. For the next several years the cost of living rose along with unemployment and inflation. Although wages rose, too, the distribution of wealth and power was widely perceived to be unequal.

Despite the efforts of the shrewd and able Aldo Moro, political sagacity was not a hallmark of the era. Italy sought in vain for a stable coalition to guide her through a particularly difficult phase of her modernization. The rapid and yet incomplete transformation of the country's largely traditional character to one more in keeping with a consumer society gave the decade its tone. On the whole, Italian culture reflected the stresses of modernization and was all but powerless to withstand their deep, unsettling thrust into the nation's psyche and mores. A process begun in the post–World War II epoch on a previously unknown scale had reached a disorienting climax by the end of the 1960s: the cities of the north, swamped by an alien population from the south, had lost their traditional character; with no period of adjustment, a new mass society had sprung into existence. Socially and culturally, the country lay in the deepest turmoil, and this condition left a mark on every feature of national life.

Against this background of collapsing fortunes, two distinct challenges to the existing system took shape during the late 1960s. Nineteen sixty-eight was the year of the powerful student rebellion in France, an event that inflamed the revolutionary passions of Italian university radicals, who already had staged their first sit-ins and protest demonstrations. The country's university system, which was severely strained anyway by a spectacular rise in student enrollments and by inadequate budgets, entered a period of violent crisis, with resounding effects inside and outside the academic world for much of the next decade. When the social structure failed to accommodate this gigantic surge of young people, protest became contagious in Italy.

During the "hot autumn" of 1969 Italy experienced the worst labor strikes in her postwar history. They were also the most numerous; never before were so many hours of work lost as in 1969. Encouraged by the dramatic gains of 1959–63, multitudes of workers balked at the modest increments won for them during the mid-sixties by their unions. Then in the late sixties they raced far out in front of their union leaders in demanding better wages and factory conditions. To gain these ends they paralyzed the country with wildcat strikes and random work stoppages. Frightened and outraged, employers demanded government action, but it was not forthcoming. With the Center-Left coalition in ruins because of fierce Socialist party in-fighting, only a minority Christian Democratic cabinet could be formed, under Prime Minister Mariano Rumor. His single-party government was too weak to deal effectively with the escalating violence. Then at the peak of the crisis came the Piazza Fontana massacre, itself the savage culmination of a series of increasingly destructive bombings.

December 12 had been a normal Friday at the Banca Nazionale dell' Agricoltura in Piazza Fontana near Milan's soaring Duomo. On other days the bank closed at 4:00 P.M., but it kept later hours on Fridays as a service to its customers. The spacious and circular main banking area was thronged with merchants and farmers queued up at a counter behind which some seventy employees worked. A little before 4:30 an individual of unsuspicious bearing entered the bank, unobtrusively left a package under the large, heavy table in the main salon, and disappeared. Seven minutes later the sights and sounds of commerce were suddenly transformed by the destructive force of seven to eight kilos of explosives in a detonation heard all over the city. One eyewitness described the bombed-out bank as "a hell of screams, of shouts, of desperation, of panic, of lamentation."[1]

The force of the bomb was so great that every object in the room became a deadly projectile, and many of the worst injuries resulted from falling shards of glass as the large windows of the bank's upper floor came crashing down. Flying chairs, blocks of marble, and typewriters produced more carnage. Sixteen people were killed outright, and ninety were wounded. Those closest to the bomb—customers standing at the heavy table filling out their bank slips—were blown to bits. One was hurled across the room and over the teller's counter, where he came down in two pieces. Another was decapitated. Limbs, horribly wrenched from their trunks, littered the bloody floor. The shoes of some victims were found with severed feet still in them. In an atmosphere permeated with the acrid odor of burned flesh, first aid arrived quickly, and the wounded were evacuated to nearby hospitals. Two priests remained behind, imparting extreme unction to the dying and absolution to the dead.

Almost immediately the police arrested two anarchists, Pietro Valpreda and Giuseppe Pinelli, and charged them with the massacre. Pinelli later died in a fall from a window at police headquarters. The authorities insisted that it was a suicide, but the Left greeted the claim with ill-humored skepticism and declared that Pinelli had been pushed to his death. These claims and counterclaims went back and forth for months along fairly strict ideological lines. Then in 1971 two radical neofascists, Giovanni Ventura and Franco Freda, were linked to the massacre. Freda, an anti-Semite of neo-Nazi sentiments but eclectic enough ideologically to envisage an alliance with the radical Left, was the leader of the Ordine Nuovo (New Order) in Padua. It was from the mental universe of the New Order that much of the violence in Italy's political life sprang.

The New Order had been created in the mid-1950s as an element of the radical Movimento Sociale Italiano (MSI). This element supported Giorgio Almirante in opposition to the MSI's pragmatic and nonrevolutionary leader, Arturo Michelini. Its members, the *ordinovisti*, were closely identified with what was known as the strategy of tension, and they acquired notoriety as the revolutionary conscience of the Italian Right. Radical neofascists had developed this strategy of tension during the postwar period, and the group most closely associated with it in the beginning was the Fasci di Azione Rivoluzionaria (FAR).[2] Tactically, Ordine Nuovo was FAR's heir. Moreover, in the tradition of their revolutionary-minded predecessors, the ordinovisti resisted any signs of moderation in the MSI.

As Michelini's grip on the party tightened, the radicals lost all hope of an MSI revolution and formed their own extraparliamentary Right group, Ordine Nuovo, in 1956. Led by Pino Rauti, Ordine Nuovo boasted several thousand members by the early 1960s. The ordinovisti established contact with Jeune Europe, led by ex-SS member Jean Thiriart, a Belgian, and with the Nouvel Ordre Européen of René Binet and Guy Gaston Amaudruz.[3] Through the 1960s Rauti's forces championed the cause of right-wing revolution in Italy.

Their vision of the world was reflected in the pages of Rauti's journal, *Ordine nuovo*, subtitled "a review of political revolution." A quotation by Mussolini, "Don't fear the storms, that which we wait will come," adorned the front page of the maiden issue, in May 1958. Europe, Rauti informed his readers, had lost its driving force and now existed as a passive entity under the control of Washington and Moscow.[4] East Europeans were trapped in a monstrous totalitarian system; Western Europeans, outwardly free, were losing their souls as American-style consumerism effected the most far-reaching social and cultural revolution in European history. The need for a revival of Europe's power and spirit was palpable, and Rauti envisaged *Ordine nuovo*, not the MSI's publications, as the catalyst for this process.

Rauti argued that the MSI had become an impediment to revolutionary activity on the right. He and his associates on *Ordine nuovo* consistently denigrated official neofascism as a nonrevolutionary force whose leaders either had no conception of Italy's danger or lacked the will to confront it. To be sure, the ordinovisti observed, the Christian Democratic government was deficient in every political and ideological element necessary for the creation of a strong and effective state, but the MSI, under the pathetic leadership of eunuchs and dwarfs, had missed its opportunity to organize a genuinely revolutionary opposition to this government.

Moreover, the MSI appeared to have no credible strategy in mind, so far as the ordinovisti could determine, for countering the Communist conspiracy, which had as its aim the subjugation of Italy to Moscow. Michelini had succeeded in creating a party not fundamentally different from any other party in a political system that deserved only to be destroyed and then succeeded by a neofascist order, but for Rauti and his friends it was a party without faith, without ideals, and without honor. Once, Rauti lamented, the MSI members, the *missini*, proudly went forward under the party's banner "like Crusaders in the land of infidels."[5] United in a political faith characterized by a reverence for what had been best in fascism, they fought, shouted, and believed. Then the vote counters took over, and the party was stricken with a disease called politics. Rauti concluded that only the ordinovisti and their allies among Almirante's radical dissenters within the MSI understood the need for a revolutionary right-wing response to Italy's dire political situation. Through the auspices of his Centro Ordine Nuovo, Rauti hoped to develop an elite corps of young men who would be "prepared and ready for any event, however drastic it might be."[6]

Despite these threatening words, Rauti and many of his ordinovisti returned to the MSI when Almirante gained control of the party in 1969. Student demonstrations in 1968 and worker strikes during the hot autumn of the next year created a political backlash from which the MSI stood to benefit at the polls. The party's prospects never seemed brighter, and Almirante's succession tempted Rauti back into the fold of official neofascism.[7] Dissident ordinovisti led by Clemente Graziani continued, however, to hold out for a revolutionary strategy. Graziani had distinguished himself as one of the most radical thinkers on the revolutionary Right, and he had made no secret of his belief in the necessity of terrorism as a means of giving birth to the revolution that would free Italy of its vile democratic order and the even worse communist future awaiting it should the neofascists not win. For Graziani the Marxist revolutionaries in Cuba and Vietnam provided the tactics that neofascist revolutionaries should adopt as their own: guerrilla warfare, with its inevitable resort to terrorism against a militarily superior foe.[8] These communist guerrillas had done no more than follow Lenin's advice about using all methods in promoting and winning the revolution. Neofascist guerrillas had much to learn from the extraordinary successes of their Marxist counterparts, Graziani advised.

Until the MSI unambiguously acknowledged the failure of its Michelini-inspired strategy, Graziani promised to follow his own revolutionary path.[9] In fact, Almirante had been forced by the pressure of Italy's eclectic right-wing politics to become what Michelini had been earlier: a pragmatist with an instinct for compromise. Never able to forgive Almirante for his apostasy to the revolutionary faith, the extraparliamentary right-wing commandos of Graziani dismissed the MSI leader as a temporizer and a politician. At the same time they continued to present themselves as the upholders of the authentic Right in an age when official neofascism had lost its revolutionary zeal.

Throughout the 1950s and 1960s numerous other radical neofascist organizations had competed with Ordine Nuovo for the extreme right-wing constituency in

Italian politics. In 1957 Giorgio Ceci and Stefano Delle Chiaie, who would earn notoriety as the "black bombardier," left Ordine Nuovo and accused Rauti of "moderatism."That same year Ceci and Delle Chiaie founded the neo-Nazi Gruppi di Azione Rivoluzionaria (GAR). In 1960 GAR became Avanguardia Nazionale Giovanile, but the courts disbanded this group in 1965. Three years later Delle Chiaie founded two new organizations: a university association called Nuova Caravella and Avanguardia Nazionale for both workers and students. As for the Avanguardia Nazionale Giovanile, it was reborn at the University of Rome in 1970, becoming shortly thereafter the most aggressive nucleus on the extreme right of the MSI.[10]

Prince Junio Valerio Borghese, the "black prince," who had been a Fascist war hero and one of the most charismatic figures on the postwar neofascist right, also became restive during the 1960s. Alienated by the MSI's growing moderation, he offered encouragement to the ordinovisti and maintained contact with them. Then, in September 1968, he founded his own radical organization, the Fronte Nazionale, with approximately three thousand members.[11] A subsequent alliance between Fronte Nazionale and Ordine Nuovo failed when Rauti led his followers back into the MSI. Borghese and his hard-core disciples were more isolated than ever. They took heart, however, from the country's mounting social tensions. The prolonged eruption of regional strife in Calabria during the summer of 1970 persuaded Borghese to gamble that the moment was right for a coup.[12] The outcome was worse than a defeat: it was a farce. Plans were laid to stage an uprising in Rome, but absolutely nothing happened. The prince fled the country. Not until 17 March 1971 did the public even learn about the episode. Borghese, sick with pulmonary emphysema and embittered over the fiasco that had smothered all his plans for the regeneration of Italy, died in exile in Spain three years later.

These radical right-wing groups—constantly distracted by their own bitter rivalries and feuds—stood for the overthrow of democracy, a preventive strike against communism, and the creation of an authoritarian order. The actual force behind this threat remained unknown. Although the accusations against Freda and Ventura in the Piazza Fontana bombing directed public attention toward the shadowy world of neofascist subversion, even its broad outlines remained indistinct. Italy was under attack by groups that wanted to smash the country's political structure, but the nature of the threat eluded analysis. After the Freda and Ventura arrests the political significance of the Piazza Fontana massacre still retained its enigmatic character. The nation's attention had been fixed on the scene of Milan's agony, but the full import of Piazza Fontana, as a portent of agonies to come, could not be taken in then.

After the Piazza Fontana bombing in 1969, the next major terrorist act did not occur until 26 March 1972, when Giangiacomo Feltrinelli, a millionaire publisher, attempted to blow up the power transmitter at Segrate, near Milan. That was not the first commando raid undertaken or sponsored by Feltrinelli. Since 4 December 1969, when he went underground to live the partisan life of his fantasies and dreams, Feltrinelli had gathered around him and financed a terrorist organization known as the Gruppi di Azione Partigiana (GAP), of ultra-Marxist provenance. The creation of this organization had been the last step in a course of action inspired by his perpetual fear of a right-wing coup engineered by the United States and the Christian Democrats, whose aim was to reimpose practical fascism on Italy.

Feltrinelli had passed nearly all his adult life trying to cultivate working-class attitudes and overcome the disadvantages of having been a tycoon's son. In his intensely ideological way of thinking, socialism was all light and purity, capitalism the socioeconomic embodiment of evil. Feltrinelli's growing conviction in the 1960s that the official parties of the Left had betrayed socialism caused him to put his fortune at the service of ultra-leftist movements and individuals. A friend and confidant of Fidel Castro, Feltrinelli patronized radical writers and sometime in 1971 established contact with a little-known group of young Marxist revolutionaries who called themselves Brigate Rosse, the Red Brigades. The extent of his support for the other splinter groups of the extraparliamentary Left—Manifesto, Potere Operaio, Lotta Continua, Avanguardia Operaia—was difficult to determine, but by 1971 Feltrinelli had established a reputation as an eccentric financier of organizations and individuals willing to work and fight for revolution in Italy.[13]

On 26 March 1972 something went fatally wrong. The bomb exploded prematurely, and Feltrinelli was blown to pieces. The press reported next day that a "Vincenzo Maggioni" had been killed, but Feltrinelli's wife knew it was her husband. Soon all Italy learned the truth and immediately indulged in extravagant speculation about how Feltrinelli had met his end. Many surmised that he had been killed by the Right or the police or secret service agencies with the death scene made to look like an accident, but nothing came of these theories. Instead, Italians began to hear more about GAP and its flanking movements on the terrorist left.

Feltrinelli's death resulted in the same kind of public attention for the extraparliamentary Left that the Freda and Ventura connection to Piazza Fontana had created for the extraparliamentary Right. Italian political life swarmed with radicals of both revolutionary traditions who rejected, on the one hand, the MSI and, on the other, the Partito Comunista Italiano (PCI) as politically senile. PCI leader Enrico Berlinguer's strictly legal political methods had intensified the long-building alienation of those left-wing militants who viewed proletarian revolution as a necessity. These dissenters charged that the Communist party, though it was a political success, stood condemned as an ideological failure; it had succeeded in maintaining a high electoral standing, but only at the cost of its Marxist identity. The party itself went on the defensive in this dispute, claiming that it had not abandoned the ultimate goal of Marxism; it merely had modernized Marxist strategy to fit the complex conditions of the present. That argument had failed to convince the extremists—a small though politically explosive minority of Italian Marxists—and the chief consequence of this failure had been the emergence of the extraparliamentary Left, whose withering critique of the PCI had plunged Italian Marxism into profound crisis.[14]

To some extent the fragmentation of the Marxist Left in Italy had developed as a variation of a traditional theme in the country's politics. From the founding of the Partito Socialista Italiano (PSI) in 1892, radicals and moderates fought over which direction Italian socialism should take, toward reform or revolution. This rift widened with time, and after World War I the most intransigent Socialists, inspired by the Bolshevik Revolution, broke away from the PSI and formed the Communist party. Factions soon appeared among the Communist followers of Amadeo Bordiga, Antonio Gramsci, and Angelo Tasca, the three dominant figures in the PCI. Fascism, not internal accord, put an end to these disputes, and after World War II the immense prestige of Palmiro Togliatti, Gramsci's lieutenant, kept the Communists more or less united.

Togliatti's policy was one of caution and accommodation with the bourgeois parties. In 1944, upon returning to his native land from Russian exile, he announced that the absence of a red army in Italy made it necessary for Italian Communists to work through legal channels.[15] In this so-called *svolta di Salerno* he proposed a government of national unity and a suspension of revolutionary class struggle; these policies inaugurated the sinuous transformation of the PCI from an extreme left-wing party to its present-day Eurocommunist character. For example, the early issues of the PCI journal, *Rinascita*, were so inoffensive that Marshal Pietro Badoglio, Mussolini's general in Ethiopia and from July 1943 to June 1944 the country's prime minister, sent an effusive letter to Togliatti, praising the publication and virtually offering his collaboration.[16]

Togliatti was far from being a moderate on all questions, however, as his passionate support of the Soviet Union in foreign policy made clear. Indeed, for many years after World War II the main threat to the internal stability of the PCI came about precisely because of Togliatti's hostility toward moderate Communist reformers such as Elio Vittorini, Eugenio Reale, and Fabrizio Onofri, who wanted to westernize the party still further by making it more democratic and by removing it from what they regarded as the baleful influence of Russia.[17] Togliatti's moderation applied only to interparty relations; within the party itself and on all matters concerning the Soviet Union he ruled as his friend and mentor Stalin would have wished.

Left-wing critiques of *togliattismo* also surfaced, however, and in a manner that bore a striking resemblance to ideological developments on the extreme right. Radical Marxists asked the same question asked by radical neofascists: do you remember revolution? In 1944 a Turin group, Stella Rossa (Red Star), called for the creation of an Italian Soviet Republic. The PCI denounced these Marxist radicals as *bordighisti* in the service of the Fascist police. In February 1945 the party showed even less sympathy toward a popular rebellion in Ragusa against the status quo. When on 6 July 1945 dissident Resistance fighters in Schio summarily executed Fascist political prisoners, *l'Unità* condemned the action as a crime. The Communist newspaper was no less explicit in its rejection of continued partisan reprisals in 1946 when such groups as the Movimento di Resistenza Popolare terrorized the countryside. Even the rebuff of the Christian Democrats in 1947 and the attempt on Togliatti's life the following year did not lessen the party's adherence to an expressly nonrevolutionary policy.

As the party abandoned all pretense of having any revolutionary antagonism toward the established order and became transformed into a mere political critic of that order, Marxist splinter groups continued to set themselves up as radical alternatives to reformist compromises. For example, during the late 1940s a Sesto San Giovanni group calling itself Volante Rossa, after the famous Resistance unit, carried out a terrorist campaign against known Fascists and prominent industrialists. Their campaign included kidnapping and assassination. For the PCI the men of Volante Rossa had succeeded only in dishonoring the purity of Resistance arms. The castigations of party leaders notwithstanding, Italian Marxism remained pregnant with revolutionary possibilities in the 1950s when radical Communists became heartened by the news from China, Algeria, and Cuba. For these individuals revolution postponed was revolution denied, and under the guidance of radical intellectuals the highly eclectic extraparliamentary Left began to take shape during the next decade. It was made up of dozens of small groups and radical publications, often in bitter opposition to one another on points of revolutionary doctrine or tactics but all exhibiting boundless enthusiasm for the idea of Marxist revolution.[18] By the late 1960s and early 1970s action groups such as GAP and the Red Brigades were preparing to make good the promises of the extraparliamentary Left's revolutionary philosophy.

The Red Brigades became the most successful and notorious of these groups, and Renato Curcio dominated its early history. Curcio had a Catholic education, and he continued to practice his faith up to within two years of being converted to revolutionary terrorism.[19] Born in 1941, Curcio arrived at the university of Trento in 1964 and began to study sociology. As late as 1965 he was still reading Jacques Maritain, but by the following year the Christian activist in him had vanished and a new kind of Marxist revolutionary was struggling to be born as he immersed himself in the works of Marx, Lenin, and Mao. Curcio became a leader among student activists in Trento, helping to edit, along with Mauro Rostagno, the *Proposta di foglio di lavoro*, which called for a new university radicalism against capitalism. They wanted to create an *università negativa* (negative university) offering *contro-corsi* (countercourses) that would negate the evil capitalist hegemony. According to Curcio, it was time to start preparing for the revolution, to set out on a journey that would resemble the long march of Mao. Curcio also collaborated on a self-styled Marxist-Leninist monthly publication, *Lavoro politico*, which was edited by Walter Peruzzi. *Lavoro politico* enjoyed prestige as the theoretical journal par excellence of the radical student movement. Its writers called for a revolutionary class war in Italy along lines prescribed by Marx, Lenin, and Mao. They held the Red Guards of China in particularly high esteem.[20] In this mental environment Curcio formed his own uncompromisingly revolutionary ideals.

He left the university in 1969 and moved with his wife, Margherita Cagol, to Milan. There they played leading roles in organizing the Collettivo Politico Metropolitano (Metropolitan Political Collective), which was founded on 8 September of that year. In Curcio's mind a direct connection existed between the student demonstrations of 1968 and the hot autumn of the factory workers in 1969. He set himself to organize these disturbances toward revolutionary ends, and that was the purpose of the collective, in which both student and worker groups participated. Curcio and Cagol brought to the collective their varied experiences in the radical student movement while such organizations as the Gruppo di Studio Sit-Siemens,

CUB Pirelli, and Gruppo di Studio IBM functioned as direct channels to the industrial workplace.[21] Thus, the collective, whose heritage would include the Red Brigades, took life from a coupling between the foremost revolutionary elements in Italy: the student protest movement and worker radicalism in the factories.

In early November 1969 about seventy members of the collective held a meeting in Chiavari, where the subject of armed violence was discussed. Curcio's presentation, "Lotta sociale e organizzazione nella metropoli," in which the collective's political line was put forth, appeared as a pamphlet in January 1970. His key concept was *autonomia*. For him autonomy was "the movement of the proletariat's liberation from the complex hegemony of the bourgeoisie."[22] He further interpreted autonomy as a fundamental political category of revolutionary Marxism, a philosophy that had as its highest aspiration "the destruction of the global system of exploitation and the construction of an alternative social organization." The long march imagery in his *Proposta* writings found renewed confirmation in this document: the transformation of Italy from its present capitalist condition to a Communist system would be long and arduous, but that process had entered its revolutionary phase. The two years 1968 and 1969 had proved this much to the satisfaction of every honest Marxist, or so Curcio believed. This was the political situation in Italy, according to him: through an elaborate corporativist scheme the bourgeoisie was trying to impose its class will on the workers, and the official working-class parties had only succeeded in making this task easier for the enemies of the proletariat. Curcio proposed that the collective should remind all true Marxists of their rendezvous with history as the avengers of the working class.

The political ideas and tactics outlined in "Lotta sociale" received a more systematic treatment in *Sinistra proletaria*, the collective's review, which began to appear in 1970. To the traditional sickle-and-hammer Communist symbols, the editors of *Sinistra proletaria* added a rifle as the most vivid indication of how serious they were about taking the war to the class enemy. Such a blatant appeal to arms alienated some members of the collective, and the group was plagued with internal dissensions and defections. Nevertheless, Curcio was able to impose a relentlessly revolutionary line on *Sinistra proletaria* and always at the expense of the "collaborationist" PCI and its union, the CGIL, which were denigrated as the pillars of the "bourgeois workers' movement." Such, according to Curcio and the most radical members of the collective, was the tragic legacy of Gramscian-Togliattian reformism on the official Communist Left. Even Lotta Continua, an extraparliamentary Left formation, found itself severely criticized in *Sinistra proletaria* as an insufficiently revolutionary force.

Sinistra proletaria called for the creation of a revolutionary organization whose leaders understood that class struggle was the equivalent of war. The Vietcong was a model organization of this kind, and the lessons of the war in Vietnam made a deep impression on Curcio. From that theater, Italian workers could learn how to answer blow for blow and how to strike first when the enemy was unprepared. Worker nuclei for defense and attack had to be created as the necessary manifestations of class struggle. Every Marxist knew—or should have known—this, but Italy was the land where communism had been subjected to interpretations of such astounding originality, particularly at the highest levels of the PCI, that even Marx's most elementary propositions regarding class war had been turned on their head to mean something totally at variance with the spirit and letter of the *Communist Manifesto* and *Capital*. The unambiguous meaning of Marx was this: for capitalism to fall, the proletariat had to lead and win a revolutionary struggle against the bourgeoisie. Revolution did not mean a piecemeal advance at the polls or in union membership; it meant destruction of the capitalist establishment and death to the pillars of that establishment. In an image dear to the writers of *Sinistra proletaria*, "the Repressive and Dirty War of the bosses" had to go down in a flaming and irreversible defeat before "the Revolutionary and Clean War" waged by the proletariat.[23]

The October 1970 issue of *Sinistra proletaria* announced the creation of the Red Brigades as "the most decisive and conscious part of the proletariat in struggle" against the institutions that administer the exploitation of the people.[24] This group claimed to represent "the first moments of the proletariat's self-organization in order to fight the bosses and their henchmen." From then on, until the journal's last issue in February 1971, the discourse of *Sinistra proletaria* became increasingly military. For example, in January Curcio and his colleagues called for the organization of a new Resistance, to finish the job left undone in 1945. Partisan action would educate the revolutionary proletariat in the ways of armed struggle, the only Marxist method of ending capitalism's hated dominion over the toiling masses. This appeal echoed a similar one made a few months earlier by the Gauche Proletarienne in France, which described itself as a new French Resistance movement.[25] The next month the Red Brigades went underground. The brief legal phase of their history was over.

Even earlier, in September 1970, the Red Brigades had become a part of the pervasive factory violence in Milan. As a result of contacts developed in the collective, they had easy access to the most radical workers in Sit-Siemens and Pirelli, where so-called study groups had been calling for an overthrow of the capitalist system. On 17 September Red Brigade terrorists destroyed the automobile of a Sit-Siemens executive; this was their first signed action under the soon-to-be famous five-pointed star. The Red Brigades set more automobiles on fire in November and December, but only on 25 January 1971 did they achieve national recognition as something out of the ordinary run of factory saboteurs. This was the spectacular bomb attack at Lainate, where they blew up three trucks. It was to be taken for granted that the PCI would condemn the Red Brigades as "provocateurs," but even the extraparliamentary Lotta Continua condemned Lainate as an anarchist act with no connection to the proletarian cause. In answer to such criticisms from the Left and the extraparliamentary Left, the Red Brigades produced a body of pamphlet literature in which they stressed the necessity of bringing down the capitalist system by force: "Just a few short years ago, were not the militants of the PCI doing similar things?"[26] The Red Brigades always insisted that they were only carrying on the revolutionary traditions of true Marxism.

The earliest communications of the Red Brigades, from late 1970 and early 1971, left no doubt about their goals in the nation's factories. They themselves defined Red Brigadism as a call to arms against the repression of the bosses. Spies and scabs they denounced by name and address, adding that such vermin deserved to be pilloried. These early documents resounded with threatening language, including the mention of assassination. There never was any doubt about the destination of Red Brigadism if the Red Brigades had their way: they promised from the beginning to destroy the capitalist system along with its upholders. The communist revolution demanded, they said, "for every eye, two eyes; for every tooth, an entire face."[27] An April 1971 Red Brigade communication called for physical attacks on the bosses, who were "vulnerable in their persons, their houses, and their organizations."[28] Though as yet unready to make life impossible for these people, the Red Brigades gave a plain forecast in 1971 of their future tactics.[29]

On 3 March 1972 the Red Brigades engineered their first kidnapping. The victim was Idalgo Macchiarini, an executive with Sit-Siemens. After a brief interrogation, they released him with a sign around his neck that read, in part, "Strike one to educate a hundred." The entire operation lasted only twenty minutes. While the mainstream press gave the kidnapping only slight attention—some major newspapers did not even mention it—this action stood out as the most ambitious and concrete example yet of what the Red Brigade strategy actually entailed. According to a leaflet later distributed by the Red Brigades, they thought of Macchiarini as "a neofascist in a white shirt" and a "functionary of the reaction."[30] Such people had to be struck down, as Lenin himself—the inspiration for the sign around Macchiarini's neck—insisted. Lenin thought that at the revolutionary moment certain bourgeois professions should be risky, and factory head was one them. Thus, the Macchiarini kidnapping was an object lesson in applied Leninism, in keeping with how the Red Brigades interpreted their entire campaign.

It was at this point, on 26 March, that Feltrinelli accidentally killed himself at Segrate. In the aftermath of this explosion, Feltrinelli's followers in GAP joined forces with the Red Brigades. Then nothing was heard from them until November 1972, when they committed a series of robberies as a means of both "taxing" the capitalist system and keeping their own organization solvent. During the same month contract negotiations between the metalworkers of Turin and Fiat gave every promise of another hot autumn. On 26 November the Red Brigades entered this struggle on the side of the workers and manifested their support by burning the automobiles of nine so-called fascists. In a Red Brigade pamphlet distributed that same day, the brigatisti claimed only to be responding to the class war declared by Fiat, which was guilty, among other things, of suspending radical workers. Sabotage of this kind was not new, but the sudden appearance of the Red Brigades in Turin did signal a dramatic expansion in their field of activities.

On 17 December 1972 the Red Brigades burned six more automobiles in the name of their war against the capitalist dictatorship. The following February, on the twelfth, they kidnapped Bruno Labate, the provincial secretary of a right-wing union. After four hours the Red Brigades released Labate, but they left him tied to a gate at the entrance of Fiat Mirafiori. The hour of his release was 1:30 in the afternoon, the time when shifts changed. Workers streamed past Labate, and no one helped him. The police had to free the victim. The Red Brigades interpreted this scene as a graphic illustration of their thesis that the workers were filled with hostility toward the capitalist system. The only thing required now was courage on the part of the proletariat's leaders to confront the bourgeoisie.

Stung by criticism from every quarter—including some organs of the extraparliamentary Left—that they were nothing but terrorists, the Red Brigades specifically answered this charge in a theoretical statement published on 11 March 1973. Just the opposite was true, they asserted; the Red Brigades were counterterrorists, reacting against the terror campaign of the capitalist forces that had showed their true character with the Piazza Fontana massacre. "To organize the resistance," the document read, "and to construct armed proletarian power are the watchwords that have guided and continue to guide our revolutionary work. What does terrorism have to do with this?"[31] Far from being guilty of "samurai" tactics, with no appreciation of working-class realities—as some extraparliamentary Left groups claimed—the Red Brigades proposed to unite all nonreformist leftists in a campaign of armed resistance to capitalism, "forces that since 1945, even though at the margins of the official worker movement, have always expressed the continuity of the working class's revolutionary thrust." Red Brigadism was nothing but the first military formation in the perfectly natural and desirable dialectic of "the armed struggle for communism."

The Red Brigades kidnapped two more executives in 1973. They explained their 28 June kidnapping of Alfa executive Michele Mincuzzi as part of their campaign against fascism in a white shirt. After subjecting their victim to a brief "proletarian trial," they let him go. Mincuzzi later reported that he had been treated humanely by the Red Brigades. Then on 10 December they kidnapped Fiat executive Ettore Amerio, also as a measure to halt "antiworker terrorism."[32] He was released eight days later with a promise from the Red Brigades that "We are only at the beginning. We are in the opening phase of a profound crisis in the regime. . . . "[33] By and large the press interpreted these kidnappings as proof that the Red Brigades were, despite their own propaganda statements, right-wing exponents of the strategy of tension.

The Amerio kidnapping coincided with a rapid worsening of Italy's economic and political problems. The Arab-Israeli conflict and the oil embargo of October 1973 had a severely disruptive effect on Italy, a country that imported 94 percent of her oil, much of it from the Middle East.[34] The imposition of austerity measures in November of that year carried over into 1974. A crisis of this kind—compounded by industrial unrest, the highest inflation rate in Western Europe, severe devaluation of the lira, ministerial instability, and political scandal—came as a godsend to the Red Brigades. It appeared to confirm their thesis that capitalist Italy was ripe for the taking. Moreover, they were not the only extremists at work on the revolutionary project in Italy. Bombing attacks of mysterious authorship continued to add tension to a deeply disturbed civic atmosphere. Under the weight of these accumulated difficulties, Italian governments fell in swift succession: Giulio Andreotti's in June 1973, Mariano Rumor's in March and then again in October 1974.

With the Italian government bobbing up and down in a broiling sea of adversity, the Red Brigades struck a blow of unprecedented force. On 18 April 1974 they kidnapped Judge Mario Sossi in Genoa. The Sossi kidnapping, code-named Operation Sunflower, represented a fantastic growth spurt for the Red Brigades: now they were attacking the state directly, in the person of a government-appointed magistrate. From 19 April to 23 May this case completely dominated newspaper headlines, as Italians received an extended course, in the form of eight communiques, on what the Red Brigades defined as the laws of proletarian justice.

Sossi, a right-wing judge who had long been an object of extraparliamentary Left diatribes, stood accused in his capacity as an unusually severe instrument of bourgeois power for crimes against the proletarian masses.[35] During the first days of Sossi's confinement, however, the general feeling in Italy was not so much fear for his safety as uncertainty over the meaning of this Red Brigade action. The kidnappers said repeatedly that they had begun the process of creating and organizing armed proletarian power, but for years after this event some highly respected authorities on Italian politics and history did not take the Red Brigadists at their word concerning the Marxist-Leninist character of their organizition. It is scarcely surprising that during the event itself contemporaries should have professed complete bewilderment over what was taking place in Genoa.

Four thousand armed men searched in vain for Sossi while the Red Brigades continued to announce the progress of their interrogation in communications from 19 to 26 April. The government waited helplessly for word from the Red Brigades on how they wanted to resolve this crisis. The Red Brigades were in no hurry to accommodate the government, for almost from the beginning Sossi's kidnapping had turned into a propaganda triumph of unexpected proportions. On 23 April Sossi himself asked the police to suspend their "useless and dangerous" search. The magistracy agreed with this request and issued an order to that effect, which the police promptly evaded as completely as they could. The unedifying polemics between judicial officials who favored the suspension and police officers who did not filled the newspapers for days. The government itself failed to offer decisive and efficacious leadership at this critical moment. On 3 May Paolo Emilio Taviani, the minister of interior, protested a little too earnestly that "our nerves are steady, they are not worn out nor will they become worn out," but in fact, as a sign of growing consternation in Genoa and Rome, the government soon stopped granting interviews to reporters.[36] This government gag order immeasurably heightened the sense of crisis.

A few days later the Red Brigades at last issued their demands. In exchange for Sossi they would require the release of eight political prisoners, members of a left-wing terrorist group XXII Ottobre.[37] Further, the Eight, as these convicts came to be known, would have to be flown to Cuba, Algeria or North Korea. The Red Brigades enclosed a photograph of Sossi, which showed him with a beard but in apparently good health. They explicitly warned, however, that Sossi's safety depended on a favorable response to their demands.[38]

Sossi had become unnerved by the trauma of captivity. He complained about being abandoned and felt anger toward the state, which lacked the courage and wisdom to protect its servants.[39] The kidnap victim now threatened that he would not die without disclosing the names of his accomplices in the crimes of which he stood accused by the Red Brigades. Sossi confessed to vague errors for which more than one man was responsible. Referring to his superiors—particularly to the attorney general of Genoa, Francesco Coco—he asserted in one message, "Everyone assumes his responsibilities."[40] Sossi's vindictive declamations reinforced popular opinions regarding the irredeemably corrupt and divided character of the Italian government—yet another propaganda windfall for the Red Brigades.

In their sixth communication, on 18 May, the Red Brigades threatened Sossi with death. If the Eight were not released in forty-eight hours, Sossi would be executed "for the crimes of which he is personally responsible."[41] After weeks of steadfastly refusing to negotiate with terrorists, Attorney General Coco declared, on 21 May, that the government would accede to Red Brigade demands, provided that Sossi went free first. Though Coco's declaration was a drastic departure from stated government policy, it at least had the virtue of being clear. Clarity became its opposite on the next day when Prime Minister Rumor appeared before the Senate and the Chamber of Deputies to denounce any effort at compromise "with a group of criminals who have hurled the most illegal direct challenge to the authority of the state."[42] Visibly moved, Rumor wanted to assume full responsibility for saying no to the Red Brigades. A stand had to be made, he proclaimed, against "an ever more bold state of criminality."

Meanwhile, Coco reiterated his offer: with the liberation of Sossi, the Eight would, in turn, be liberated. This was the government voice to which the Red Brigades chose to pay attention, and after thirty-five days of confinement Sossi went free on 23 May 1974. Now it was Coco's turn to demur, and he kept the Red Brigades on tenterhooks while deciding what to do about the Eight. First, he averred, Sossi's injuries, mental and physical, would have to be diagnosed. Second, the government faced an insoluble problem with the Eight: where could it send them? No government or embassy wanted this group, he said. Third, Prime Minister Rumor had condemned all government dealings with terrorists. In truth, Coco concluded, it would not be possible to release the Eight after all.

Sossi reacted furiously to Coco's decision. Upon his release, the embittered Sossi had refused even to see the attorney general, believing him to have been unconscionably laggard in securing an exchange of prisoners. Now Coco was adding insult to injury by implying that Sossi might not be in his right mind. Sossi rejoined that Coco himself was old and tired, lacking zeal and even ordinary competence during the kidnapping ordeal.[43]

Sossi's bitter recriminations dominated Italian political life in the aftermath of the judge's release from the people's prison. Although murder had been averted, the state was made to look feeble, spiritless, and disorganized. The protracted dispute between Coco and Sossi had the effect of covering the judiciary with ridicule. Moreover, the Italian government as a whole was seen in a brutally unflattering light: an adamant refusal to negotiate had been coupled later with a parallel willingness to negotiate, only to end in a decision to dishonor the negotiated settlement. It was as though the Red Brigades had to deal not with one government but with several; this was the greatest lesson of all for Italian terrorists in the Sossi affair. As the Red Brigades themselves expressed it in their last Sossi communication: "during these thirty-five days the contradictions of the various state organs have been manifested."[44] Perhaps for some time into the future the government would be able to muster tactical strength, the Red Brigades concluded, but in the long run "strategic weakness" would be its undoing.

Only five days after Sossi's release, right-wing terrorists resumed their offensive. On the morning of 28 May 1974 a crowd of approximately twenty-five hundred people gathered before the Brescia City Hall in the Piazza della Loggia to hear a speech by Franco Castrezzati, a trade union official. The crowd at this antifascist political rally might have been even larger but for the threatening weather. As rain began to fall, some of Castrezzati's listeners sought shelter under a nearby portico. Here a terrorist bomb had been placed in a refuse container. At 10:12 A.M. Castrezzati's voice was drowned out by a terrifying roar.

Screams of agony and shouts of panic pierced the din that followed. As the smoke cleared away, the extent of the carnage could be seen. A man and a woman lay next to a fountain, their heads blown off. Next to them was the lacerated corpse of another woman. A little way off the remains of a man were crumpled into a ball of burned flesh and clothing. Eight people were killed; 102 were wounded, many—as in the Piazza Fontana massacre—by shards of blown-out windows and other flying debris.[45] Although the authorities immediately launched a search for suspected Ordine Nuovo terrorists, the motives and the identity of the people responsible for this terrorist bombing have not yet been established to the satisfaction of a law court.

Bombers struck again a little more than two months later. At 1:23 in the morning on Sunday, 4 August, the Rome-Brenner Italicus express train, filled with *ferragosto* vacationers, was rocked by a terrific explosion as it passed through a tunnel on the approach to Bologna. Twelve people died in the blast; forty-eight suffered serious injuries.[46] Thirteen-year-old Mauro Russo, badly injured in the explosion, watched in horrified helplessness as his three-year-old brother was burned alive. His mother and father were also killed. Several of the dead remained unidentified for days.

On 5 August a group known as Ordine Nero (Black Order) claimed responsibility for the Italicus explosion. In 1973 the courts had ordered the remnant Ordine Nuovo to disband, but by the following year Ordine Nero had taken over where the ordinovisti had left off, as champions of the violent Right. The Italicus and Brescia bombings completely eclipsed the Red Brigades, and indeed the latter seemed to derive their paramount importance from the role they played in furthering the radical Right's designs. The redoubtable anti-Communist interior minister Taviani publicly recanted his long-held belief that Communists represented the greatest danger to the state. "I and they have changed," he conceded.[47] The bombs of Brescia and Bologna had destroyed some of his most deeply held beliefs about Italian politics. Now he professed to believe, as many Italians did at the time, that the major terrorist threat to the country came from neofascist radicals.

Even in the immediate aftermath of the earlier Red Brigade murder of two missini in Padua on 17 June, Taviani had not thought to include the brigatisti among the subversive forces then making war on the Italian government. Although the killings had not been intentional,[48] they were the first murders for the brigatisti, deeds which, along with the Sossi kidnapping, signaled an ominous change from the days of the early seventies when the public thought of the Red Brigades, if it thought of them at all, as ideologically infatuated pranksters spray-painting revolutionary slogans on factory walls. Taviani reflected a trend among political analysts and government experts to minimize the importance of the Red Brigades and to pay no attention to the group's propaganda statements. Journalists joined in this enterprise. Stories of no journalistic merit whatsoever began to circulate on the theme that Curcio was probably part of the *trama nera*, or fascist plot—and this despite the unambiguous ideological pronouncements of the Red Brigades. Curcio's capture on 9 September 1974 did nothing to correct these misconceptions. Journalists continued to put Brigate Rosse in quotation marks, as though this form of terrorist activity were really the manifestation of one fascist hallucination or another.

Thus by late 1974 the distinctive faces of Italian terrorism—one black, the other red—had revealed themselves, but the revelations had yet to gain full acceptance. On the eve of the period when Red Brigadism would pose the greatest challenge to the political stability of Italy in the republic's history, the nature of this threat remained the subject more of misleading speculation than of solid fact. The very idea of Marxist-Leninist fanatics actually taking up arms against the Italian government seemed preposterous and was, therefore, the subject of much ridicule. Because of this fundamental misconception about what was happening in Italy to the left of official Marxist precincts, neofascism received credit for powers it did not possess. The five-year period that began with the Piazza Fontana bombing ended with the conviction firmly in place that Italian terrorism was essentially a product of neofascist machinations. The truth began to emerge slowly in 1975.

TWO

■■■■

Surging Red Brigadism

1975–1977

With Curcio's capture and imprisonment in 1974, Italians were subjected to the first of many premature in memoriam pronouncements regarding the Red Brigades. It was taken for granted that his enigmatic organization would never be heard from again. Curcio himself had described Red Brigadism in plain language, but his words had made almost no impression. The public was told by its political and opinion leaders that the Red Brigades were almost surely something other than what the authors of the group's propaganda statements repeatedly said they were. Now, after Curcio's arrest and that of his second-in-command, Alberto Franceschini, the issue of Red Brigadism appeared to retain only an academic significance.

The fortunes of the Red Brigades continued their sharp descent in October and November 1974. Though Red Brigade fugitives in Milan violently resisted arrest and succeeded in killing carabiniere officer Felice Maritano, four of them, including Roberto Ognibene, were captured on 15 October. Three weeks later the police arrested Alfredo Bonavita, who had been helping direct the Red Brigades since Curcio's capture. The organization now appeared to be utterly leaderless and without the capacity to generate suitable replacements for Curcio, Franceschini, and Bonavita. If there had been any doubts concerning the state's victory over the Red Brigades before, the events of October and November removed them completely.

The next three months were almost tranquil. In late November an explosion in Savona killed one and wounded eight, but the prevailing mood afterward was one of relief that a greater loss of life had been averted. Not until 18 February 1975 did the public sense that its optimism of the previous fall might have been unwarranted. On that day Mara Cagol and three other Red Brigadists walked up to the prison in Casale Monferrato, where Renato Curcio was incarcerated. A two-story building with facilities for forty-five inmates, the prison was the most dilapidated correctional facility in Italy. Moreover, Curcio had been given complete liberty to go anywhere on the institution's premises, make unlimited telephone calls outside, and have full and unregulated visitation rights. A journalist observed, "More than a prisoner, Curcio resembled a terrorist on sabbatical."[1]

The guards at the entrance perceived nothing out of the ordinary because it was Tuesday, visitors' day. Cagol and her three companions gained entry without undergoing even a minimal search. Suddenly the unsuspecting guards found themselves in the line of fire from a machine gun that Cagol had been hiding under her coat. The guards did what they were told as two of Cagol's companions also brandished machine guns while a third cut the institution's telephone wires. In this way the four terrorists subdued the entire nineteen-man security force and rescued Curcio.

The liberation of Curcio created a sensation. Coming not long after the shocking theft of Raphael's *Muta* and *Flagellazione di Cristo* from Urbino's Palazzo Ducale, the escape prompted one politician to comment sarcastically that the prisoner "had been guarded as though he were a Raphael."[2] Italy's antiquated prison system and the government's failure to take even the most basic precautions with captured terrorists became the subjects of scornful journalistic inquiries. In the best Italian tradition government officials publicly hurled scathing charges of incompetence and negligence at each other.

Two days later the Red Brigades, buoyed by the return of Curcio and the discomfiture of Italy's leaders, announced that henceforth they would vigorously prosecute their war of resistance against the Christian Democratic puppets of Gerald Ford and Henry Kissinger. In the brigatista's mind the evil work of traditional though hopelessly discredited fascism was now being performed by its close relative, "democratic" fascism, behind which the United States stood as the guiding force. The Christian Democrats and their allies worked merely as the district managers in Italy of the parent imperialist corporation with its headquarters in Washington. Revolution, the Red Brigadists maintained, was the only possible Marxist response to this state of affairs. In their own words of 20 February 1975: "The task of the revolutionary vanguard today is that of combatting, beginning in the factories, counterrevolution in all of its manifestations. . . . Let us liberate and organize all the revolutionary forces for the resistance against the white takeover. Armed struggle for communism."[3]

Once again the Red Brigades had produced a document that rendered the origins and objectives of the movement as clear as language could make them. It had arisen as a movement in despair with the Italian Communist party, the PCI, which recently had made public what had long been evident to discerning people in Italy: its desire for a historic compromise with the Christian Democrats. The Communist party leader Enrico Berlinguer now professed a belief in class collaboration. The working class, he claimed, could not triumph without the help of other classes. Furthermore, political isolation had been the fatal mistake of the Italian Left in 1922. Berlinguer's ideas crystallized around the party's new theme of independence from Moscow in search of the democratic way to socialism by means of a strategy of reform. Therefore, the party offered to work with all popular forces, including Catholics and Socialists.[4]

The Red Brigades flatly rejected this offer as a monstrous perversion of Marxism, and they were not the only ones who reacted to Berlinguerian ideas in this way. Many Communists expressed disenchantment with their party's moderation and were left ideologically homeless by Berlinguer's revisionist shifts. In *Unsettling Europe* Jane Kramer depicts the disturbed surprise of aged Communists in "San Vincenzo" when no one sang the Internazionale at the local Festa dell' Unità.[5] It had always been sung before; why not now? The answer, of course, was that the party no longer maintained a revolutionary profile; it had long since begun collaborating with industrialists and Catholics. For all the fundamentalist Marxists in Kramer's "San Vincenzo," the party's about-face was nothing less than a sacrilege, and their reaction typified that of Communists all over Italy for whom Marxism had been an evangelical faith. Nationwide the movements of the new extraparliamentary Left reacted against what their members viewed as the fall from revolutionary grace of the PCI.[6] Even the moderate Communist Umberto Terracini scolded the PCI for withdrawing too hastily and too far from a traditional Marxist position. "In short, for me the class struggle is not a particular of secondary importance," he sarcastically commented.[7] Very far to the left of Terracini, the Red Brigades would find recruits and a sympathetic audience among the revolutionary-minded who now ridiculed the PCI as a beached whale.

The Red Brigades remained quiet for a few months. Then, on 15 May, they were responsible for a major tactical innovation in the terrorist war on the state. Three masked Red Brigadists confronted Massimo De Cairolis, a lawyer, at gunpoint in his Milan office. A prominent Christian Democrat, he stood accused by the three intruders of counterrevolutionary machinations against the proletarian classes. Thus indicted, De Cairolis was handcuffed, gagged, and made to stand against a wall. One terrorist took careful aim and shot him in the leg. Then all three of the masked gunmen took flight. This was the first of many *gambizzazioni* (kneecappings).

By the late spring of 1975 terrorist episodes had become commonplace, and no longer could each one be featured on page one of the newspapers. On 4 June, however, the Red Brigade kidnapping of Vittorio Vallarino Gancia, a liquor millionaire, dwarfed all other news stories. The brigatisti abducted him near his villa in Piedmont. Twenty hours later the carabinieri caught up with them near Acqui Terme. A fierce gun battle ensued and lasted for half an hour. As usual the terrorists were extremely well armed. The carabinieri were on the receiving end of two hand grenades; one of the explosions blew off the arm of a lieutenant and severely injured his left eye. A lance corporal also fell critically wounded. At this high price Gancia was restored to freedom.

The terrorists suffered a grievous loss as well: Renato Curcio's wife, Mara Cagol, was killed. Curcio himself survived the gun battle and escaped. Speculation now ran rampant in Italy on the dialectical progression of Cagol from a conservative Catholic girlhood, characterized chiefly by good grades in school and a critically acclaimed talent as a guitar player, to a rendezvous with violent death.

Born in Sardagna, near Trento, on 8 April 1945, Mara had been the delight of her archly Catholic shopkeeper parents. Singularly devout in the profession of her faith, she seemed destined for a musical career, particularly after 1961, when she finished third in a national music contest. Concerts at the Filarmonica di Trento followed, and in 1963 she went on a tour of France, where her concerts were well received.[8] While not intending to abandon her musical career, she decided to enter the University of Trento to take courses in the immensely popular sociology department. Here she met Curcio; with him she was converted to an extremely militant form of communism. At Curcio's side and always in his shadow, she participated in the endless student demonstrations and sit-ins of the middle and late 1960s. She also performed very ably in her studies, completed a highly praised thesis entitled "Qualification of the Work Force in Phases of Capitalistic Development," and graduated with highest honors. After their marriage, the Curcios moved to Milan to experience working-class life.[9] They helped found the Metropolitan Political Collective and became the most famous leaders in the early history of the Red Brigades.

Rumors abounded at the time of Cagol's death that a miscarriage she suffered in Milan tipped the balance in her mind toward ever more radical forms of revolutionary protest, but it would require an excessively ingenious psychohistorian to trace the origin of her terrorist activity to the anguished sensibilities of frustrated motherhood. Cagol's concept of a cleansing revolutionary apocalypse had begun to take shape during her university days. Milan, a city she loathed as a monstrous excrescence of capitalism, was merely the scene of dénouement in her ideological development. Mara, along with Curcio, long since had become convinced that the capitalist system should be destroyed by any means at the revolutionary proletariat's disposal, including the most violent. The Red Brigades were the translation into fact of these ideas, to which Mara made major contributions.

In a 6 June 1975 in memoriam message the Red Brigades bade Mara farewell, calling on all sincere revolutionaries who were struggling for worker autonomy and communism to honor the fallen leader's memory by imitating her example: "May a thousand arms reach out to pick up her rifle."[10] Mara's death had been a tragic price for them to pay, but not so high as to make them prefer the slavery of salaried labor and the dictatorship of the bourgeoisie in its fascist and democratic variants over the communist destiny of mankind, which could only be achieved by revolutionary class war.

The summer and fall of 1975 passed without serious terrorist incident, but then on 11 November a group calling itself Potere Proletariato Armato shot Milan businessmen Valerio Di Marco three times in the legs. This shooting, which took place before two hundred people, introduced the Italians to yet another gang of left-wing terrorists. Before the decade ended, no fewer than 597 groups, of the Left and the Right, made attempts to disrupt Italian political and institutional life.[11]

Meanwhile, the Red Brigades continued to sustain crippling losses. Fabrizio Pelli, twenty-three years old and one of Curcio's most talented lieutenants, was captured in Pavia on 26 December 1975. Susanna Ronconi, also twenty-three and destined to play a highly dramatic role in the subsequent history of Italian terrorism, barely escaped capture in the same raid. In what appeared to be a crowning misfortune, Renato Curcio was recaptured following an 18 January 1976 gun battle with police in Milan. Once again journalists and political commentators began tolling the bell for Red Brigadism.

Indeed, for the next few months all was relatively quiet. Then beginning in April 1976, Red Brigade sabotage lit up the skies, with a billion lire worth of damage at Fiat Mirafiori on 3 April in Milan and a two billion lire firebombing at Fiat in Turin eleven days later. On the sixteenth Fiat suffered its third act of sabotage for the month while the "Squadra Mara Cagol" set fire to a warehouse in Rome owned by the Standa department store chain. Five days later Giovanni Theodoli, president of the Unione Petrolifera Italiana and Chevron, was accosted in the middle of Rome by terrorists belonging to a group called the Nuclei Armati Proletari (Armed Proletarian Nuclei) and shot eight times. Then on 29 April left-wing terrorists of uncertain affiliation assassinated Enrico Pedenovi, the provincial counselor for the Movimento Sociale Italiano (MSI) in Milan. In a retaliatory attack the following day, nine neofascists assaulted a leftist youth, Gaetano Amoroso, and stabbed him to death.

With Italian terrorists once again giving proof of their unanticipated power to survive, the Turin trial of captured Red Brigadists began on 17 May 1976. The proceedings got under way with the accused taunting the judges and putting them on notice that the Italian court system itself, not the Red Brigades, should be on trial. A spokesman for the prisoners read a declaration inviting all armed communist organizations to make the trial an occasion for political and military confrontation as well as for class unity. The communist attack, he said, should be carried by the fighting party to the heart of the state.[12] The judges found the people of Turin strongly disinclined to participate as jurors, and the trial was postponed numerous times.

True to their threatening word, the Red Brigades did not remain passive objects of the state's judicial system. Instead, with the trial already sputtering, they struck a blow that, more than any other act up to this time, established their credentials as the unrivaled terrorist organization of the day. The Red Brigades had long promised to settle accounts with Judge Francesco Coco, Genoa's attorney general, the man who had gone back on his agreement in the Sossi kidnapping case. The Red Brigades had released Sossi in exchange for Coco's promise that eight imprisoned terrorists would be given their freedom, but in the end these terrorists had remained in jail. Such an insolent affront to the people's justice could not go unanswered, and on 8 June 1976 the Red Brigades gave their answer.

It was a brilliantly sunny and warm day in Genoa. In accordance with his workday custom, Coco left his office on Via Pammatone for a midday meal with his family. He was driven home by his new driver, Antioco Dejana, and was accompanied by his bodyguard. The bodyguard, Giovanni Saponara, got out of the car with him, and they started up the *salita* Santa Brigida to the family home while Dejana parked the car nearby. Five terrorists, armed with pistols and machine guns, were waiting for the pair and began firing before Saponara could even make a move toward his holster. Both men fell dead instantly. Parts of Coco's head were blown away. At the same time Dejana—who by an evil chance had started his new job that day—was killed while sitting in the car. Coco's horrified wife and daughter were the first to behold this scene of slaughter.

The next day Curcio announced in the Turin courtroom: "Yesterday we put to death Coco, enemy of the proletariat."[13] Prospero Gallinari later rose and began to read the official Red Brigade declaration on the Coco operation: "Yesterday, on 8 June 1976, armed nuclei of the Red Brigades executed the executioner of the state, Francesco Coco. . . . "[14] Guido Barbaro, the president of the court, interrupted Gallinari and ruled him out of order. Gallinari continued anyway: " . . . and also the two mercenaries who had to protect him." Amid loud tumult, the judge ordered him removed from the courtroom.

Subsequent investigations into Coco's murder revealed that as late as 1976 imprisoned Italian terrorists were treated just like other prisoners. Curcio and his group, for example, had permission not only to use typewriters but also to make unsupervised telephone calls. In all probability, these investigators surmised, Curcio had merely telephoned Coco's death sentence to Red Brigadists on the outside. The state had not yet grasped the nature of the threat posed by the Red Brigades, although Coco's shocking murder did have the effect of a fire bell in the night.

With the shock value of left-wing terror then exceeding all previous records, the radical Right could and did remain in the background. The Red Brigades and ideologically related terrorist groups were, in effect, carrying out the neofascist strategy of tension by proxy, and this development made it possible for the radical Right to husband its resources. It was as though the communist bogeyman of neofascist rhetoric had actually taken shape before the democratic strawman of that rhetoric. There was no need for the Right to blow up trains or banks now. By the force of events unleashed by the radical Left, the Italian people might yet be pushed into the arms of a latter-day Mussolini who would promise them stability and order. Every unanswered blow by the Red Brigades and the rest of the leftist terrorists helped confirm the thesis of the radical Right that the government lacked the intelligence, the will, and the power to protect Italy from the armed fanatics of the Marxist underworld. *Tanto peggio, tanto meglio.* Things were getting worse—and therefore better.

Nonetheless, the machine-gun death of Judge Vittorio Occorsio in Rome at 8:40 A.M. on 10 July 1976, just as he took the wheel of his car on the way to work, came as an electrifying reminder of the extreme Right's continuing presence in Italian life. Welcome as the assistance of the terrorist Left had been, it was not always selective enough for the precise needs of the radical Right. Occorsio, for instance, had been prominently connected with judicial investigations of right-wing terrorism. He had a particular interest in Ordine Nuovo and its successor organization, Ordine Nero. Occorsio had gotten too close to the truth about the connections between these groups and individuals in the secret services as well as in the judiciary.[15] For once in recent months the actions of the terrorist Left were supplemented by an action of the neofascists. Moreover, the timing of this act— just two days after the fall of Aldo Moro's fifth and final government, which had been anemic since birth on 23 November 1974—was an added bonus for radical right-wing subversives, who relished exploiting the republic's ministerial crises.

For the next several months the terrorists of both extremes appeared to be following their respective designs in a most languid manner, but even without campaigns of systematic violence these individuals could count 1976 a success. This was because the government, now guided by Giulio Andreotti, wounded itself as badly as any series of terrorist acts could have. Scandals of omission and commission gravely weakened the government. There was nothing it could be expected to do about the terrible sequence of severe drought and torrential rain that summer, but its poor responses to a devastating earthquake in Friuli and a poison gas disaster in Seveso, near Milan, were subjects of withering criticism all over the country.

In that same year two international scandals broke upon the Italian government. First, it was revealed that from 1948 to 1976 the U.S. Central Intelligence Agency had contributed seventy-five million dollars to anti-Communist parties during Italian elections and that from 1963 to 1972 Exxon Corporation had spent from forty-six to forty-nine million dollars for the same purpose.[16] Soon afterward Christian Democratic and Social Democratic officials in Italy were indicted for taking bribes from Lockheed in the sale of Hercules C-130 airplanes. Economic crises accompanied the political scandals: the trade deficit worsened, inflation climbed along with unemployment, and the Italian economy could only be sustained by a series of loans from the International Monetary Fund, the European Economic Community, Germany, and the United States. The Red Brigades, now down to no more than fifteen members, and the numerically exiguous right-wing bombers could and did take heart from the national distress for which they both offered a violent epuration.[17]

The year 1976 ended with fierce fighting between terrorists and policemen in Rome and Milan. The Nuclei Armati Proletari killed a policeman in Rome on 14 December. The following day Milan police raided the Sesto San Giovanni home of Walter Alasia, long suspected of being a brigatista. The police arrived late at night at the door of the house where Alasia lived with his parents and brother, Oscar. The bewildered father let the officers in, and they proceeded to Walter's bedroom. He was waiting for them and fired several pistol shots. Two policemen fell to the floor dead or dying.

Walter Alasia, in turn killed by other officers, was described as a young man without a history, or at least without an apparent history. Neighbors remembered him as cultivated and courteous. His father, a member of the PCI, had been reassured when Walter agreed with his denunciations of the Red Brigades as "delinquents." The elder Alasia had noted with approval his son's decision to stop reading *Lotta continua* and other extraparliamentary Left newspapers. Yet all the while, Walter—only twenty years old when he died—had been leading a double life, a seemingly dutiful and compliant son on one hand and a Red Brigade terrorist on the other.

Alasia's case appeared to be a vivid illustration of what the sociologists Sabino Acquaviva and Mario Santuccio described in *Social Structure of Italy* (1976) as the tragedy of Italian education: "People come to the end of their studies equipped with an out-of-date culture that proves an anomaly in the society in which they have to earn their living."[18] Alasia had been a student at the neighborhood Istituto Tecnico Industriale Statale (ITIS). Once a prestigious technical school whose graduates seldom failed to obtain lucrative jobs, ITIS by the early 1970s was paralyzed by the open-admissions policy that afflicted Italian higher education generally. For Alasia, as his future biographer, Giorgio Manzini, would remark, the school "became a factory of malaise, of desperate frustration."[19] Alasia and his fellow radical students at ITIS, alienated by the reformist tendencies of the PCI and inspired by Lotta Continua, Potere Operaio, Avanguardia Operaia, and other dissident groups promoting the myth of Marxist revolution on the extraparliamentary left, made up lists of proscribed teachers—elitists who were hard graders. These youths disrupted the school by running through the halls during classtime with megaphones, inciting other students to overthrow the reactionary educational system. When Alasia and his friends did deign to attend classes it was only to provoke the teachers, either by turning their backs on them or by moving their chairs out into the hallway, chanting revolutionary slogans as they left.

School could offer Walter Alasia nothing but a way station on the road to revolution against a system that he hated past the power of endurance. He was a young man who slept with loaded weapons under his bed, dreaming dreams of whose existence no one in his family—not even the brother who shared his room— even suspected. "My son," his father said in the aftermath of Walter's murders and death; "now I know that I did not know him."[20]

The next year, 1977, began on an ominous note for Italy when the Red Brigades received a ransom of one-and-a-half billion lire for kidnapped industrialist, Pietro Costa. This money financed the organization's increasingly ambitious plans for 1977 as the country's political and social environment continued to deteriorate. The economy was dominated by the aftermath of the 1976 lira crisis, when the currency suffered a 30 percent devaluation. Industrial production fell by nearly 8 percent, while unemployment rose by the same amount. The ups and downs of the economy subjected the political system to severe strains, and in 1977 the entire society, with the universities in the forefront, reached the most remote limits of its patience.[21] Upheavals unprecedented in scope stunned the country and left it supremely vulnerable to terrorist attack from extremist groups, whose ranks now began to swell. These new recruits and supporters came to terrorism in a mixed mood that included both alienation with politics (the elections of 1976 had resulted in a nationwide rejection of the extraparliamentary Left parties) and exuberance over the country's mounting physical violence, which seemed to portend revolution.[22] The doom of the republic, long prophesied by Marxist and neofascist radicals, appeared to be at hand, emanating from the streets of the capital itself.

A conspicuous difference between university life in Italy and the United States is that the American idea of a centralized campus does not have a precise equivalent in the Italian *città universitaria*, or university city. At the University of Rome, for example, many of the school's faculties, or departments, are scattered far beyond the limits of the university city. This means that when students engage in political protests their activities are not confined to a relatively isolated college yard; instead, large zones of the nation's capital can be overrun with street fighting between protestors and policemen.

Rome experienced the first of many such street battles on 2 February 1977. It began with a neofascist attack in the university city that left one Communist wounded. A counterattack was mobilized against the headquarters of the extreme right-wing organization Fronte della Gioventù, located in the Piazza Indipendenza near the university's teachers' training college. Two thousand extraparliamentary Left youths assembled for this assault. The police intervened in an attempt to avert further bloodshed, but an officer was shot and mortally wounded. A fellow officer fired answering shots, hitting two protestors in retreat. All Rome went into shock over these scenes of guerrilla warfare, but it was just the beginning.

The revolutionary fires smoldered for a little more than a week and then broke out again on 10 February. Christian Democratic offices in the Piazza del Gesù sustained the worst damage, as numerous commandos of the ultra-Left, striking virtually without opposition, left four wounded victims and tens of millions of lire worth of fire damages. Other politically inspired eruptions occurred all over the city, with major attacks on MSI headquarters and the Monte Sacro Standa department store.

Another week passed as political tensions in and around the university continued to mount. On 18 February Luciano Lama, the Communist secretary of the Confederazione Generale del Lavoro (CGIL) appeared at the university city for a speech. At PCI headquarters it was imagined that this would be a day of triumph for the party, but as the proceedings got under way Communist officials became by turns bewildered and angry in the face of the extraparliamentary Left's taunts and jeers. Even before Lama's speech, youths began to chant sarcastically, "More work, less pay," in reference to the secretary's plea for realism in labor negotiations with capitalists. Other chants, equally sarcastic, rose from the constantly swelling crowd of university students: "More huts, fewer houses" and "All power to the bosses." These sarcasms provoked a hostile reaction from PCI members in the audience, who retorted: "Away, away members of the new bourgeoisie."[23] The level of political discourse was not raised when the extraparliamentary Left targets of this sneer responded with "Away, away members of the new police."

The university's Piazza della Minerva resounded with these abusive refrains as Lama mounted the speaker's platform. Reciprocal insults between the official and the extraparliamentary Left could still be heard as Lama commenced speaking, at 10:30 A.M. Here and there in the crowd verbal taunts led to punches and kicks. One PCI security guard, concerned for the safety of those on the platform, turned his extinguisher on some of the militants, whose fury then became uncontainable. Lama continued to speak, but all attention was now directed toward the members of the PCI security guard, who had become targets of potatoes, pieces of wood, and chunks of asphalt. Lama hurriedly concluded his speech, and only with great difficulty could the PCI committee be escorted to safety beyond the reach of a hate-filled, violent mob of student radicals.[24] The truck on which the speaker's platform had been mounted was turned over and destroyed. The students, who obviously had come prepared for a demonstration of this kind, drew clubs, crowbars, tire irons, and monkey wrenches. Only after university rector Antonio Ruberti called the police, at 12:30, could the situation be brought under control. The police had to use tear gas to disperse the crowd. Meanwhile, the Faculty of Letters became converted into a temporary infirmary for care of the wounded.

The day of rage at the University of Rome caused a national reaction of consternation and soul-searching as the country sought to understand the causes of student malaise and violence. The attack on Lama was seen as a microcosm of Italy's disaster in the field of higher education; the university system had arrived, in the words of the minister of public education, "at permanent chaos."[25] Of the country's one million university students, relatively few could enter the job market prepared for gainful employment. At the University of Rome, where 200,000 students matriculated, many of the professors openly admitted that their school had become a factory of illiteracy and discontent.[26] What the University of Rome suffered in elephantine proportions, other public universities experienced in varying degrees of seriousness. The whole system had become a spawning ground for radicals, and from such large reservoirs of alienated youth the terrorists had been able to recruit many followers.[27] The connection between student violence and terrorism was palpable.

Disturbances continued at the University of Rome, and on 5 March 1977 ten thousand radical students battled with policemen for more than four hours. Once again the violence spread beyond the university precincts into adjoining neighborhoods. In the ensuing melee two policemen fell with bullet wounds. Three other policemen suffered multiple contusions. The police counterattacked with tear gas and routed the students. Still, the university remained a live volcano. The next day the Academic Senate temporarily closed down the entire university.

The scene of the student rebellion then shifted to Bologna, where on 11 March four thousand students gathered to protest carabiniere violence in the death of a twenty-five-year-old member of Lotta Continua, Pier Francesco Lorusso. He had been killed during a student protest meeting over university reform, and afterward the radicals went on a rampage. Violent incidents erupted along the elegant Via Rizzoli, the address of Bologna's most luxurious shops; few showcase windows were left unbroken, and expropriations became the order of the day. A stone-throwing mob assaulted the prefecture, and only with tremendous difficulty did the police turn it away. The city's train station became the scene of even more violent altercations; dozens of people were wounded, and the police arrested more than twenty demonstrators.[28]

The impact of Lorusso's death reverberated throughout Italy, and on the following day—a rainy Saturday—students from twenty-five cities arrived in Rome for a gigantic protest. At 4:00 P.M. the protestors began their march from the Piazza Esedra to the Piazza del Popolo. Most of the fifty thousand participants had not come to Rome for an armed confrontation with the police, but as usual during this period a protest of moral indignation quickly turned to violence. Fights, stonings, and fires ravaged the procession route. Police and radicals exchanged gun shots. No one was killed, but panic seized most of the students as they fanned out in disarray across the entire city. In the Piazza Venezia alone, four to five hundred terrorized marchers surrendered with their hands held high or folded on top of their heads.

Battles between the police and hard-core revolutionaries continued far into the night, and in the next day's early morning light the city looked like a deserted battlefield. Countless stores, bars, and restaurants had suffered damage; burned-out shells of automobiles were smoldering in the streets; cartridges from machine guns, rifles, and pistols littered the sidewalks. Here and there Molotov cocktails had been left unused. Everywhere there was the smell of tear gas. Full-scale urban guerrilla warfare had come to the streets of the nation's capital.

And not only in Rome. The violence in Bologna had escalated as well. An assault by extremists on an army barracks had netted one hundred rifles, fifty pistols, and stores of ammunition. The police then took to the streets in full riot gear, complete with bulletproof vests. They invaded and closed Radio Alice, an extra-parliamentary Left station that had called for revenge against the murderers of comrade Lorusso and whose broadcasters actually had been directing Bologna's revolt, ordering Molotov cocktails where they were needed. Police reinforcements from half of Italy had to be brought to Bologna, but the situation remained wildly out of control. For a time, before the arrival of decisive reinforcements, it appeared that the radicals might make good on their threat to destroy the PCI's showcase city, which extraparliamentary Left writers for years had called The Communist Disneyland. "The junta of Bologna," these radicals jeered, "is red only with shame," not because of any serious application of Marxism to the city's social and economic problems. [29]

Such spectacular disturbances lent credence to the thesis of left-wing terrorist groups that the moment of communist revolution was at hand. They saw in the war-torn streets of Bologna and Rome proof that political violence in Italy had acquired a vital connection with society. This violence was not what the government said it was: the criminal work of a few crazed fanatics. The events of March 1977 had disproved that thesis. In fact, revolution was in the air. The question now for such groups as the Red Brigades was how to give the revolution proper direction. Italian communists had to find an answer to Lenin's famous question: what is to be done?

Lenin himself was never one to wait passively for events to take their dialectical course, and his willingness to take a hand in furthering the cause of revolution was a characteristic that his admirers in the Red Brigades sought to imitate. Contemporaneous with Rome's "black Saturday," Bologna's riots, and related disturbances from Brescia to Palermo, left-wing terrorists continued to attack the state. With this campaign of systematic violence they sought to give proper guidance to the country's revolutionary impulse, according to the principles laid down by Lenin. The Red Brigades, the Armed Proletarian Nuclei (NAP), and related revolutionary organizations imagined that they were working to achieve precisely this end during the violent March of 1977. On 12 March a group calling itself the Brigate Combattenti shot and killed Giuseppe Ciotta, a twenty-nine-year-old police officer in Turin. NAP terrorists killed a twenty-one-year-old policeman, Claudio Graziosi, in Rome on 23 March.

Terrorist kneecappings in Rome and Pisa closed out the bloody month, and then April began with the sensational kidnapping of Guido De Martino in Naples. The son of Francesco De Martino, who for years had been a leading figure in the Socialist party, Guido was set free after forty days of imprisonment. But his release was secured only after payment of a ransom of reportedly one billion lire. [30] Critics of the ransom payment charged that the De Martino case set a fatal precedent by encouraging more political kidnappings. The elder De Martino admitted that the blackmail payment was a defeat, but at least he had his son home.

The Red Brigades even managed to use the trial of Curcio and other captured brigatisti to demonstrate the helplessness of the state and, simultaneously, to encourage the belief that the revolution was gaining momentum. They promised to sabotage the trial and publicly threatened with death all lawyers who participated in the proceedings. On 28 April terrorists assassinated Fulvio Croce, the seventy-six-year-old president of the Lawyers' Association and the man in charge of selecting the public defenders for indicted Red Brigadists. In answer to the murder of Croce, all the lawyers of Turin agreed to act as public defenders of Curcio et al.

Despite this show of solidarity by the lawyers, Turin was a city dominated by fear, its people literally immobilized in a state of siege. The 2 May murder of two policemen by terrorists heightened tensions over the Curcio trial, and on the following day Guido Barbaro, the president of the Corte d' Assise, ruefully announced the court's failure to find a sufficient number of jurors. "With this," he lamented, "terrorism has won; the state has been defeated."[31] Judge Barbaro had beseeched the prospective jurors to do their duty, but of three hundred candidates only four would serve. One frightened man told him: "You have chosen this for your profession. We no."[32] In truth it would have been asking too much of human nature to expect judicious deliberation from men and women scared out of their wits.

The Red Brigades pressed the advantages they had gained in the Turin trial fiasco by launching a campaign against their most implacable foes in the media. On 2 June 1977 in Genoa they attacked the vice-director of *Secolo XIX*, Vittorio Bruno, shooting him five times in the legs and twice in the arms. The same day other terrorists in Milan shot Indro Montanelli, the director of *Giornale nuovo*, four times in the legs. The Red Brigades marked TGI news director Emilio Rossi for a kneecapping of unprecedented ferocity. He stood accused of using his influential position to spread lies about Italy's new resistance fighters. On 3 June they shot him twenty-two times in the legs. The bones were smashed to pieces, and doctors doubted that he would ever walk normally again.

Stymied in Turin, Italian authorities in the following month transferred the Curcio trial to Milan. Once again the Red Brigades promised to disrupt the proceedings. Their target this time was Mario Trimarchi, the sixty-seven-year-old first president of the Court of Appeals, but they failed to penetrate the thick wall of police protection surrounding him. Instead the terrorists settled for an attack on two of his carabiniere bodyguards, who were shot in the legs a short distance from the place where Indro Montanelli had been kneecapped. The public impact of these shootings was great, and all Milan braced for another wave of Red Brigade violence.

As the Curcio trial got underway in mid-June 1977 with maximum obstructionism on the part of the defendants, who loudly threatened the lawyers and judges with death, hugely destructive fires were set at the Magneti Marelli and Sit-Siemens business firms on 19 June. These fires burned out of control into the following day, when the Squadre Operaie Combattenti attacked a Sit-Siemens department head, Giuseppe D'Ambrosio, in front of his home. The terrorists shot him twice in the left leg and once in the right thigh. Elsewhere in the city on that day terrorist bombs destroyed or severely damaged nearly two dozen new Fiat automobiles.

The 23 June sentencing of Curcio to seven years in the penitentiary, to be served in addition to sentences he had received from courts in Bologna and Reggio Emilia, brought Italy no respite from the Red Brigades' campaign of terror. Knee-cappings and other terrorist assaults continued to occur from Friuli to Sicily during late June and early July. Each of these attacks would have received extensive news-paper coverage even less than a year before, but by the summer of 1977 stories on terrorism were beginning to read like war bulletins, some of them receiving only single-line mention.

On 1 July the terrorists suffered a major reverse in Rome. Home of Michel-angelo's *Moses* and the chains of St. Peter, the ancient church of San Pietro in Vincoli has always attracted vast crowds of tourists and religious pilgrims in the summertime. The church was also practically next door to the carabiniere barracks. Nevertheless, Antonio Lo Muscio and three other members of NAP, called *nappisti*, sat down, laughing and joking, on the church steps. Too late, they realized that the carabinieri had closed in on them. Lo Muscio bolted toward buildings in the direction of the Colosseum, but he fell with six bullet wounds—the fatal one behind his left ear—not twenty meters from the church and right in front of the University of Rome's Engineering Faculty. Two captured women, Franca Salerno and Maria Pia Vianale, resisted arrest and howled insults at the carabinieri who silenced them with a rain of blows from their service revolvers. The fourth member of the group escaped.

Lo Muscio's death virtually eliminated NAP as a vital force in Italian terrorism. The Nuclei Armati Proletari had been founded in 1970 by young Neapolitan uni-versity students, mostly of middle-class background and even from the same neigh-borhood. The historic nucleus was made up of young men and women who had been friends since childhood: Alfredo Papale, the son of a general; Maria Pia Vianale, the daughter of two teachers; Giuseppe Gentile, the son of poor peasants from Matera but adopted by a petroleum company executive, Pasquale Schiavone; Pierdomenico Delli Veneri, the son of a brick-works industrialist; Nicola Pellacchia, the son of a lawyer; Vitaliano (Vito) Principe, the son of a teacher. Lo Muscio had not been part of the original group, but he had been one of the first recruits and had inherited the leadership position as, one by one, most of the original *nappisti* fell in action or went to prison.

According to their propaganda statements, the nappisti stood for the liberation of the *non garantiti*, or, in the phrase of Frantz Fanon, one of their favorite authors, "the wretched of the earth."[33] They despised the PCI and even the extraparlia-mentary Left parties as feckless apologists for the status quo. Violent, unremitting revolution was the only answer to neocapitalist corporativism, which the official Left, according to the nappisti, had the effrontery to call "our democracy." They wanted to go back to the pristine sources of communist revolution, and with this ideal in mind they set up their own little politburo.

For a while it was all wildly radical talk in a neighborhood bar. Then they started to read George Jackson and Carlos Marighella.[34] From these sources the nappisti learned about prisons as a reservoir of revolutionary manpower. They then established contacts with prisoners in various parts of Italy. In Perugia, for example, where a high degree of politicization among convicts had already occurred, Fiorentino Conti led the Red Panthers; he soon became a major NAP leader. Martino Zichitella and Pietro Sofia, two Sicilians who had grown up in the north, followed the same path to positions of leadership in NAP. Lo Muscio himself had become politicized in the Lecce prison, where the nappisti recruited him to their cause.

By the early 1970s NAP had become a clearly defined revolutionary organization, made up essentially of three nuclei: the student radicals of Naples and the convicts in Perugia and Lecce. From such disparate and seemingly immiscible materials one of Italy's most violent terrorist campaigns was formed. In these early years Sergio Romeo, a former convict and a student—with a foot at each pole of NAP's bipolar world—acted as the group's go-between. He became the first nappista to be killed. He died, along with Luca Mantini, in a gun battle with carabinieri on 29 October 1974 during a foiled robbery attempt.

In addition to expropriations of the kind Romeo and Mantini were attempting, the nappisti carried out numerous acts of political terrorism; attacking Christian Democratic headquarters in Naples, blowing up the automobiles of government and police officials, and kidnapping judges and businessmen.[35] This NAP offensive did not last. The organization suffered a disastrous blow on 11 March 1975, when Vito Principe blew himself up while working on explosives. Alfredo Papale was badly injured in the blast. Police discovered numerous incriminating documents in the debris, and a roundup of many nappisti swiftly followed.

As if to prove that it was still a vital organization with an unimpaired capacity to terrorize the state, NAP waited scarcely a month to attack and wound the Christian Democratic regional counselor for Lazio, Filippo De Iorio. Then on 6 May they kidnapped Judge Giuseppe Di Gennaro, the official responsible for the electronic center of the prison administration. A few days later nappisti prisoners Pietro Sofia, Giorgio Panizzari, and Martino Zichitella in Viterbo barricaded themselves in a room with three hostages. They attempted to bargain their way out of jail in exchange for their own hostages as well as a promise that Di Gennaro would be released. The authorities refused to negotiate. Both NAP actions came to nothing. Di Gennaro was released without conditions, and the Viterbo jail-break attempt ended peacefully.

Their own explosives and gun battles with the police continued to take a bloody toll on the nappisti. On 30 May 1975 a bomb exploded in the hand of Giovanni Taras, and he was killed. Then, on 8 July, officer Antonio Tuzzolino shot and killed the sister of Luca Mantini, Annamaria, as she was trying to kill him. Four months later he was shot and paralyzed in a NAP reprisal. Despite their thinning ranks, the NAP realized the dream of Pierdomenico Delli Veneri on 1 March 1976 by joining forces with the Red Brigades in a wave of simultaneous attacks on carabinieri stations in Milan, Turin, Genoa, Naples, Florence, and Pisa. Other joint actions under the Red Brigade sign of the encircled five-pointed star and the NAP hammer and sickle at the center of a star reportedly followed throughout the spring.

With the arrest of Giuseppe Schiavone, the petroleum executive's son, in July and Pierdomenico Delli Veneri, the industrialist's son, in September, NAP was an organization without its historic nucleus. Now its leadership passed to common criminals, notably Lo Muscio and Zichitella, who for some time had been on the loose. Both met death in combat with the carabinieri. Zichitella apparently was killed by accident at the hands of Lo Muscio during a police ambush attempt on 14 December 1976. Then seven months later, with Lo Muscio's death at the church of San Pietro, one of the last embers of a conflagration sparked by radical talk in a Neapolitan bar was extinguished.

A subsequent police investigation of Lo Muscio's hideout revealed that the nappisti had not merely chanced to be sitting on the steps of San Pietro. They had been waiting there for university rector Antonio Ruberti to emerge from the Engineering Faculty, where he had gone for a teachers' meeting. The nappisti had already prepared a statement claiming responsibility for an attack on him. Alongside the NAP signature on this statement was that of the Red Brigades, documenting once again the working alliance between these two terrorist groups.

The elimination of the Nuclei Armati Proletari as an effective ally of the Red Brigades did not materially alter the nation's assessment of left-wing terrorism as a growing threat. The NAP had always been a distinctly junior partner in this alliance, and the Red Brigades remained in the field, an adversary of proven capacity. Moreover, a horde of related left-wing terrorist groups vied with each other for pride of place in the revolutionary vanguard alongside the Red Brigades. The nappisti had fallen, but "the thousand arms" of Red Brigade rhetoric were reaching out to pick up their rifles. Terrorist kneecappings, beatings, and car burnings continued to pile up during July 1977. Then, following a *ferragosto* lull during which even Italian terrorists went on holiday, the violent campaign against the institutions of Italy's democracy dramatically widened.

THREE

▬▬▬▬▬▬

Living the Revolution

On 19 September 1977 commandos of Azione Rivoluzionaria ambushed *l'Unita*'s Leone Ferrero in Turin and shot him five times in the legs. This kind of kidnapping had become commonplace in Italy, but the attack on Ferrero was noteworthy in the highest degree. He was the first Communist journalist to fall before terrorist gunfire. His attackers claimed that they had "punished a bastard . . . at the service of the regime."[1] Here, in a phrase, was the essence of things for the most radical exponents of the revolutionary Left in Italy during the late 1970s: the Communist party men in grey flannel suits had betrayed the revolutionary cause, and they had to be pushed aside, brutally if necessary, to make room for authentic Marxist revolutionaries.

The radical or extraparliamentary Left was a vital but ill-defined force in Italian politics. It had given rise to political sentiments and ideological expressions of great variety.[2] While not characteristic of the movement as a whole, proterrorist convictions—or, at any rate, a comprehending tolerance of terrorism—were conspicuous at the 22–24 September 1977 extraparliamentary Left rally in Bologna. The atmosphere was dense with anger and violence. Graffiti on university walls told the story well enough: "Zanghieri [the Communist mayor of the city] = shit" and "PCI = spies." And this was just what the extraparliamentary Left thought of the official Left.[3] Their slogans for the Christian Democrats and other conservatives were unprintable.

Six thousand policemen were present to cope with a crowd expected to reach forty thousand. Helicopters and carabinieri kept the entire city under surveillance, but most of the speeches and meetings were scheduled to take place at the university and in the Palazzo dello Sport. Even before the rally began a young member of Lotta Continua was shot accidentally by a friend, and the *bolognesi* prepared for what they feared would be three riotous days. The opening deliberations appeared to confirm the worst fears of the authorities as thousands screamed "Free Curcio!" In the face of all predictions, the three days passed without major incident, although one journalist tellingly noted that the real story in Bologna lay in the mere presence of so many thousands of young people at an ultrared convention.[4] They had a program of dreams and rage. They stood against the Italian status quo to which the PCI declared itself firmly attached, and some of them were ready to ignite the revolution without further ado. The Bologna rally pointed unmistakably toward the place where terrorist groups were getting some of their most militant recruits.

While it would be an oversimplification to say that the extraparliamentary Left was the lengthened shadow of Raniero Panzieri (1921–64), this intellectual did exercise a pervasive influence on the movement at a crucial stage in its history, during the early 1960s. His own political outlook was formed by the ideological disputes of the 1940s. For the rest of his life he sought to develop a revolutionary tactic that would protect the integrity of Marxism. His ideological itinerary possesses a high historical value for anyone interested in the mentality, so strikingly in evidence at the Bologna convention, that gave rise to the revolutionary assault on the Italian state in the 1970s and 1980s. In a short but intense career Panzieri attempted to live the revolution of Marxist prophecy. It was an example that inspired emulation. Living the revolution became the vital impulse for a heterogeneous generation of 1960s Marxist radicals. Some of them rested content with academic inquiries about capitalism, whereas others demanded—as the tactically innovative Red Brigades would later demand—the immediate and violent overthrow of capitalism. Panzieri's story illuminates them all.

Panzieri launched his career with some serious disadvantages for a young man graduating from high school in 1938. To begin with, he was Jewish, and that made a state university education impossible until close to the end of the war. He did take some classes in philosophy and economics at the Vatican's Pontificium Institutum Utruiusque Juris, which was the only school where Roman Jews of his generation could enroll in advanced courses. With the fall of fascism in 1943 he began reading Marx, and the next year he joined the Socialist party (PSI). Employment as a book editor in the Centro di Studi Sociali immediately followed, and Panzieri began to write book reviews for various left-wing publications.[5] By the fall of 1945 he had completed all his course work at the Vatican school but refused to accept suggested changes in his thesis. On 26 October he enrolled at the University of Urbino, and four days later he received highest honors for his thesis, on Morelly, "L'utopia rivoluzionaria nel settecento: il *Code de la Nature* (1755)."[6]

With his formal schooling finished, Panzieri plunged more deeply into Socialist politics and intellectual life. His instinctive radicalism was apparent during the debates that preceded and continued through the stormy 1946 Socialist Congress in Florence, where the delegates argued over postwar strategy. He sided with Lelio Basso, who led the fight against the moderates at the congress, the social democrats captained by Giuseppe Saragat. Panzieri agreed completely with Basso's rejection of reformist or "humanitarian" socialism as a policy line for the Socialist party. Socialism, the youthful Panzieri wrote, meant the proletarian struggle to suppress the existing state of things—capitalism—and he went so far as to condemn Saragat's revisionism as nothing but an attempt by the bourgeoisie to capture socialism from within.[7] Not long afterward the social democrats seceded from the party, a departure that in Panzieri's view left the Socialists more ideologically coherent and more seriously prepared to wage a struggle on behalf of Marxism. Indeed, now Panzieri could see no reason for the two proletarian parties to oppose each other, and he enthusiastically favored an aggressive Popular Democratic Front against capitalism's gigantic offensive in the postwar years. His writings from this period reveal that he considered a leftist takeover in Italy not only possible but imminent.

Though Panzieri was a radical *bassiano* at the time of the Florence congress, he soon took up an even more extreme position under the influence of Rodolfo Morandi (1902–55), the so-called puritan chief of the Socialist party's left wing.[8] Morandi responded to Panzieri's admiration by paying tribute to his young friend's brilliant promise as a Socialist leader.[9] Panzieri became Morandi's protégé, and in postwar Italy such a relationship could only result in distinct advantages for a budding left-wing intellectual. One prestigious job after another came Panzieri's way. In 1946 he was named editor-in-chief of *Socialismo* as well as secretary of the Institute of Socialist Studies, which Morandi directed. He lived in Bari for a time, working on behalf of left-wing Socialist groups while contributing articles to the party newspaper, *Avanti!*, and editing the *Bollettino dell' Istituto di Studi Socialisti*, which in November–December 1947 was succeeded by *Studi Socialisti*, also under Panzieri's editorship. He was already calling for a Socialist plan to confront capitalist society "in dissolution."[10] Moreover, Panzieri used these publications as vehicles for his stridently anti-American view of the Marshall Plan, which he denounced as "this vast program conceived and conducted by the reactionary forces of world capitalism. . . . "[11]

The Socialist hierarchy, recognizing the young man's enormous potential, increased his responsibilities as a committee chairman at numerous regional and topical party conferences. But in July 1948, following the PSI's XXVII Congress in Genoa, Panzieri fell under a cloud as moderates dislodged his radical supporters from positions of power and influence. Once again he moved to confront reformism, and in an unpublished 1948 essay, "Rivoluzione catastrofica e rivoluzione permanente," he wrote that "the true Marxist-Leninist theory of permanent revolution" was enunciated by Marx from 1843 on and then repeated in the *Manifesto*, *Capital*, and the *Critique of the Gotha Program*. "Marxism," Panzieri concluded, "develops with rigor and coherence, in an ideological and historical continuity to which the works of Lenin and Stalin are tied."[12] This was the legacy that the Socialists now dared to betray, he lamented. Panzieri even considered joining the Communist party and made inquiries about working for Edizioni Rinascita, but then decided to make no political changes while waiting to see what would develop in both of the workers' parties.

That fall he married Giuseppina Saija and shortly afterward began a new life at the University of Messina as a teacher of philosophy. Panzieri owed this opportunity to Galvano Della Volpe (1895–1968), a maverick Marxist philosopher of esthetics on the faculty who was calling for a radical re-reading of Marx, made all the more necessary, he believed, by the unfortunate but total triumph of the old-line Communist leader Gramsci's philosophically odd and rudely provincial notions of what Marxism meant.[13] The two men planned to publish a Marxist review in Sicily, *Critica materialistica*, but it never appeared. Still, next to Morandi, Della Volpe exerted the greatest intellectual influence on Panzieri during the late 1940s and early 1950s.[14] In Messina, too, he continued his intensive study of Marx, translating the second book of *Capital* in collaboration with his wife.[15]

Panzieri's commitment to Marxism was strengthened even more by his efforts to combat Sicily's "giant misery" than it was by any purely intellectual experience.[16] Continued fluctuations in the PSI's intramural politics, between moderate and radical elements, convinced Panzieri that hope existed for the Socialists after all, and at Morandi's urging he began to work for the party's renewal by promoting a series of directives in support of peasant land seizures. Panzieri became involved in these revolutionary activities at a time when the Mafia routinely disposed of peasant organizers by assassinating them.[17] Rejecting radical left-wing criticism of the peasant movement as nothing more than an anticommunal land hunger with no revolutionary potential in recognizably twentieth-century terms, Panzieri established a principle of procedure that he followed for the rest of his life: before making a political judgment about the people, first make an informed intellectual judgment.[18] In effect, he was asking to be shown a Socialist intellectual with enough knowledge of actual working and living conditions in Sicily to speak with confidence about the revolutionary potential of the masses there. Panzieri proposed to become the first such intellectual, and that meant a long period of study and observation. An attentive and objective observer would see, he later claimed, that in fact Sicilian protest was a vital part of the democratic struggle in Italy, to be understood on its own terms and fostered, not dismissed as an inconvenient and undesirable permutation of the dialectic.[19] From these experiences, fraught with great personal danger to himself, Panzieri derived the lasting conviction that political theory must never be separated from the actual life experiences and needs of the proletariat.

Promoting the peasant struggles in Sicily as the undefiled essence of socialism, Panzieri made a deep impression on the delegates to the XXIX Party Congress, held in Bologna 17–20 January 1951. This congress was a great personal triumph for him, and shortly afterward he accepted the party's nomination as the regional secretary for Sicily. Panzieri barely had begun to savor this triumph when, in June 1951, government authorities put him on trial for instigating peasant land seizures, but he was released by the court for lack of evidence.

The University of Messina also released him at about this time. He was marked as a man of extreme controversy, and politics no doubt played an important part in the university's decision.[20] Yet the land seizure trial and Panzieri's subsequent highly publicized involvement in organizing strikes of sulphur miners and field workers near Palermo sharply advanced his political career. In a party struggling to define a place for itself in the shadow of the PCI's vast bulk, his deeds in Sicily could hardly go unnoticed. Aided by the powerful support of Morandi, who from 1951 to 1955 was vice-secretary of the PSI as well as president of the Socialist caucus in Parliament, Panzieri rose swiftly in the party's national hierarchy. In 1951 he was appointed director of the PSI's propaganda section. The 1953 PSI congress in Milan elected him to the Central Committee, and in April of that year he took over as editor of the party gazette, *Propaganda socialista*. A few months later Panzieri moved back to Rome, where new party duties brought about a reorientation and a diversification of activities for him, but well into 1954 he continued to work actively on behalf of Sicilian land reform, and the issue would always concern him in a special way.

In 1955 two events occurred that vitally affected Panzieri's career. First, he resigned as the PSI propaganda minister to lead the party's cultural affairs section. This appointment opened up a vast range of new or relatively unfamiliar theoretical problems for him. Second, Morandi died on 26 July, a loss that deprived Panzieri of his staunchest supporter in the party. As a result of the first event he began to concentrate his formidable intellectual energies on the question of how politics and culture are connected; his articles on this theme appeared in *Mondo operaio*, a journal founded and directed by Pietro Nenni (1891–1980). As a result of the second event Panzieri was compelled to seek new allies in the party, and with this end in view he set about to work with Nenni. In the fall of 1955 the two men, accompanied by other Socialists, went on a ten-day trip to China, an experience that provided the highly impressionable Panzieri with a large inventory of revolutionary symbols and ideas.[21] After two days in China he noted in his diary, "I cannot remove from my mind the thought that this country is or at least will soon become the keystone of the world."[22] In a later diary entry he added that China "is preparing in gladness a revolution for the world."[23]

It was the dying Morandi himself who had enjoined Panzieri "to stay close to Nenni" in the interests of party unity. By this time Nenni had become one of the truly grand old men of the Italian Left, an immensely admired figure whose charismatic reputation covered a multitude of ideological ambiguities, and Morandi correctly observed that his personality was a major force in keeping the party together as a leftist entity.

Nenni began his career as a Republican, and in 1911 participated with the left-wing Socialist Mussolini in a strike against the Libyan War. Four ears later Nenni campaigned for intervention in World War I, and after the war he supported D'Annunzio's filibustering expedition in Fiume. In 1919 Nenni again joined forces with Mussolini, helping to establish the Bologna *fascio*. But very soon afterward he perceived fascism's rightward lurch and resigned. Two years later he joined the PSI, and although the party continued to be his political home for life Nenni was always a restless, searching spirit. The struggle against fascism absorbed and channeled his energies for the next twenty-five years, but after world War II he stood at the center of the storm that buffeted and sundered the PSI over the party's relationship with the PCI. Nenni stood for working-class unity regardless of party labels and was prepared to suffer a decidedly ironic split in the PSI rather than yield on this issue.[24]

Mondo operaio came into existence on 4 December 1948 for the avowed purpose of restoring and promoting working-class unity among all parties of the Left.[25] Insignificant at first because of Nenni's defeats at the hands of his PSI rivals, *Mondo operaio* suddenly became the dominant ideological organ of the party in mid-1949. Nenni was named PSI secretary in May of that year, and thereafter *Mondo operaio* took the lead in voicing party positions on all the major domestic and foreign policy issues of the day.

In the first seven years of its existence *Mondo operaio* struggled, as all Socialist and Communist newspapers and journals did during that period, against the United States-backed Christian Democratic hegemony in Italy. The John Foster Dulles–Alcide De Gasperi (1881–1954) combination proved impregnable, however, and even after the Christian Democratic leader's fall from power in 1953 his successors kept the old system alive if not well. Checkmated by American money and by the deep-rooted conservatism of the Christian Democratic masses, the PSI and the PCI worked to keep their own ranks united and optimistic about the long-range prospects of the working-class movement. With the country's economic boom furnishing abundant proof that the American connection worked on a level everyone could see—the only level of interest to the majority of Italians—the PSI and the PCI could do little more than hope for the inevitable crisis and catastrophe of capitalism that would bring the Left to power.

A crisis was, in fact, gathering momentum, but it did not emanate from the West or produce the conditions necessary for the collapse of capitalism. Stalin's death in March 1953 inspired hagiographic eulogies in Togliatti's *Rinascita*—no modern-day pope was ever given a more glorious send-off in *Civiltà cattolica*—but Italian mourners in Moscow were struck by the cold, formal character of the funeral. Indeed, one of them, Giorgio Amendola, later recalled that destalinization really began on the day Stalin died.[26] Reality became officially recognized in the Soviet Union with Nikita Khrushchev's 1956 "secret report" to the Communist party, a document subsequently published by the U.S. State Department. His lengthy account, based on the research of numerous government commissions, portrayed Stalin as a criminal lunatic who had perpetrated acts of genocide on a scale that defied belief.[27] These disclosures, leaving no doubt about the falsity of Stalin's purge trials or about his systematic distortions of history, shocked the Communist world.

Ten years after the Twentieth Party Congress at which Khrushchev gave his report, Nenni recalled that it had provoked "a crisis of enormous proportions [which] is still now far from being resolved."[28] Nenni had been no less emphatic in 1956 as he began a forced move toward a reconciliation with Saragat and the moderate Socialists. In a March editorial for *Mondo operaio* he declared that the palpable failure of the Soviet Union to democratize itself called into serious question the usefulness of the Soviet model.[29] The following July he wrote that the denunciation of Stalin could only be the barest beginning for the Soviet rulers; if the country failed to transform itself into a humane, democratic society it would continue to stand solely as a monument to the perversion and ruination of Marxist ideals.[30]

Panzieri wasted no time in expressing his views on these Soviet developments. In May 1956 he recognized that degenerations had occurred in the Soviet system; the question now concerned the source of the problem.[31] By November, following the publication of Khrushchev's report, Panzieri was much more anxious over what he described as "the crisis of communism."[32] He emphasized "the radical contradiction between socialism and Stalinism," with the latter understood in Panzieri's mind as an ensemble of "dogmatic and oppressive structures of ideology and political actions."[33]

Early in 1957 Panzieri added his voice to the *Mondo operaio* debate on the significance of the Twentieth Congress. He had been a regular contributor to *Mondo operaio* for some time, but the Thirty-Second National Congress of the PSI, held in Venice 6–10 February 1957, appointed him coeditor of the journal, succeeding Francesco De Martino as Nenni's editorial colleague.[34] In some respects Panzieri's analysis of destalinization reflected Nenni's views. Panzieri, too, was appalled by "Stalinist degeneration and the terrible violation of Socialist legality."[35] He called for "a Marxist analysis that would shed light on the structural foundation of the long and tragic degeneration that took place in the Soviet Union."[36] In other words, Panzieri, like Nenni, refused to take the easy way out of the dilemma posed by destalinization; not a single man was at fault, but an entire system. It was this system—a one-party dictatorship with a self-perpetuating ruling group at its center, responsible to no one—that required the closest scrutiny now.

By the time of Panzieri's first *Mondo operaio* editorials in the winter of 1957, the situation in Russia seemed even more grim than during the Twentieth Congress the previous February. First, Polish workers' strikes in Poznan on 28 June 1956, with eighty people killed and thousands injured, had been followed by the semi-successful attempt of Wladyslaw Gomulka's government to introduce nationalist reforms while nevertheless bound by the terms of the Warsaw Pact.[37]

Then on 23 October an even more profound disturbance rocked the Soviet Union's East European empire when Hungarians launched a revolutionary movement that culminated in an attempt to break away completely from the Warsaw Pact. The Kremlin was prepared to live with Gomulka so long as he did not touch the fundamentals of Poland's relationship with the Soviet Union, but the Hungarian rebels were presenting an intolerable challenge to Soviet hegemony. Khrushchev swiftly intervened with an army of tanks and artillery. Thousands of Hungarians died and tens of thousands went into exile as the country was forced to continue its loveless embrace of Stalin's heirs.[38] Imre Nagy, the prime minister who on 1 November had declared Hungary's withdrawal from the Warsaw Pact, was shot as a traitor. The same fate befell other members of the Nagy government.

The gallant but futile resistance of Hungarian workers and students produced a wave of indignation against the Soviet Union and all who attempted to defend Khrushchev's actions. Togliatti, still a keeper of the Soviet faith, witnessed a substantial desertion of the PCI by intellectuals, academics, artists, and journalists, including the editor-in-chief of *Rinascita*, Renato Mieli, over "the events of Hungary." Popular support for the party did not diminish, but the novelist Elio Vittorini, echoing Sartre's bitter abjuration of the Soviet catechism in *The Ghost of Stalin*, expressed the despair of the intellectuals when he lamented the quite definite end of all hope for "a democratic and liberal communism."[39] The vaunted Marxist passage from formal liberty to actual liberty had led to the worst and bloodiest tyranny on record in the Stalin period, and now the very men who lately had delivered suspiciously sanctimonious preachments on the evils of Stalinism proved that the Kremlin was a school for the unteachable.

Panzieri himself had no doubt about "the tragic character" of the Hungarian disaster.[40] He agreed with Nenni that the Soviet Union was the fallen daughter of socialism. Yet Panzieri had never been consumed by a burning passion for the

Soviet system; in Italy the feeling that the USSR was the proletarian light of the world had tended to be the religion of Communists, not Socialists.[41] Nevertheless, for Marxists everywhere the Soviet Union had been the "fatherland of all the world's workers,"and Panzieri was sensible to the implications of Hungary's agony for Marxism as a whole.[42] The Italian *fare come in Russia* and the French *les Soviets partout* had not been mere slogans; they had been articles of faith for an entire generation of Marxists.[43] Now this faith experienced the most severe emergency in its history, and to many observers the parallel between the Soviet Union in 1956 and the Catholic Church in 1517 was manifest. No less than sixteenth-century Christians, twentieth-century Marxists sought to explain the sudden demise of orthodoxy. Certainly after Moscow, Poznan, and Budapest the intellectual life of the Italian Left—and of the Left all over Europe—revolved around the question of how to make sense out of that "unforgettable 1956."[44]

An initial show of party unity notwithstanding, the two editors of *Mondo operaio* were soon identified with the poles of this debate in Italy. Panzieri began with the same premise that Nenni did: Stalinism had put Marxism in bad odor. But how should destalinization be accomplished? What should be its results? The two colleagues offered radically different answers to these questions. Whereas Nenni called for more democracy as an antidote to Stalinism and to the regrettably existent legacy of Stalin in Russia, Panzieri called for more Marxism-Leninism, emphatically rejecting the idea, as Morandi had before him, that Marxism could ever be reduced to social democracy. Reformism had always been and always would be an irredeemable error because it contradicted what Marx himself had said about the dialectic of history. Only revolution could bring about a socialist state; this, for Panzieri, was the inviolable core of Marxism. Therefore, the socialist answer to Stalin's "bureaucratic and dogmatic degenerations" had to lie in the authentic revolutionary traditions of Marxism, not in what to his mind were the fallacies of social democracy.[45]

To solve the problem created by destalinization Panzieri proposed to dispense entirely with the intellectualistic revolutionary-reformist, or maximalist-minimalist, party traditions and—as he had done in Sicily—to go to the people for political instruction. He theorized that in Italy, at least, the controversy over destalinization was only a symptom of the Left's chronic disease: the obsession of the country's Marxists with factionalism. To his way of thinking the deeply distressing posthumous exposé of the mass murderer who in life had been praised to the skies as the epitome of Marxist man had merely exacerbated internecine party machinations, most unhappily to the advantage of those Socialists and Communists he esteemed the least. Panzieri lamented that Italian working-class parties and movements habitually viewed themselves "as closed formations, each one a bearer of its own 'class truth,' each one a depository of a fixed Marxist Word."[46] This was all very religious and, consequently, very anti-Marxist, he complained. In so saying Panzieri was repeating and stressing Morandi's ideas about the dangers inherent in the *partito-guida* (party guide) concept, which had led inexorably to Stalinism. The lesson of 1956, then, was plain: Marxists had to restore "to the Italian workers' movement its own autonomy and a clear consciousness of that autonomy."[47] In other words, "new forms of direct democracy" would have to be created, though these should never be confused, as in Nenni's case, with bourgeois democracy.

The first step toward an authentic Marxism-Leninism, Panzieri asserted, would occur with "the direct participation of the workers at the base of the party."[48] By this he meant that revolutionary democracy could only come about as a result of a profound change *within* the Marxist political tradition, hitherto characterized by the incessant bickering of intellectual and political elites.. Panzieri's central idea was that only the workers themselves could impose silence on the chatterboxes whose slogans and clichés reverberated to no serious purpose in Italian political life. Until that inner revolution occurred, capitalism would be safe. Unless the proletariat itself attained, expressed, and acted upon revolutionary consciousness in strict accord with the indispensable formulas of Panzieri's paramount heroes, Marx and Lenin, the upholders of the status quo could sleep and dream in peace. These were the essential elements in Panzieri's personal crusade that had for its motto "Back to Marx and Lenin." The main strategy for this crusade was "worker control" of the revolution, not only after the revolution had taken place, but while it was taking place and always thereafter. The factory, Panzieri believed, would be the incubator of this revolution, which could only succeed as a socialist revolution under the watchful eyes of the workers themselves.[49]

Since Panzieri's writings at this time had as one of their primary objectives the annihilation of Togliatti's notion of an alliance between the working class and the enlightened bourgeoisie, it came as no surprise when the PCI counterattacked in the pages of *l'Unità*. In July and August 1958 the Marxist historian Paolo Spriano spoke for the PCI in denouncing Panzieri's views as impractical where not patently wrong.[50] All he had done, according to Spriano, was to take the cobwebs off the hoary errors of Trotsky and the anarcho-syndicalists and, with the light of discovery shining in his eyes, present them as the fresh fruit of his own genius.[51] It was all well and good to insist that party activity should be the prolongation and fulfillment of the proletariat's spontaneous existence, but what did such high-sounding phrases actually mean? How, exactly, did Panzieri propose to change the party structure? Was he calling for an end of the party or, conversely, a supraparty organization of all leftist groups? If the latter, would he not be left with the same old problems, only in an even more magnified form?[52]

Panzieri devoted the remaining years of his life to an attempt at formulating comprehensive and detailed answers to these questions. In 1958 all he could see clearly was that without a return to the factory council and to the revolutionary traditions of Italian Marxism the triumph of social democracy on the left and of neocapitalism in society as a whole could be anticipated with certainty.

Soon afterward Panzieri was clear on one other matter as well: he could no longer collaborate on *Mondo operaio*. He resigned from the journal early in 1959, just before his split with Nenni became public, at the party congress in Naples, 15–18 January. The ever-adaptable Nenni, dismissing the entire Soviet system as an irretrievable disaster, won an unconditional victory for the forces of moderation in the Socialist party. This was only one signal among many in the late 1950s that destalinization had resulted in the virtual abandonment of the Italian Left's revolutionary challenge to capitalism, even as a rhetorical device. The revolutionary confidence of an entire generation had been inundated by a floodtide of scandals originating in the Soviet Union, and Italian Marxists could even be heard discussing Lenin's "errors" as well as the "horrors" of Stalin.[53] Nenni was now on the point not only of supporting the Christian Democratic government but of joining it as well. Panzieri thought this move would be an annihilating calamity for socialism. Nenni eventually became a member of Aldo Moro's Center-Left government, on 5 December 1963, but long before this Panzieri had condemned his politics as "truly shameless . . . a series of contradictions . . . and lies."[54]

Not only Nenni and the PSI but also Togliatti and the PCI plainly spoke now of Marxism as an evolutionary process.[55] What had long been practiced as a virtue made necessary by the strategic realities of postwar Europe now quite suddenly became a virtue on its merits alone. It only required the death of Togliatti in 1964 for his successors, Luigi Longo and especially Enrico Berlinguer, to push the Communist party toward its Eurocommunist position of conspicuously shunning class revolution in favor of class collaboration and complete political pluralism. No one in the PCI cared to put it quite this way, but Eduard Bernstein, the author of the seminal *Evolutionary Socialism* (1899), had come out the clear winner over Lenin in the struggle to determine which tradition—the reform or the revolutionary—would guide the party's political strategy.[56]

Panzieri had been watching these tendencies grow in the working-class parties since the Twentieth Congress of the Soviet Communist party, but only in the summer of 1958 did he fully realize what had happened on the Italian Left: the PSI and the PCI had ceased to be Marxist in any meaningful sense. On 1 August 1958 he wrote to his friend Maria Adelaide Salvaco, "I am disappointed and embittered."[57] His last months as editor of *Mondo operaio* were torturous. He seemed to be the only person in the office who still believed that socialism meant attacking the bourgeoisie, not joining it. In one of his last pieces for *Mondo operaio*, published on 3 March 1959, Panzieri observed: "We are ever more convinced that the central theme of the Italian worker movement remains renewal. But the winners at Naples have been shown to be searching for the new only in the exasperation of the old. By multiplying illusions the true construction of the Italian Left always becomes more difficult."[58]

Panzieri then surveyed the literary publications of the Left in the hope of finding both a job and a vehicle for his own articles, but he soon concluded that virtually all of the so-called Marxist newspapers and journals in Italy were either corrupted by reformism or blinded by dogmatism.[59] His health and finances always precarious, Panzieri managed to survive thanks to an editorial job with Einaudi, but it necessitated a move from Rome to Turin in April 1959.[60] Turin, with its incessant rain and smog, together with what for Panzieri were the odious social consequences of neocapitalism at its worst, overwhelmed him. His correspondence during this period betrayed a deepening sense of alienation.[61] To Maria Adelaide Salvaco he wrote laconically, on 3 October 1959, "Here cold, smog, and monopoly."[62] For him Turin would always be "the neocapitalist concentration camp in which my honest family lives and cries."[63]

His greatest disappointment, though, was caused by the Socialist party. For fifteen years Panzieri had worked indefatigably in the ranks and at the top of the PSI, but in that same October he vowed to leave it, or "at least [its] directing organs."[64] What had driven him from the offices of *Mondo operaio* earlier in the year continued to prey upon Panzieri's mind, and his invective against former colleagues, now fully "assimilated" in an obscene "contest of conformity," became savagely vituperative.[65] If anything, the PCI was even more contemptible in his view, as Togliatti continued "to mystify" working-class problems in a politics of reformist evasion.[66] Other PCI leaders, such as the long-time editor of *l'Unità*, Pietro Ingrao, who had the audacity to call for "a gradual passage to socialism," he rudely dismissed as "mad sheep."[67]

Panzieri's outrage over the fading revolutionary fervor on the left was shared by small groups of alienated Marxists in several cities scattered across the peninsula, and by the end of 1959 they had begun looking to him for intellectual leadership.[68] The rightward movement of Nenni and Togliatti was bound to leave some Marxists dissatisfied and ideologically homeless. The revolutionary tradition, sedulously nurtured for generations by the PSI and PCI, could not be ordered out of existence by party decrees; after the decrees were promulgated the tradition remained, and adherents were not lacking to sustain it. From this last group came Panzieri's new constituency.

Such was the origin of a unique movement that would culminate two years later in the publication of *Quaderni rossi*, a journal destined to have a great impact on the extraparliamentary Left. At the very beginning of his estrangement from *Mondo operaio* and the PSI, Panzieri recognized the need for a new journal that would unite the working-class movement while simultaneously refuting the false alternatives of reformism and catastrophism. The chief problem of the working class, he continued to believe, was the reconquest of "full autonomy, the revolutionary autonomy of the worker movement."[69] Not a single Italian journal or party stood squarely on that premise, and this was the ground that Panzieri and his fellow Marxist dissidents staked out for themselves.

The "comrades of the Quaderni Rossi" joined together as a national alliance of study groups and labor agitators nearly two years before their journal appeared. In the words of Vittorio Rieser, a contributor to all six issues of *Quaderni rossi*, Panzieri attracted leftists from diverse backgrounds, "in the PCI, in the PSI or in no party, in the CGIL (Confederazione Generale Italiana del Lavoro) or in no union."[70] Panzieri personally led a seminar in Turin devoted to a discussion of *Capital*. He thought of the book as "a 'sketch' of socialist sociology."[71] In December 1959 Panzieri reported to a younger colleague, Alberto Asor Rosa, a leader of the Quaderni Rossi group in Rome: "Here these comrades carry on union work and research with great zeal."[72] Their first major project was to conduct a sociological inquiry into the workers' conditions at Fiat.[73] Panzieri explained to Asor Rosa, "A work of this type, systematic but not academic, is the essential condition for realizing the other perspectives of [our] work: we will have a concrete reference point even for the activity of ideological elaboration, and the homogeneity of the group will be solidly founded."[74] Panzieri's use of the phrase "other perspectives" euphemistically concealed the group's passionate commitment to the development of a revolutionary socialist strategy that would enable the workers "to struggle against this undertaking of [capitalist] rationalization."[75] The bourgeoisie, with its reformist allies, wanted "to integrate" the workers into the capitalist system, to make them "collaborators," but the comrades of the Quaderni Rossi set themselves to oppose this, to find and to augment those pockets of worker resistance where Marxism still meant revolution.[76]

Although Panzieri saw "all the roads blocked" in the official leftist camp, he had no intention of forming his own small sect.[77] He spurned the suggestion that he and his "four cats" should form a party—as if the Left needed yet another faction.[78] Panzieri protested that his aim had always been to unite the Left, and he proposed to do this by undertaking a Marxist examination of capitalist society, which could then be used by all Marxists as the sound basis for a new socialist program of unity. He also wanted to publicize the Chinese alternative to Soviet communism.[79] With these objectives in mind Panzieri began to take positive steps early in 1960 toward founding a new journal as a publishing vehicle for the research that the Quaderni Rossi colleagues were carrying out. However, he lamented to Salvaco on 25 March 1960 that "ideologically this group is as far as possible from being homogeneous."[80] They had certain negative positions in common, notably "the coarse reformism" of the PSI and the rigid party structure of the PCI, but Spriano's questions in the *Mondo operaio–l'Unità* debate were still open. In a letter of 14 October 1960 his good friend Luciano Della Mea wrote of the objectives of *Quaderni rossi*: "The discourse of the review is a class discourse that is in search of readers and support and class participation."[81] As an editorial program this was suitably vague to cover the manifold ideological differences of which Panzieri himself was fully aware. Nevertheless, as the harsh Piedmontese winter of 1960 ended, Panzieri dared "to hope."[82]

His desire for a new journal was gratified in June 1961 when the maiden issue of *Quaderni rossi* appeared.[83] The first organizing session had taken place during the previous October, and Panzieri had described it in exceptional detail to Asor Rosa on 26 October.[84] He asserted that *Quaderni rossi* had five goals: to articulate "a unitary position" for the Left, to formulate "a revolutionary political strategy," to refute the false alternatives of reformism and catastrophism, to develop a strategy for the realization of direct democracy, and to analyze the reality of the working class with the aim of destroying "the current myths of neoreformism." These assertions were in keeping with a subsequent policy statement in the journal: "*Quaderni rossi* is not therefore a review in the normal sense of the term, but it is above all one of the instruments of collective political work that has multiple aspects and does not subordinate itself to the 'journalistic' exigencies of a review."[85] Panzieri made it clear in a letter to Salvaco that he did not want *Quaderni rossi* to remain merely "a provincial sheet."[86] To accomplish its aims, the journal would have to penetrate the south and, eventually, the entire Marxist world.[87]

For the present Panzieri and his *Quaderni rossi* friends, armed with the facts and figures of worker strikes and alienation in Turin, claimed to be in the vanguard of labor's offensive against capital, as the revolutionary conscience of the Left.[88]

Panzieri noted with mounting concern, however, that the journal's staff could not agree on the nature of the crisis in Italian society, let alone on the best way for the workers to meet it. All his collaborators were deeply affected by the labor unrest of 1960–61; but did present trends indicate that capitalism was entering a period of irreversible decline or, rather, a period of intense rationalization in a dramatic bid to eliminate revolutionary consciousness among the workers? Either conclusion could be drawn from the journal's first issue.[89]

Panzieri's own contributions to *Quaderni rossi* showed the deep impression that the Frankfurt School of Marxism had made on him, particularly on his thinking about two vexed questions: first, why generations of Marxist prognosticators had failed to understand the hidden strength of capitalism and its seemingly uncanny knack of sidestepping the destiny of general crisis and definitive collapse to which Marx had condemned it; and second, why such a belief in the inevitability of this destiny was even more erroneous in the last half of the twentieth century than ever before. In December 1959 Panzieri had met Theodor Adorno in Stresa at the International Congress of Sociology, a meeting that he later described to friends in adulatory terms.[90] It was Friedrich Pollock's theory of state capitalism, however, that became the centerpiece of Panzieri's analysis of both these questions.[91] Panzieri learned from Pollock that while technology had been the secret weapon of capitalism all along, this economic system's increasingly refined modes of planning were now destroying the very possibility of revolution in advanced capitalist countries.

In his first article for *Quaderni rossi*, "Sull' uso capitalistico delle macchine nel neocapitalismo," Panzieri applied to the Italian situation Pollock's major argument that technology and economic planning under government direction could very well contain capitalist contradictions indefinitely.[92] In other words, controlled by capital, technology augments the triumph of its master and seals the dependence of the workers, dulling their revolutionary consciousness and incapacitating them for their historic mission as formulated by Marx.[93] The workers were suffering from something worse than alienation: false consciousness. Neocapitalist mass culture had confused them—raising the working class, as Flaubert had noted a century earlier, "to the level of stupidity attained by the bourgeoisie." But now *Quaderni rossi* would try to set this deplorable situation aright with its watchwords of "worker control," signifying an acceleration of class war, class consciousness, and class power against capitalist development. This was precisely why *Quaderni rossi* would stress praxis as well as theory, to reawaken "the destructive force of the working class, its capacity for revolution."[94] If the proletarian revolution were not inevitable, it would be necessary to make it so.

The official Left greeted *Quaderni rossi* with varying degrees of contempt and hostility. The PCI's Giorgio Napolitano condemned the first issue as a nebulous compilation of "simplifications, distortions, and inexactitudes."[95] The whole enterprise, he analyzed, suffered from a hopelessly utopian character that was made all the more ludicrously fanciful because Panzieri et al. proclaimed with such cloying solemnity that they were dealing only with the hardest of facts. These dreamers of a dangerously absurd dream could not see beyond the entrancing facade of their own gaudy intellectual formulations. Moreover, they were completely blind to the most pressing fact of all in working-class politics: the absolutely indispensable need for a system of alliances with other classes in Italian society. Paolo Santi, also of the PCI, ridiculed the journal as "a distortion of Marx."[96] All Santi could see in *Quaderni rossi* was a deadly combination of theoretical jargon and aggressive intolerance for anything but its own ensemble of contradictory and breathlessly banal theses.[97] These voices on the official Left unanimously rejected the *Quaderni rossi* idea on the grounds that it threatened the workers' movement with "castration."[98]

Such predictable criticisms notwithstanding, Panzieri was generally pleased with the first issue of *Quaderni rossi*. But on 24 March 1962 he confessed, in a lecture delivered on the occasion of launching a Quaderni Rossi group in Siena, that the journal was still too timid.[99] He was more convinced than ever that a revolutionary potential existed in Italy—the very element now completely ignored by the PSI and the PCI, both of which were lost in a wilderness of doctrinal errors. While touching again on some of the same points that he had stressed in his *Quaderni rossi* article— that the greatest possible misconception about the historical process was to think of modern technology as neutral, as the disinterested creation of truth-seeking scientists when, in fact, every scrap of technology corresponded to the perceived needs of capitalism—Panzieri now asserted that the working-class struggle was still the most profound fact in contemporary Italian politics, and only *Quaderni rossi* had even made a start toward taking it into account. Nevertheless, he insisted that the journal would have to go much further in promoting "a Marxist vision of reality," in calling the working class directly to the struggle for socialism. The comrades of the Quaderni Rossi should not only write about revolution; they should also promote it actively. But Panzieri warned against trying to make the revolution "in one act alone, in one day alone." In fact, the process of revolution would be "very difficult and laborious," involving first of all the exceptionally arduous task of "the unitary composition of class." Above all, Panzieri concluded, "Our tactic must not repeat old models; it must be a new tactic adequate to this situation, the tactic of the worker movement today."[100] Whether or not this new tactic would call for a global attack against capitalism remained to be determined by *Quaderni rossi*–style research work in other countries.

The new tactic sought by Panzieri began to take shape in the light of Turin's violent metalworkers' strike later that spring and summer. Worker disunity at Fiat, arising from factionalism between the three major unions—CGIL, CISL (Confederazione Italiana Sindacati Lavoratori), and UIL (Unione Italiana del Lavoro)— had left the plants largely under the paternalistic control of Vittorio Valletta, the president of the company and the power of darkness in the Left's demonology.[101] Valletta had been with Fiat since 1921, called to the company by Agnelli in the aftermath of the disastrous occupation of the factories. One of the few professional managers in Italy, Valletta was deeply influenced by the American industrial model, and he developed plans for Fiat that would make Turin the Italian Detroit. His greatest success came after World War II, when the fabulous sales record of the

"600" revolutionized private transportation in Italy. During this period of exceptional expansion, Valletta acquired the image of "an orchestra conductor who, with baton in hand, masterfully directed a plant of more than 100,000 workers."[102]

By 1962, however, worker resentment against this arrangement had brought on serious labor disturbances. Fiat workers resumed their historic role as the vanguard of Italy's labor movement.[103] Vittorio Rieser later recorded that while interviewing Fiat workers in 1960–61 Quaderni rossi investigators had discovered "a high degree of internal tension, a series of latent and even open conflicts, but [these] were not organized or connected with each other."[104] The workers, he added, were even bitterly critical of their unions, whose leaders, incidentally, soon took a dark view of Quaderni rossi investigations into factory conditions. Worker morale hit bottom after the defeat of a February 1962 strike, and a metalworkers' strike on 12 June quickly collapsed when union leaders failed to reach an agreement among themselves.[105] However, by late June this internal bickering had ceased, and the three unions were able to present a united front against management.

On 7 July the metalworkers went out on strike, setting off a chain reaction of worker disturbances that threatened to engulf the entire city in violence. From the very beginning the "events of July" more closely resembled a riot than a strike. When the UIL agreed to a separate peace with the company, those workers still on strike attacked the offices of the "yellow union" in Piazza Statuto, setting off a wild melee. Miraculously, no one died, but many people were injured as screaming, rock-throwing strikers and their sympathizers exchanged insults and curses with the police, who further responded with tear gas attacks. After a lull on Sunday, violence flared up the following day, 9 July, in still more bloody confrontations between strikers and police. A rampaging mob broke street lamps, smashed store windows, blocked trams, and erected barricades. Police and carabinieri reinforcements had to be called in from as far away as Padua and Bologna. The police stopped 1,141 people and arrested forty, many of whom were armed.[106] Order was not fully restored until some days later when the allied unions won a compromise settlement.

The most astonishing feature of the strike was the spectacle of the PSI and the PCI censuring the Quaderni Rossi group for its revolutionary activities, with Panzieri himself personally condemned for infantile leftism, spontaneism, and anarchosyndicalism. A comparatively restrained Palmiro Togliatti decried the Piazza Statuto violence, asserting that the workers had nothing to gain by provoking bloody clashes with the police.[107] The main question on Togliatti's mind was who would profit from such disturbances. Surely the police had behaved with their customary brutality, but there had been "elements of provocation" on the other side.

Togliatti did not name these elements, but Paolo Spriano, Panzieri's nemesis since their debate in the pages of l'Unità and Mondo operaio, pointed an accusing finger at the Quaderni Rossi radicals. The crowd in Piazza Statuto that night, he wrote, was not made up of workers but of "professional provocateurs, fascists, criminals, and hooligans."[108] Their acts of vandalism "carried the signature of organized provocation at the service of the antiworker and anti-Communist cause." Admittedly, Panzieri had not condoned their lawlessness, but Spriano charged that by continuously undermining the PCI and the CGIL in calling for more "revolutionary" action the Quaderni Rossi groups had stimulated "the events of the Piazza Statuto."[109] Spriano articulated the reform attitude of the PCI, that the huge industrial cities overflowed with desperate young people who required no further instigation to destructive action.[110] At the very least the Quaderni Rossi comrades were guilty of unconscionable behavior, proving that they had "a meager sense of self-control."

As of this moment the constituent elements of an extraparliamentary Left clearly became part of Italy's consciousness and, soon afterward, of her political reality as well. This phenomenon has been growing ever since, characterized chiefly by the desire—in Stefano Merli's words—"to recover and to rethink the anti-institutional formulations of revolutionary Marxism, national and international, from Marx to Luxemburg, to the Soviet Lenin, to the Gramsci of the [factory] councils and critic of bureaucracy, to the Morandi of direct democracy and of the politics of class."[111]

Indeed, for the more ardent Quaderni Rossi spirits the great strike of 1962 flashed as their blinding light on the road to Damascus, confirming them in their revolutionary faith and tantalizing them, according to Alberto Asor Rosa, with visions calling up "the general reconquest of class consciousness."[112] Asor Rosa was in Turin for a meeting of the *Quaderni rossi* staff when the strike erupted, and his diary for the next three days was later published in the maiden issue of *Cronache dei Quaderni rossi*: a companion publication that Panzieri's associates hoped would serve as a rapid means of communication between the widely scattered Quaderni Rossi groups.

Asor Rosa recorded in his diary that the meeting quickly turned into a strategy session on what to do about the situation at Fiat, and the group decided to promulgate a prostrike pamphlet, "Agli operai della Fiat," reaffirming "the necessity of worker unity."[113] The pamphlet was addressed not to the union leaders but to the workers themselves, on the grounds that only the workers could decide their own destiny. Here was the proletariat's choice, according to the *Quaderni rossi* staff's analysis:

> Either return to a condition of isolation and disunity, in which the despotism of the master will again have a free hand and will result in, as before or worse than before, cuts in hours, arbitrary qualifications, dismissals, transfers, in short all the insupportable arbitrariness that the Fiat master has exercised against the workers;
> *Or become the conscious vanguard of a strong and united working class.*[114]

Clearly the strike was a watershed: "You have in your hands not only the key of this struggle of today, but the key of the future struggle of the Italian proletariat." The *Quaderni rossi* enthusiasts then hastened to join the picket lines, as much in an attempt to radicalize the confrontation as to comprehend it.[115]

Asor Rosa noted that he and his *Quaderni rossi* friends shared the "utmost enthusiasm" about the city's "atmosphere of serene victory." In an Italian Marxist's variation of Wordsworth's paean to the French Revolution, "Bliss was it in that dawn to be alive / But to be young was very heaven," Asor Rosa rhapsodized, "At this point I cannot do less than say how fortunate I am: before my very eyes the grandiose myth of Italian neocapitalism is falling with a great clamor." He even allowed himself to hope that "perhaps the Fiat worker is today in the vanguard not only of the Italian proletariat, but of all the proletariat in the industrially developed countries," for "here the laceration has happened: the Fiat worker has torn his ties with the capitalist collective, he is 'outside,' there is no doubt, the network of capitalist relations." The strike was, Asor Rosa continued, "the most important political experience of the postwar period: an experience which we had foreseen and waited for with confidence, but the reality of it made it become infinitely more clear and concrete to us."

As for the Piazza Statuto violence, Asor Rosa attributed it mainly to the "blind" overreaction of the police. Undeniably the strikers had gotten carried away in damaging factory property, in harassing scabs, and in resisting the police, but in view of the long-standing oppressive conditions at Fiat, he contended, the "immense rage" of the proletariat was understandable, and for him Piazza Statuto signified, above all, "an expression of [worker] consciousness and power." He ridiculed the PCI thesis that worker violence in Turin had come about solely through *Quaderni rossi*'s provocation. How, Asor Rosa asked, could a handful of intellectuals—many of whom did not even live in Turin—have orchestrated the activities of 250,000 striking workers and of their families, friends, and diverse other supporters? No, Piazza Statuto was a product of historical forces, not of conspiracy or of provocation. To assert either one of the last two propositions was to try to diminish the crisis of capitalism, and for the PCI to associate itself with such a "stupid and calumnious maneuver" left no doubt in Asor Rosa's mind that the party had lost all sense of working-class realities, which could only be understood in the light of abiding Marxist truths on the nature of class warfare.[116]

The September 1962 issue of *Cronache dei Quaderni rossi*, devoted almost exclusively to news about the strike, included additional declarations of the group's unlimited euphoria. One team of *Quaderni rossi* writers described the strike as "an expression of worker autonomy" that had succeeded in terrorizing the Fiat masters.[117] Two other *Quaderni rossi* authors joined Asor Rosa in condemning *l'Unità*'s hysterical analysis of the Piazza Statuto riots in terms of a tragically real if unacknowledged PCI capitulation before the forces of Italian neocapitalism.[118]

Panzieri's own views were reflected in an article signed QR, in which the author scornfully rejected the Communist interpretation of Piazza Statuto, suggesting, in effect, that the party leaders would do well to reread —or possibly just to read— Marx, who would teach them that social disturbances involving masses of workers could not come to pass with the wave of a magic wand by some conspiratorial group.[119] Such broad-based phenomena could only be explained in social terms, and in fact Piazza Statuto was the eruption of a class volcano in society. The party, it was charged, had largely ignored the 400,000 recent immigrants in Turin except at election time. Squalor, exploitation, cultural deracination, and despair had impelled worker action at Piazza Statuto, and only a party sunk in ignorance of Marx's obvious meanings and of the tenor of life in Turin's working-class ghettos could come to any other conclusion.

In November 1962 Panzieri proclaimed that the metalworkers' strike had reawakened the proletariat's will to resistance.[120] Neocapitalism, he continued, was worse than fascism because of its greater subtlety, but now the workers had begun to perceive the necessity of rejecting this evil hegemony. The "deepening of consciousness" had begun, and now *Quaderni rossi* would seek to spread the good news. In July of the following year he counseled that the workers must do more than merely respond to the neocapitalist hegemony; they must anticipate it and frustrate it in every way. In short, "the most advanced form of class struggle [is] insubordination of the capitalist plan."[121] Panzieri typically warned against an endless repetition of theoretical statements: "We cannot, therefore, limit ourselves to theorizing and idealizing the worker 'refusal' . . . because the revolutionary political struggle of the working class is now being born. . . . "[122] The time had come for "the positive elaboration of *a plan* of struggle that invests the entire society and manifests itself more clear-sighted than the thinking of the collective capitalist."[123]

When he wrote in this manner Panzieri seemed to be encouraging those radicals in the group who wanted to do something more than sit around a seminar room discussing the recondite points of Marxist theory. However, Panzieri's call for revolution was louder in some ears than he intended it to be. As a preface to his remarks on the summer of 1962 Panzieri carefully noted that the strike had not resulted in a revolutionary victory for the working class. The strike, after all, had been settled. Therefore, more *inchieste* (investigations) would be required before *Quaderni rossi* could safely recommend a plan of working-class action. Panzieri's recommendation was the sticking point in the subsequent history of *Quaderni rossi*.

Romano Alquati, a *Quaderni rossi* writer, later recalled that almost from the beginning the staff had been divided into two groups: a component "immediately political" in Turin and a "sociological component" in Rome. Panzieri managed to keep them together for a time, but after the Turin metalworkers' strike the politically minded comrades called for a more explicitly revolutionary line, and they visibly began to lose patience with *Quaderni rossi* staff members who advised caution.

Panzieri had long been aware of the potential for such a clash, and as early as May 1962 he had expressed concern about the utopian mentality of some of his colleagues. To Alberto Asor Rosa he expressed his anger over "the sight of the revolutionary will of some comrades negating itself for the lack of adhering to reality [and] of recognizing the most obvious and evident things. . . . "[124] Yes, Panzieri concluded, "a revolutionary line" might now be opened, but not without an "understanding of the 'precise objective structure' of capital at this stage of [its] development." In this way Panzieri had hoped to cure the congenital maladies of the radical Left, that is, the refusal to come to grips with things as they were and a corresponding passion to formulate new jargon for Leninist ideas. These ideas had worked brilliantly in the Russia of 1917, but Panzieri scoffed at the belief that they could be mechanically introduced in contemporary Italy's totally different historical situation.[125] That Italy needed Leninism, Panzieri had no doubt, but a Leninism reinterpreted to meet the objective needs of Italy in the present. That meant, for a start, more factory investigations, which would teach Marxists how to collect and to use empirical data. As things now stood, Panzieri charged, Marxist ideas were not connected to anything in reality, only to dogmas that were in too many cases embarrassingly threadbare where not positively useless.[126]

Tension mounted between the rival *Quaderni rossi* factions through the fall of 1962 and the winter of 1963. Attempts to smooth out these factional differences culminated early the next summer when the entire staff participated in publishing a special number of *Quaderni rossi–Cronache operaie*, but no agreement could be reached on what to do next. In August the staff gathered in Milan for a last attempt at compromise. Here once again, and more forcefully than ever before, Panzieri spoke against prematurely stoking the fire of revolution. Such an action, he warned, would "severely damage the prospect of a left-wing worker movement in Italy."[127] Italian workers were simply unready for the kind of political organization that a full-scale revolution would require, and for this reason he spoke against those comrades who presently saw the possibility of an immediate "raising of the workers' struggle to a more political, revolutionary level." To make sure that this point was not lost on his listeners he repeated it at the end of his remarks, expressly condemning the "formation of a revolutionary vanguard of the masses." To provoke "agitation" out of season was to misunderstand that genuine Marxist revolution involved "a series of steps"; it was also to fight a battle on terrain ideally suited for a catastrophic defeat of the proletariat. Panzieri claimed to want revolution as much as the next Marxist, but revolution based on reality, not on mere "ideological constructs."[128]

In 1963 a break occurred that subsequent attempts at compromise failed to heal, and a new, even more radical journal came into existence: *Classe operaia* (January 1964–March 1967), a forerunner of the most important voice on the extraparliamentary Left during the 1970s, *Potere operaio*.[129] The war cry of this secessionist "journal of workers in struggle" was "death to ideology."[130] As Vittorio Rieser observed, the metalworkers' strike had inspired these radicals to believe that "a qualitative political leap" had taken place in the revolutionary consciousness of the working class.[131] Now, Panzieri's former antagonists on the staff of *Quaderni rossi* affirmed, "forms of direct political action could be introduced into the class struggle." What forms would such action take? Rieser was very specific: "Work stoppages, acts of sabotage, wildcat strikes, sometimes even the refusal of participation in strikes proclaimed by the unions came to be considered as the essence of this political action."[132] Panzieri was left with a rump *Quaderni rossi* staff that continued to publish the journal as well as *Lettere dei Quaderni rossi*, a bulletin of their activities and a vehicle of "correspondence and permanent discussion that would assure the collective character of the work of *Quaderni rossi*."[133]

Actually, the *Quaderni rossi* staff had been reduced even earlier by a defection of those members who clung to the belief that it was possible to reawaken the revolutionary consciousness of the traditional working-class parties. These schismatics included Vittorio Foa, Giuseppe Murraro, Luciano Della Mea, and Giuliano Boaretto.[134] A second schism arose from the problem that Alquati and Rieser described. The leader of this group was Mario Tronti, whose *Operai e capitale* (1966) became one of the sacred texts for student rioters in 1968.[135] Tronti's book evolved from concerns expressed in his first *Quaderni rossi* article, "La fabbrica e la società."[136] Tronti argued that under neocapitalism all society would eventually become a factory without walls, with every aspect of life falling under the aegis of the system: "that is, all society living as a function of the factory and the factory extending its exclusive dominance over all society." The radical rationalization of capitalist society was in progress, and he called for a direct struggle against such a *dominio*: "And in fact on this point it is no longer only possible, but it becomes historically *necessary* to plan the general struggle against the social system inside the social rapport of production, to place *bourgeois society* in crisis from within *capitalist production*." Every effort would have to be made to resist the integration of workers into this system, "carrying the class struggle to its maximum level." He believed that the only way to oppose "capitalist development" was through "revolutionary development"; the workers had "to organize themselves as a revolutionary class." Tronti was proposing for Italian workers nothing less than the tactic of absolute noncooperation with the capitalist system that Frantz Fanon had proposed only the year before in *The Wretched of the Earth* for Third World victims of colonialism: "Under the colonial regime, what is true for the Arab and for the Negro is that they should not lift their little fingers nor in the slightest degree help the oppressor to sink his claws deeper into his prey."[137]

Tronti and Panzieri differed on a number of key theoretical points besides the matter of direct intervention in the political arena, and eventually personal rancor spoiled their relationship.[138] Certainly by the summer of 1963 Panzieri was using what for him was scathing rhetoric in attacking Tronti's "very Hegelian" views, which amounted to "a fascinating summary of an entire series of errors that the worker Left might commit in this moment."[139] Tronti was arguing that capital, "a vampire [that] lives only by sucking on profit," did not even have "an objective existence"; for him the working class alone mattered in the dialectic.[140] In his view capitalism was all husks and skeletons—detritus to be swept away without worrying about the future, which would take care of itself. Panzieri laughed at such ideas, scorning them as ridiculously extremist and irresponsible nostrums. He kept asking the *trontiani* where the basis in society was for "a strategy of global revolution." Did they not see, he warned, the ruinous potential for mythogenesis in a dogmatic and undocumented celebration of working-class revolution? Tronti and the left-wing *Quaderni rossi* comrades, it seemed to him, were calling for worker sabotage "that for many decades the working class has applied in diverse situations, in diverse moments, and that is the permanent expression of its political defeat."[141] In the long run there would be a worker revolution, but for now the proletariat had to prepare itself thoroughly for that struggle.

As early as May 1962 Panzieri had explained to Asor Rosa, one of the future secessionists, that he was adamantly opposed to "disordered activism," to "spontaneity," to "these positions of nervousness."[142] Because anarchism struck him as both a crime and a blunder, Panzieri was convinced "of the necessity not to concede [anarchists] any space within our position."[143] Theirs was "the path of isolation," Panzieri warned, and now that the question of political violence was beginning to emerge as an option for some of his colleagues he took up what he perceived to be a strict Leninist position: "the authentic terror of all the people" was justified, but individual, uncoordinated acts of violence were anathema to him.[144]

The question of the hour was beyond Panzieri's formulation, however, at least in the judgment of the *Quaderni rossi* radicals: all Marxists were bound to oppose violence lacking historical perspective—that was the error of Bakunin—but in 1962–63 Tronti et al. wanted to know whether or not the moment for the active organization of Marxist revolution, which by the very nature of its struggle against capitalism would contain destructive elements, had arrived.

Also included among the secessionists was Antonio Negri, destined to become the most controversial Italian Marxist of his time. Negri, always first in his class during childhood and adolescence, had enjoyed a brilliant career at the University of Padua, where he earned his degree in 1955. Thereafter he became the assistant of Enrico Opocher, the university rector, who would say of him, "No one in Italy knows Marxism as he does."[145]

Although Negri began to develop a reputation as one of the most aggressive radicals in Italy, he did not break completely with l'Intesa, the organization of university Catholics, until the late 1950s. An old priest later recalled that as a youth Toni was "assiduous" on points of doctrine, a fervent organizer of "manifestations in honor of St. Anthony," and a dedicated student of St. Thomas.[146] Catholic politicians had their eyes on him, and a young deputy from the Veneto, Mariano Rumor, called him an "outstanding youth."[147] The conservative politics of Pope Pius XII alienated Negri, however, and cut him adrift from the church. Thereafter he sought out Danilo Dolci in Sicily and lived on a kibbutz in Israel for a time, vainly searching for the realization of his Christian-inspired ideal of a harmonious community.[148] There is a parallel between Negri's career and the careers of Renato Curcio and Mara Cagol, who also left adolescence as devout Catholics only to repudiate their religious heritage in favor of secular Marxism, arriving at their ultimate ideological destination by traversing the Catholic Left to a point in Italian politics where Catholicism no longer had meaning and where the world of radical Marxism began.[149]

In 1958 Negri joined the PSI, but this attachment only lasted for a short time as he, like Panzieri, recoiled from the Socialist party's increasingly moderate, reformist character. Contemporaneous with Panzieri's launching of the Quaderni Rossi movement, Negri—by then completely converted from Catholicism to Marxism—was editing a far-Left newspaper, *Progresso Veneto*, in which he relentlessly attacked existing working-class unions and parties for their patently nonrevolutionary character. *Progresso Veneto* attracted a group of like-minded intellectuals in Padua, and toward the end of 1962 they joined forces with militant Socialists in Venice who were already connected with Panzieri's group and engaged in conducting *Quaderni rossi*-style factory investigations in nearby Marghera. In this way Negri entered Panzieri's orbit.

Their coupling, though intense and even passionate in a thoroughly sublimated political way, did not long endure. Negri later explained why he was drawn to

Panzieri and why the two men eventually parted company. In the beginning Negri was completely dazzled by Panzieri's intellect and deeply impressed by his political sophistication. Language failed to express Negri's admiration for the one man in Italy who had kept the flame of Marxism burning while the PCI and the PSI had betrayed the Marxist cause of proletarian revolution.[150] He had exposed the fraudulent character of academic Marxism in Italy as mere ideological posing by certain elements of the bourgeoisie who hypocritically wanted to keep their snug places in society while simultaneously cutting a bold revolutionary figure in the lecture hall.[151] He had destroyed the myth of the party in Italy and had shown how it must be subordinated "to the autonomy of class."[152] For Negri, Panzieri was unquestionably the most creative thinker of the Italian Left from 1956 to 1962. During those years he had inspired a whole generation of young Marxists with a vision of Marx that was totally outside "the historicist Gramscianism of the academic Togliattians." Some of Negri's own ideas on *autonomia* proceed in a straight line from Panzieri's thought, as *Il dominio e il sabotaggio: sul metodo marxista della trasformazione sociale* (1978) and other works by the University of Padua professor make clear. Romano Alquati accurately noted in 1980 that Negri was Panzieri's "most orthodox disciple."[153] And in 1983 Negri himself acknowledged that Panzieri's thought "was good fuel for my brain."[154]

Nevertheless, Negri pointed out that under Panzieri "*l'autonomia operaia* did not find its own political representation," and this failure lay at the heart of the *Quaderni rossi–Classe operaia* split.[155] In Negri's view, Panzieri could not follow his ideas about worker autonomy to their logical conclusion. Panzieri had said that the workers were by nature antagonistic toward capital, but Negri criticized him for not seeing that they were outside it as well. This was another way of saying that Panzieri could never visualize the actual means by which the workers would take power, the only step that Negri and Tronti were interested in taking.[156] These two firebrands balked at the prospect of offering nothing more than an inquiry into the manifold ills of capitalism.[157] In effect, they were refusing to continue as Panzieri's graduate students; in their minds the development of revolutionary consciousness was sufficiently advanced for social analysis to be succeeded by political action. As Negri said repeatedly in later years whenever he was asked to comment on the origins of his radical Autonomia Operaia movement, "Piazza Statuto was our founding congress."[158] Panzieri, in Negri's judgment, had failed to draw the correct political conclusions from this revolutionary event. By failing to propose a specific plan of attack on capitalism, Panzieri admitted—to the satisfaction of Negri and the other radicals of *Quaderni rossi*—that he was seriously interested only in supervising research projects, not in leading a revolution. That is what Negri meant when he later accused his old mentor of contaminating the revolutionary moment with "positivist ideologies."[159]

Apprised of these charges, Panzieri reacted with a sense of injury and with a protest that he, too, was a revolutionary, though he did not want to skip the necessary stages of revolution. That had been the tragedy of Russia, and he did not want to see it repeated in Italy. For the present, he insisted, *Quaderni rossi* had to concentrate on showing what was wrong with Italian society and on convincing the Italian Left that the journal's program was correct. Tronti and Negri determined that such a passive policy would play into the hands of the bourgeoisie; when the workers of Fiat had taken to the streets in 1962 it became evident that the time for organizing the revolution had arrived. Twenty years after these events Negri remembered that with Piazza Statuto it was as though "Venus had emerged from the water."[160] Panzieri, too, saw hopeful signs in the events of Turin, for the strike revealed the alienation of the working class, which was a force that might be used to propel a Marxist revolution; still, it would be premature to take to the streets until the whole field of Italian capitalism had been surveyed.

Meanwhile, Panzieri insisted, it would be an act of faith for any Marxist to assert, on the basis of the 1962 metalworkers' strike, that Italy was ripe for revolution. That the workers had signed a contract and had gone back to work caused Panzieri to ridicule the celebration of Piazza Statuto as the Italian equivalent of the Soviet of Workers' and Soldiers' Deputies in Petrograd. Italy in 1962 was not Russia in 1917, or even in 1905. No less an authority than Marx had expressed a very clear opinion on "spontaneous" political activism to the anarchist writer Wilhelm Weitling: "To excite the workers without giving them reasoned arguments is quite simply to deceive them. To awaken fantastic hopes can lead only to disaster, not deliverance."[161] These were Panzieri's exact sentiments, which he expressed with increasing anxiety as the Quaderni rossi radicals continued to call for a class war, to the very end of the end, against the capitalist enemy.

Vittorio Rieser, one of Panzieri's supporters, put the controversy this way: the Quaderni rossi factions were arguing from different premises—Negri et al. that the political strategy of the working class should be based on the subjective revolutionary needs of that class alone, Panzieri that this strategy should proceed from an objective analysis of capitalism.[162] The new or extraparliamentary Left has conducted this intramural debate ever since about how the promised land of communism is to be reached, through the raising of worker consciousness or the instigation of worker revolution. It is a debate that has waxed and waned through the intervening years, but its essential contemporary terms were set by the Quaderni rossi disputants.

One of the principal ironies of contemporary Italian history is that in the very real revolutionary activities of 1968 and after, the catalyst of revolution was not the working-class movement, which remained by and large loyal to the ever more moderate PCI and PSI, but the student movement. The historical impact of the student movement is a lesson in the constant surprises that history affords.[163] Men turn to the past for guidance about the future, but it is always the unforeseen and the unpredictable that diminish history's value as a practical guide for sorting out current events. The really amazing thing about political prognostications in the first half of the 1960s is that no one—not even the radicals of Classe operaia— thought to mention the students as a likely source of political agitation, and Marxists were the least prepared of all for what happened in Italy after 1968.[164] According to original Marxist theory only reaction and frivolity could be expected from the sons and daughters of the bourgeoisie en masse, but, in fact, they were the ones, in and out of school, who mounted an organized threat against the Italian state and society, a threat that continues to exist in the extreme extraparliamentary Left form.[165] Through their direct participation in the plethora of industrial strikes during the "hot autumn" of 1969 the students also helped to radicalize the workers, who as a class, however, ignored the ideological call for a perfect revolution and instead channeled their radicalism into specific demands for wage increases and improvements in the workplace.[166]

Panzieri, no less than Tronti and Negri, remained blind to the students as a force in politics, but his judgment about the workers was more astute than that of his antagonists on *Classe operaia*. Panzieri always believed that the workers were the only conceivable historical agent for revolution; however, he correctly surmised how far removed they were from a true class consciousness. They lacked a political sense; and, as he observed in a letter to Luciano Della Mea, "that which is not admissible is the lie of positing the existence of a politically oriented force . . . in the worker movement that does not yet exist."[167] The insights of the Frankfurt School into the problem of false consciousness had enabled him to understand why the vast majority of Italian workers had no adequate conception of their role in history. Moreover, from Mao Tse-tung, no less than from the Frankfurt School, he learned that only with correct revolutionary theory would correct revolutionary practice be possible.[168]

Here was where Panzieri believed that he had scored a telling point in his debate with those who wanted revolution and not further sociological inquiries: correct theory, according to him, was revolution or, at the very least, it was more important for a true socialist revolution than any political or violent act. In 1958 he and Lucio Libertini had written that "ideology is the first condition of the existence of a class party because it is its political conscience."[169] He meant that without a firm basis in theory the politics and the violence would have to end badly, as they had under Stalin in the Russian Revolution. Soviet Russia served as his paradigm for failed revolutions, just as the United States did for triumphant capitalism. Italy had its own capitalists to worry about, but it could never defeat them with methods that had produced the Russian Gulag. Panzieri lived long enough to conceive what he thought was the right idea for revolution; nevertheless, more public exposure and debate were required before he could participate in provoking the holocaust of capitalism.

By the summer of 1963 Panzieri had alienated the most vital forces of the Italian Left. Condemned by the official Left for his utopianism, he had become the object of patronizing address by the *Quaderni rossi* alumni, who thought that his ideas were passé. Yet these sorrows had come only as the single spies of the battalions that descended upon him in the months ahead. He lost his job at Einaudi in October 1963, partly over a dispute arising from his ardent insistence on the desirability of publishing *L'immigrazione meridionale* by Goffredo Fofi, who was a collaborator on *Quaderni rossi*. Panzieri's superiors rejected his recommendation and, adding insult to injury, accused him of having used Einaudi "merely as an instrument for an ideological-political battle" with singularly unproductive results for the firm.[170]

Out of work, the chain-smoking and severely insomniac Panzieri entered a period of acute financial crisis, which only began to be relieved in the summer of 1964, when he obtained a position with the Nuova Italia publishing firm. Unfortunately, the ravages of the preceding months had totally undermined his health, which had never been vigorous, and on the morning of 9 October 1964 he died of a cerebral embolism at the age of forty-three. The official Left limited itself to perfunctory announcements regarding his "unexpected death."[171] But Fofi, so recently the beneficiary of Panzieri's selfless support and now a co-editor of *Quaderni piacentini*, another major journal on the extraparliamentary Left, would not allow what he scornfully referred to as the "workers' parties" to forget their role in this tragedy. In a eulogy of flame and wrath he called them to account:

> We do not want to recall here the exceptional intellectual and human qualities of Panzieri. They are very familiar to those who knew him and to the rest they would sound rhetorical (and Panzieri was a man devoid of rhetoric). We only want to deny the general opinion according to which Panzieiri died "unexpectedly." It is not true. His death has been the consequence, has marked the success of that thorough and proper moral lynching operation to which for years, from the time he began *Quaderni rossi* . . . , the "workers' parties" subjected him, with their bureaucrats, union leaders, etc. Moreover, in the previous winter he had lost his editorial position. But grave wear and tear and heavy financial burdens had not induced him to spare himself, to concern himself with his own affairs. By this he was broken, this deeply pessimistic and perhaps desperate man who knew how to cheer anyone who approached him.[172]

To the last Panzieri remained a restless searcher for Marxism undefiled by compromise or error.[173] Certainly he merited Negri's description of him as the Socrates of the extraparliamentary Left.[174] It is an image that he would not particularly have liked, however. No doubt he would have preferred to go down in history as the movement's Lenin, but Panzieri was too critical a thinker to develop the kind of unswerving faith needed to direct a violent revolution and too concerned about demystifying Marx for the comfort of the many Marxists who criticized his growing ideological eclecticism, marked by what they interpreted as an excessive fondness for empiricism.[175] In fact, Panzieri repeatedly called for a theoretical confrontation between Marxism and modern sociology, and after 1962 he showed an increasing willingness to admit that neither Marx nor Lenin had written the last word in the book of the future.[176] For Panzieri Marxism-Leninism remained "the science of revolution," but especially in his final period he came to believe that the hoary formulations of Marx and Lenin on this or that problem of capitalism could only be objects of veneration for Marxists who refused to become adults.[177]

Tronti and Negri were right to conclude that Panzieri would always find a reason to say "not yet" to the call for revolution. Tronti attributed this overdeveloped sense of caution to "some petty bourgeois residues" in Panzieri's background, whereas Negri believed that Panzieri had committed intellectual suicide, first by invoking revolution without having any real idea of what he was doing, second by recoiling in palpable distress at the sight of what political violence actually meant when it erupted in the streets, and third by failing to recognize or acknowledge toward the end of his life that he was rapidly retreating from revolutionary positions.[178] In other words, while Panzieri was a roaring lion in his study and in seminar rooms, he sadly turned into a bleating lamb when pressed to translate his thought into action.

Still, Panzieri was the major pioneering ideologist of the most revolutionary Italian political development of his time. The literature of the extraparliamentary Left reflects Fabrizio Cicchitto's 1971 declaration that it was from *Quaderni rossi* that "at bottom the extraparliamentary Left took its inspiration."[179] The thousands of extraparliamentary Left Italian youths at the Bologna convention in September 1977 understood history and the world essentially in the radical antireformist terms that Panzieri had done so much to advance. Moreover, it cannot have been a coincidence that so many terrorists of the 1970s had been alumni of one extraparliamentary Left faction or another. The extraparliamentary Left was not always or even mainly terroristic, but a revolutionary desire for the destruction of capitalism characterized its virulently antireformist program, which in some extreme left-wing minds issued in both the contemplation of violent strategies and their execution.[180]

The *Quaderni rossi* experience shows us the Italian extraparliamentary Left in embryo. The journal began as an inquiry into the nature of things in a capitalist society, but in the manner of Marx himself the most consistent staff members could not rest content with a mere understanding of the world; they felt compelled to change it as well. All of them, including Panzieri, dreamed of the perfect Marxist revolution, and in that still innocent time they never imagined that such a dream might produce monsters.

Panzieri cannot be held responsible for the violent actions that marred some later extraparliamentary Left groups, and Negri rightly insisted that the founder of *Quaderni rossi* was temperamentally and intellectually averse to the violence without which revolution is inconceivable.[181] As Merleau-Ponty observed in *Humanism and Terror,* "an action can produce something else than it envisages"; nevertheless, he added, "political man assumes its consequences."[182] The historical issue here is not the question of blame, but rather how the interplay between ideas and actions unfolds in a concrete social setting. In this particular case we can conclude that Panzieri started something he did not finish, even taking fright toward the end at the revolutionary project to which many of his ideas were being applied. Negri insisted all along, quite factually, that there was no getting away from Panzieri's influence during the seed-time of the radical workers' autonomy movement—from which, we must add, a jungle of extraparliamentary Left plants, including some poisonous ones, sprouted. Panzieri surely would have understood the 1969 lament of Adorno, whom he so admired: "I only built models. How could I suspect that people would try to turn them into reality with Molotov cocktails?"[183]

Nevertheless, almost to the end of his life Panzieri believed in the myth that in revolution the people's violence could only be heroically moral and restricted to class enemies. Typical of this personal belief was his boyish enthusiasm at the feet of Chou En-lai during his 1955 visit to China when the Chinese leader regaled him and other Italian Socialists with the story of how "one hundred thousand enemies were destroyed on a single day."[184] Panzieri noted in his diary that "these reminiscences provoke clamorous outbursts of laughter. But not for primitive or sadistic [reasons]. It is absolutely natural. It is a great communist leader, modern, young, a little crude perhaps, who *lives* the revolution."[185] Living the revolution: these were words to fire Panzieri's imagination, but shortly before his death he discovered that they signified the Left's most delusional abstraction. The *Quaderni rossi* experience enabled him to see that there might be something other than heroic violence in the revolutionary tradition after all. Such was the education of Raniero Panzieri during the last two years of his life.

Turin in 1962 dispelled his naive illusions about the nature of revolution, but by that time he had surrounded himself with revolutionary ideologues fanatically disposed to make good the political promise of his philosophy; in so doing they helped set in motion forces that would smash the elaborate safeguards that their erstwhile leader elevated to a place of honor in his own theory of revolution. To this brilliant and sensitive man belongs the distinction of having summoned a new generation of Marxists to the contemplation and the practical application of pure Marxism, but not every individual who responded to Panzieri's trumpet call had his sense of awe before the dialectic of history.

Explosion at the Banca dell' Agricoltura in Piazza Fontana, Milan, December 12, 1969. (ANSA Photo)

All photographs by courtesy of Massimo Faraglia, archivist, *La Repubblica*, Rome.

Scene of the abduction of Aldo Moro in Via Mario Fani, Rome, March 16, 1978. (AP Wirephoto)

The discovery of Aldo Moro's corpse, May 9, 1978.

A scene of devastation at the Bologna train station, August 2, 1980.
(ANSA Photo)

Explosion at the Bologna train station, August 2, 1980. (ANSA Photo)

A wounded woman just removed from the rubble, Bologna train station, August 2, 1980. (ANSA Photo)

FOUR

Aldo Moro and Italy's Difficult Democracy

Extraparliamentary Left violence, unexpectedly muted in Bologna, exploded nationwide at the end of September 1977 in response to the murder of Walter Rossi, a Lotta Continua militant, by neofascists in Rome. Ten thousand demonstrators marched on the Rome headquarters of the youth organization of the Movimento Sociale Italiano (MSI). In Milan, Bologna, Verona, Padua, Bergamo, Nuoro, and Catanzaro, MSI headquarters buildings also came under attack, and some were burned out. Rossi's funeral in Rome on 3 October was the occasion for sporadic gunfights all over the city. A policeman was shot in the back, but not fatally. For the next several days the extraparliamentary Left continued its protest against the MSI in Rome, resulting in the burning of cars, the destruction of shops, and violent confrontations with the police. Another hot autumn had begun in the nation's capital.

For several months Aldo Moro, Italy's foremost political leader, had been viewing the political violence with a haunting presentiment of disaster.[1] The kidnapping of Guido De Martino, the Socialist leader's son, in April had had a desolating effect on Moro. The former prime minister had begun to fear that he or members of his family might be similarly victimized by terrorist groups. Eleonora Moro later observed that her husband had begun to compile his "testament." He had done so in an episodic manner that never failed to surprise and terrify her. Every ten or fifteen days, beginning in April and "always in the evening in moments of great peace and silence," Moro, without looking up from his newspaper, had made testamentary remarks, such as "If you should have need of a notary, this person is someone you can depend on" or "I would like my books to remain together [in a collection]" or "If you have need of counsel . . . of someone to whom you can open your heart, you can turn to this person, who is a friend."[2]

Moro had never been one to talk this way, but the events of 1977 had prompted numerous changes in his behavior. Giovanni Moro later recalled that at about this time his father had started taking care every evening to close the window shutters completely. He also had shown much greater concern than ever about varying the schedule of his comings and goings. His office on Via Savoia had been protected with armor plate and bulletproof windows.

Moro's passion for security became even more ardent after 16 November, when the terrorist event of the year took place in Turin. On that afternoon Carlo Casalegno, a former Resistance fighter who had become one of the most respected journalists in the country and was vice-director of *La Stampa*, fell with four bullet wounds in his face. To the Red Brigadists who shot him, Casalegno was "a servant of the state" and "an active agent of the counterguerrilla campaign."[3] Casalegno recently had attacked terrorist groups in some spirited editorials. Critically wounded, he regained consciousness later that afternoon, but the devastation to his face was so extensive that he could not speak. He improved somewhat the next day, even managing to communicate by pen and paper; however, the doctors would not operate because of his weak heart. After thirteen days of unceasing agony, on 29 November, Casalegno died.

While Casalegno was fighting unsuccessfully for his life the Red Brigades perpetrated, on 17 November in Genoa, the second left-wing terrorist attack against a member of the Italian Communist party, the PCI. Forty-one-year-old Carlo Castellano had been active on the Catholic Left before joining the PCI. To the terrorists of the ultra-Left he was the kind of "communist" they abhorred, a Berlinguerian par excellence who sought to soften the workers' resistance to capitalism. Members of the Red Brigades shot him nine times: eight bullets in the legs and one in the abdomen. Castellano was forced to undergo fourteen operations over a two-year period. He later recalled the look in the eyes of his assailants: "Eyes filled with so much hatred as if I were a wild animal to be killed, not deserving the slightest pity."[4]

The terrorist violence of November left Moro aghast. He told his wife that Italy was now at war. To Franco Di Bella, the director of *Corriere della sera*, Moro confided: "We are living in terrible moments. . . . It is as though we are in the catacombs."[5] He was under no illusions, then, about his enormous personal danger. After all, Moro stood out in the arena of Italian politics as the paramount leader of the very Christian Democratic establishment that left-wing terrorist groups had vowed to destroy. Born in 1916, Moro, the former president of FUCI (Federazione Universitaria Cattolica Italiana), rose swiftly in the Christian Democratic party ranks: parliamentary deputy at age thirty, undersecretary of foreign affairs at thirty-two, president of the party's parliamentary group in the Chamber at thirty-seven, minister first of justice and then of public instruction at thirty-nine, party secretary at forty-three, prime minister at forty-seven. A politician of his long experience and high skill could not fail to draw the necessary conclusions from the threat of Red Brigadism.

Though no longer in an official government position, Moro remained a conspicuous target for subversive forces because of his well-deserved fame as the man for "difficult passages" in Italian political life. He was the only Christian Democratic leader who had the temperament and the vision to bring the party's contentious factions together, while at the same time his reputation for honesty in a party not known for high ethical standards enabled him to reach out to the other parties as a credible champion of compromise. He was a master at the art of persuasion.[6]

The liberal Catholic Moro believed that by espousing a policy of cooperation with the PCI he had made implacable enemies in the United States and Italy among those individuals and groups who at any cost wanted to keep the Communists out of the Italian government. Moro had shocked many people in his own party as well as some secretaries of state and national security advisers in Washington when he professed to see a difference in kind as well as in degree between Berlinguer and Stalin.

In the early 1960s he had made the same impression on both sides of the Atlantic by taking the initiative in forming an alliance between the Christian Democrats and the Socialist party. However, on this occasion Moro had the official support of the United States government, which hoped that an opening to the relatively moderate Left would lead to greater stability in Italy. From 1963 to 1968 he led various Center-Left governments. In a speech on 16 September 1964 he underscored the necessity of resolving "the problem of political stability in our country."[7] In his view this problem aggravated all of Italy's other difficulties.

Much of the intellectual inspiration for Moro's policy had come from the 1961 papal encyclical *Mater et magistra*, but neither John XXIII nor Moro foresaw the magnitude of the difficulties besetting the Center-Left line.[8] The pope's appeal for the efficacious intervention of the government in the economy as a measure necessary for the reduction of social strife between classes and regions marked out a broad area of convergence between Catholic and Socialist reformism. The Socialist party, however, was not united when it entered the Center-Left coalition. Pietro Nenni's position was always weak because powerful forces within his party chafed at his arrangement with the Christian Democrats. Moro, on the other side, had the benefit of a more united party, but in order not to lose this advantage he could ill afford to make any concessions in social or economic policy that might threaten his party's unity. The result was a frustrating stalemate for both members of the coalition.

The 19 May 1968 elections ended in a decisive defeat for Moro's Center-Left government. Although the Christian Democratic party fared well enough, the divided and demoralized PSI was crushed. Now out of power and pushed to the margins of his party, Moro began a period of agonizing political readjustment. The student demonstrations and worker strikes of 1968–69 drastically affected his thinking. These developments focused Moro's attention on the need for a completely new approach to Italy's worsening political problems. He became the principal spokesman for a thesis hitherto unthinkable in Catholic politics: in Italy's present circumstances the Christian Democrats had to consider an opening to the Communist Left. On 29 June 1969 Moro delivered a pathbreaking speech on this subject in Rome before the XI Congress of the Christian Democrats. He argued that the party had to remain a popular force and not become a conservative one; to do that it had to remain open to all sincerely democratic forces, including the PCI, which had proclaimed its desire to participate in a free and pluralistic political system.[9] Moro had always been a relentless anti-Communist. It is true that he had made an issue of formulating his argument against Communists in aggressively democratic terms, always taking care to dissociate himself from reactionaries. Nevertheless, in 1963 Moro had insisted that before the Center-Left alliance could be formed the PSI would have to break completely and unequivocally with the PCI. Thus it was ironic that at the end of the Center-Left interlude Moro began to look for a way to effect a reconciliation between the two grand antagonists of Italian politics.

For Moro the disagreeably hard fact of political life in Italy could be taken in with a glance at the PCI's performance in recent national elections: 25.3% of the vote in 1963, 26.9% in 1968, 27.2% in 1972, 32.4% in 1975, 34.5% in 1976.[10] Meanwhile, the Christian Democratic party's share had fallen to 35.5% in the 1975 election, its poorest showing since 1946. Arguably more a protest against the perceived misgovernment and corruption of the Christian Democrats than a positive endorsement of the PCI, which enjoyed all the enormous advantages of the opposition in difficult times, this election still confirmed Moro's belief that the era of his party's domination of Italian political life had ended.[11] The PCI could no longer be quarantined. The safety of Italy's democracy in an age of "mortal risks" depended on the inclusion of this large and growing force in the government itself.[12]

The veteran anti-Communist leader proposed his *compromesso storico* (historic compromise) in a spirit of resignation. He had spent nearly thirty years in search of the right political combination that would ensure the demise of the PCI. Nothing had worked. The PCI was growing because it represented something vital in the country. Moro now understood fully what few other Christian Democratic leaders could even begin to contemplate, and he moved with his customary caution and skill toward an understanding with the PCI. Always a fervent Roman Catholic, he professed an irreconcilable aversion toward the PCI's strictly materialistic vision of man and society.[13] At the same time he recognized that unalterable political facts had sharply circumscribed his party's room for maneuver, and that was the point for the politically pragmatic Moro. He turned to the PCI with a sense that there was no other practical thing to be done.

Right-wing Christian Democrats and other conservatives, along with their patrons in the United States government, condemned Moro's opening to the PCI. According to these individuals, Moro had been deceived by an obvious ploy of Eurocommunism. Although reticent about the details of his relationship with the "wily" Moro, Henry Kissinger, for example, asserted in *White House Years* that the opening to the Communists was woefully misguided.[14]

Historically, United States administrations had not limited their participation in Italian politics to verbal protests. As the Pike Report made clear, the CIA had played a devious and illegal role in Italy by supplying antileftist groups with $65 million from 1948 to 1968. In the 1972 elections alone, $10 million had been spent this way.[15] Moro feared that United States resistance to his strategy would follow this historic pattern and perhaps go even further. He addressed his fear in an unpublished article written early in 1978. Moro professed continued and undiminished loyalty to the alliance with the United States but said that Washington had not yet learned the distinction between advice and criticism on the one hand and interference on the other.[16] He believed that the United States government and his domestic enemies were doing everything in their very considerable power to implicate him in the Lockheed scandal, which had begun to break in late 1975. According to Moro's own estimate this attack on his reputation and his political collaborators was the price demanded for the coalition he had envisaged with Berlinguer. Another Christian Democratic leader, Giulio Andreotti, noted in his diary that Moro became deeply worried about the anti-Eurocommunist movement. He feared that agents from various foreign countries were working for their own cold war ends in this campaign of vilification, which, if successful, would completely destroy the political equilibrium of Italy.[17] Washington in particular seemed bent on destroying the one development in Italian politics calculated to give the country what it needed most: time in which to cope with its staggering problems. However, nothing could shake Moro's resolve to work with the PCI, particularly after the party's impressive gains in the 1976 elections.

To the ex–prime minister, who clearly perceived his own vulnerability as a condition arising on the radical Left from the symbolic association between the name Moro and the Christian Democratic hegemony and on the American-backed right from his notoriety as a philo-Communist, events occurring in early 1978 brought fresh discouragement. The campaign to tarnish his name in the Lockheed scandal continued. Even more immediately troubling was the nationwide eruption of terrorist burnings, knifings, and shootings. In his last speech, on 28 February, Moro confessed: "I believe in the emergency, I fear the emergency."[18] Subversion in the factories had reached unprecedented proportions on 4 January when Major Carmine De Rosa, a fifty-two-year-old carabiniere on leave and in charge of security at Fiat, was shot in the face, neck, and chest at pointblank range and killed. The Operai Armati per il Comunismo and the Nuclei Armati Comunisti took credit for this action, calling De Rosa "a spy for the establishment."[19] On the morning of the De Rosa assassination hundreds of terrorist leaflets carrying the title "Buon anno padrone!" were found inside the Fiat plant. According to this literature, De Rosa bore the responsibility for "the militarized structure constructed at Fiat, for the coercion of work, and for espionage against the workers."[20] The terrorists explained the assassination as "an attack that aims to destroy the vital mechanisms of capitalist command over work."

Like the violence of 1977, that of early 1978 possessed two characteristic features: precise terrorist attacks, such as the De Rosa killing, and a pervasive political gang warfare that became especially virulent in Rome. There, armed bands of extra-parliamentary Left and Right youths roamed the streets, leaving burned cars, smashed windows, and bloodied bodies in their wake. Both kinds of violence reinforced the impression that Italy had arrived at a moment of revolutionary crisis, and extremist leaders of the Left and the Right concluded that the momentum of the situation was in their favor. The gang violence in Rome appeared to have a life of its own, unconnected to any kind of terrorist plan, but simultaneous attacks against Fiat in Turin and the business community elsewhere were a different story. Kneecappings, beatings, and kidnappings occurred at a furious pace throughout January 1978.

To the list of preferred terrorist targets, which up to this point had included mainly newspapermen, industrialists, and policemen, the terrorists now added judges. Riccardo Palma, sixty-three years old and a judge since 1947, had distinguished himself as the leading authority on the country's prison system. Following a flurry of convict breakouts across Italy in the early and mid-1970s, he had been given the responsibility of organizing security in the entire penal system. With this objective in mind, Palma had just completed a tour of the prisons in Piedmont. The Red Brigades, demonstrating a perfect acquaintance with Palma's routine, killed him on 14 February with bursts of machinegun fire at the door of his car. Shortly afterward the terrorists announced in a telephone call that they had just executed "a servant of the multinationals."[21]

The following month Turin began holding a heavily publicized Red Brigade trial. The police went to novel extremes in providing security. Eight thousand armed men stood guard around the old Lamarmora barracks courthouse. The courtroom itself looked like the center ring in a circus as fifteen caged defendants, including Renato Curcio, clenched their fists and gesticulated wildly, shrieking insults at the judges and the jury. Turin, after its shame and failure to find jurors in 1977 trials, had found its courage now, and six jurors—two women and four men—prepared to do their duty; eight supplementary jurors were also available. A Red Brigade propaganda statement denounced these men and women as a "lynch mob"; its authors warned: "To the jurors we say, with great clarity, that in this voluntary capacity as a special tribunal we consider them responsible for their actions and consequently we will hold them accountable."[22] On the opening day of the trial a courtroom spokesman for the Red Brigades contemptuously denounced the "armed democracy" and the "revisionists" who had manufactured a campaign of hysteria against the true communism of the Red Brigades.

Almost from its beginning the Turin trial was totally eclipsed by terrorist actions of a hitherto unimaginable magnitude. The first of them occurred on 10 March at 7:55 A.M. in Turin itself. A commando group of terrorists confronted fifty-one-year-old Rosario Berardi, the city's marshal of public security, in Largo Belgio. He reached for his gun and succeeded in pulling it from its holster, but not in time to fire a shot. The first terrorist bullet struck Berardi in the nape of the neck, and then six more shots tore into his body. The Red Brigade posthomicide message was brief: "The trial must not go forward."[23] A city already agitated profoundly by the Red Brigade trial staggered under the blow of Berardi's death—its fourth political homicide in less than a year.

The violence in Turin heightened Moro's sense of foreboding. In compensation, however, he could point to a new national coalition government. Moro, the guiding spirit of this compromise, had succeeded in overcoming the bitter resistance of diverse opponents to his opening to the Communist Left, including opposition from elements in his own party, elements in parties traditionally allied to it, and—most bitter of all—the United States government. Against this array of powerful antagonists Moro had won his point, that an agreement with the Communists offered the republic its best chance for improved equilibrium. He fully understood that the American phobia on this subject could never be cured, but in his opinion the historic compromise offered Italy its only hope for political stability.

On the morning of 16 March 1978 Moro prepared to help celebrate the installation of the new government, which would be led by Giulio Andreotti and supported by the PCI. The ex-premier, still the leader of the Christian Democratic party, was scheduled to appear in Parliament at 10:00 A.M. He and his bodyguards set out in two cars from the family apartment on Via Forte Trionfale in Rome's Monte Mario section. His chauffeur for eighteen years, forty-three-year-old Domenico Ricci, drove Moro's dark blue Fiat 130 along the route to the nearby Church of Santa Chiara, where the political leader began each day with a few moments of quiet prayer. Moro sat in the back seat, directly behind Ricci, reading the morning newspaper. On Ricci's right was Marshal Oreste Leonardi, nicknamed Judo, Moro's long-time bodyguard. Three additional bodyguards traveled behind them in an unmarked cream-colored Alfa Romeo: twenty-five-year-old Giulio Rivera, twenty-five-year-old Raffaele Jozzino, and thirty-year-old Francesco Zizzi, who had joined Moro's security force that very day.

Moro and his retinue had made this same third-of-a-mile drive countless times before without incident. On this day, as the Fiat 130 approached the intersection of Via Fani and Via Stresa, a woman driving a white car began to back into Via Fani from Via Stresa, in front of the Moro vehicles. Ricci tried to avoid the car but slammed into its right rear end. Rivera, driving the Alfa Romeo, made it a three-way collision, but there was little damage to any of the cars.

The woman driver and her male companion bolted from their car toward positions on either side of the Fiat 130 and began pouring automatic weapon fire into the front seat area. Ricci and Leonardi were killed instantly. Simultaneously, several men dressed in light blue airline uniforms sprang from their cover near a deserted bar, blasting away with submachine guns at the Alfa Romeo. A half-dozen or so more terrorists assisted in holding back traffic and covering the assault commandos. Fifteen to twenty seconds later the massacre was over: Rivera died as he tried to radio for help; Zizzi, mortally wounded, died unconscious at the hospital within a few hours; Jozzino, the only one of Moro's men who managed to draw a gun and shoot it, crawled out of the car but was shot in the head by a terrorist specially positioned for just such a contingency.

While blood ran on Via Fani, the terrorists took Moro, alive and apparently unhurt, into a waiting Fiat 132. Without suffering a single casualty and scarcely even an inconvenience, they whisked him away down Via Stresa to Via Trionfale and eventually to Via Massimi, where he was transferred to a van. In yet another masterful touch they had sabotaged all the telephone lines in the neighborhood. A full forty-seven minutes passed before the Italian police began to mount systematic roadblocks. For the next two months the ordeal of Aldo Moro would dominate the national life of Italy.[24]

At Montecitorio the country's political leaders reacted to the news with varying degrees of shock and outrage. Giuseppe Saragat, the former president of the republic, called it "the most terrible deed that has struck Italy since the end of World War II." Tina Anselmi, the minister of public health and a close friend of Moro, interpreted the attack as a declaration of "civil war." Ugo La Malfa, president of the Republican party (PRI), agreed: "We are in a state of war, and therefore it is necessary to prepare an action recognizing the state of war." What he meant by this was "martial law and curfews." Emergency laws were desperately needed, including the death penalty, La Malfa asserted. Ciriaco De Mita, a future Christian Democratic president and prime minister, simply collapsed on a divan and without a word began to cry.[25]

Between 10:00 and 11:00 A.M. on the day of the attack, the Red Brigades made six telephone calls claiming responsibility for the murders and the kidnapping. Forty-eight hours later authorities were directed to an underground passageway in Largo Argentina, where they found terrorist communication number one, including a photograph of Moro before an encircled five-pointed Red Brigade star. The world learned that Moro had been placed in a people's prison because he was "the most authoritative leader, the undisputed theorist and strategist of the Christian Democratic regime, which for thirty years has oppressed the Italian people."[26] Considered to be a henchman of the multinationals and "closely tied to imperialist circles," Moro embodied the Christian Democratic party, which the communist vanguards, as the Red Brigades styled themselves, had long regarded as "the most ferocious enemy of the proletariat." In opposition to this "imperialist project" the Red Brigades claimed to have launched a "CLASS WAR FOR COMMUNISM." Their strategy would be "TO CARRY THE WAR TO THE IMPERIALIST STATE OF THE MULTINATIONALS." Further, they would "DESTROY THE STRUCTURES, THE PROJECTS OF THE IMPERIALIST BOURGEOISIE, ATTACKING THE POLITICAL-ECONOMIC-MILITARY PERSONNEL WHO REPRESENT IT." The hour of communist revolution had struck, and the Red Brigades urged all communists "TO UNIFY THE REVOLUTIONARY MOVEMENT, CONSTRUCTING THE FIGHTING COMMUNIST PARTY."

When the state's trial of the Red Brigades resumed in Turin on 20 March, Curcio yelled in the courtroom: "Moro is in our hands."[27] He then added: "The real trial is taking place elsewhere. A much more serious trial is at another place. Moro is in the hands of the proletariat, and the whole state will be on trial." When the public prosecutor ridiculed the notion of the Red Brigades as the authentic voice of the proletariat, calling them nothing but "an armed band," Curcio replied: "A band that holds Moro, that will try Moro, the DC [Christian Democrats], and the entire political class of Italy."[28]

While the new government of Giulio Andreotti swiftly passed severe antiterrorist measures and mounted the largest police manhunt in Italian history, the Red Brigades struck again, in Turin, wounding the former mayor of the city, Giovanni Picco, in the legs and shoulder. It was the first of many other terrorist incidents during the Moro kidnapping. In this way the Red Brigades demonstrated their ability to fight simultaneously on more than one front in the war against the state.

The attention of the nation and the world remained fixed on Moro. Red Brigade communication number two, received on 25 March, repeated that Moro, long "the point man for the bourgeoisie," would be subjected to "PROLETARIAN JUSTICE."[29] Moro himself was heard from at last on 29 March in confidential letters to his wife, his secretary, and Minister of the Interior Francesco Cossiga. The letter to Cossiga contained a threat. Moro told the minister that he had no intention of dying a martyr's death. His family needed him, and he called upon the party to formulate a prisoner exchange, to be negotiated by the Vatican. Reminding Cossiga, with whom he had been especially close, of "our collective action," Moro insisted that it was not right for him to be held solely responsible.[30] A lasting controversy sprang up over whether or not this was the real Moro or some brainwashed and tortured shell of a man the world once knew.[31] That some researchers have found an intellectual correlation between Moro's prison letters and his other writings seems to be a trivial discovery at best. More to the point is an awareness of the absolute, unmanning terror in which Moro lived from the moment he was kidnapped. To his credit, he did not yield to this terror, but what human being would not have been affected by it?

An instructive parallel with the Moro kidnapping is provided by the Mario Sossi kidnapping in 1974. Sossi claimed that throughout his ordeal he stood in mortal terror of the Red Brigades. They subjected him to physical violence in the beginning and psychological torture throughout. Until the very hour of his release he feared that the terrorists would murder him. His "trial" consisted of hectoring tirades by the people's advocates, who busied themselves not in proving a case but simply reciting one. These interminable sessions left him with "a sense of impatience, frustration, and castration."[32] As for the integrity of his communications to the outside world, Sossi stated flatly that they were influenced from first to last by what he thought the Red Brigades wanted to hear.[33] The conclusion to be drawn from Sossi's experience is that in life and death situations only heroes or martyrs choose to be true above all else to an abstraction. For most men in his circumstances, intellectual and political consistency lacks compelling force; it acquires importance only insofar as it furthers the victim's chance for survival.

So it must have been with Moro. Since he expressly refused to play the role of hero or martyr, it is reasonable to take him at his word. The main theme of Moro's communications was his desire to be reunited with his family. No other objective mattered to him as much, and his arguments were means to that end, not illustrations of a political thesis.

In their third communication, a few days after the second, the Red Brigades explained the historical significance of 16 March: "the capture and trial of Aldo Moro is nothing but a moment, important and elucidating, of the Revolutionary Class War that the armed communist forces have assumed as a strategy for the construction of a communist society."[34] In other words, the revolutionary moment of communist prophecy had struck: "Comrades, in this historic phase, at this point of crisis, the practice of revolutionary violence is the only policy that has the real possibility of confronting and resolving the antagonistic contradiction that pits the metropolitan proletariat against the imperialistic bourgeoisie." As for the prospects of victory in this struggle, the Red Brigades offered their own record of success as an indication of what the future held: "it is possible to beat it [the state] to death . . . , it is possible to annihilate it strategically."

Andreotti, supported by the PCI and the United States, adopted a hard line and refused to negotiate with the Red Brigades.[35] The government and, overwhelmingly, the media portrayed Moro as a tragic victim whose increasingly bitter letters of recrimination were to be regarded as either extorted statements or the ravings of a man shattered by psychological and physical torture.[36] When on 2 April ailing and aged Pope Paul VI pleaded publicly to the "unknown men" of the Red Brigades for the prisoner's life, hardliners complained that this gesture of a Moro family friend was a great victory for the terrorists.

Communication number four arrived on 4 April, together with a letter from Moro for the Christian Democratic leader Benigno Zaccagnini. The Red Brigades still presented no specific demands to the government but aimed most of their words at the nation's "true communists." The terrorists had thought that the kidnapping of Moro would detonate a revolutionary explosion in Italy. That nothing of the kind had happened, that even the normally sympathetic or at least understanding radical Left had pronounced the kidnapping an act worthy of imbeciles, had thrown the Red Brigades on the defensive, and now they sought to explain, in dialectical terms, what they were trying to accomplish.

"In the imperialist state," they began, "reformism and annihilation are integrated forms of the same function—preventive counterrevolution."[37] The official Communist party in Italy had fallen into the gross error of reformism, and in the aftermath of that tragic fall every genuine communist had to rediscover Marxist truth. Things had reached such a sorry pass in Italy that the PCI "is also and above all at the service of the imperialist state." To the Red Brigades, communist revolution meant the violent dismantling of the capitalist state, and that was the only thing it could ever mean. Every other tactic only served the capitalist hegemony. The Red Brigades signed off with a resounding "PROLETARIANS OF ALL COUNTRIES UNITE."

Moro, in his letter to Zaccagnini, called for negotiations with the Red Brigades: "I am a political prisoner [and] your brusque decision to close down any discourse relative to other persons similarly detained places [me] in an unsustainable position."[38] Moro claimed that he had always been against inflexibility on matters of prisoner exchange, and his present views, therefore, could not be attributed to Red Brigade pressures. "And in truth," he added plaintively, "I also feel a little abandoned by all of you." Moro was not alone in the struggle to break the government's hard line. His wife worked indefatigably toward this end. Moreover, in the political arena Bettino Craxi's Socialists, dissident elements within the Christian Democratic party, various extraparliamentary Left groups, and some independent intellectuals attempted to promote negotiations with the Red Brigades for Moro's life. However, this motley alliance had recourse only to arguments of moral persuasion. They lacked what their adversaries in this debate had: power.

On 10 April, Red Brigade communication number five announced that prisoner Moro had divulged vital information regarding "the antiproletarian strategy, the bloody and terroristic plots" of the government. All the hideous truth was coming out now, and "NOTHING MUST BE HIDDEN FROM THE PEOPLE."[39] Moro, in a companion letter, continued to advocate negotiations—the "soft line." Meanwhile, in keeping with their strategy of continuous additional terrorist action during the Moro crisis, on 7 April in Genoa the Red Brigades ambushed and wounded Felice Schiavetti, the president of the provincial Industrialists' Association. They shot him five times in the legs. Four days later the same terrorist group assassinated Lorenzo Cotugno, a thirty-one-year-old guard at the prison where Curcio was an inmate. Cotugno had been marked only for a kneecapping, but he drew his gun and severely wounded one terrorist, twenty-eight-year-old Cristoforo Piancone, and grazed another one before falling with mortal wounds. Piancone, a former inspector at Fiat and a veteran of the Lotta Continua movement, was left behind at the scene.

In communication number six, received on 15 April, the Red Brigades announced the termination of Moro's trial, "a stage in the CLASS WAR FOR COMMUNISM."[40] The indictment against the Christian Democratic party and its allies of the so-called Left had been fully confirmed by the facts, and thanks to Moro's testimony, they wrote, the whole sordid mess was at last clear and on record. Then came a dreaded pronouncement: "ALDO MORO IS GUILTY AND IS THEREFORE CONDEMNED TO DEATH." Moro's obituary notice arrived three days later, as communication number seven. It said that Moro had died by his own hand; the corpse could be found in the icy depths of Lake Duchessa, some fifty miles northeast of Rome. This document turned out to be a sadistic forgery. Moro was still alive. The authentic communication number seven arrived on 20 April, and it denounced the 18 April document as a fake. The Red Brigades then stipulated that they would free Moro in exchange for "communist prisoners."[41] They gave the government forty-eight hours to begin negotiating toward this end. On the same day, in Milan, Red Brigade terrorists coolly murdered Francesco Di Cataldo by shooting him in the head four times as he stood waiting for a bus. Di Cataldo had been the marshal of the Milan prison guards.

To avert death himself, Moro employed all of his enormous negotiating skill in a desperate effort to win his freedom. On 21 April he wrote another letter to Zaccagnini in which he accused his party of forsaking him: "Is it possible that all of you are agreed in wanting my death for a presumed reason of state . . . almost as a solution for all the country's problems?"[42] He insisted that his fate lay in the party's hands: "Whether or not the condemnation is carried out depends on you. . . . If you do not intervene a chilling page would be written in the history of Italy. My blood would fall on you, on the party, on the country." Moro warned Zaccagnini: "Don't look at tomorrow, but at the day after tomorrow."

The next day Pope Paul VI issued a personal appeal "to the men of the Red Brigades: to restore the honorable Aldo Moro to liberty, to his family, to civil life."[43] He begged them "on bended knee" to liberate Moro: "Men of the Red Brigades, allow me, the representative of many of your countrymen, to hope that in your souls there still resides a victorious sentiment of humanity." Religous and humanitarian entreaties had no impact on the Red Brigades, and in communication number eight, of 24 April, they listed the names of the prisoners they wanted in exchange for Moro: Sante Notarnicola, Mario Rossi, Giuseppe Battaglia, Augusto Viel, Domenico Delli Veneri, Pasquale Abatangelo, Giorgio Panizzari, Maurizio Ferrari, Alberto Franceschini, Renato Curcio, Roberto Ognibene, Paola Besuschio, Cristoforo Piancone.[44] The Red Brigades insisted on an immediate, clear reply; otherwise the Moro death sentence would be carried out.

At the same time Moro sent a third letter to Zaccagnini. "We are almost at zero hour," he wrote; "it is more a matter of seconds than minutes."[45] Of the men in power, Zaccagnini was his only hope, but should the party decree his death Moro made the following request: "I ask that neither authorities of the state nor party men should participate at my funeral. I ask to be followed by the few who really cared for me and are therefore worthy to accompany me with their prayers and their love."

Moro's letters to Zaccagnini, along with a simultaneous supplication to the Red Brigades on the prisoner's behalf by United Nations Secretary General Kurt Wald-heim, provoked bitter polemics in Rome. By this time government hard-liners and their supporters in the PCI, who all along had opposed negotiations on the grounds that this was the only way to bring about the final crisis and defeat of terrorism, felt free to claim that the recent letters by Moro were not authentic at all. They had been written by a man either tortured or drugged. There was of course no evidence in support of this charge, but the logic of the hard-line position was compelling: the Red Brigades had no interest in transmitting Moro's thoughts about his situation; they were interested only in humiliating and destroying him in order to further their revolutionary campaign against the state. Therefore, wittingly or not—and for most of the hard-liners it was the latter—Moro was playing the game of Italy's deadliest enemies. The country could not be expected to play that game along with him.

On the other side of the fence in this debate, doves of mixed breeds urged negotiations as the only way to save Moro. Bettino Craxi launched his plan to negotiate with the terrorists, calling for the release of some political convicts and the improvement of conditions in the special antiterrorist prisons. The extraparlia-mentary Left, now fully alive to the mortal danger it faced in its publicly perceived role as the ideological ally and chief source of recruits for the terrorist Left, mounted a frantic campaign to dissociate itself in thought, word, and deed from the Red Brigades. This eclectic ensemble of parties and groups called for the government to negotiate and, at the same time, exerted pressure on former friends and colleagues in the terrorist groups to spare Moro.[46] Prime Minister Andreotti utterly rejected all pronegotiation arguments. In a television address he stated his government's view that to negotiate would mean fatally compromising Italy's political institutions by giving in to terrorism.

Moro sought to assist the doves. In two letters to his family dated 25 and 27 April, he lamented the failure of his party to save him. So many democristiani had been loyal to him in "the happy hours" of power, but where were these summer soldiers now?[47] Moro also denied that he had been brainwashed in the people's prison: "I have not been coerced, I am not drugged, I write with my style ugly though it may be . . . with the usual penmanship." People must be made to believe that this is his authentic voice, he wrote; otherwise the sentence of the people's court would be carried out. Then Moro added: "I die, if my party so decides, in the fullness of my Christian faith and in the immense love for an exemplary family that I adore and hope to watch over from on high in the heavens."

The authoritative voice of former president Giuseppe Saragat now joined that of Craxi in urging negotiations. Saragat, long a leader of the Social Democrats and one of the country's foremost elder statesmen, declared that Moro's letters from the people's prison could not be ignored or undervalued. Moreover, it seemed to him that "no democratic form of power could exist outside the sense of humanity and pity."[48] Therefore, Craxi was "completely right to explore all the . . . difficult ways that might lead to the salvation of Moro." Saragat concluded by observing that an inflexible refusal even to make an attempt to save Moro would be a sign of the very weakness and fear that the hard-liners claimed to abhor.

At the same time the Moro family announced its break with the Christian Democratic leadership, declaring that the attitude of the party "is completely insufficient to save the life of Aldo Moro."[49] The announcement singled out Christian Democratic leaders by name for a feckless "attitude of immobility." The family then called for a convocation of the party's national council to deal with the Moro case. Craxi pressed this initiative and on 2 May met with the leaders of the Christian Democrats. He outlined his one-for-one plan of a prisoner exchange, but the meeting degenerated into an acrimonious dispute when the leaders demanded further "guarantees" before the party could proceed with negotiations. Craxi stormed out of the conference, shouting, "There is someone in this room who wants Moro dead, and I'm going out and cry it in the streets."[50]

Craxi's initiative lost force the next day when one of the most respected members of his own party, Sandro Pertini—the old Resistance fighter and future president of the republic—supported the hard line. To negotiate, he said, would be the end of Italy's democratic institutions. Having been a witness to Mussolini's takeover in 1922, Pertini announced that he did not intend to be present a second time at democracy's demise in Italy. Even more devastating to the doves was the media report of a woman described only as "a widow of Via Fani." Sickened by the thought of dealing with the terrorists who had killed her husband, she promised to burn herself to death publicly in front of her two children if any of the terrorists were freed.[51] Andreotti, emboldened by these expressions of solidarity for his policy, rejected Craxi's one-for-one release plan.

Nevertheless, Craxi's denunciation of the Christian Democrats expressed and continues to express the feelings of many regarding the ordeal of Aldo Moro. Numerous authors have repeated his charge and a few have based entire books on it.[52] Moro was abandoned to his fate, in this interpretation, because it was expedient to do so. The prospect of his removal from the scene was one to gladden the hearts of his numerous enemies in Rome and Washington. This thesis is fascinating, but it lacks compelling proof. On the other side, Andreotti's moving account of his ordeal in following the hard line as the only way to keep the governing coalition intact during the worst crisis in the republic's history contains nothing inconsistent with the stark realities and dreadful choices facing him.[53]

Simultaneous kneecappings on 4 May of a Milan business executive, Umberto degli Innocenti, and a Genoese union official, Alfredo Lamberti, were followed the next day by Red Brigade communication number nine. It announced that the battle initiated on 16 March with the capture of Aldo Moro had reached its conclusion. For the Red Brigades the ultimate meaning of the Moro affair was this: "The state of the multinationals has revealed its true face, without the grotesque mask of formal democracy; it is that of the armed imperialist counterrevolution, of the terrorism of mercenaries in uniform, of the political genocide of communist forces."[54] According to the Red Brigades, the state's violent actions were only "the convulsions of a beast that is mortally wounded." The past fifty-one days had reinforced the Red Brigades' thesis: "To extend the activity of combat, to concentrate the armed attack against the vital centers of the imperialist state, to organize in the proletariat the Fighting Communist Party is the right path to prepare the final victory of the proletariat, to annihilate definitively the imperialist monster, and to construct a communist society." In this valiant struggle against the protofascist Christian Democratic state, the Red Brigades proclaimed that they were now compelled by the misdeeds and inaction of their adversary to carry out Moro's death sentence. With this document Moro sent a last farewell to his family, impugning without hope the "absurd and incredible behavior" of the Christian Democrats.

In desperation the Moro family begged President of the Republic Leone to pardon one brigatista in exchange for Moro. He agreed in principle but demurred on legal grounds. Enmeshed in the Lockheed scandals that would drive him from office on 16 June 1978, Leone felt that he could do nothing. In the terrorist camp, too, dovish counsels failed. The so-called *duri* of the extraparliamentary Autonomia movement warned the Red Brigades not to kill Moro. The autonomi, whose relationship with the terrorists had been tantalizingly vague, said that Moro's murder would be "outside every dialectic and revolutionary logic" as well as "a gross political and strategic error."[55] Moreover, "the cadaver of Moro" would serve the parties of the state as "a mystical body." It would be a godsend to the foundering Christian Democratic regime.

While the Red Brigades maintained an ominous silence, the country's political leaders continued to squabble over what to do next. Individuals belonging to the Christian Democratic faction led by Amintore Fanfani began to make public statements criticizing the hard line, but the party chiefs who mattered most resolved to do nothing until the forthcoming elections of 14 May were out of the way. For their part the Red Brigades grew increasingly afraid that the people's prison would be discovered, and they decided to end the drama. By this time Moro had stopped shaving and had begun to take only liquids. His deep bag of tricks was empty, and he awaited his fate.

The historical record contains thousands of contradictory pages on the final days of Aldo Moro, and in such a circumstance it is not surprising that legends have arisen. The details of the murder itself remain obscure, a continuing subject of examination and investigation. What is known is that Moro died on the morning of 9 May, shot by two terrorists firing a Scorpion machine-pistol and a Beretta. Riddled with wounds, he hemorrhaged to death.[56]

The Red Brigades saved their biggest shock for the finale. A red Renault containing Moro's body was parked in a spot almost precisely midway between the headquarters of the Christian Democratic and the Communist parties, on Via Caetani. The political symbolism in this taunting mockery of the Italian authorities, whose gigantic fifty-four-day manhunt had proved fruitless, made up in dramatic force what it lacked in subtlety. The party most like a nemesis to the working-class revolution and the party most responsible for the betrayal of that revolution were now linked by Moro's death. Their political linkage had been the last achievement of Moro's political life, and for the Red Brigades the deeds of 9 May constituted the people's verdict on crimes against the revolution.

The audacity of the Red Brigades stunned the country. In an area teeming with policemen the terrorists had managed to deposit the corpse of the country's most powerful political leader—"the ultimate provocation," as the newspapers called it. If they could do that to Moro, to whom could they not do it? Certainly, on that day very few Italians would have cared to turn to the police for protection against terrorism. Whatever the Moro affair might lead to in the long run, at that moment the Red Brigades had an aura of Mafialike invincibility.[57]

At 12:10 P.M. the Red Brigades informed Moro's university teaching assistant, Franco Tritto, where the body could be found. Tritto was so devastated by the news that his father had to carry the message to Moro's family. Eventually, the heavy word came down to the Christian Democratic hierarchs, solemnly assembled in their headquarters at the Piazza del Gesù, where they were debating their next step in the Moro crisis. Fanfani was in the midst of his imploring remarks on Moro's behalf when Zaccagnini interrupted the meeting to take a message from Interior Minister Cossiga, who had the particulars. A hopelessly quiet assembly listened to Zaccagnini's report, and then Christian Democracy wept.

Many of the leaders walked down to the street for a look at the grisly dénouement of the tragedy they had been living for fifty-four days. What they saw would be made famous by a photograph of Moro's body, shortly to make its way around the world and then, not long afterward, into Western civilization textbooks. There was Moro, wrapped in an orange blanket, turned on his left side with his legs bent behind him. He was partly covered by a dark overcoat, his left hand visible on his chest, his head resting on his left shoulder.

Renato Curcio announced from his cage in the Turin courtroom that "the act of revolutionary justice administered to Aldo Moro was the highest act of humanity possible in this class society."[58] Expelled from the courtroom for this sensational remark, Curcio added, on his way out the door: "This is only the beginning. You have not understood what will happen in Italy during the coming days and months."

On this day, however—the first of the so-called *dopo* Moro period—the immediate struggle was between the Moro family and the state for control of the Christian Democratic leader's body. The state wanted to give Moro a martyr's funeral, but the widow and her children contemptuously rejected this plan. Instead, they wrote that there would be "no public manifestation or ceremony or discourse; no national mourning, neither a state funeral nor a commemorative medal. The family closes itself in silence and asks for silence. On the life and death of Aldo Moro history will judge."[59] Not even the request of the personal representative of Pope Paul VI, Cardinal Poletti, much less the earnest entreaty of Zaccagnini, could turn Eleonora Moro from her desire to honor the last wishes of her husband. An official memorial service was held at St. John Lateran, with the pope officiating but without the body or the members of Moro's family present.

Aldo Moro was interred on 10 May 1978 in the *campo santo* of the parish church in Torrita Tiberina, north of Rome, where the family had long maintained a country retreat. It was a peasant's funeral, with only the closest friends and family in attendance, as Moro had wished. No music was played. The old parish priest spoke briefly, and the entire ceremony lasted only forty minutes. It rained and hailed the whole time.

FIVE

7 aprile 1979

By the time that University of Padua political science professor Antonio Negri was arrested, on 7 April 1979, as the putative leader of the Red Brigades, the chilling prophecy of Renato Curcio had already come to pass. The imprisoned terrorist had warned that the Moro affair was only the beginning; the worst terrorist violence was yet to come. Indeed, the Red Brigades gave the country no time at all to take in the full meaning of 9 May 1978, let alone to recover from it. May and June of that year were filled with acts of industrial sabotage, kneecappings, and murders. The most spectacular of these acts occurred on 21 June in Genoa. Antonio Esposito, a thirty-six-year-old police officer who had been investigating terrorist assassinations, was sitting on a crowded bus reading his newspaper when two youths walked up to him and began shooting. Esposito, hit in the face, the neck, and the chest, slumped dead to the floor of the bus. Absolute panic erupted among the more than twenty passengers, who fell back in horror as the gunmen leaped from the bus and disappeared. Commenting on the terrorist murderers of Esposito, a fellow policeman exclaimed, "Actually, we are demonstrating that we do not know how to combat them."[1]

In response to the national clamor for decisive action against the worsening terrorist violence in Italy, the government, on 11 August 1978, gave General Carlo Alberto Dalla Chiesa virtually unlimited power as the nation's chief of antiterrorist operations. A brilliant carabiniere general, the fifty-eight-year-old Dalla Chiesa had spent many years in Sicily fighting the Mafia. In the mid-1970s he had been entrusted with the mission that led to the arrest of Curcio. With his latest assignment, the general would only be responsible to the minister of the interior. In a sign of the times, the Dalla Chiesa appointment provoked no opposition from any of the parties, all of whom—in a rare display of unanimity—had become convinced that terrorism had to be brought to the ground. The Red Brigades in particular had succeeded too well in the Moro operation; they clearly possessed a degree of subversive power that could no longer be tolerated. The state now attempted to direct the full force of its power against them.

Dalla Chiesa's first major victory in his new command came on 13 September 1978, when thirty-year-old Corrado Alunni, the go-between for the Red Brigades and another increasingly prominent terrorist group, Prima Linea, was captured.[2] A factory worker at Sit-Siemens from 1967 to 1974 before going underground, Alunni was the emblematic figure of *operaismo* (workerism) in Italian terrorism.

Political violence was in the factories, battening on the alienation of many workers, particularly of the younger generation. The factory had become second only to the university as a source of manpower for terrorism in Italy.

The capture of Alunni, while heartening to the forces of law and order, was hardly a turning point in the struggle against terrorism. Sensational Red Brigadist kneecappings and murders, particularly of Italian businessmen, continued through-out the fall of 1978. As the government fought back, making arrests and raiding hideouts, the immediate effect was to provoke the terrorists into violent reaction, as though to prove to the revolutionary faithful that despite its best efforts the state was in no condition to postpone the day of revolution. If the diverse terrorist groups of the Left agreed on anything during this period it was the necessity of maintaining the atmosphere of crisis, for only in such an atmosphere could the revolution take shape. Therefore, each blow from the state had to be answered with counterattacking blows from the terrorists, and in this way 1978 drew to a convulsive close. For example, on 10 October Giuliano Tartaglione, a magistrate who served as Italy's director of penal affairs, was killed with a bullet in the head. The next day Alfredo Paolella, a professor of criminal anthropology and an expert on the prison of Pog-gioreale, died in the same way. Judge Fedele Calvosa was murdered in a Via Fani–style ambush on 8 November. The many kneecappings and other maimings of that autumn could not compete for front-page space with events as spectacular as these murders. Reports on terrorism were beginning to be printed in the newspapers as bulletins from a far-spreading front.

In Turin the terrorist campaign against Italy's prison system continued to take a bloody toll in murderous attacks against prison guards and officials, but the new year, 1979, opened with a pair of assassinations that once again dramatized the salient importance of radical extraparliamentary Left thinking in the history of Red Brigade–Prima Linea–style terrorism, and these deeds occurred in Genoa and Milan. Guido Rossa was an Italian Communist's Communist, and by any standard an exemplary human being. A highly skilled mechanic at Italsider, he distinguished himself as an active union member. To these accomplishments Rossa added the varied gifts of a Renaissance man in work clothes: he was a world class alpinist, a photographer of outstanding ability, a fluent writer of topical factory articles, a sculptor, and a painter. Politically, he fervently supported Berlinguer's antiterrorist line. In keeping with his party's commitment against terrorism, Rossa denounced a fellow factory worker, Francesco Berardi, for passing out Red Brigade literature at Italsider.[3] Berardi had been working as a *postino*, the lowest rung on the terrorist ladder, but Rossa's disclosure of his "mailman" activities infuriated the Red Brigades. For some months Rossa lived with the fear of Red Brigade retribution, and it finally came on 24 January 1979 when they shot him to death in his car.

Spontaneous strikes and demonstrations erupted in all the major factories of Genoa. Sixteen thousand workers from Italsider alone took to the streets and de-nounced the "Fascist/Brigadists." President Sandro Pertini personally conferred the medal of gold on Rossa, and at his nationally televised funeral a half-million people, including 200,000 workers from all over Italy, lined the streets of Genoa to pay their respects. Anger over this terrorist act exceeded the public displays following

Moro's death, and Rossa's murder was unquestionably the greatest single public relations miscalculation of the Red Brigades in their history.[4]

Not to be outdone, Prima Linea struck a blow in Milan with scarcely less impact than the Rossa murder, and again the victim belonged to the Left. Emilio Alessandrini was one of Italy's most fearless and respected judges in the war on terrorism. This thirty-seven-year-old magistrate—a non-card-carrying socialist—had been involved in several terrorist cases, of the Left and the Right. His name had appeared prominently on captured Red Brigade documents as an inveterate foe of their organization. Only five days after the Rossa murder, a group of piellini shot Alessandrini to death in his car.

During that terrible winter of 1979 the self-styled avengers of the proletariat claimed victims from every level of society. Although their general strategy remained the same, not all terrorist acts proceeded from coolly calculated strategic considerations, as in the 16 February murder of a forty-three-year-old jeweler, Pierluigi Torregiani. Several days earlier, Torregiani had been waiting in line at a Milan pizza shop when a hold-up occurred. Using a pistol he was carrying to protect his gems, he sprang into action and foiled the thieves. In the ensuing gun battle two of them were killed. For this action Torregiani attracted national press attention as "the sheriff of the bourgeoisie." Newspapermen, avid for a novelty in the day's news, spread that image far and wide.[5] Terrorists belonging to the Proletari Armati per il Comunismo (PAC) responded to Torregiani's "provocation" on 16 February. He died at the door of his shop with a bullet in the head. His fifteen-year-old son was critically wounded and paralyzed for life. PAC promised that all collaborationists would suffer the same fate.

If revenge became an independent variable in some terrorist acts during this period, the strategists of revolution sought to incorporate all such attacks in the furtherance of their grand design: the overthrow of capitalism and the creation of a communist order. This was always the ultimate goal of left-wing terrorism, although different groups on the violent radical left quarreled with each other over how to achieve it.

Then, on 7 April 1979, the media hailed an event which, they said, signaled a decisive breakthrough against this network of revolutionary violence. In Milan eight to ten heavily armed policemen arrested Toni Negri on the charge that he was "the supreme leader of the mysterious Red Brigades."[6] Fifteen of Negri's intellectual and political associates were arrested on the same day in Rome and Padua, including Emilio Vesce, the director of the extraparliamentary left-wing Radio Sherwood; Franco Piperno, the author of prorevolutionary articles in *Preprint* and *Metropoli*; and Oreste Scalzone, the director of *Metropoli*. Negri and his entourage were accused of helping organize and direct the Red Brigades.

Overnight the Italians were divided on "*7 aprile*" into *colpevolisti* (those who held that Negri et al. were guilty) and the *innocentisti* (those who held that the opposite was true). Negri's Autonomia movement screeched its indignation against this "PCI provocation," but the guilty thesis received a powerful boost on 12 April when three young members of the Padua section of Autonomia died in the accidental explosion of a bomb they had been making. On the thirteenth, twenty-seven terrorist acts—against carabiniere barracks, private houses, and party headquarters—were reported in Vicenza, Padua, Treviso, Rovigo, and Venice. The authorities and many others were convinced that these attacks had been unleashed by Auto-nomia, an accusation the organization heatedly denied. The controversy over Au-tonomia has not yet been stilled, but even to begin the process of fathoming the case of Toni Negri we must return to where we left him, as one of Panzieri's leading antagonists in the *Quaderni rossi* schism that culminated in the creation in 1964 of *Classe operaia*.

Negri and his principal *Classe operaia* colleagues, Mario Tronti and Alberto Asor Rosa, continued to bask in the revolutionary glow of the July 1962 metal-workers' strike. Two years after the event they were still analyzing its meaning. The strike had taught them to exchange blow for blow with the Boss, to inhibit the collaboration of workers with him, to diminish his factory output, to lessen his profit, to frustrate his political and economic plans. To compensate for the pathetic failure of all the unions, wildcat strikes were the order of the day.[7] *Classe operaia* counseled the workers to attack their class antagonists and escalate the confrontation between themselves and the bourgeoisie until the Marxist revolution completely broke through the restraining bonds of capitalism. Negri and the others did not call for a dialogue with capitalism but rather a total war with it: "We ourselves want to liquidate the problem [by] constructing a unitary line of struggle against the padrone di Stato!"[8] The numerous pamphlets that *Classe operaia* published and distributed in the mid-1960s, with such provocative titles as "Our Struggle Must Become Massive and Violent," clearly expressed the unabashedly revolutionary character of the journal, and no single event gave the staff writers more encouragement for their belief in the imminence of revolution than the Turin metalworkers' strike of 1962.

Despite the fierceness of this strike, the revolutionary voice of *Classe operaia* seemed to be emanating from a point beyond the most distant horizon in the panorama of Italian civic life. It is true that in 1964–65 Italy experienced an economic downturn after a five-year miracle of unprecedented growth that had brought the country to the threshold of full employment and had resulted in enor-mous wage gains for workers. Moreover, in that same two-year period the newly formed Center-Left coalition governments of Aldo Moro—made up of both Socialist parties, the Republicans, and the Christian Democrats—suffered from the relentless opposition of the PCI and the MSI, as well as the internal hostility of conservative Christian Democrats and left-wing Socialists. The PSI even had to endure a schism of its most radical members as they formed the Italian Socialist Party of Proletarian Unity (PSIUP). These political pressures exacerbated the inevitable squabbles be-tween the constituent elements of the governing coalition. As the economy began to decline, causing a flight of capital, foreign trade deficits, instability of the lira, and growing unemployment, the Christian Democrats resisted the PSI's call for thoroughgoing reforms, and this resistance subjected the coalition to grave stresses.

The downturn proved temporary, however, and by the end of 1965 economic and political equilibrium were restored. By and large the workers remained deaf to the siren call of revolution, and the university students as a group had no coherent political program or interests. As an exercise in Marxist polemics, *Classe operaia* had much in its favor, but the journal was connected to nothing significantly threatening to the status quo.

Classe operaia possesses an interest for us mainly because of the light it sheds on an important stage in the ideological itinerary of Negri, whose academic career was already brilliantly launched. With even more élan than Tronti and Asor Rosa had, Negri sounded the exultant note of revolution in *Classe operaia*.[9] In his specific recommendations on how the revolution should proceed, Negri spoke in recognizably Panzierian accents. The first thing to be done was to go back to the pristine moment of the Russian Revolution itself. Lenin, in the young Negri's estimation, was still the indispensable guide for Marxist revolutionaries everywhere because no one had done more than the Bolshevik leader in demonstrating how a proletarian revolution could actually be made to work. According to him, the Bolshevik Revolution had been the greatest breakthrough event in the Left's entire history, which since 1917 could scarcely be understood apart from the transforming Russian experience. This was not to say that Italians should use Lenin's same blueprint in constructing their revolution, but the spirit of Leninism—understood by Negri as an unqualified rejection of democratic reformism and a simultaneous affirmation of class warfare—had to be recaptured if socialism were to triumph in Italy.[10]

Of the three major *Quaderni rossi* alumni who founded *Classe operaia*, Tronti was the first to abandon the revolutionary project as Negri defined it.[11] His defection brought about the demise of the journal in March 1967. *Contropiano*, a new theoretical journal edited by Negri and Asor Rosa, appeared in January 1968. This was the year of the great student explosion in France, an event that inflamed the revolutionary passions of Italy's university radicals, who already had staged their first sit-ins and protest demonstrations. *Contropiano* interpreted the sharp escalation of student radicalism as one more piece of evidence for its thesis that profound and irresistible anticapitalist forces existed in the West.[12] The students were part of "a tremendously vast arc of interests" with a revolutionary potential, the realization of which depended on a rigorous application of the "worker science" principles enunciated by Marx.[13]

Negri took the intellectual lead on *Contropiano* in celebrating the totality of Marxist-Leninist analysis, still the only system, he believed, that offered a complete explanation of capitalism, its works, its contradictions, and its inevitable demise.[14] In the Negri of *Contropiano* we again hear echoes of the "hard" Marx, the raging prophet of hatred for capitalism's fiendish hegemony of exploitation. What, he began, was the proper answer to capitalist violence, the violence of joblessness, of strike-breaking policemen, of all the well-documented ills that we justly associate with the bourgeois order? The answer for a Marxist-Leninist was inescapable, Negri continued: this capitalist system, the primary cause of evil in the modern world, remained what it had been for Marx and Lenin, "the fundamental object of worker subversion." Revolutionary counterviolence was justified, he professed, because the bosses use the laws and the police to perpetrate violence against the workers who must defend themselves by developing violent techniques of their own. For Negri this was "the only way to escape the spiral of infinite evil." He proposed to take the paragon of revolutionary masters, Lenin, at his word: "Smash the weakest link in the chain." Negri received this commandment as a message sealed with seven seals.

Negri's shrill call to proletarian arms deeply troubled the other *Contropiano*, staff writers who were still unsure about the correct revolutionary strategy for the working class. Negri's fiery vehemence and frightening clarity brought them up short. Negri invariably inflicted a crisis of conscience on the people around him. He had an astonishingly deft way of forcing them to confront what in his mind was the heart of Marxism: do you believe in revolution, and what are you, personally, prepared to do about it? With Negri, people could not equivocate indefinitely. Sooner rather than later the red hot iron of his logic would mark a person's heart and mind in service to the cause or against it. Asor Rosa, for example, wheeled around and broke into a full gallop to the PCI, of which he became a member in good standing. It came as no surprise when the following declaration appeared in the second issue of *Contropiano*: "For substantial divergences relative to the political stand of the review, as of this number Antonio Negri is leaving the staff."[15]

By 1969 Negri's university was teeming with students who yearned for the revolutionary discipline of which he more than anyone else in the country appeared to be the master. The alienated and disillusioned young at the University of Padua found in him an electrifying interpreter of Marx who left them in no doubt about the violent nature of Marxist revolution. Having become an *ordinario* in political science in 1967 at age thirty-four, Negri was perfectly cast for the role of a charismatic communist don, his tense, nervous body pulsating with an extraordinary energy and vitality. A pair of horned-rim glasses beneath a shock of long jet black hair suggested a professorial air, but Negri convincingly struck the pose of a revolutionary prophet in his fiery lecture-dramas.[16]

The inspirational Negri came to symbolize Padua's reputation as a center of left-wing radicalism. Once a sleepy provincial city known primarily for its university, the Basilica of Sant' Antonio, and the Giotto frescoes in the Cappella degli Scrovegni, Padua had experienced a dramatic surge of economic growth and social change in the postwar period. The tensions generated by this transformation, as well as by the sudden swelling of the university student body, exploded in the late sixties. During the next ten years violent neofascists—who long had enjoyed a home in Padua—and revolutionary neo-Marxists turned the city into one of the chief spawning grounds for Italian terrorism.

Throughout this period Negri was never without a journal. He helped launch *Potere operaio* in the fall of 1969 as the successor to *La Classe*, which had been the original ideological organ of diverse Potere Operaio groups scattered in Pisa, Porto Marghera, Rome, Milan, Porto Torres, and Turin. *Potere operaio* gave voice to the most radical mentality in Italy, and to peruse its pages is to take an excursion through the exotic intellectual realms that ideologically preceded the great leftist terror of the middle and late 1970s. A weekly publication at first and then a monthly, *Potere operaio* not only conditioned the thought of an entire generation of radical left-wing intellectuals; many former *potopisti* (members of Potere Operaio) were later found in the ranks of the Red Brigades and of other terrorist organizations. *Potere operaio* is, therefore, a uniquely well-endowed example of the interaction between thought and practice during Italy's age of lead. Tactical and legal questions aside, its view of the world became an extraordinarily suggestive mental starting place for thousands of Marxist revolutionaries in Italy, some of whom became protagonists in the country's tragedy with terrorism.

To the *Potere operaio* writers, whose articles appeared anonymously, the entire capitalist world—beginning with the United States—appeared to be on the precipice of revolution. Berkeley and the nationwide aftermath of the Free Speech Movement seemed to be only one source of revolutionary disturbance.[17] Even more threatening were the ghetto riots in Detroit and other U.S. cities, which Negri and his colleagues interpreted as portents of capitalism's final crisis.[18] The lurid television images of this violence convinced them that every black person in the United States was either actively engaged, through the agency of the Black Panthers and the League of Revolutionary Black Workers, in constructing ghetto soviets or shortly would be a revolutionist ripe for conversion to the Marxist-Leninist cause. Moreover, the Vietnam War seemed to confirm the impression of an indecisive power staggering blindly on the road to extinction. Looking at the United States, the potopisti were a collective Edward Gibbon surveying the decline and fall of Imperial Rome, except that in the United States the barbarians were already inside the gates—in the ghettos and on the campuses—while from afar the Vietcong were showing the world how to smash the American imperium.

Look to the Vietcong, *Potere operaio* counseled, for this communist organization had proved conclusively how "it was not at all adventurism to shoot high-level state functionaries, that it was not adventurism to assault police stations in order to procure arms and . . . to execute those high state authorities hated by the urban and rural proletariat."[19] Its brilliant success against U.S. imperialism had made the Vietcong an example of "incalculable value for the revolutionary Left of the world." *Potere operaio* concluded that the Vietcong was winning its war because it had always adopted a policy of maximum force.[20]

According to Negri's analysis, as the heartland of multinational corporativism went, so would go the outlying parts of the system. There was only one capitalism and one workers' struggle. This was where Italy came under consideration in the pages of *Potere operaio*, as "the Vietnam of the West."[21] The "hot autumn" of 1969 gave the potopisti added confidence in this political conviction. According to them Italy was charged with a revolutionary tension, just waiting for someone steeped in "the science of Leninism"—always the journal's equivalent for "the necessity of struggle"—to lead an attack against the state.[22]

At issue now was not the question of consciousness or of mental preparation, but rather of physical attack, "immediate and spontaneous." This meant the creation of an Italian version of the Bolshevik party that would lead "the formidable offensive of the workers" without respect for "order and procedures."[23] Only with a solidly established revolutionary organization could the question of political intervention "emerge from the catacombs," where, presumably, Panzieri and the *Quaderni rossi* had left it.[24] The revolutionary party, "leninisticamente," would answer capitalist violence with worker violence and would bring into being the communism that Marx himself defined as "the real movement that abolishes the present state of things."[25] *Potere operaio* graphically conveyed its meaning on this point by publishing a photograph of Fiat's Agnelli looking straight at a superimposed image of a worker about to throw a flaming Molotov cocktail.[26]

In September 1970 Negri's organization began to schedule conferences on how "to practice the art of insurrection" in order to destroy the bourgeois state and to replace it with a dictatorship of the proletariat. The first Potere Operaio conference was held jointly with II Manifesto, another extraparliamentary Left group, and they both agreed that it would be fatal to wait for a revolutionary crisis to develop; this crisis would have to be provoked.[27] A follow-up conference was held in Milan on 30–31 January 1971, and in their joint resolution II Manifesto and Potere Operaio announced their intention to establish a "new revolutionary party," with political committees to be set up in the factories and the proletarian neighborhoods.[28]

On 24 September 1971 approximately one thousand Potere Operaio organization delegates, representing fifty-seven sections and 108 cells, convened in Rome's Palazzo dei Congressi and dedicated themselves to the creation of an insurrectionary party "as the key with which to open the revolutionary process."[29] Revolution entailed a constantly accelerating "anti-institutional violence" until the volume of proletarian protest had risen from the present prerevolutionary levels to the next stage of the dialectic. To the authorities and to every political party from the PCI to the MSI, Potere Operaio had now left no doubt at all about its terroristic character, but the potopisti refused to be put off the scent of revolution by the united remonstrances of the Italian establishment. In fact, Negri and the potopisti regarded such reproofs as confirmation that Potere Operaio had taken the correct course, which was to follow the straight and narrow path of Marx and Lenin to revolution, not the broad highway to working-class slavery on which the ideologically degraded PCI and the antiproletarian Christian Democrats were fellow travelers.

Negri warmed to the battle with his enemies of the official Left, particularly the PCI, to which *Potere operaio* routinely referred as the party of "the red bourgeoisie" whose idea of communism was on display in the "Marxist Disneyland" of Bologna and in such Potemkin villages as Ferrara, where workers could no longer afford to live.[30] The PCI had duped the workers with a brazen misrepresentation of Marx, Negri and his potop colleagues reproached; the party had mystified "the reality of class" and its naturally ordained violence against the capitalist order by resorting to the tiresome fiction of "extraneous forces" leading the workers astray.[31] In analyzing this worker violence *l'Unità* fell back on that singularly unenlightening cliché in Italian politics: *chi paga?*—who was paying for the worker violence? If that were to be the level on which the PCI chose to examine society, *Potere operaio* professed that it could only respond with a cliché of its own: *"chi vi paga"*—who is paying you to keep a lid on the boiling caldron of factory life in Italy?[32]

Negri and his potop colleagues argued that the violence of the workers and the unemployed was too widespread and full of rage to be the work of isolated minorities. The PCI ostrich could not intelligently analyze proletarian rock throwing and factory sabotage because it was not in a position to see or hear them. All it could do from its below-ground angle of vision was to repeat the same hackneyed litany, that the workers were patient and good—except for the unruly few who had drunk deep from a spring poisoned by *Potere operaio*. The journal replied that the violence was real and constantly intensifying, now moving "onto the terrain of illegality" with numerous episodes of sabotage and physical violence against executives and scabs.[33] These events would go on multiplying in a wave of "violent insubordination" as a prelude to revolution itself, but poor Enrico Berlinguer, the Italian Communist leader for whom Lenin's *State and Revolution* had not yet been written, lacked even a faint awareness of this world that was sure to come. Negri would later say of Berlinguer that between him and a real Marxist there is "the difference that shoots through a water pistol and a 'P-38'."[34]

One week after the Rome gathering Potere Operaio sponsored a congress in Florence of delegates from all over the world "to organize a new revolutionary International." They hoped to synchronize worker struggles on a global basis, and their exemplar was Chairman Mao, whose reputedly sage observation about power coming from the barrel of a gun was the subject of many a discourse in Florence. The Chinese Cultural Revolution, these delegates told each other, had illuminated the Marxist truth that "violence is the only instrument for the mass expression of proletarian interests" and that "the dictatorship of the proletariat must be periodically reaffirmed by the open violence of the masses."[35]

Such rhetoric and a simultaneous increase of violent action in the factories and on university campuses caused authorities to believe more firmly than ever before that a direct connection existed between Potere Operaio and the country's worsening problem with terrorism. On 12 December 1971 they arrested a dozen potopisti in Milan, prompting an angry editorial from *Potere operaio*. To Negri and his fellow radicals it was ludicrous to argue that anyone who took violent action against the state could be dismissed as a terrorist, for such an argument meant that every revolution is wrong and that history can only move forward on the strength of the good intentions unchallengeable authorities possess—very reassuring for the status quo.

For the writers of *Potere operaio* the proper question to be asked was not "do we employ political violence," which is another way of asking do we want to end capitalism, but rather "when or under what conditions do we employ violence." Negri and the others professed to give a Marxist answer to this question: "To organize the revolutionary civil war is a fundamental duty of all Communists."[36] Political violence, then—which every existing regime finds a way to brand as terrorism— is legitimized when "the prospects of victory for the proletariat" come clearly into view. Thus, when the hour of doom strikes for the capitalist order it becomes politically wanton for communists to remain aloof from the struggle. The potopisti took turns ridiculing anarchist violence for its defensive and sporadic character, but they all agreed that history had reserved a place of honor for communist violence which anti-Marxists of the Left and Right vainly sought to confuse with their mystifications. It was this last form of violence that *Potere operaio* intended to promote.

Among the readers who took a warmly appreciative interest in *Potere operaio* were the followers of Giangiacomo Feltrinelli in the Gruppi d'Azione Partigiana (GAP) and of Renato Curcio in the Brigate Rosse. These groups chose the journal as the vehicle best suited to publish their terrorist propaganda statements. While denying charges by the authorities that *Potere operaio* was linked to the *gappisti* or the *bierre*, the journal clearly stated that its opposition to the terrorist groups had nothing to do with the question of violence—for "without a theory and practice of violence the revolutionary movement cannot succeed"—but with the uses to which violence should be put and, above all, with the question of timing.[37] The potopisti had always believed that without violence "the proletariat is mutilated, castrated in the concrete possibility to liberate itself."[38] Therefore, when Feltrinelli and Curcio called for a violent assault against imperialism at home and abroad no one on *Potere operaio* could seriously raise an objection in principle, especially since the journal itself would urge its readers to attack "this army of bureaucrats who compensate for their human inferiority by treating common people with sadism."[39] Against such beasts of prey, "whose very existence had long been a ferocious menace" to humanity, "violence and revolutionary terror" must be employed.[40]

In short, the bureaucrats who ran the capitalist structure always deserved what they got, and *Potere operaio* expressly called for the creation of conditions in Italy that would make any ruling-class job—policeman, factory executive, judge—"a risky profession."[41] Curcio's vision of a *contropotere* of the workers contradicted nothing in *Potere operaio*; indeed, with the early Red Brigade kidnappings the journal found itself in unreserved sympathy: "They are new forms of worker struggle, in the cities, that are rapidly gaining ground; this practice of organized violence on the part of the proletariat is rendered obligatory by the growth of the class conflict and by its characteristic of violence."[42]

Such a claim did not mean that Negri and his colleagues approved of everything the gappisti and the bierre were doing. If they had, that would have been something wholly novel in the contentious world of Italy's revolutionary politics. Still, while noting that the potopisti proposed a more varied strategy against the capitalist order than anything envisaged by the clandestine terrorists, in 1972 *Potere operaio* recognized kindred spirits in Feltrinelli and Curcio, for the kidnappings and the acts of sabotage had "if in an imperfect way" expressed "a necessity, an urgency" in the revolution.[43]

In fact, the political assumptions of these nascent terrorist groups, that Christian Democracy and fascism and official communism were different faces—deserving to be smashed—of the same ugly hegemony, had been created in their present form by *Potere operaio*. The early actions of the gappisti and the bierre corresponded more or less well with the major ideas, if not the specific recommendations, of Negri and his neo-Leninist potop associates, who always claimed early bolshevism as their major inspiration. *Potere operaio* had called for the organization of active mass resistance against the capitalist exploitation of the workers and against the nonaction of the worker parties; the GAP and the Red Brigades claimed to be developing strategies for the attainment of these goals.

As for the later assertion of Negri and the other potopisti that they had never expressly recommended terrorism, their own journal contains decisive evidence to the contrary—at least from the point of view of anyone who wished the Italian republic well. We have already seen numerous instances of the journal's broad tolerance for terrorism. This tolerance frequently shaded into an identification with terrorist methods. For example, when Wasfi Tall, Jordan's prime minister, was slain on 28 November 1971, *Potere operaio* commented "The pig Wasfi Tall has paid his bill with the Palestine resistance movement."[44] The potopisti made no effort to distinguish between the treatment that Jordanian and Italian pigs should receive. The *Potere operaio* message on this point was clear: terrorism had to be counted as a legitimate weapon in the proletariat's arsenal—not the only weapon, as the Red Brigades and the GAP seemed to believe—but the subsequent claims by Negri and his collaborators, that they had opposed Feltrinelli and Curcio because of GAP and Red Brigade violence, contradicts the real *Potere operaio* experience.

Although the last issue of *Potere operaio* appeared in November 1973, the journal had ceased to be published regularly in the spring and early summer of 1972. As the final editorial pointed out, "a strong internal difference of opinion" had long paralyzed *Potere operaio,* and this conflict had arisen, as with so many of the intramural battles of the extreme Left, over the question of how to organize the revolution.[45] Negri had been in the hottest part of these battles for more than ten years. He had collaborated on the flagship journals of the extraparliamentary Left in the hope of furthering the cause of a proletarian revolution, but each one of them, including *Potere operaio,* had become bogged down in sterile debate and hopeless deadlock. Ironically, this time it was Negri who, in opposition to Franco Piperno—the secretary of Potere Operaio—counseled patience among the potop faithful. Ardent as ever in his revolutionary beliefs, Negri now conceded that more time might be required for the revolution than he had previously thought.[46]

In July 1973 four hundred potop delegates, representing sixty sections and one hundred cells, gathered at Rosolina, where the organization formally dissolved itself. Later that summer, from 28 July to 4 August, Negri convened a seminar at the University of Padua with the objective of creating the guidelines for Autonomia Operaia, an organization made up of radicals from Porto Marghera, Padua, and Milan that had been created some months earlier in Bologna.[47] The *atti* of this Padua gathering were published in the 112-page final issue of *Potere operaio,* and Negri's mood at this time can be summed up in the journal's last words: "We have rejected the group and its logic in order to be in the real movement, in order to be in the organized autonomy [of the workers]."[48]

Since the articles published in *Potere operaio* appeared anonymously, it is impossible to determine from this source alone exactly what Negri's attitudes were at that time. But he published a collection of essays in 1972, *Crisi dello stato-piano comunismo e organizzazione rivoluzionaria,* which reveals that his thinking had been reflected accurately in the journal. The central question for Negri all along had been how Marxists should proceed in bringing about the fall of capitalism. The Marxist answer, he offered, lay in the intensification of "the working-class struggle." Negri believed that history could be trusted to show the working class when the hour of deliverance was at hand, for "problems, when they are real, can in no way be repressed."[49] In its own time and way the proletariat would sweep away the capitalist system, and then the people's party would be assigned the role of "interpreting and conducting the will of the appropriating masses against the [capitalist] enterprise, against the factory command. . . . "[50]

In *Crisi dello stato-piano* Negri professed bewilderment when self-proclaimed Marxists attempted to define Marxism as something other than a violent, revolutionary overthrow of capitalism. Such people always elicited an indignant rebuke from him for their imperfect, incomplete, or dishonest reading of Marx. If Marxism were to be taken seriously, the doctrine had to stand for what its founder intended that it should, and this meant the physical destruction of capitalist tyranny, not the evolutionary minuet of reform-minded Berlinguerians—who should at least have the honesty and the wit to recognize their fall from Marxist grace on all vital questions of the dialectic.[51] Reformists were fond of saying that times had changed and therefore Marxism must change with them, but for Negri this was an enervating cliché that struck at the heart of Marx's system of historical analysis and political practice: the central reality of class struggle. The irreducible minimum in Marxism, Negri held, consisted of this point, that the working-class struggle is still the essential element of history, and Marxists now had to lead the workers "directly, immediately against the state."[52]

Negri contemptuously dismissed those old women of both sexes who affected to swoon with surprise at his Marxist insistence on violence as the motor of history. From Machiavelli on, political analysts increasingly had recognized force as the primary agent of historical change, and anyone in this day and age who believed that violence was the sort of thing that only bad people and evil systems engaged in had no understanding of history or no intellectual honesty. Indeed, to Negri the most infantile and yet widely believed mystification of the present moment was the pious declaration of the "vital Center" that violence and terror existed as the unique products of ideological extremism of the Left and the Right.

Negri countered that capitalism lived and breathed through violence by the very nature of the exploitative economic arrangements it imposed on the people. Capitalist millionaires and their lap dogs in the media and the research institutes wanted people to believe that Marxist revolutionaries were all neurotic "true believers," but Negri saw the authentic followers of Marx as the protagonists of history's noblest struggle, to replace the soulless circumstance of capitalism with a socialist order promising the full realization of man's humanity. The tycoons had demonstrated their willingness to use every form of violence to protect the status quo, all the while hypocritically sputtering moral outrage as the Left employed Marxist-prescribed counterviolence. That is what Negri meant when he denounced the moralizing spokesmen of the bourgeoisie for their selective outrage. The same moralists turned a blind eye toward the global violence of capitalism and the way in which this criminally irrational system was turning the world into a vast prison house. Humanity lay throbbing in the death grip of capitalism, and now—before it was too late, Negri urged—Marxists had "to rediscover the Leninist privilege of taking up the cudgel"; to refrain from doing so would condemn the workers "to a fate not less sterile than the evil fate of the class adversary."[53] Hegemonic violence was disfiguring mankind, and Negri proposed what he called not a modernized version of Marx's message, but Marx's message itself: a counterhegemonic violence that would restore man to his true nature. Therefore, he concluded, "Every spontaneous, semispontaneous, and organized act of appropriation is transformed into an action of militant attack against the dominion that capital reproduces through punctual and determined provisions."[54]

The rise of Autonomia Operaia brought yet another extraparliamentary Left journal into existence, *Rosso*, which published scorching analyses of Italy's deteriorating political and economic situation during the 1970s. Indeed, a serious slump in the economy had begun in 1970, and it aggravated political and social tensions. Then came OPEC's fourfold oil price increase in 1974, an action that forced the almost entirely oil-dependent Italians to deplete their reserves of gold and foreign exchange. For the rest of the decade the economy suffered from high rates of inflation, major balance-of-payments difficulties, low rates of economic growth, rising unemployment, double-digit inflation, a severe devaluation of the lira, and a steep rise in the cost of living. With all economic figures in the red, Italy could sustain itself only by taking out a series of loans from the International Monetary Fund, the European Economic Community, Germany, and the United States.

Conflicts over economic policy contributed to the collapse of Aldo Moro's last Center-Left coalition government in 1976. With the more than decade-old Center-Left formula increasingly unworkable, the atmosphere of political uncertainty became heavier, just when criminal kidnappings, student demonstrations—in some cases involving hundreds of thousands of people—and terrorist violence were becoming worse than ever. Even nature frowned on the Italians. In that same year Friuli groaned under the impact of a devastating earthquake in which more than one thousand people were killed. In Seveso, near Milan, a cloud of poison gas added a man-made disaster. Failing in both cases to provide swift and effective relief to victims, the political leaders of Italy felt the wrath of an outraged populace. Then, after scandals involving CIA payments to Italian politicians and Lockheed bribes in promoting the sale of Hercules C-130 airplanes had added virtuoso refinements to the government's image of incorrigible venality, there seemed to be no humiliations left for the men charged with running the country.

Italy's increasingly critical economic and political problems in the 1970s fired Negri's imagination, and *Rosso* documents how he and his Autonomia Operaia colleagues envisaged Italy's coming revolution. In their attempt to broaden the base of Italy's revolution, the writers of *Rosso* professed to eschew the "group" in favor of "class," conceived in the broadest sense. Through *Rosso* Negri became identified with the extra-Marxist concerns of the Italian New Left, which had been the object of *Potere operaio*'s scorn.[55] *Rosso* took up the cause of prisoners, defended drug use, tolerated homosexuals, advocated women's rights including abortion, and campaigned for sexual freedom of every kind, with a consistently negative critique of the family as a bourgeois institution organized in such a way as "to inculcate in us the terror of our sexual needs and to make us believe that only the consecration of GOD and of the STATE renders sexual love legitimate between persons."[56] Indicative of *Rosso*'s point of view on marriage and family was the 20 December 1975 cartoon of a beetle-browed Mary in the traditional manger scene over the caption, "I didn't want him." The journal prided itself on a policy of sexual iconoclasm, even adopting as one of its mottoes "Toccarsi è bello" (Masturbation is beautiful). Moreover, marijuana smoking was equated with factory absenteeism as an emblem of struggle against capitalism.[57] The utopianism of primitive bolshevism mixed well with the campus radicalism of the 1970s, and *Rosso* appealed to this mood by proclaiming, "Communism is a society where no one is oppressed or repressed, where one's needs will be freely satisfied."[58] The journal repeatedly asserted, "WE WANT EVERY-THING."

Nevertheless, the traditional revolutionary character of Negri's Autonomia Operaia was not obscured by *Rosso's* fashion-conscious appeal to the counterculture radicalism then in vogue. The journal plainly stated that Autonomia Operaia meant "the refusal of capitalist work and of the reformist strategy that preaches the reconciliation to work"; the PCI of Berlinguer and Amendola thus was once again condemned for its betrayal of the revolution. Negri and his colleagues held that if these men—with their refusal even to consider revolution as a possibility—were right, then Marx was wrong.[59] For *Rosso* the revolution was everything: all anti-capitalist forces—in the factories, schools, neighborhoods, and jails—had to be united, though not centralized, on the issue of worker autonomy. As for the role of violence in this revolutionary process, only one point mattered, the readers of *Rosso* were informed: the usefulness of violence in furthering the proletarian cause.

Certainly by 1974 Negri and his Autonomia Operaia circle were expressing their opposition to the excessive and even monomaniacal emphasis of the Red Brigades on terror as the sole means of bringing about the revolution. *Rosso* insisted that violence had to be "useful and functional," not be based on anarchist myths about the sacred power of spontaneous revolutionary acts. Yet even in 1975 *Rosso* condemned the terrorist violence of the Red Brigades more as an error than as a sin, a problem of emphasis rather than of character. In October Curcio's confederate Alberto Franceschini was still honored with the term of "comrade."[60] The following month *Rosso* praised Red Brigade kidnapping operations as the legitimate and powerful blows of the proletariat against capitalism's hegemony. It had been a good thing for the Red Brigades to capture Vincenzo Casabona, the head of personnel at Ansaldo Meccanico Nucleare, for he was the liaison between the factory and "the band of criminals that goes by the name of Antiterrorismo e Nucleo Speciale dei Carabinieri."[61] And what had the Red Brigades done with Casabona after all but interrogate him, after which "he was released in the garbage dump of Recco, a most congenial place for lackeys of the bourgeoisie like him." The Red Brigades might be going too far, *Rosso* conceded, but at least they had gone in the right direction, toward the "armed struggle for communism."

As the first major trial of the Red Brigades got under way in Turin during the fall of 1975, *Rosso* condemned the prosecution's argument that Curcio and the other defendants were criminals. According to the journal's editorials of this period, the Red Brigadists were revolutionaries in the Marxist sense of the term because they had attacked capitalism in the name of the proletariat and of communism. In an age of paralyzing conformity, when it was becoming increasingly difficult to tell the difference between Communists and Christian Democrats and even missini, the Red Brigadists had dared to be different by actually doing what Marx and Lenin expressly commanded their followers to do: defend the proletariat by cracking the skulls of the capitalists. Of course, the PCI and its sorry crew of reformist intellectuals recoiled before this truth; the mere mention of it could not fail to call to mind what they once must have known was the core belief in the Marxist system—revolution. Now the Communist party was engaged in the nefarious misrepresentation of Marxism as a populist catchall and had been fully transformed as a prop for bourgeois democracy. To Negri and his associates on *Rosso* nothing in the imagination of Lewis Carroll could rival this tissue of PCI-invented absurdities. Therefore, Marxism belonged much more to the Red Brigadists in the Turin courtroom than to such grey-flannel men in Berlinguer's entourage as Giovanni Agnelli's "dear friend," the CGIL's Luciano Lama.[62]

Rosso, like its immediate predecessor, *Potere operaio*, published propaganda statements of the Red Brigades. For example, Franceschini's open letter about the "collaborationist" PCI appeared in the 29 November issue.[63] According to him, the PCI was still busy baking, as it were, its own brand of fortune cookies, a harmless confection in appearance but with the promise of a cryptic revolutionary message inside which the cognoscenti would understand. It was a product from which only Berlinguerians–long a term of opprobrium in the Red Brigade lexicon—could derive any physical nourishment or mental stimulation.[64] Without a trace of subtlety, Franceschini warned that the reformist pigs in the PCI, now trying to degrade the Red Brigade revolution by criminalizing it, would not be forgotten by the proletariat. Commenting on the Franceschini case, *Rosso* could only lament "the climate of psychological terror" created by the state in its nakedly reactionary plot "to criminalize the armed struggle."[65]

Following the capture of Curcio on 18 January 1976, *Rosso* counseled the establishment press not to take excessive delight in what many journalists were calling a mortal blow to the Red Brigades. Despite capture, Curcio was still an indestructible symbol of revolution to his militant followers, the journal insisted.[66] Negri and his colleagues were only too proud to salute this Marxist militant with "a clenched fist."[67] To be sure, they did not always agree with his tactics, but the men and women of *Rosso* were always scanning the horizon for signs and portents of revolution. Curcio was to them what a barking two-headed frog would have been to a soothsayer in the time of Shakespeare: a herald for "enterprises of great pith and moment." The *autonomi*, the members of Autonomia Operaia, saw every riot and breakdown of law and order as exhibits in their case for revolution, but Curcio was especially prominent in this regard.

Amid mounting violence, the Red Brigade trial opened in Turin on 17 May 1976, and *Rosso* published the following declaration of Curcio and the other defendants: "We consider the lawyers who accept the nomination of the court to be *collaborationists*; therefore we invite them to renounce formally and publicly the charge given them; if they accept collaboration with the court of the regime, they will assume all responsibility before the revolutionary movement."[68] It is true that other newspapers and journals published this declaration, but *Rosso* made a point of identifying its authors as comrades. Several months later a horrified Turin learned exactly what the Red Brigade threat meant when seventy-six-year-old Fulvio Croce, the man put in charge of selecting public defenders in the Curcio trial, was barbarously murdered.

Even after the Croce assassination *Rosso*, while condemning the errors of the Red Brigades, allowed that their strategy was understandable.[69] Citing quotations from Marx on the need for revolution if the workers were ever to lose their chains, *Rosso* still in the summer and fall of 1977 interpreted Red Brigadism as one tactic in the necessary assault on capitalism. That September *Rosso* commented: "Not here in discussion are the accumulated historic merits of those [Red Brigade] comrades in demonstrating that the armed struggle is not only necessary, but possible for the destruction of capitalist power."[70] *Rosso* only wished to criticize a certain "incomprehension" on the part of the Red Brigades regarding the other tactics that were open to the resistance movement. In other words, the capitalist machine must be smashed, but not in the precise way that the Red Brigades were doing it.

Rosso also published propaganda statements of the Nuclei Armati Proletari (NAP), the prisoner-oriented terrorist group of the mid-1970s. Identified by *Rosso* as comrades, the nappisti claimed to be standing on a platform of prisoner autonomy, with the objective of recruiting the victims and outcasts of capitalist society for action in the final proletarian assault on the citadel of reaction. Bakunin's anarchist theories about the suitability of convicts as the shock troops of revolution were exhumed from the pages of the *Revolutionary Catechism* and presented by nappisti spokesmen as an exciting theoretical innovation. Marx himself had been shocked by Bakunin's blatant political appeal to murderers and thieves, but these early NAP documents revealed no interest in old theoretical battles. All that mattered to the nappisti was the proletariat's need for men who had experience with guns and who were not afraid to use them.

During the 1970s *Rosso*, the Red Brigades, and the Armed Proletarian Nuclei differed over tactics, but they all interpreted the world from the same revolutionary viewpoint: internationally, the U.S. and the USSR were seen to be competing with each other to determine which form of slavery—neocapitalism or neo-Stalinism—would subjugate the world; domestically, Italian politicians strutted and fretted, but Italy had no real independence. The country was locked into an imperial system whose subtlety was its strength and from which there would be no escape save by revolution. With the PCI destroyed as a working-class party, the Left had become a vacuum which Autonomia Operaia, the Red Brigades, the Armed Proletarian Nuclei, and numerous other radical groups proposed to fill with a genuinely revolutionary presence.

By 1976 the nature of the terrorist challenge by the bierre and the nappisti was at least unambiguous, but experts voiced differing opinions about Autonomia Operaia's true intentions and capabilities. Some thought it was the last pathetic caricature of Italy's revolutionary tradition, while others, including the major analysts of the PCI, condemned Negri's organization and journal as the core elements in the country's terrorist problem. *Rosso* answered these charges by insisting that Autonomia Operaia had never been anything more than a loose federation of students and workers whose only common element consisted of a shared hatred for the present overlords of Italy and their inhuman system.[71] From this highly varied constituency—which in addition to the students and workers included the subproletarian elements of the great cities, the unemployed, the underemployed, and the alienated professionals—would come, *Rosso* believed, the directions for how Italy should go about the task of revolutionizing itself. The journal hardly made a secret of its revolutionary character. Nevertheless, the staff ridiculed the notion that Negri was the cause of the country's political violence. They rejoined that the system was the problem and that Negri's crime lay in his fearless and accurate analysis of the very structural and institutional arrangements responsible for the real terror in Italian life, beside which the actions of the Red Brigades were hardly worth mentioning.[72]

In the public mind, however, Autonomia Operaia had become a specter indistinguishable from that of terrorism, and on 21 March 1977, when alarm over the spectacular student demonstrations in Rome and Bologna was at its height, police officers arrested Negri and several of his colleagues at the University of Padua's Istituto di Scienze Politiche. Two hundred fifty of General Dalla Chiesa's men combed the city in search of Autonomia terrorist suspects, and by the end of the operation seven more arrests were made. *Rosso* denounced the police action as a declaration of civil war, on one side of which were ranged "the forces of repression, the parliamentary parties, the unions" and on the other "the revolutionary organizations, all the movement."[73] Negri and his friends were soon released, a sign to *Rosso* that the carabinieri could not imprison "the communist class struggle," which had demonstrated its force and mass appeal in Rome and Bologna.[74] Indeed, the long-awaited revolution appeared to be in the offing, and to its readers *Rosso* proclaimed the need to mobilize now in order to affirm "the revolutionary process in our country."[75]

The events of 1977 provoked within Autonomia what *Rosso* itself described as "the schism between insurrectionary and gradualist lines of conduct."[76] The oldest extraparliamentary Left story was again being repeated. Actual violence invariably shocked and inhibited some members of the organizations vociferously espousing the cause of revolution while, with equal regularity, radicalizing still further a number of their colleagues, who, in the aftermath of physical assaults on the establishment, believed themselves to be surging forward on the crest of an unstoppable revolutionary wave. The inevitable divorce would then occur between those who wanted to proceed more cautiously and those who embraced revolution with intensified passion, proposing to advance now, sleeplessly vigilant, to final victory. A rift opened up along these lines in the ranks of Autonomia Operaia during the summer of 1977, followed by calls for a new *inchiesta* to determine the actual situation of the workers.

This fundamentally Panzierian proposal calls to mind the connection between what *Rosso* thought it was trying to do and the example act by *Quaderni rossi*. As part of its theoretical justification for revolution *Rosso* even invoked the name of Raniero Panzieri. It republished some passages from his 1962 theses on Lenin as the wise advocate of Marxist revolution whose theoretical acuity penetrated to the heart of Gramsci's disastrously wrong humanist interpretation of Marxism.[77] Gramsci's Marxism with a human face had deprived Marx's doctrine of the one element most critical for its survival: the necessity of revolution. Once this was gone the even more pathetic neo-Gramscian sophistries of Berlinguer and Amendola were inevitable. "Honor to Comrade Panzieri," *Rosso* rhapsodized, for he had been a pioneer in the movement, so badly needed in Italy, to supplant Gramsci with Lenin.[78] Panzieri, therefore, had been "a formidable comrade who had produced a new theory and practice for the working class, a theory and practice that was verified by all the revolutionary movement in succeeding years."

Rosso's intentions regarding a Panzieri-style *inchiesta* never bore fruit, and in 1978 the journal became totally absorbed in its attempt to analyze the unexampled violence that erupted in Padua, particularly at the city's long-troubled university. Entire departments ceased to function during the winter of 1977–78, and Luciano Merigliano, the rector of the university, publicly referred to the Political Science Faculty and the Magistero as "these lost sheep."[79] Psychology, with ten thousand students and the resources to handle only one thousand, also inspired doleful pronouncements from the rector. On 18 February the political science chairman, Sabino Acquaviva, conceded:

> Here the only real and constant presence is that of the autonomi. Among the professors there is an incredible absenteeism, and of the two thousand enrolled students only about seventy attend more or less regularly. This was once a department, it became an examining room, and is now a grading room, a dispenser of academic titles devoid of market value.[80]

He concluded that these conditions nullified the very possibility of a mental life in his school: the place was culturally dead and professionally disqualified. A teacher simply could not do his best work—or any work at all—if he were in habitual fear for his personal safety.

Increasingly, "antiproletarian professors," including members of the PCI and PSI, came under physical attack at the University of Padua. In February three professors were beaten up for their refusal "to accept the 'political control' of examinations and to give an automatic passing grade (*il voto garantito*)."[81] Armed autonomi students roamed Via del Santo, where the Political Science Faculty was located, threatening teachers suspected of bourgeois political and pedagogical views.[82] For example, Severino Galante, a PCI member of working-class origins and an assistant professor of political science, received numerous death threats by telephone at night and could not take a walk in Padua without seeing his name spray-painted on the walls of the city as one marked for revolutionary punishment.[83] One memorable slogan from this period was "To shoot at the professors is our duty."[84]

The violence in Padua reached a climax during the summer of 1978. In July a group known as the Ronde Proletarie took credit for Molotov cocktail attacks against the residences of two "reactionary" professors. That same month, on the tenth, a powerful explosive device went off before the entrance of an institute under the administrative control of the Political Science Faculty. Professor Acquaviva's bitter letter of resignation as chairman of the faculty was published the next day.[85]

The day after that, ten to twenty autonomi pummeled Professor Marco Sambin of the Psychology Institute and then did the same thing to Professor Carlo Arslan, who had bravely rushed over to help his colleague.[86] Eleven terrorist attacks occurred in Padua on 13 July. (During all of 1978 the city witnessed 279 episodes of political terrorism.[87]) Rosso expressed approval of attacks on those professors who were "particularly zealous" in their antiproletarian initiatives.[88]

Nineteen seventy-eight was also the year Rosso broke completely with the Red Brigades. The Moro assassination in May provoked the following editorial outburst in Rosso: "Red Brigadism [is] the senile illness of communism."[89] Now the Red Brigades were said to be in error strategically as well as tactically. What formerly had been the criticism of one comrade to another over points of procedure now became transformed into an obliterating condemnation; lacking the correct principles of class analysis, the Red Brigades had embarked upon a campaign of destabilization that might have worked in a backward country but not in the seventh largest industrial power in the world, Rosso readers now learned.

In the tense atmosphere of the Moro affair, Rosso made haste to declare a "most profound" break between Autonomia Operaia and the Red Brigades. But, as the University of Padua historian Angelo Ventura, himself destined to be wounded by local terrorists on 26 September 1979, would tellingly observe, Autonomia's 1978 rejection of the brigatisti ("every last residual rapport has fallen," autonomi leaders insisted) "at the same time confirms a rapport that had existed until then."[90] Moreover, Walter Tobagi, a journalist soon to be murdered by ex-autonomi terrorists, correctly insisted that Autonomia's sudden rejection of the Red Brigades could not be taken at face value, for there remained "a decisive element in common: the political use of violence."[91] Tobagi accurately interpreted Autonomia's position: "The slogan 'Neither with the state nor with the Red Brigades' becomes transformed in this manner: 'Against the state, independently of the Red Brigades, but also with them as with all revolutionaries, with all combatants for communism.' "

Negri, now forty-five, attracted increasing national attention as the intellectual mentor and leader of Autonomia Operaia. His prestige vastly augmented by an invitation from Louis Althusser to give a course of lectures on the Grundrisse at the Ecole Normale Supérieure from November 1977 to June 1978, Negri cut an exceptionally dashing figure in the eyes of those who by the power of his word felt transported to the promised land of communism. He had made a mark on his time, and not only in the university world. Well connected in high society through his marriage to Paola Meo, daughter of an architect, this tribune of the people lived in lavishly funded artistic disorder, with one beautiful residence on Milan's chic Via del Boccaccio and another in the historic center of Padua near the Piazza delle Erbe. From these mansions of privilege—emblems of that peculiarly Italian upper-middle-class revolutionary bohemia, all malice and disdain for the class enemy who lives next door—Negri's Autonomia movement reached into the factories of Porto Marghera, Milan, Turin, and Genoa, where antiunion, prorevolutionary Comitati Unitari di Base (CUB) were founded.

In several books written during the Rosso period, Negri uncompromisingly defended the revolutionary rationale for sabotaging and undermining the capitalist state.[92] The most notorious of these books was *Il dominio e il sabotaggio: sul metodo marxista della trasformazione sociale* (1978). In this fierce little treatise he assumed that "the self-valorization of the proletarian class is above all the destructuralization of the enemy totality."[93] There could be no compromise, no dialogue, no commerce of any kind with the representatives of the money system. In the capitalist world, the state structured and the workers destructured; that was all. Shootings, sabotage, strikes, absenteeism, deviant behavior, criminal behavior, and the refusal to work all contributed to the destructuralization of the capitalist economy.[94] Wherever capitalist valorization broke down, proletarian valorization was augmented: "And no pity for the enemy."[95] For Negri, properly politicized violence fostered the ultimate good of mankind. Hence, as he wrote in *Proletari e stato* (1976), "the necessity of a militant avant-garde force, capable of deepening . . . and continuing the crisis and of blunting . . . the violence of the bosses."[96] Negri has been called "the master of ambiguity," but that reputation, if it is deserved, does not arise from his books.

The terrorist potential in Negri's Autonomia program was always sizable, and later even he would admit that his books—the most violent of them, at any rate, the ones he referred to as "bad literature"—nurtured the tearing passion of the age. For this he would apologize during his trial, but Autonomia Operaia never retracted its policy of diffuse violence. During the three months before Negri's arrest, eighty-one terrorist episodes occurred in Padua.[97] In March 1979 Oddone Longo, president of the Faculty of Letters and Philosophy, and Guido Petter, a psychology professor in the Magistero—both members of the PCI—were savagely beaten by Autonomia students in separate incidents. When a reporter, investigating these attacks, tried to interview some psychology students, he was told by one of them, "Go, go and tell Gabriele [Di Stefano, a colleague of Petter and also of the Left] that his days are numbered. Sooner or later we'll split his head open, too."[98] For those who were on the receiving end of these threats and blows, 7 *aprile* was a day of deliverance.

As Professor Sabino Acquaviva noted in a 1983 interview, whatever one might think about Toni Negri—whether he was guilty, partly guilty, or not guilty at all of the charges leveled against him—in retrospect the arrests of 7 April could be seen as a turning point in the city's reign of terror during which all professors except those visibly a part of Negri's entourage were at risk.[99] Autonomia violence, until then a scourge of civic and university life, perceptibly declined and soon became a scarcely recognizable shadow of its former self.

The same could not be said about Red Brigade violence, which continued to rob Italy, in a prodigious manner, of domestic tranquility and many of her best men for another two years and more. The virtual cessation of the one violence and the unchecked growth of the other strongly suggest that Autonomia Operaia and the Red Brigades were not exactly the same thing but were different parts of the same thing, distinct yet connected by a common ideological parentage and by similar goals. Their differences existed on the level of tactics, and even there it requires the mind of someone steeped in the doctrinal complexities of the Italian revolutionary tradition to determine exactly where the Red Brigades failed to heed Negri's strident call for "destabilization and destructuralization." For a long while there was an unmistakable kinship, if once removed, between Negri's theory and the practice of the Red Brigades. Numerous former autonomi who passed into the ranks of terrorism later commented on this relationship, but it is at least conceivable, as Negri charged, that these people were liars as well as murderers. Also against him in this dispute, however, is the *Rosso* record, and that cannot be argued out of existence.

Books and journal articles by themselves, even when reinforced by vindictive reminiscences about the role of Potere Operaio and Autonomia Operaia in leading thousands of youths into the blind alley of terrorism, fail to do full justice to the complex issues in the age of lead. Beyond Negri's at least partly suspect argument that "the senile, the bored, the fanatics, the hysterics, and the romantics"—people he referred to collectively as "i grunf," who understood nothing and whose behavior contributed to his misfortunes—had subjected his views to vile distortion, his full story is much more complicated than anything contained in his writings or in the utterances of former admirers and worshippers who singled him out as the first cause of their errors and crimes.[100] Men of brutal deeds, like all other men, march to the beat of somebody's drummer, and Negri's booming revolutionary message gave people bent on violence against the state a justification for their world view. However, so long as people continue to be held personally responsible for their actions, there will be limits imposed on any *cattivo maestro* explanatory model of terrorism.

It is wrong to demonize Negri. The gifts of even the most brilliant actor would be wasted without an audience attuned to his performance. Neither Negri nor his radical associates could have had the enduring impact they did in Italy without precisely this kind of vast approving assembly of spectators that encompassed university students, factory workers, professional elites, and the unemployed. By contrast, radicals in the United States during the same period lacked this kind of popular support and understanding. The Vietnam War defined the epoch and the opportunities for radicalism, which were far more limited than most people at the time realized. On college campuses, for example, where the Left attempted to create its own movement, the fundamental issue of the day proved to be not the war but the draft, which affected college-age students. The obligation to defend imperialism, rather than imperialism itself, created extreme unrest, which vanished overnight when the apparatus of the student draft was dismantled. Thereafter, radicalism continued to exist on college campuses, as it still does, but more as an exercise in cultural nostalgia than as a serious political movement with a well-developed awareness of how the neocapitalist establishment is to be transformed into a classless society.

Anyone who worked or studied in a U.S. university during the late 1960s and early 1970s will recall the conspicuous presence of professors and graduate students à la Negri—ardent radicals in love with the idea of revolution. That the American Negris either disappeared by the late 1970s or only managed to survive as easily recognizable specimens from a bygone era suggests a condition of infertility in the humus of U.S. culture for this kind of ideological radicalism. For reasons that only history can explain fully, revolutionary ideas face a virtually invincible challenge in the United States from the combined forces of cultural inheritance and self-assured political and economic power structures. Neutralizing this complex of forces will evidently require a far greater shock than even so desolating a blow to civic and psychic life as the Vietnam War.

In Italy, however, Negri's revolutionary ideology was already anticipated in the minds of his multitudinous admirers, some of whom found their way into terrorist groups. In Negri the revolutionary generation of the 1970s found a spokesman of supernal brilliance for its hammer, sickle, and rifle vision of an alternative society—a latter-day sequel to other visions of the same general character which had seized previous generations of Italian radicals. Negri spoke a political language in which his audience was completely fluent; his success depended not on an issue or a moment, but rather on his extraordinary ability to convey the traditional message of revolution in a way that made it come alive for thousands of young Italians.

The search for answers to the historical questions about contemporary left-wing terrorism in Italy cannot be limited to Negri's words and books. He simply pointed in the direction of a brave new world, and, as in every revolutionary movement, not all who were inspired by the quest for paradise came equipped with a discriminating intellect, a highly developed sense of irony, and firm convictions about the sanctity of human life. Some only heard the call to revolutionize and then let their instincts do the rest. The history of left-wing terrorism in contemporary Italy is about such individuals, but we must ask ourselves why so many Italians heeded this call in the first place. The answer must be that Negri and other radical intellectuals succeeded in giving expression to the genuine anxieties and hopes of many thousands of individuals in a political culture suffering from a deep historic crisis.

SIX

The Blast Furnace
of Terrorism

1979–1980

Whatever 7 *aprile* may have represented in the history of Italian terrorism, it did not signal a turning point in the war against the Red Brigades or Prima Linea. These organizations even increased their attacks against the state. On 3 May 1979, for example, fifteen terrorists launched a guerrilla attack against the party seat of the Christian Democrats' Rome Committee, in Piazza Nicosia. They killed a policeman, wounded two others, and set off a bomb in the building. The government, in a declaration of war against terrorism that revealed the true nature of the threat facing Italy, then mobilized fifty thousand soldiers to guard bridges, dams, electrical centers, and transmission wires. Yet the pace of kneecappings and explosions quickened throughout the spring, and the fear grew that Italy might be succumbing to guerrilla warfare.

With the onset of summer the Red Brigades astounded the country by perpetrating one of their most audacious assassinations. The Rome column of the Red Brigades had been taking heavy losses in General Dalla Chiesa's campaign of attrition against terrorism. As always in adversity, the Red Brigades struck back with redoubled fury, and on 13 July they shot a high carabiniere officer, fifty-two-year-old Colonel Antonio Varisco. With this death, Dalla Chiesa lost one of his most capable deputies.

The hope engendered by the media in the aftermath of 7 *aprile* that Italy's long nightmare with terrorism might be over had long since collapsed. It was not the end or even the beginning of the end. In place of hope, fear and bewilderment returned with renewed vitality. The fear was understandable, but the Red Brigades themselves had indicated in the previous year exactly what they proposed to do and why; then they had acted on that proposal. In "Risoluzione della Direzione Strategica," dated February 1978 but not published until July of that year, the Red Brigades—citing Marx on the Paris Commune and Lenin on capitalism—called for an all-out attack on the dictatorship of the bourgeoisie. "For this," they proclaimed, "we define ourselves as 'Marxist-Leninists.' "[1] They knew that they had involved themselves in a class war of "long duration," but in the end Christian Democratic Italy, the servant of the United States, would fall before them.

The Red Brigades were particularly anxious to purify the Left by unmasking reformism as preventive counterrevolution: "Reformism is not a policy of the working class, but a policy of the imperialist state against the metropolitan proletariat."[2] To them the Italian Communist Party had simply degenerated into a "social democratic party," with Marx and Lenin no longer in evidence. It had cheerfully accepted its assigned function in the neocorporativist state as the amiable and wholly controllable representative of the workers. Rather than exacerbate the crisis of capitalism and lead the workers to communism, the PCI encouraged a rapprochement between the classes. The capitalist system was to be kept safe at all costs; this was the policy, in its essentials, of Berlinguer and Lama.

It was not the policy of the Red Brigades. They, *marxisticamente*, prescribed revolution as the only cure for the disease of capitalism: "In this historic phase, at this point of the crisis, the practice of revolutionary violence is the only policy that has a real possibility of confronting and resolving the antagonistic contradictions that pit the metropolitan proletariat [against] the imperialist bourgeoisie."[3] This bourgeoisie resembled a beautiful actress trying to remain young by "stopping history," but the dialectic was relentless. The Red Brigades viewed themselves as the heralds of that dialectic's next phase, all in accordance with Marx's fundamental interpretation of history. They denied the accusation of terrorism. How convenient for the bourgeoisie if revolution and terrorism should become synonyms, if every attack on the capitalist establishment could be dismissed as an act of "criminal deviation." The Red Brigades, far from being terrorists, were the revolutionaries of Marxist prophecy; terrorism was the profession of those capitalist exploiters who battened on the misery of the toiling masses all over the world. The proletariat had no choice but to revolt, and that meant destroying the imperialist state so that a dictatorship of the proletariat might be created: "To go beyond the crisis means communism," and this last they defined as the reorganization of work and social relations in terms of "the people's needs."[4]

The immediate question before the Red Brigades, or "the organized vanguard of the metropolitan proletariat," concerned "the right tactic." Lenin's question "What is to be done?" had become their own. They answered it in a way that threw a bright light on the violent *biennio*, 1978–79: "The principal tactic of the guerrilla in this stage [of history] is the disarticulation of the enemy's forces." This meant the physical destruction of the personnel who "maneuver the vital centers of the state." Politicians, businessmen, police and military officers, and mass media executives all fell under the Red Brigade proscription. Such individual attacks would lead to progressively more complex assaults until full-scale guerrilla war swept across Italy. Through the process of revolution, revolutionaries and the "Fighting Communist Party" would emerge; these were the essential preconditions for the complete annihilation of capitalist imperialism, the authentic scourge and terror of the world.

This was the Red Brigade justification for the more than 2,100 acts of political violence in 1977 and for 350 more such acts during the month of January 1978 alone, in fifty provinces and cities. From Moro to Varisco the objective of the Red Brigades had never varied: "the construction of the Movement of Resistance" with which to smash capitalist Italy, "the weak link in the imperialist chain." The proletarians of the world had to unite:

> Carry the attack to the imperialist state of the multinationals
> Disarticulate and destroy the centers of the imperialist counterrevolution
> Create and organize everywhere proletarian armed power
> Reunify the revolutionary movement in the construction of the Fighting Communist Party.[5]

Contrary to repeated assertions in the media about the "delirious" and "raving" character of Red Brigadism, the clarity of this discourse was its distinguishing feature. This February 1978 resolution was in part a term paper on the Marxist-Leninist roots of Red Brigadism, complete with apposite quotations and footnote references. On the tactical level the Red Brigades professed to be doing in Italy what Lenin had done in Russia. There was nothing abstruse or even highbrow, in a theoretical sense, about their writings, least of all in this seminal resolution. Nevertheless, the myth of Red Brigadism as a form of fascism or as a creature of the CIA continued to vie with demonstrable facts in the arena of public debate.

In that same summer of 1979, though, Red Brigadism experienced a major schism, and thereafter the movement could never be reduced to a single line of reasoning or action. On 25 July *Lotta continua* published an anonymous article, later attributed to captured Red Brigadists Valerio Morucci and Adriana Faranda. It contained a scathing indictment against "the Strategic Direction" of the terrorist organization. In addition to a pervasive problem of "too much arrogance and too much presumption," the Strategic Direction's greatest error, according to Morucci and Faranda, lay in mistaking the Italy of 1979 for 1919 Russia or, worse, 1949 China.[6] Experts interpreted their statement as the consummation of a rupture within the Red Brigades between the *movimentisti*, who demanded a more organic relationship between the communist vanguard and the masses, and the *militaristi* of Mario Moretti, who were content with a symbolic relationship.[7] The real beginning of this split had occurred during the Moro crisis, for the organization's strategic objectives in that operation had not been reached. A period of sharp internal questioning had culminated in the Morucci-Faranda denunciation.

These two dissidents appealed to the imprisoned Curcio and other similarly circumstanced members of the Red Brigade historic nucleus for support against "the strategic deformation" of Moretti. On 11 August, Curcio et al. dismissed their appeal in a verbal torrent of rage and ridicule. "Signorino Valerio Morucci" and "Signorina Adriana Faranda," described as "poor idiots utilized by the counterrevolution," found themselves stripped of membership in the Red Brigades.[8] Curcio et al. also denounced "the ideological rubbish" and "the destructive discourse" of those immersed in "the sacred texts of some university professors in search of violent emotions." So much for Autonomia Operaia. To Curcio and his associates, the autonomi appeared as "innocent children," who in their newspapers played at revolution while all along the real thing had been Red Brigadism. Strait was the gate of revolution and narrow the path leading to it.

The loud shattering of Red Brigade unity was followed by the even louder din of terrorist actions in Italy. With the passing of *ferragosto* doldrums a new campaign of violence began. On 21 September 1979 Carlo Ghiglieno, a Fiat executive in charge of automobile planning, fell dead under a barrage of Prima Linea bullets. The police lashed back three days later, at first without realizing they were doing so. Late that afternoon the police received an anonymous telephone call regarding some suspicious individuals who had been observed changing license plates on a car in Rome's Via Vetulonia. A squad car raced to the scene. The officers found two young men and a young woman apparently stealing a car. No sooner did one of the officers ask to see some identification than he fell to the ground with a bullet wound in the leg. His fellow officers returned the fire, hitting the young man at the wheel of the car in the head, abdomen, and legs. The two other suspects started running in different directions and a deadly chase ensued in this crowded quarter filled with women and children taking late-afternoon walks. The young man eluded his pursuers, but Mara Nanni was captured. Only when she declared herself a political prisoner did the police realize that they had not merely interrupted a gang of car thieves at work. In fact, Nanni belonged to the Red Brigades, and her critically wounded companion was Prospero Gallinari, a participant in the Via Fani massacre and the executioner of Aldo Moro.

Padua erupted in violence again on 26 September when terrorists attacked forty-nine-year-old Angelo Ventura, a professor of history and political science at the university. An active Socialist, he served as director of the Veneto's institute for the history of the Resistance. Ventura had been one of Toni Negri's most outspoken adversaries at the university, and both before and after 7 *aprile* he had written fearless articles sustaining the thesis that a connection existed between terrorism and Autonomia.[9] The bespectacled professor stood out as the prototype of what the autonomi had in mind when, with apologies to Lenin, they spray-painted on the walls of Padua, "Punish one teacher to educate a hundred."[10]

In this incubator of extraparliamentary left-wing radicalism, Ventura could not have chosen more powerful or implacable enemies. Constantly terrorized by the threat of violence, he always went about armed with a pistol. On this day he needed it. As he emerged from his home early in the morning, two young men on a Vespa approached him, and one shot at his feet, wounding him. Ventura fired five answering shots, but only to scare off his attackers, not to hit them. He later told a reporter: "I hope never to shoot anyone. The first feeling that I experienced was one of profound humiliation for this absurd shooting scene in a country that was once civilized "[11] To the Fronte Comunista Combattente, though, Ventura was simply another "collaborationist" and "servant" of the capitalist state. "Nothing will go unpunished,"they warned; "collaborationists and provocateurs are on notice."[12]

Turin was also the setting for terrorist reprisals in the autumn of 1979. On 4 October gun-toting youths kneecapped Cesare Varetto, the director of union relations at Mirafiori. Less than fifteen hours later, four unmasked Prima Linea terrorists invaded a regional office of the Praxi company. They were all about sixteen or seventeen years old. One of the four, wearing sunglasses, stayed behind in the hallway to guard the *portinaia* while the others entered the office proper. Although completely terrorized, this woman later described him as a nice young man who spoke very well. "I am not a thief," he told her. "We want to change the world, not to do harm."[13]

Meanwhile, his three companions—two boys and a girl—held the office employees at gunpoint. "We are proletarian communists," the youths announced with solemnity. They then demanded to see the office manager, who was not present. Another worker, Pier Carlo Andreoletti, stepped forward to ask if he could do anything. After tying up all but two of the other workers with plastic cord, the youths ushered Andreoletti and the two unbound employees into the bathroom. There they ordered Andreoletti to sit on the edge of the bathtub. With his two co-workers looking. on, the youths shot him in the legs.

Later that morning, while doctors operated on Andreoletti in Turin's trauma center, Prima Linea claimed responsibility for the shooting and directed authorities to a refuse container in Borgo Dora, where they found a five-page propaganda statement. In this document the piellini promised a harsh fall campaign of "proletarian terror" in order to disrupt "the new science of capitalist command."[14] To be exposed in this campaign were the monstrous fallacies and contradictions of capitalism with a human face. Capitalist officers (executives) were given a choice: "either desertion or annihilation." The composition was signed by the *gruppo di fuoco* Barbara Azzaroni and Matteo Caggegi.[15]

In an attempt to rid its factories of saboteurs and terrorist informers, Fiat fired sixty-one workers on 9 October 1979. One week later Curcio and twelve other Red Brigadists, on trial in Florence, answered Fiat by promising an intensification of the terrorist war against *il padronato*—the combined oppressors of the people, with Fiat and Alfa in the lead. One of the terrorists on trial attempted to read the group's four-page statement, but the presiding judge stopped him almost at the beginning. All the prisoners were ordered out of the courtroom, but they left a copy of the document behind. Replete with quotations from Stalin and Mao, it was published in the newspapers the next day.[16] The police then braced themselves for the promised wave of terrorist attacks.

They did not have long to wait. In cities throughout the country numerous terrorist groups, all sharing the basic revolutionary philosophy of the Red Brigades and Prima Linea, combined in a mighty offensive during the terrible months of November and December 1979.[17] Rome was hit hardest. In November terrorists killed and wounded policemen in the name of proletarian justice, a fate that some of their uniformed colleagues in Genoa shared. For sheer terrorist spectacle and bravado, the piellini of Naples distinguished themselves on 1 December. Ten or so of them, including two women, assaulted a building complex that housed the office of the district inspector for the prisons of Campania, Molise, and Basilicata. Armed with machine guns, pistols, and bombs, they completed a paramilitary operation in which thirteen people were overpowered, a policeman pistol-whipped and kneecapped, and one of the three buildings in the complex blown up. Ever since the trial of NAP's historic nucleus had begun a few days earlier, the city had been preparing itself for terrorist actions, but nothing of this magnitude.

All across the Veneto terrorist actions exacted a heavy toll, with more than twenty separate attempts on 3 December alone. In Padua terrorists blew up a dozen automobiles; Christian Democratic offices were the targets of Molotov cocktail attacks and pistol shots; even insurance offices and supermarkets came under assault. In Vicenza a bomb went off at the *Giornale di Vicenza* building, shattering windows; the cars of two journalists were destroyed. Rovigo's *Il gazzettino* was also the site of a terrorist explosion. Violence scarred Padua again the next day. Rioting autonomi, desperately seeking to recapture their revolutionary prestige, put more offices and cars to the torch. Armed with rifles, pistols, and Molotov cocktails they chanted, "We have returned to the piazza for communism."[18]

Of the six stages in guerrilla warfare—sporadic terrorism, diffuse terrorism, the emergence of a network of terrorist groups, unity of action between these groups, creating partisan areas of intensive action. and controlling those areas—Italy had witnessed, in varying degrees, all save the last.[19] Even on this sixth point an act by Prima Linea on 11 December made it obvious that if the terrorists did not yet control cities such as Turin the police no longer controlled them either. At three that afternoon ten piellini, commanded by two women and armed with machine guns and pistols, seized the Istituto di Amministrazione Aziendale at the University of Turin. This was a graduate school in the university, offering a master's degree in business administration. At first the students failed to take in the seriousness of the intrusion. One of them asked a female terrorist, who was not older than nineteen, "May I address you formally or informally?"[20] "Please address me formally," she replied, taking hold of the young man and shooting him in the leg. Others were kneecapped—five professors, all Fiat and Olivetti executives, and five students. Before departing, the terrorists told the students that "the system is wrong, it is necessary to destroy it," and they called on them "to do as we do, we are ready to welcome you." The ordeal lasted forty-five minutes, and the police arrived only to find the wounded in pools of their own blood, the remaining students suffering from traumatic shock—many of them weeping or screaming hysterically—and Prima Linea slogans on the blackboard. Later that day Prima Linea announced that it had successfully attacked a bunker of capitalism as part of its violent campaign "against the business ruling class."

In response to the worsening violence of late autumn, Prime Minister Cossiga convened a meeting of the Council of Ministers on 14 December that lasted more than seven hours. The ministers adopted measures that had no precedent in the history of the republic. Most dramatic of all was the announcement that carabiniere general Edoardo Palombi would be the new prefect of Genoa, the first military man ever to hold this civilian office. They also nominated new prefects for Milan and Turin, the other two cities identified as major theaters of terrorist conflict. In addition General Dalla Chiesa became commander of the carabiniere's 25,000-man Pastrengo division, with military responsibility for the entire north. The council further decided that stop-and-search orders for people suspected of terrorism could now be prolonged by order of a magistrate; moreover, the detainees could be interrogated without the presence of a lawyer. Penalties for terrorism were stiffened, including an automatic life sentence for the murder of public officials. Conversely, penalties were lessened for terrorists who cooperated with the police.[21]

These extraordinary announcements in Rome had to share the day's headlines with news of continued Red Brigade attacks on Fiat that included the kneecapping of a foreman, a 500-million-lire robbery, and the wounding of a guard. Turin's nightmare continued on the fifteenth, when two carabinieri suffered wounds in a gunbattle that left suspected piellino Roberto Pautasso, twenty-one, dead. However, later that day it was the Red Brigades who called *La Stampa*: "Red Brigades here. Comrade Pautasso, executed tonight [was] assassinated by the carabinieri. For every fallen comrade five carabinieri will be killed."[22]

The year of perpetual terror, with 2,513 attempts in all (compared with 2,379 for 1978, the second worst year for terrorist violence in Italy) ended with some important victories against terrorism and some momentous revelations about it. On 18 December, General Dalla Chiesa moved against three Red Brigade hideouts and captured six leading members of the Turin column. Three days later authorities apprehended leaders of Autonomia Operaia and former members of Potere Operaio. In connection with these last arrests Carlo Fioroni, a terrorist imprisoned in Matera, made damaging accusations on 26 December against Toni Negri. He began by saddling Negri with all the crimes for which the former University of Padua professor had already been indicted by the state. According to Fioroni, who had been a close associate of both Feltrinelli and Negri, the Autonomia leader had proclaimed the necessity of a "Mafia-like productivity" against the capitalist state.[23] With this end in mind, Fioroni continued, Negri had met Curcio several times in an attempt to develop a common revolutionary strategy.

Fioroni's revelations made headlines well into the new year. The essence of his testimony was that the origins of left-wing terrorism in Italy could be found in the journal *Potere operaio*. Just read that publication, he said; the whole story was there in embryo. The prototype of a species of ex-terrorist known as *i pentiti* (the repentant ones), Fioroni further asserted that when Potere Operaio disintegrated in 1973 some members of the organization drifted into terrorism and others into Autonomia Operaia, but both groups of ex-potopisti continued to work toward the same revolutionary ends, differing only on tactical details. Although terrorism meant revolution now while Autonomia meant revolution soon, the line between the two was much greater in theory than in practice, as the ideological itineraries of numerous bierre and piellini documented.

Fioroni made other charges against Negri as well. He accused him of masterminding a series of robberies and kidnapping plots to raise money for Autonomia, which was always in financial difficulty. The most serious of these plots unfolded on 14 April 1975 with the kidnapping of Carlo Saronio, himself a member of Potere Operaio. According to Fioroni, Negri believed that Saronio's family would pay a huge ransom for his release. Though Fioroni was a good friend of the intended victim, he went along with Negri's plan. Politicized criminals of Negri's acquaintance performed the kidnapping. Saronio died accidentally when his captors held a chloroform tampon over his face too long.[24] This unforeseen development did not prevent the kidnappers from demanding—and receiving—470 million lire from the Saronio family. The death of Saronio apparently caused the scales to drop from Fioroni's eyes, although cynics saw in these accusations only a cowardly attempt to shorten the twenty-seven-year sentence he had received for his part in the kidnapping.[25] Negri heatedly denied everything, blaming his woes on magistrates tied to his nemesis, the Communist party.

Despite Dalla Chiesa's victories and Fioroni's disclosures at year's end, the seemingly boundless staying power of the terrorist phenomenon continued to manifest itself as a new decade dawned. On 6 January, Piersanti Mattarella was slaughtered in the presence of his wife and children on the way to mass. A brilliant star in his generation of political leaders, he was at forty-five the president of the Sicilian Region and the head of the island's Christian Democrats. Since the death of his mentor, Aldo Moro, Mattarella had been in the forefront of those Christian Democrats calling for a dialogue with the PCI. The Sicilian Communist leader, Pio La Torre, called this murder the most important act of political terrorism after Moro. Indeed, at his funeral Mattarella was called "the Sicilian Moro." La Torre also pointed an accusing finger at what for many was still an unimaginable alliance; the Mafia and terrorist organizations had a mutual interest, he claimed, in eliminating honest and faithful servants of the state. Moreover, who more than Mattarella, La Torre asked, favored a Christian Democratic opening toward the PCI, and who more than the terrorists and the Mafia opposed this opening? It was not clear at that moment who had killed Mattarella, but in the mind of La Torre and, increasingly, in the minds of others, the Mafia and the terrorists had become natural political allies.[26]

The police suffered frightful casualties in January: in Milan three of them were machine-gunned to death by the Red Brigades; in Rome a powerful explosion from a bomb set by the Ronde Comuniste at a carabiniere barracks injured eighteen officers; in Genoa, Prima Linea and the Red Brigades assassinated carabiniere colonel Emanuele Tuttobene and his driver Antonino Casu while severely wounding army colonel Luigi Ramundo, who lost his left eye. Meanwhile, the terrorist campaign against capitalist "officers" continued with the murders in Mestre of Montedison executive Silvio Gori and in Milan of Paolo Paoletti, a technical director of Icmesa. January 1980 ended with two simultaneous bomb explosions in a factory on the outskirts of Turin. The blast killed one security guard and gravely injured another. A spectacular fire then raged out of control for hours. On the first day of February, in the same city, Fiat security guard Carlo Alba, on the eve of becoming a pensioner, was shot and killed during a terrorist assault on the factory.

A week later Italy's elderly and venerated president, Sandro Pertini, issued a nationwide appeal for a new Resistance against terrorism and violence. The Red Brigade answer to Pertini came from the barrel of a gun in Rome on 12 February 1980, an unusually brilliant and warm day for that time of year. At 11:40 A.M. Professor Vittorio Bachelet, the fifty-four-year-old vice-president of the magistracy, former president of Catholic Action, and intellectual luminary among progressive Catholic thinkers in the Moro galaxy, left his University of Rome classroom, recently renamed Aula Moro. The atrium of the Political Science Faculty, its walls covered with the usual graffiti slogans in favor of this or that extraparliamentary group, swarmed with students at that hour. In this busy place a man and woman in their early twenties confronted Professor Bachelet while he was speaking with one of his assistants. Without a word the woman fired four .32-caliber pistol shots at point-blank range into Bachelet's stomach. Then her male companion shot three times and leaned over close to the fallen professor's body to administer a coup de grâce in his right temple. These shots, which were not muffled by silencers, caused pandemonium as shrieking students dived for cover. Someone in the crowd yelled that a bomb was about to explode. These shrill words added the last touches to a scene of extreme alarm, and in the confusion the terrorists easily got away. Shortly afterward Father Adolfo Bachelet arrived at the university and gave his brother last rites.

The next day newspaper headlines announced the loss of one of the leading men in Italy's democracy, and on front pages was a photograph of Bachelet's corpse with his blood streaming in the groves of academe. The aged historian, A. C. Jemolo, commenting on the murder, quoted Italy's first Nobel Prize-winning poet, Giosuè Carducci: "Our country is vile."[27] Jemolo asked, "Who could have imagined the abyss into which we have fallen?" He concluded that for the Italy of today, infinitely more than for the nineteenth century of Carducci's day, it was "the hour of satan."[28]

The state rebounded from the Bachelet tragedy by inflicting a heavy blow against the Red Brigades. On 20 February General Dalla Chiesa announced the capture of Rocco Micaletto and Patrizio Peci, two of the most wanted and feared Red Brigade chiefs.[29] The severity of this setback impelled the Red Brigades to react quickly in order to offer fresh proofs of their continued effectiveness. A few days later they staged a holdup in Rome at the Bank of the Ministry of Transportation, which netted them 550 million lire. On 28 February they kneecapped Roberto della Rocca, an executive who worked for Cantieri Navali Riuniti in Genoa.

Then from 17 to 20 March terrorist groups assassinated three judges: Nicola Giacumbi in Salerno, Girolamo Minervini in Rome, and Guido Galli in Milan. The death of Galli, shot in the back outside a classroom at Milan's Università Statale, where he was about to give a lecture, caused great shock because of his fame as a leftist judge. However, judges of nearly every political opinion expressed outrage over this terrorist act, coming so hard on the heels of the Giacumbi and Minervini murders. Judges' associations nationwide reported severe and growing problems of demoralization; they demanded that exceptional measures be taken. As one judge remarked, "Three homicides in four days, at this point words are no longer enough."[30] Italy remained trapped in an atmosphere of civil war.

It was a war that the Red Brigades and related groups believed they could win, but the problem of the pentiti turned the tide against them. Peci's capture was followed almost immediately by his public defection. Information provided by this one-time leader of the Turin column and member of the Strategic Direction brought carnage to the organization. To begin with, he informed police about the location of a major terrorist hideout in Genoa. Acting on that information, the police surrounded a building in a residential quarter of the city on 28 March. The five occupants of the hideout appeared to be on the verge of surrendering but instead opened fire, gravely wounding an officer in the right eye. A murderous volley of carabiniere gunfire left not a single person alive in the apartment. Killed were Anna

Maria Ludmann, a thirty-three-year-old language teacher known as Carla in the Red Brigade movement, Lorenzo Betassa, Luca Nicolotti, Pietro Panciarelli, and Riccardo Dura. From this point forward the Red Brigades always marked Peci as "the infamous one."[31]

Peci's confessions eventually resulted in the smashing of numerous Red Brigade hideouts, the discovery of huge arms deposits, and the death or arrest of dozens of terrorists in Turin, Milan, Biella, and Ravenna. His testimony continued to fuel Dalla Chiesa's spring offensive against Red Brigadism, its hitherto solid mass now scarred by devastating fissures. Peci talked to the police for more than two hundred hours and threw a powerful light on the tactics of the Red Brigades. Their deep tactical strength through the years, nowhere illustrated more brilliantly than in the Via Fani massacre, lay in a zealous attention to detail. They prepared the attack on Moro for six months, with full-scale rehearsals as a regular part of the training. Moro's enormous symbolic value to Christian Democracy attracted them, but his perfunctory security arrangements, which did not even include a bulletproof car, made him an especially inviting target for the Red Brigades. As for Moro himself, Peci said that the political leader carried himself with high dignity throughout his imprisonment and trial, responding only in the most general terms to the people's advocates.[32] Peci also provided detailed information about many of the other foremost terrorist assassinations of the 1970s, but his lugubrious who-was-murdered-by-whom catalogue remained incomplete. Even within the organization secrecy enveloped every operation. Nevertheless, thanks to Peci authorities at least had the start of a program for the actors and their roles in the tragedy of terrorism.

The most valuable portion of Peci's testimony concerned the organizational structure of the Red Brigades. He claimed that the entire organization consisted of five hundred individuals, divided into "regulars" and "irregulars." A column existed for each geographical area, five in all—Turin, Milan, Genoa, the Veneto, and Rome—with one leader for each. The columns were further broken down into brigades of two to five operatives. Some of these brigades dealt only with logistics by providing cars, weapons, and safehouses, while others were *gruppi di fuoco* kidnapping, kneecapping, and murdering the capitalist enemy. The entire organization continued to be divided into small, sealed compartments so that acts of betrayal and police infiltration would result only in local damage.[33]

The Red Brigades was not the only terrorist organization in Italy to suffer from betrayal during the winter and spring of 1980. In late April a former piellino, Sergio Zedda, told the authorities everything he knew about his former colleagues. His *pentimento* resulted immediately in thirteen arrests. Zedda, a first-year law student with excellent grades, revealed that he had become converted to the faith of the new Left, had moved by what to him was a series of logical steps to the terrorist cause, and only too late had taken in the ghastly import of his conversion and its consequences. Through his testimony the police acquired more evidence to show that Prima Linea had connections with Action Directe in France as well as with the Red Brigades and Autonomia Operaia in Italy. Zedda described the latter as a reservoir of manpower for terrorism, echoing Peci's assertion that Autonomia Veneta was one of the most dangerous organizations in the country. About Toni Negri he had only two points to make: the University of Padua professor did not have any direct relationship with Prima Linea, but some of his political ideas did influence the thought and action of the piellini.

Zedda's revelations about Prima Linea—and, in the next month, those of Roberto Sandalo—opened up what had been a closed chapter in the history of Italian terrorism. The group originated on the fringes of Lotta Continua, which itself had come into being in 1968 as an essentially Marxist organization of students and workers. Lotta Continua sprang from the same revolutionary culture that produced Potere Operaio and many other extraparliamentary Left groups in that period. Reformism was the enemy for them all.[34] No less than Potere Operaio, the Turin-based Lotta Continua group called for a Marxist revolution against capitalist Italy. In so doing it advocated an escalation of factory violence and an intensification of the conflict between workers and policemen throughout society. "Continuous struggle" meant "general struggle." Bloodshed would be inevitable, and when a policeman, Antonio Annarumma, died in a riot on 19 November 1969 the newspaper *Lotta continua* held that in class conflicts the workers were always right. While sharply critical of the Red Brigades for their clandestine character, Lotta Continua did recognize them in the early 1970s as *compagni*. In the Marxist-Leninist manner of Potere Operaio, Lotta Continua held that violence was an intrinsic part of the revolutionary process. The real debate between these extraparliamentary Left groups arose over when, not whether, violence should be unleashed against the bourgeois order. For example, *Lotta continua* had led the extraparliamentary Left campaign against officer Luigi Calabresi, accused of murdering Guiseppe Pinelli, a Piazza Fontana suspect; when a terrorist killed him in 1972 the newspaper editorialized that although "political homicide is certainly not the decisive weapon for the emancipation of the masses . . . , just as armed clandestine action is not the decisive form of class struggle in the phase we are going through," nevertheless "these considerations absolutely cannot induce us to deplore the killing . . . , an act in which the exploited recognize their own will to justice."[35]

In fact, the Calabresi editorial caused such a forceful backlash against *Lotta continua* and such dissension within the organization that nothing as inflammatory as this ever appeared again in the newspaper. While still revolutionary in theory, *Lotta continua* became an increasingly moderate force of the extraparliamentary Left, but important elements within the organization rejected moderation. The politics of zealotry produced deep lacerations in Lotta Continua. When the June 1976 elections ended in victory for the hated Christian Democrats and the despised PCI and a crushing, completely unexpected disaster for the extraparliamentary Left, polemics within Lotta Continua became more acrimonious than ever. The organization soon afterward dissolved itself. For many radicals the country's rapidly proliferating terrorist groups now cast a particularly guileful spell. Moreover, many former members of Lotta Continua formed small groups, called *circoli*. These circles were based in diverse working-class neighborhoods of Turin. They eventually developed Communist Committees for Worker Power with their own journal, *Senza tregua*. Prima Linea became the fighting formation of these committees and, given the rhetoric of *Senza tregua*, their logical consequence.[36]

In the beginning Prima Linea distinguished itself from the Red Brigades by claiming to lead the revolutionary forces of the piazza and by disdaining Curcio's methods of sporadic gestures against the establishment. That was in 1976, before the Red Brigades had developed the resources and the plans for a systematic assault on the heart of the state. Even then, though, Prima Linea was a cockboat in the wake of the Red Brigade man-of-war. In practice the revolution of the people, Prima Linea style, meant Molotov cocktail attacks against Christian Democratic offices and the like; the first of these occurred on 6 October 1976. Such early manifestos as "Let Us Construct the Communist Committees for Worker Power" gave no indication of originality. Prima Linea appealed to Marx and Lenin and to the Resistance; in other words, to the same revolutionary mystique which the Red Brigades and dozens of lesser left-wing groups represented.[37] Prima Linea, along with the Red Brigades and the others, claimed to be doing to capitalism what the Partisans had done to the Fascists and the Nazis. In the minds of these terrorist leaders both battles belonged to the same war: the long and mortal struggle between capitalism and communism. The carabinieri and the business executives of Fiat were Fascists who had changed their uniforms since 1945 and, therefore, legitimate targets of attack for a new generation of partisans.

On 12 March 1977 the piellini killed a police officer, Giuseppe Ciotta. It was their first assassination, but they remained in the shadow of the vastly more destructive Red Brigades. Then the Moro kidnapping produced an identity crisis in Prima Linea, as it did in the Red Brigades. Some piellini were filled with admiration for the deed, whereas others experienced only inquietude. When the Red Brigades asked for support from Prima Linea in the form of diversionary kidnappings, robberies, and assassinations, the latter suffered from so much internal dissension that it had to refuse. Following Moro's death Prima Linea did establish an alliance with the Formazioni Combattenti Comunisti (Communist Combatant Formations), one of the armed groups created by former autonomi.[38] A period of intense Prima Linea violence then began, the most sensational act of which was the 29 January 1979 murder of left-wing judge Emilio Alessandrini. That produced a wave of indignation against Prima Linea, even within the so-called movement.

Prima Linea never recovered its former élan, and in the fall of 1979 some of the group's leaders openly called for a retreat from the *lotta armata*. These disenchanted ones argued, in effect, that the people obviously had jilted the piellini at the altar of revolution. Indeed, the people appeared to be unaware that they had been invited to the service. Prima Linea, according to this revisionist view, had been engaged in a long and ridiculous soliloquy, which for the sake of everyone concerned should cease at once before any further preposterously inapposite "revolutionary" actions occurred. Somehow the piellini had gotten the analysis all wrong. The dialectic was not where they thought it was.[39]

By then it was already too late to regroup. The revelations of the pentiti, beginning with Peci, who had known some piellini, and culminating with Zedda and Sandalo, brought almost total ruin to Prima Linea. The police arrested all of the group's major leaders, including Marco Donat Cattin, who had to be extradited from his refuge in France. He was the son of Carlo Donat Cattin, a powerful

Christian Democratic politician who, ironically, long had been one of the party's most implacable anti-Communists. The twenty-seven-year-old Donat Cattin had broken with the family and had rejected his bourgeois past completely. Troubled and alienated, Marco had drifted into the world of extraparliamentary Left radicalism and in 1977 went underground with Prima Linea. He became one of the group's most proficient killers. Public amazement over this arrest gave way to shock when the elder Donat Cattin and Francesco Cossiga were charged with aiding and abetting Marco's escape to France. Both politicians eventually survived the case, and Marco himself became a pentito.

Despite the loss of manpower and arms, the Red Brigades and surviving remnants of Prima Linea immediately resumed the offensive, and for every pentito-directed Dalla Chiesa raid in the spring of 1980 the revolutionaries responded with a fury born of desperation. As part of their campaign to wipe out experts of "counter-guerrilla warfare," they shot and nearly killed a prison architect on 2 May. Within the next two weeks they killed a policeman, seriously wounded one Christian Democratic official, and murdered another.

May ended with a reminder that the Red Brigades continued to inspire revolutionary youths with the plan they had presented to public view in their "Risoluzione della Direzione Strategica." In that document they for once had quoted Gramsci: "The worker must always know that the bourgeois newspaper (whatever its [ideological] tint) is an instrument of struggle charged by ideas and interests that are in contrast to his. . . . the press is constantly influenced by an idea: to serve the dominant class, that translates itself into a fact: to fight the working class."[40] The Red Brigades claimed to have learned from Italy's most venerated Marxist master that in capitalist societies the major newspapers functioned merely as channels of communication for the establishment. Italy's vaunted freedom of the press was really a smokescreen that enabled capitalism to obscure the *paese reale* of the working class. A vivid contemporary example of this nefarious process could be observed in the media campaign to discredit "the guerrilla movement" by criminalizing it.

Stimulated by this Red Brigade mentality and desirous of gaining admission to that organization by impressing its leaders with a bold action, a group known as the XXVIII March Brigade in honor of the fallen in Via Fracchia attacked and killed Walter Tobagi on 28 May 1980. Only thirty-three, Tobagi had been a highly praised correspondent for many years on the *Corriere della sera* as well as a prolific author of books and a teacher of contemporary history at the Università Statale in Milan. Tobagi had written penetrating articles about the radical Marxist culture from which left-wing terrorism had emerged in Italy.[41] He approached the subject of terrorism from a Christian and reform socialist viewpoint, arguing that the ferocious intellectual intolerance of radical Marxist teachers had led in a straight line to the ferocious deeds of impressionable youths.[42] Tobagi saw this connection in much the same way that André Malraux interpreted the relationship between Professor Gisors and Ch'en in *Man's Fate*: the terrorist's rationale for his actions had to come from somewhere, and only at the cost of distorting the truth could the mental links between the terrorist and his *maître à penser* be obliterated, even when this last had no physical involvement with the actions themselves.[43] Unlike Malraux, Tobagi scorned terrorists, and his articles on them were completely unsparing of their sensibilities. For this they hated him. He long had been a target of diverse terrorist groups, and in the end it was the upstart XXVIII March Brigade that killed him.

A few days later his killers explained what had been on their minds. First, the XXVIII March Brigade authors cited the Gramsci quotation on bourgeois journalism that they had copied from the "Risoluzione della Direzione Strategica" of the Red Brigades. Tobagi's assassins understood this to mean that establishment journalists—prostitutes at best and state terrorists at worst—make their living at the expense of "the proletariat and of their armed vanguard."[44] In other words, the capitalist press was by nature incapable of either wanting to know the truth or discovering it. As Gramsci said, its concerns are profit and control; every other task it essays is related to those two functions of power or hegemony. The men of the XXVIII March Brigade further observed that Tobagi had relished his role as the character assassin of communist revolutionaries. "The communist methodology" had impelled them, they claimed, to attack and to destroy such information centers as the one for which Tobagi wrote. He himself was the very archetype of the class enemy, whom "the instruments of Marxist analysis had permitted us today to specify and to annihilate. . . . "[45] This would be the fate, they said, of all the Tobagis.

The Tobagi assassination left no uncertainty about the continuing menace of terrorism. The general public had succumbed to the euphoria engendered by Dalla Chiesa's April and May raids against dozens of terrorist hideouts. It was hoped that Peci, Zedda, Sandalo, and the other pentiti had put their former organizations into the dustbin of history, or at least on the path leading to that destination. Then the appeal made by former piellini such as Fabrizio Giai to cease the armed struggle because it did not correspond to anything real in the country had begun to create the impression that the nightmare would soon stop.[46] But the terrorist deaths and maimings of May, culminating in the murder of Tobagi, caused these hopes to disappear almost as quickly as they had been formed.

SEVEN

The Children of the Sun

On 28 May 1980, the day of Tobagi's murder in Milan at the hands of Marxist revolutionaries, a group of right-wing terrorists shot and killed Franco Evangelista in front of the *liceo* Giulio Cesare in Rome. The thirty-seven-year-old Evangelista, called Serpico after the character played by Al Pacino in a film of the same name, had become famous for his numerous arrests of drug dealers. He was sitting in a police car on a routine patrol of this neofascist hotbed when two terrorist assassins started shooting at him. His partner, Giovanni Lorefici, suffered critical wounds in the same attack, and in a related shooting a school guard fell with near-fatal bullet wounds in the stomach, back, and head. Although neofascist terrorists had murdered another policeman earlier in the year, Evangelista's assassination captured public attention as an event emblematic of radical neofascism's return to terrorist prominence.

Neofascist terrorists killed again on 23 June 1980. Their victim this time was Judge Mario Amato, who had been the government's principal investigator of right-wing terrorism. In a dossier on this political phenomenon Amato had claimed that black subversives were reorganizing according to the red subversive model. His superior, Judge Giovanni De Matteo, who counted among his friends and social acquaintances some notorious neofascists, deemed this information unworthy of police notice. Amato's report fell victim to the same official obstructionism that had derailed one investigation after another into black terrorism. Now he lay dead next to a bus stop with a bullet behind his right ear.

The circumstances of Amato's death instigated a violent polemic in Italy. Why had this vulnerable man, threatened on all sides by fanatical organizations from which he in heroic loneliness had sought to protect society, not been given police protection? His superiors denied him carabiniere security guards and a bulletproof car on the grounds that other, nameless, judges were more exposed. Many critics wondered aloud whether some of these superiors, notably Judge De Matteo, might have desired this end for Amato and conspired to bring it about. De Matteo was even accused of passing along the particulars of Amato's secret investigation to the lawyers of neofascist defendants in diverse terrorist cases.

On the next day a Nuclei Armati Rivoluzionari (NAR) leaflet proclaimed that this neofascist organization had killed Amato to demonstrate how the radical right-wing revolution had "no need either of hideouts or of great organizations: three faithful comrades of good will are enough. And if there are not three, two will do."[1] The same document contained a blistering indictment of the extreme Right, including its so-called violent groups. NAR denounced these last for their verbosity and inertia. Required now were action and will, not program statements for the benefit of the old women who with trembling hands and shattered nerves timidly led the MSI along its shameful parliamentary course. The mysterious NAR proposed itself as the agent that would guide the revolutionary Right to a decisive victory over its enemies.

Resurgent right-wing terrorism still appeared to be an affair of unconnected violent acts, vastly less serious than the statistically overwhelming terror of the Red Brigades and Prima Linea. However, on 2 August 1980, at the start of the *ferragosto* holiday, neofascist terrorists succeeded in completely reestablishing their stature as public enemies deserving of comparison with extreme left-wing fanatics. At 10:25 A.M. an ear-splitting bomb explosion ripped through the Bologna train station. The entire left wing of the station, including the roof, was reduced to ruins above an immense crater in the floor. Eighty-five victims died in the explosion or as a result of it. Two hundred more were wounded, many horribly.[2] Windows were blown out in nearby buildings, and outside the station two taxi drivers sustained fatal wounds.

Inside the station children flew through the air like rag dolls. Many people were blinded, and some victims went to the hospital with their lungs in plain sight. For hours doctors ministered to sufferers who lost arms and legs. The dead were soon removed to the morgue, where a reporter observed the cadavers of many small children clad in short pants, brightly colored shirts, and beach sandals.[3]

In the days that followed, an outraged nation clamored for action against black terrorists. Since the mid-1970s they had worked in the shadow of the Red Brigades and other left-wing terrorist groups, but after 2 August violent neofascists found themselves in the spotlight once again, as they had been from 1969 to 1974. Eventually, numerous pentiti would come forward with testimony implicating themselves and their former colleagues in the twilight world of black terrorism.[4] They stated in the authoritative language of the adept what scholars of right-wing literature had learned from their studies: with massacres like the one in Bologna, neofascist terrorists hoped to create a prerevolutionary situation. In answer to the question of who actually set the explosives, witnesses offered conflicting testimony, but they did confirm the suspicions of those authorities who had long viewed the alumni and fellow travelers of Ordine Nuovo as the chief instigators of a strategy of tension, including bomb attacks against Italy's democratic order. A whole crowd of fanatical Julius Evola devotees and neonazis—including Paolo Signorelli, Franco Freda, Claudio Mutti, and Stefano Delle Chiaie—became the subject of police and journalistic inquiry.

The official reference to Evola in the aftermath of the Bologna train station bombing highlighted the prominence of this neofascist thinker in radical right-wing circles. Certainly in the thirty years prior to his death in 1974 he had been the premier thinker of the extraparliamentary Right. Evola developed his ideology as a response to certain definite political, social, and psychological realities in twentieth-century Italian life. It is of the utmost importance to understand the nature of his appeal to those Italians who from a neofascist perspective view contemporary Italy as a society bent on suicide, who believe themselves to be the protectors of a traditional civilization infected with the disease of modernity. To them the infection is so advanced that only the most drastic measures will be of avail.

Evola was born in 1898 into an aristocratic Roman family. A brilliant student with a talent for art, he very early developed a taste for iconoclastic literature. Dmitry D. Merezhkovsky's fin de siècle trilogy, Christ and Antichrist (1896–1905), demolished the Catholicism that he had inherited from his parents.[5] The resulting void in his mind was quickly filled by the aphorisms of Nietzsche, whose critique of modernity became and remained the centerpiece of Evola's thought. Otto Weininger, Carlo Michelstaedter—a suicide at age twenty-three in 1910—and Max Stirner gained admittance to the youthful Evola's literary pantheon because of their Nietzschean dissent from the egalitarian, humanitarian, and conformist values of modern bourgeois society (in Stirner's case it was anticipatory), which they proposed to replace with a code of aristocratic morality.[6]

Still in his teens, Baron Evola fought as an artillery officer during World War I on secondary fronts and then became the leading Italian representative of the Dada movement in art and literature.[7] Even before the war he had been drawn to the Italian literary avant-garde, then under the high-spirited direction of Giovanni Papini and Giuseppe Prezzolini, and to Filippo Tommaso Marinetti's Futurist movement in art.[8] Evola ultimately found the Futurist esthetic "too loud and showy," but the Dada movement of Tristan Tzara and André Breton suited his artistic sensibilities perfectly.[9] After the war he plunged into a whirl of Dada activities: reading his extremely avant-garde poetry—to the accompaniment of music by Schönberg, Satie, and Bartok—in the Cabaret Grotte dell'Augusteo, which was Italy's version of Zurich's Cabaret Voltaire, the birthplace of Dada; exhibiting his Dada paintings in Rome's Galleria Bragaglia as well as in Milan, Lausanne, and Berlin; and collaborating on the Dada Journal Revue Bleu.[10]

His avant-garde notoriety after World War I has caused many of his contemporary admirers to conclude that Evola went through a decadent period before discovering his true conservative voice, but he always resisted this interpretation of his early life. Visitors to his Roman palazzo home on Corso Vittorio Emanuele could hardly fail to notice the numerous Dada paintings always on display, and Evola strongly insisted in his autobiography that Dadaism could not be dismissed as a "sin of my youth."[11] The Dada movement, Evola recalled, spearheaded a frontal attack on the rationalist cultural values of the bourgeoisie, always the true enemy of conservative elites.[12] The Dadaists intended to excise all passé art forms, and in 1920 that meant the Victorian-Edwardian residue of middle-class culture and morality. Only with such an excision, they believed, would a new and better world be possible. For Evola, then, Dada was not art but the dissolution of art as a preparatory stage for "a superior state of liberty."[13]

Evola, recognizing that avant-garde art was rapidly becoming undermined by commercialism and hardened into an academic convention, anticipated Marcel

Duchamp's extreme Dada gesture and in 1922 gave up painting completely. At the same time he followed the example of Rimbaud and renounced poetry as well. Evola then began those "transrational" philosophic studies that would occupy him for the rest of the 1920s: *Saggi sull'idealismo magico* appeared in 1925, *L'individuo e il divenire del mondo* and *L'uomo come potenza* in 1926, *Teoria dell'individuo assoluto* in 1927, and *Fenomenologia dell'individuo assoluto* in 1930. All purported to defend philosophical idealism, which in Evola's parlance meant that "the world is my representation" or "the ability to be unconditionally whatever one wants."[14] In practical terms these ideas signified that the limits of the "real" world were self-imposed and could be eliminated easily by the "absolute individual" who had achieved complete control over himself through wisdom.[15] Hegelian and Schopenhauerian concepts made a deep impression on him, and Evola concluded that through a hierarchy of stages a society of absolute individuals could achieve unity with the One—"the ultimate synthesis," or "the perfection of perfection."[16]

Evola's shift from painting and poetry to philosophy suggests something of the restlessness that characterized the "lost" generation of 1914.[17] Like so many other artists and intellectuals of the postwar period, Evola failed to adjust to civilian life, and his artistic-intellectual career during the 1920s may be summarized as a series of experiments in what he called "transcendence." He rejected the same bourgeois social and cultural values that had alienated Robert Graves, John Dos Passos, Ernst Jünger, and Julien Benda—but in Evola's case this alienation assumed a totally uncompromising form. His postwar quest for a personal philosophy of transcendence led him to Oriental studies, and he became a student of magic, the occult, alchemy, and Eastern religions.[18] In 1924–25 Evola published numerous articles on mysticism in *Atanòr* and *Ignis*, journals dedicated to "initiate studies," and then in 1927 he founded the Gruppo di Ur, an association of Italian intellectuals who desired to treat "the esoteric and initiate disciplines with seriousness and rigor."[19] Although his three-year affiliation with this highly unconventional *cénacle* of spiritualists gave him a lifelong reputation as a theosophist crackpot, Evola contemptuously rejected theosophy as a degenerate caricature of ancient wisdom in *Imperialismo pagano: il fascismo dinnanzi al pericolo euro-cristiano* (1928) and, more systematically, in *Maschera e volto dello spiritualismo contemporaneo* (1932). Evola condemned the spiritualist sects of his age because, according to him, their "old soul" mentality led to a pathetically self-indulgent form of escapism into a drowsy nirvana. He, on the contrary, proposed a philosophy of utter wakefulness and vigilance on this plane of existence, the only one with which he was seriously concerned.

In the late 1920s he had a fateful encounter with the work of the French Orientalist René Guénon (1886–1951), whose *La crise du monde moderne* (1927) inspired Evola to organize his fragmentary and increasingly dyspeptic thoughts around a central concept, the critique of modernity.[20] He called Guénon "the Descartes of esoteric studies" and "the true master of modern times."[21] Certainly the Frenchman's aggressively antimodern philosophy was the point of departure for *La rivolta contro il mondo moderno* (1934), Evola's most important book. At the time this work was almost completely ignored.[22] Eventually it became and remains a cult book of the extreme Right—not only for Italian reactionaries but, in translation, for their political counterparts nearly everywhere in Europe.

Evola wanted to explain "the decadent nature of the modern world," with decadence understood as a decline in spiritual values and a corresponding rise in materialism.[23] In tracing the origins of this decadence he singled out the intellectuals—first in the Greece and Rome of antiquity—who, by their relentless questioning, had brought about the decline of traditional values. But the traumatic disorientation of the West, Evola asserted, had resulted mainly from the humanist movement, the Renaissance, and the Protestant Reformation.[24] Renaissance anthropocentrism signaled the demise of organic medieval society, and Western man had been trapped in a modern version of Plato's cave of shadows ever since.[25] According to Evola, the Enlightenment had vastly augmented the triumph of liberal humanism, and the whole sorry process had achieved an apotheosis with the French Revolution: democracy, socialism, and communism had become inevitable after that, and with them the eclipse of order, culture, and tradition. World War I, the Russian Revolution, and World War II were merely addenda to the disaster of 1789. By 1945, he pointed out in a later edition of the book, it could be said that modernity had eliminated Europe "as a subject of great world politics."[26]

Italy had the contemptible distinction of inaugurating this decadent dialectic. Even before the humanist movement and the Renaissance, the Communes had sabotaged first the idea and then the physical existence of the Ghibelline Empire. Evola deeply admired Frederick I, who had affirmed "the supranational and sacred principle" of empire against the anarchy of the Communes.[27] Far from celebrating the patriotic legend of the Communes, Evola denigrated it, insisting that Werner Sombart was right to call Florence "the New York of the Middle Ages."[28] For Evola the rising of the Communes had been essentially a movement of the Third Estate and therefore a preview of the French Revolution. More immediately and in strictly Italian terms the revolt against the empire plunged Italy into a long night of chaos, civil war, and regionalism at the expense of organic unity. While Spain, England, and France emerged from the Middle Ages under the guidance of strong national monarchies, Italy tore itself apart during the reign of the *signorie* and of a cynical, opportunistic church.[29] The subjugation of the peninsula by foreigners irrepressibly followed, and when, after four centuries, national unification did occur it came about as a conquest by Piedmont, not from any desire on the part of the Italian people. Now, seventy-five years later, Italy was still struggling to establish a true polity.

The victim of the historical process by which Europe, under Italy's lead, had modernized itself was the world of tradition. Evola thought of this world in essentially Platonic and Nietzschean terms of transcendence. Claiming the authority of both Plato and Nietzsche, he asserted that "progress" is powerless to change certain fundamental truths about men and society, especially the need for hierarchy, caste, monarchy, race, myth, religion, and ritual—categories subsumed in *La rivolta contro il mondo moderno* under the rubric "virilità spirituale." To lose this spiritual virility was to become incapable of generating true order; hence the retreat of modern man from cosmos to chaos. Evola cited Toynbee with approval: when the spiritual center is no more, civilization begins to disintegrate, and by 1934 the disintegration of Europe had proceeded very far, with the Soviet Union and the United States menacingly poised on its flanks.[30]

The obvious question here is, whether Evola viewed fascism as a cure for the ailments caused by American capitalism and Soviet communism. Up to a point he did. Nonetheless, in *Torre*, his 1930 fortnightly political review, he denounced the demagogic tendencies rising to the surface of official fascism. "We would like," Evola wrote in an editorial, "a fascism more radical, more intrepid, a truly absolute fascism, made of pure force, inaccessible to any compromise."[31] This view endeared him to [radicals] in the Fascist movement, but not to the pragmatic Mussolini, whose censors, according to Evola, ruthlessly suppressed the journal and subjected the staff to a campaign of character assassination. For months Evola felt compelled to maintain a group of bodyguards, made up of like-minded radical Fascists. The journal died out after five months and ten numbers, the last one published on 15 June 1930. Italian fascism, it seems, had as little tolerance for opposition on the right as on the left.

The fanatically anti-Semitic editor of *Vita italiana*, Giovanni Preziosi, who had deeply admired the *Torre* experiment, introduced Evola to Roberto Farinacci, the Fascist chief of Cremona and, after 1933, the cynosure in Italy for pro-Nazi sentiment.[32] At about the time that *La rivolta contro il mondo moderno* appeared, Evola began his collaboration with Farinacci's radical Fascist Cremona newspaper, *Regime fascista*. He edited a page entitled "Diorama filosofico," where some of the most important thinkers on the international right discussed problems of Fascist philosophy. Included among the contributors were Paul Valéry, Gottfried Benn, Gonzague De Reynold, Sir Charles Petrie, Prince Karl Anton Rohan, Othmar Spann, Edmund Dodsworth, Friedrich Everling, and Albrecht Erich Günther.[33] René Guénon authorized the translation of his essays and of passages from his books for publication as articles in *Regime fascista*. Farinacci himself set the tone for Evola's third-page section of the newspaper by writing the first "Diorama" piece, "Formare l'Italiano Nuovo," in which he called on Fascist intellectuals to consecrate their work to "a new classical mission."[34] Evola's own contributions to this page often stressed the need for a more aggressive, imperialistic foreign policy; on the eve of the Ethiopian War, for example, he counseled Mussolini to transform Italy into a "warrior nation," one that would appreciate and admire "the sacred valor of war."[35]

With Farinacci's protection, Evola resurrected the *Torre* idea in *Regime fascista*. Evola then became the *cremonese* editor's candidate to succeed Giovanni Gentile as the philosopher of true fascism.[36] The succession never took place, but Evola's relationship with *Regime fascista* lasted until the fall of fascism in July 1943. On the day that Italy formally defected from her alliance with Germany, 8 September 1943, Evola was in Berlin, and he was among the first to see Mussolini after the dictator's liberation from prison by Otto Skorzeny. Thereafter, Evola became actively involved in the creation of the Salò Republic. His aristocratic sensibilities were injured, however, by the ostentatious efforts of Mussolini's new government to modify fascism with the catchwords of democracy and socialism, as interpreted by the highly inconsistent intellect of yet another Socialist turned Fascist, Nicola Bombacci.[37] The Congress of Verona, where the ideological patchwork of fascism in extremis took place, elicited Evola's stern disapproval, and yet he had to admire "the combative and legionary side of Salò, the decision of thousands of Italians to remain faithful to [their] ally and to continue the war."[38] He observed that "in the history of post-Roman Italy such a phenomenon was nearly unheard of."[39]

Nevertheless, since the mid-1930s Evola had felt that his "natural environment" was in Germany. His books had enjoyed a *succès d'estime* among right-wing German intellectuals, and after 1934, when Evola lectured at the University of Berlin and at the city's Herrenklub, he became an increasingly admired and sought-after speaker in those circles. According to him, fascism had attained its most sublime form in Germany because the country's traditional thinkers, such as Arthur Moeller van den Bruck, Ernst Jünger, and Gottfried Benn, had been taken seriously by the National Socialist regime. His admiration for Hitler far surpassed any that he ever expressed for Mussolini. The contrast, he thought, between Hitler's SS and the Moschettieri di Mussolini (Musketeers of Mussolini) was or should be a source of acute embarrassment for every virile Italian. What Evola liked most about Nazi Germany was the "attempt to create a kind of new political-military Order with precise qualifications of race," and he longed for an elite organization in Rome comparable to Berlin's Herrenklub.[40]

Returning to Rome with Farinacci on 18 September 1943, Evola began to organize the Movement for the Renaissance of Italy, a forerunner of the radical right-wing groups that proliferated in Italy after World War II.[41] But when Rome fell to the Allies in June 1944 Evola fled to Vienna, where, in his own words, "I sought to work in a mode analogous to that in Rome," by continuing to participate in the Nazi struggle against the forces of bourgeois capitalism and Bolshevik communism.[42] Working with Fascist leaders all over Central Europe, Evola performed vital liaison services for the SS as Nazi Germany sought to recruit a European army for the defense of the Continent against the Soviet Union and the United States.[43] During an aerial bombardment of Vienna he suffered a crippling injury, and medical problems resulting from this wound forced him to remain in Austria until after the war was over.

Despite his passionate involvement in various Fascist causes, Evola always refused to join the Fascist party.[44] Membership in the party no doubt would have advanced his career, but for reasons set forth clearly in *Il fascismo: saggio di una analisi critica dal punto di vista della destra* (1970) Evola thought that fascism was at best a halfway house on the road to a genuine state.[45]

Evola declared that the greatest merit of fascism was "to have realized in Italy the idea of a state, to have created the bases for an energetic government."[46] The Fascist motto "Everything in the state, nothing outside the state, nothing against the state" met with his enthusiastic approval. Men must belong to a traditional, organic, hierarchical order, he pontificated. According to him, Mussolini promised such an order and seemed to be working toward its realization; at least the duce got rid of the *partitocrazia* of democratic regimes and parliamentary reform.[47]

Certainly, Evola continued, Fascist corporativism represented a vast improvement over the chaos of laissez faire capitalism and the regimentation of Soviet Marxism. Therefore, he could write that whatever flaws may have existed in Fascist corporativism, "the direction . . . can be considered as substantially positive."[48] Moreover, Mussolini had persevered heroically in his efforts to instill discipline in the Italian people—"discipline and the love of discipline"—in order to avoid "the perils of the bourgeois spirit."[49] The glory of fascism, Evola believed, lay in its generation-long war against the "bourgeois race" on behalf of Roman ideals, and as late as 1941 he was still hoping that the process of *fascistizzazione* would correct the manifold defects of the Italian people.[50] Even after 1945 he maintained that in theory "Fascist reforms presented a rational and plausible character."[51]

Nevertheless, he lamented that *fascismo reale* fell tragically short of these theoretical goals.[52] The regime did not succeed in creating a traditional state, and in fact did everything possible to minimize the roles of the monarchy and the aristocracy. Evola insisted that Mussolini should have been Vittorio Emanuele III's "loyal counselor," not the king's rival for power.[53] The Fascist party itself should have been disbanded in 1922, when Mussolini took office, and become one with the state instead of continuing to function as a parallel state.[54] Not only did the party remain in existence; it became a mass organization and increasingly demagogic. The cult of the duce offended Evola, and he observed that the longer the party held power the more fatuous its slogans became. "The duce is always right" appealed to the lowest common denominator in Italian society, not to the elite where fascism should have aimed its message.

In addition, fascism compromised itself in an entente with the Catholic Church. In 1928 Evola had declared: "The identification of *our* tradition with the Christian and Catholic Church is the *most absurd* of all errors."[55] The Lateran Accords of the next year confirmed his worst fears about fascism, and he called it a "laughable revolution."[56] Most damaging of all to fascism from Evola's point of view was "a heavy bureaucratic centralism," characterized by extreme inefficiency and venality. The regime simply did not produce "a sufficient number of men who were equal to certain high exigencies . . . and capable of promoting the development of the positive potentialities . . . contained in the system."[57] In other words, Mussolini had promised the right things but had only managed to make a start on delivering a few of them when the calamitous finale of World War II overtook him.[58]

Because Evola had influenced the regime's racial laws, he felt obliged in *Il fascismo* to comment on his reputation as a racist. As early as 1935 Mussolini had enthusiastically noted Evola's articles on race, beginning with "Razza e cultura" in *Rassegna italiana*. When Mussolini read his book-length treatise on the subject, *Sintesi di dottrina della razza* (1941), the duce was so favorably impressed by it that a subsequent printing carried the title *Sintesi di dottrina fascista della razza*.[59] The two men met at last in September 1941, and Mussolini promised to support Evola's projected Italian-German journal, *Sangue e spirito*. However, by then the dictator was already caught in the vortex of defeats that would smash his regime and leave fascism hardly more than a phantom of its former self. *Sangue e spirito* never appeared.

Evola wrote *Sintesi di dottrina della razza* with two fundamental problems in mind: the Jews and Ethiopia. Not an anti-Semite in the formal sense of the term, Evola did loathe Jews.[60] The distinction in his thought between anti-Semitism and anti-Jewishness is worth noting: he had a horror of the "corrosive irony" in Jewish culture and bewailed its effect on Europe; however, he did not then leap to the main anti-Semitic position, that Jews are responsible for what is wrong with the world.[61] Evola believed there would always be a problem with the Jews as long as they retained a preponderance out of all proportion to their numbers in the political, economic, and intellectual life of the West.[62] Moreover, Jewish intellectuals had played a large part in demolishing the foundations of Europe's traditional culture, and Evola did not choose his words carefully in condemning them for it. [63]

Although Evola concurred with the anti-Semites on their assertion concerning the strongly marked Jewish tendency to denigrate lofty ideals by ascribing every human activity to economic and sexual motives, à la Marx and Freud—the two archetypal Jewish intellectuals—he nevertheless charged that Hitler's theories about Jews, inspired by gross misconceptions of history, amounted to a "demagogic aberration."[64] In his judgment Nazi musings on the race question never rose above a low level of polemicism and expediency. The Nazis were right, Evola thought, in claiming that through a combination of money and guile the Jews worked to subvert Aryan spirituality, but he rejected the conspiracy theory for this subversion.[65] He contended that the Jews, especially now that Judaism had degenerated into a secular ethic of professional advancement and mammonism, felt both envy and hatred for Aryan ideals of faith, loyalty, courage, devotion, and constancy; however, this feeling was an instinctual reaction—they compulsively "poison, soil, and debase all that is held to be high and noble" (*per la sua stessa natura, cioè senza propriamente volerlo*).[66] Certainly, the Jews had risen to lofty heights of power and influence in the modern world, but for Evola that was merely a symptom of contemporary decadence, not its essence, as Nazi anti-Semites claimed. The real problem, as he had written earlier in *La rivolta contro il mondo moderno*, began with the rise of rationalism, first in antiquity and then, more tragically, in the Renaissance: humanists and Protestants had dramatically accelerated the historical process of which Jews had merely taken advantage. For Evola the Jewish problem was just one element in a much larger phenomenon.[67]

Leaving aside Hitler's paranoia on the question of the Jews, Evola insisted in *Sintesi di dottrina della razza* that racism could have positive results if the concept were interpreted primarily in Nietzschean terms of spirit rather than in biological terms of blood. For example, Aryanism, like Semitism, was not a race, as the Germans untenably claimed, but an attitude, an idea, a vision of the world.[68] Evola did not doubt that there were inferior peoples, and his remarks about the Ethiopians, lately terrorized into colonial subjection by Mussolini's legions, revealed how fully he shared the vision of Fascist imperialism. The most elementary powers of observation, he wrote, should convince any honest person that some races possessed a "dominant" character while others were intended by nature to be slaves. Therefore, the principles of social Darwinism, updated and streamlined by fascism, should be applied to all areas of what would later be called the Third World. Although biology did, in fact, matter to Evola, his precise position was that race must not be understood *solely* as a biological condition; it was a spiritual condition as well.[69] Like Evola, Mussolini worried about the problem of race mixing in Ethiopia, but the dictator's main racial preoccupation from 1921 on was to create "a new type of Italian," to introduce a higher civic consciousness in the Italian people and thereby create a new breed of man in Italy.[70] Evola's achievement in his writings on race was to provide Mussolini with a theory of "Nordic *Romanità*," which the duce then selectively used for his own ends.[71]

Another point must be added, then, to Evola's list of positive Fascist features: the regime's attempt to create a race imbued with "a traditional and antimaterialistic conception of human nature."[72] As so often happened with Italian fascism, however, theory did not presage practice, and Evola complained that nowhere did Mussolini fail more conspicuously than in his program to improve the race. He doubtless would have agreed with Hindenburg's remark that Mussolini would never be able to make anything but Italians of Italians.[73] Evola theorized that in Italy Nordic elements coexisted in perpetual anarchy with African and Mediterranean elements, and for him this complete absence of psychic equilibrium was the key to understanding the complex, creative, and infuriating history of the Italian people.[74]

Evola concluded his analysis of racism in Fascist Italy by affirming, "it was not fascism that acted negatively on the Italian people, on the 'Italian race,' but vice versa: it was the people, this 'race,' that acted negatively on fascism. . . ."[75] For Evola the betrayal of Mussolini on 25 July 1943 by the Fascist Grand Council and then the horrible confusion of the country, culminating in a desolating civil war between Communist partisans and Fascist loyalists, "fully revealed the inconsistent and damaged human component [that] had been hidden behind the facade of fascism."[76] How utterly unlike the Germans, who because of their "love for discipline" fought on "until the end without a lament and without a rebellion," he caustically remarked.[77] Croce had been right about fascism: it was a "parenthesis" in Italian life; but Evola believed it was a "heroic" one for all its shortcomings.

Evola regarded the Allied liberation of Italy as an unmitigated disaster because it meant that the country had fallen again into the mainstream of liberal development. And yet, at the same time, he was pleasantly surprised upon returning home to find so many young people interested in him and his books.[78] This belated recognition should not have been completely surprising to him. As Mario Tedeschi noted in his memoir, *Fascisti dopo Mussolini*, the very completeness of official fascism's failure opened the door wide for right-wingers whose reputations had not been ruined during the war.[79] By this standard the noncommittal and elusive Evola was perfectly situated to play an important role in the postwar intellectual and political life of the extreme Right.

Although he shared the antiliberal and anti-Communist resentments of Guglielmo Giannini's ephemeral right-wing Uomo Qualunque (Common Man) party in the years immediately following the war, Evola continued to reject party labels.[80] This rejection applied even to the extreme right-wing Movimento Sociale Italiano, with its symbol of a flaming tricolor above (it was said) Mussolini's funeral bier, founded on 26 December 1946 by ex-Fascists who had been active in the Republic of Salò, typically at the second and third echelons.[81] For the most radical of the missini leaders the resolutely antiparty Evola existed as an oracle. Giorgio Almirante hailed him as "our Marcuse—only better."[82] Pino Rauti, the leader of the *evoliani* in the MSI, exalted Evola as the paramount intellect of the age and based much of his own writing on Evola's *La rivolta contro il mondo moderno*.[83]

Through articles in *La rivolta ideale*, the MSI's leading newspaper during the late 1940s, as well as in other party publications and in the notorious pamphlet *Orientamenti* (1950), Evola goaded the missini in the same way he had goaded the Fascists, always toward a more radical theoretical position. In these pieces he stressed the "legionary spirit" and the "warrior ethic."[84]

Orientamenti was a précis of the political books that Evola would write during the 1950s and 1960s. According to him, all Europe had now become afflicted with the tragic condition that for centuries had been Italy's destiny: to be the passive, inert object of stronger, outside powers. For him the twentieth-century analogue of Italy's catastrophic experience during the French and Spanish invasions of the fifteenth and sixteenth centuries was the U.S.-USSR condominium on the Continent. The Italians had been forever cursed by the moral devastation produced by these earlier invasions; their country had remained profoundly disoriented at its core from that day to this, Evola argued. Now he saw all Europe coming down with the dreaded symptoms of this Italian psychological and cultural disease, characterized by "a general moral anesthesia."[85]

Orientamenti proposed to show how European man could rise again. First, he would have to renew himself spiritually by rejecting the "sad pig" image that contemporary psychiatrists had fashioned for him and by embracing an aristocratic conception of life. The "New Man" would have to learn how "to choose the most difficult way . . . how to struggle even knowing that the battle was materially lost."[86] He and his brothers in "the new battle array" would see in capitalism and bolshevism degrees of the same illness, just as the U.S. and the USSR were two branches of the same evil. The circle of Marx and Madison Avenue would have to be broken by what in Evola's mind was still the vital force of corporativism.[87]

Although Evola wanted his followers to have "the courage of radicalism," at this time he cautioned against subversion on the grounds that it would not work and would condemn the aristocratic revolution to failure.[88] Instead he called for "intransigence of the idea" and "readiness in advancing with pure forces when the right moment strikes." In 1950 Evola was willing to leave the concrete forms of the new order in abeyance: "the essential task is to prepare silently the spiritual ambience in which a new form of authority might take shape."[89]

Strong-minded antifascists scoffed at Evola's public disclaimers against subversion, and in April 1951 agents of the Ufficio Politico della Questura arrested him, along with twenty other neofascists, for trying to revive the Fascist party. Moreover, he was specifically accused of having been "the maestro, the inspirer" of the Fasci d'Azione Rivoluzionaria (FAR), a violent shadow organization of the MSI.[90] After six months of imprisonment Evola et al. came to trial, and the state pointed to him as "the spiritual father of all the defendants."[91] The public prosecutor demanded an eight-month sentence for him, but Evola, his monocle shining, had little trouble proving that he had never belonged to the Fascist party or to any neofascist organization and that he had specifically opposed subversion, in *Orientamenti*. Naturally, not all readers would understand the message correctly; but Evola asked what writer could be held responsible for how people interpreted his books.[92] The government case against him came to nothing, and the other defendants received either light or suspended sentences.[93]

Evola continued to agitate for radical right-wing causes, and in 1956 Rauti's founding of Ordine Nuovo, made up of members who had been repelled by the increasingly moderate line of the MSI, came about as a result of Evola's inspiration and was modeled on the Nouvel Ordre Européen.[94] Ordine Nuovo continued the radical right-wing strategy of tension, begun in the postwar period by FAR and characterized by indiscriminate explosions and acts of aggression against Communist organizations. By the late 1960s Rauti's organization, with its fasces and double-ax symbol, boasted five to six thousand adherents in dozens of provincial groups, with particular strength in the Veneto, Campania, and Sicily. Evola later referred to Ordine Nuovo as the only political group in Italy "that doctrinally had held firm without descending to compromise."[95]

During these postwar years Evola remained an independent intellectual, but he exerted a definite and historically verifiable influence on those right-wing Italians who despaired at the prospect of an Italy in thrall to American capitalism and endangered by Soviet Marxism.[96] Militant right-wing youths in post-Fascist Italy compared their fate with that of Dante, who had lamented the collapse of the Ghibelline order.[97] The generation of 1945, as they called themselves, hailed Evola as the "celestial warrior" whose work made sense of what for them were ruined times.[98]

It was for this generation that in 1953 Evola summed up his thoughts about the Christian Democratic regime in *Gli uomini e le rovine*.[99] Prince Junio Valerio Borghese, a Fascist war hero, the idol of neofascist youth groups, and one of the most influential postwar figures of the extreme Right, first as president of the MSI and then as a tireless promoter of extraparliamentary organizations and coups, wrote an introduction for the book, accurately describing it as "a cry of protest."[100]

Evola argued that the fundamental right-wing task in the postwar period was that of counterrevolution or, more accurately, conservative revolution.[101] The task entailed two objectives, one political and the other ideological. The political objective involved out-maneuvering the Italian agents of U.S. capitalism and Soviet Marxism, for this is how Evola described the Christian Democratic party and the PCI, respectively. As for the ideological objective, Evola in effect took a leaf from Gramsci's *Prison Notebooks*, namely, the ideas of hegemony and counterhegemony. The results of World War II had left the Christian Democratic party and the PCI in political and intellectual control of Italy; this, for Evola, was the hegemony of the hour. He proposed a counterhegemony led by men capable of saying no to all the ideologies that were derived from "the immortal principles of 1789," the world of ideas from liberalism to bolshevism. Such men would be a minority—only a few would listen to "the word of order"—but, fortified by "a general vision of life and by a rigorous political doctrine," these reactionary supermen could retrieve the world that fascism had lost. [102] This is what he meant when he addressed his appeal to those men who "are rising from the ruins" to constitute a new order.

Evola could not counsel his readers to look for leadership from existing political institutions. Even the Right, "as presently constituted," offered authentic conservatives little solace and no hope for ultimate victory. [103] The MSI and the Monarchist party understood neither Marxism nor the world in which this ideology had made breathtaking advances. Evola prided himself on his knowledge of both. He took enormous pleasure in pointing out what he called the obnoxious and tendentious assumption of Marxists that they alone were motivated by a selfless pursuit of truth and justice, whereas conservatives merely acted from class interests. For him this was the fairy tale at the heart of scientific socialism, and he insisted that Marxist "realism" was in fact nothing more than a mythology. Here Evola reminded Marxists of a point made earlier by Karl Mannheim in *Ideology and Utopia*, that Marxism was itself only a hypothesis, an ideology, not an irrefutable truth that entitled its spokesmen to adopt an attitude of disdainful arrogance toward the spokesmen of all other ideologies. [104] This was not even to mention the laughably coarse oversimplifications at the core of Marxist psychology, with its unreal and unbelievable emphasis on the mode of production in human affairs, Evola complained.

Nonetheless, the depressing truth—polemically analyzed in *Gli uomini e le rovine*—was that Italian conservatives had played into the hands of the Left by attaching their cause to the destiny of "capitalist piracy and cynical, antisocial plutocracy." [105] Evola insisted that the conservative revolution should be based not on bourgeois sociopolitical structures but on "a general conception of life and of the state, . . . on values and interests of superior character, clearly transcending the levels of economy and of 'classism.' " [106]

For the rest of his life Evola continued to diagnose the problems of Europe in a manner consistent with the analysis in *Gli uomini e le rovine*: Western man was sick unto death from an existential dread of the future. In *Cavalcare la tigre* (1961) he revealed himself to be more depressed than ever. [107] "The desert is growing," he averred, quoting his adored Nietzsche. [108] It seemed irrefutable to him that the farther along man progressed into the modern period—the more "liberty" he enjoyed—the worse things became. Such liberation as modern man had experienced since the death of God had failed to satisfy his deepest wants, and Evola interpreted the widespread abuse of alcohol, drugs, sex, and work itself as feverish attempts to compensate for inner loneliness; these abuses obviously reflected a negative psychic and existential situation. As for women's liberation, that most progressive of all modern developments, he tersely defined it as "the renunciation by woman of her right to be a woman." [109] Feminism, he believed, could only appear as a reaction to an unmanly age when men surrendered their male prerogatives by default to an ever more intolerant and sexually imperialistic feminist movement. [110]

Above all, the conspicuous decline of the modern city proved to him that the values of modernity had failed; they had taken away from man his dignity and his very identity in exchange for the dubious freedoms of debauching himself and ruining his environment. The invalidating flaw in these values lay in the assertion that all men are created equal. The attempt to design social, economic, political, and cultural institutions in conformity with that primordial error resulted in cruel and perpetual frustrations for the masses, who neither could be nor wanted to be free. The most visible consequence of the false and pernicious freedom characteristic of the modern world, Evola contended, was a degree of cultural and psychological disorientation not seen since the collapse of the Roman Empire. He concluded that there was a fundamental dishonesty at the core of democratic theory, an unwillingness or an inability to test its philosophical abstractions against what we knew—by the middle of the twentieth century—to be true about man and society. For Evola, the complete disjunction between democratic theory and reality condemned democratic society to an endless round of crisis, chaos, and terror.

To document his thesis about progressive democratic societies, Evola cited the well-known brutality of American life. A country such as Switzerland could be democratic, though even there a pall of bourgeois sameness had been the most noticeable result of democracy. In a heterogeneous country like the United States, where "the most degenerate people from Europe had gathered," such an absurd political theory, he thought, had produced the hideous urban jungles made world famous by American novels and films.[111] Evola studied the literature of the beat generation, and he derived extremely pessimistic social conclusions from the books of Jack Kerouac and the young Norman Mailer. He felt sorry for the beatnik and the hipster because instinctively they were reacting in a quite natural, human way to the immoral institutions, social practices, and "culture" of consumer society, but, pathetically, these "rebels without a cause" had failed to develop a coherent philosophy and plan of action. Unlike the "anarchists of the Right," the American dissenters had no serious alternative to the existing state of things, only a petulant, egotistical, and insipid desire to set themselves off from the thickheaded multitude. Their existential despair amounted to nothing but an expression of futility, making them the last pitiful product of bourgeois capitalism, not the point of genesis for a salutary transformation of society, "an object of study in the general picture of an epoch's pathology," not the Sturm and Drang alarum for a brave new world.[112]

Evola judged Sartre's terminal disgust with the bourgeois world as the quintessential literary expression of the depersonalized and dehumanized culture of twentieth-century Western man. Existential alienation had been inescapable in a society that deprived man of moral bearings, and these could only be found in the traditional values of courage and honor for the few, obedience and discipline for the many.[113] Ultimately, there could be no hope for the West unless it retraced its missteps and succeeded in creating a sane order based on transcendence, by "confirming spiritual stability against temporality."[114] A serious contemporary philosophy would have to go beyond existentialism, which merely reflected the present crisis without solving or transcending it. Existentialists had only succeeded in creating a new jargon for the philosophical question that they had pretended to solve, the question of authenticity; but Evola asked who decides what an authentic existence is. To raise this question implied a metaphysical answer; to set it at rest necessitated a particular metaphysical answer, the one arising from traditional and antimodern values, or so he believed. Admittedly, few in today's world would be receptive to such a vision of life, for his ideas went against the grain of practically everything sacred and sensible to modern man. Nevertheless, Evola continued to believe in those few people who "by temperament and vocation still think, in spite of everything, about the possibility of a rectifying political action."[115]

Evola's recommendations raise two immediate questions: What, in concrete political terms, did he have in mind by calling for a return to tradition? And what does that have to do with the everyday realities of contemporary Italian politics—was he merely a far-from-amiable crank, or did his subjective vision of the world and history make a significant impression on society?

First, Evola advised his followers to withdraw completely from the illusory world of national politics, now dominated by democratic, parliamentary, and socialist forms.[116] By national politics he meant the official institutional life of the nation states, themselves thoroughly conditioned by that most odious product of the satanic French Revolution: nationalism.[117] At first glance, Evola's aversion here seems paradoxical because nationalism is generally viewed as a right-wing force. To view it so, however, requires that we ignore the enormous and largely realized revolutionary potential in European nationalism during the first half of the nineteenth century, as well as in Third World nationalism today. In Europe nationalism was a ram with which the Left of that time battered the old order, and parallel phenomena are now in progress all over the Third World. Evola identified completely with men such as Metternich and Bismarck—aristocrats who in his judgment viewed nationalism as a frightful modern development.[118] The premonitions of these Central European leaders had proved tragically correct, but now that Europe's world hegemony had been crushed as a result of the Continent's wholly destructive and lunatic obsession with nationalism, Evola invoked Vico's principle regarding cycles in history: when one cycle reaches its nadir another begins.[119] In other words, the very ashes of World War II concealed the materials for a new European order.

Evola found evidence for this assertion in the creation of foreign Waffen-SS units. Tens of thousands of international volunteers had fought alongside German soldiers in defense of the Continent against Soviet and U.S. invaders.[120] By the end of the war the Waffen-SS had consisted of forty divisions and 594,000 men.[121] As of 1 October 1944 this elite corps had lost 320,000 men.[122] The major foreign units in the Waffen-SS were the French Charlemagne, the Flemish Langemark, the Walloon Wallonie, the Dutch Landstorm Nederland, the Albanian Skanderberg, the Muslim Handschar, and the Croatian Kama. There were also three Cossack divisions, some Caucasian and Turkestan regiments, an Indian legion, two Rumanian battalions, one Bulgarian battalion, and one Norwegian battalion. A number of Arab volunteers served in the Thirteenth Bosnische-Herzegovinische SS Gebirgsdivision. Approximately, 6,000 Danes, 10,000 Norwegians, 75,000 Dutchmen, 25,000 Flemings, 15,000 Walloons, and 22,000 Frenchmen served in the Waffen-SS.[123]

Evola argued that this supranational military organization, reminiscent in his mind of the "ascetic warriors" in the Order of Teutonic Knights, signaled Europe's continued "spiritual virility."[124] It was this kind of international cooperation by European reactionary elites that Evola had in mind when he called for a new supranational militancy against the postwar Soviet and American occupiers of Europe.[125] All men opposed to the bourgeois world of modernity were potential recruits for this army of the conservative revolution, and Evola felt encouraged by the emergence of the British National party and the National Socialist movement in England, the Movimiento Nacional in Spain, the Vlaamse Militanten Orde in Belgium, the Organisation de l'Armée Secrète and the Nouvel Ordre Européen in France, the Legion Europa in Austria, and Fasci di Azione Rivoluzionaria and Ordine Nuovo in Italy. The emergence of these European fascist groups signified that a broad constituency for reaction existed, and Evola incited them to confront the Left and Center in a struggle for power. By revolutionary struggle the tradition had been lost; by revolutionary struggle—and only by such struggle—it could be restored. In practical terms the restoration of the tradition thus meant taking the war to the enemy, and by that Evola meant total war.

Second, concerning Evola's impact on the Right, it is never a simple matter to determine a writer's influence on politics, but in his case an abundance of fragmentary evidence—most notably the large number of radical neofascists whose ideological itineraries either began or ended with him—indicates that the books and ideas under discussion here have not been merely one man's sound and fury, signifying nothing.[126] Evola himself had written that the traditional "vision of the world is not based on books, but on an interior form and sensibility having a character not acquired, but innate."[127] In his own books, however, he depicted this vision by means of powerful symbols and images, thereby providing the radical Right in postwar Italy with a distinct intellectual coherence.[128]

Three generations of extreme right-wing youths identified Evola as their *maestro segreto.* In a fascinating memoir entitled *Autobiografia di un picchiatore fascista,* Giulio Salierno, the Communist writer who passed his teen-age years in the late 1940s and early 1950s as a right-wing terrorist, described Evola's influence on him and on his comrades from the MSI youth section of Colle Oppio in Rome.[129] Born into a "typically bourgeois Roman family," Salierno joined the MSI in the late 1940s over the issue of Trieste, which had been taken away from Italy after World War II. The issue of unredeemed Trieste served as a rallying point for the extreme Right, and Salierno noted that the intransigent nationalism of the MSI possessed an irresistible appeal for him. At section headquarters all was secrecy and sacred rites, with no end of Fascist salutes against a backdrop of war memorials to "the fallen of the RSI," illuminated crosses, Fascist eagles, and an immense portrait of Mussolini.[130] Fascist guest speakers could induce hysterical applause from these young men, and Salierno recalled the occasion when former General Graziani had them screaming: "Marshal, we are ready, we are here. One order, one order only, and we will all take up arms again."[131]

By 1952 Salierno had become secretary of his section, and his greatest ambition was to kill Walter Audisio, the executioner of Mussolini. This plan came to nothing because on 15 June 1953 Salierno, while trying to steal a car in Rome, killed a young man. He fled to France and eventually joined the Foreign Legion, serving with numerous ex-Nazis. Arrested by Interpol in 1954, he was extradited to Italy and put on trial. From then on his story is one of upward movement. While in prison he enrolled in a university, the first inmate to do so in Italy. He wrote *La spirale della violenza,* which became famous, and since then numerous other works of his authorship have been published. Liberation came in 1968, a reward for good behavior.

There is a memorable scene in his autobiography recounting Salierno's de rigeur visit with other young missini to Evola's home as though on pilgrimage to an ancient guru high in the Himalayas.[132] Salierno recalled that the crippled Evola held forth as an oracle in the suffocating heat of a small room, never deigning to look at his audience and frequently falling into long silences. Then the low voice would begin again, with Evola giving the wide-eyed boys a firsthand account of how he personally had advised Goebbels on a variety of matters and of what Hitler actually had said about this or that.

The séancelike performance overwhelmed Salierno and his friends. Here sat a man who had been a protagonist in "that legendary epic poem of the millenarian Third Reich."[133] Some of Evola's charisma did evaporate, Salierno noted, when in the midst of his rambling discourse a servant brought him dinner, which he unceremoniously devoured, "noisily lapping up the soup."[134] Still, Salierno agreed completely with the two major points of Evola's political analysis: to affirm the aristocracy of superior beings and to extirpate the communist cancer with "iron and fire."[135] This meant that bombs and physical attacks had to be part of their strategy against the communists. "Violence," Evola remarked in answer to a question by Salierno, "is the only possible and reasonable solution. . . . "[136]

Romano Cattaneo, who in 1974 eulogized Evola for *Il Conciliatore,* recalled the anguish of the right-wing youths belonging to the post–World War II generation: "We were born in time to suffer through the end of a badly lost war and burning inside of us was the desire for something that transcended the misery of those days and of those that would follow."[137] He praised Evola's *Orientamenti* and *Gli uomini e le rovine* as torch-bearing manifestos for a dark age. For him and like-minded Italians, Cattaneo recalled, "*Gli uomini e le rovine* and then the vast earlier and later work of Evola radically changed our being," providing a clear alternative to "an increasingly plebeian and tyrannical society."

The generation of 1968 accorded him, if anything, an even more enthusiastic reception, and this was the beginning—in Pino Rauti's words—of "a real and true Evola 'boom.' "[138] Almirante's comparison of him with Herbert Marcuse fit perfectly because Evola became that generation's patron saint of counterrevolution in much the same way that his hated adversary came to speak for the New Left. For example, on 15 November 1966 *Riscossa,* the notorious neofascist periodical of Brescia, hailed Evola as a master who was "firm in [his] principles; inaccessible to any concession; indifferent before the fears, the convulsions, and the acts of prostitution" in the present age.[139]

Furthermore, the radical right-wing activist Franco Freda based much of his seminal neofascist work, *La disintegrazione del sistema* (1969), on Evola's *Cavalcare la tigre.* This tract was the fleshed out version of a discourse presented before a meeting of the European Revolutionary Front in Regensburg, West Germany, on 17 August 1969. In it Freda expressed the essentially Evolian view that Europe had been crippled by two thousand years of the Judeo-Christian infection. He further explained that for the past two centuries the ideological germs of the French Revolution had transformed a serious situation into a critical one, and now Europe suffered from the worst conceivable kind of dictatorship, that of the business class. Freda, along with Evola, held that this dictatorship would have to be overthrown if Europe were ever to reclaim her greatness. Evola provided the philosophical starting point for this quest, but Freda proposed to supply something that had been missing in the work of the master: a practical revolutionary manual. Inevitably, he reasoned, revolutionaries must move beyond principles to the operative level of politics, and they must ask themselves, what tactics will provide the desired results.

In this spirit of applied Evolianism Freda described how "the destruction of the bourgeois world" could be accomplished.[140] In brief, "the nervous center of the bourgeois system" had to be attacked with the utmost violence: "in a political soldier, purity justifies every hardness, altruism every act of cunning, while the impersonal character [of the] struggle dissolves every moralistic preoccupation."[141] From such a recommendation, the radical right-wing reader could easily reason to Piazza Fontana, the Bologna train station, and the other bombing attacks in Italy from 1969 to the present as well as to every other act of neofascist violence during that period. Freda, who even counseled a tactical alliance with groups of the extreme Left, presented his argument in a way that made all conclusions but terrorism illogical.

In another right-wing manual of the period, *La lotta politica di Avanguardia Nazionale* (1974–75), the so-called black bomber, Stefano Delle Chiaie, portrayed his followers in Avanguardia Nazionale as an Evolian "elite of heroes."[142] Moreover, when Clemente Graziani, the leader of the Movimento Politico Ordine Nuovo (MPON), following Pino Rauti's return to the MSI in 1969, sought to defend the need for a truly revolutionary right-wing organization in Italy, he patterned his argument, in *Processo a Ordine Nuovo, processo alle idee*, on Evolian ideas. The bibliography of this tract was made up almost entirely of books by Evola. Graziani stated succinctly that "the work of Ordine Nuovo from 1953 to today has been that of transferring Evola's teachings to the political plane."[143] On the question of violence, he reminded his readers, "We are not Christians." No, they were revolutionaries who in the civil war that had already erupted would fight: "we intend to react, in a virile manner, responsibly, but to react. . . . "[144] Graziani did not oppose violence on principle; but then he asked who did. Perhaps not even the bourgeois revolutionaries, who through violent acts against the established order of their day had founded the modern Italian state, now in its death agony.

Finally, Adriano Romualdi, the brightest star in the firmament of the Italian extraparliamentary Right before his death at the age of thirty-three in an automobile accident on 12 August 1973, singled out Evola in 1971 as the intellectual hero of militant neofascism.[145] Evola's books, many of which had been out of print for years, were reissued in the late 1960s, and while the academic community and the world of official politics ignored him the young of the revolutionary Right found in his philosophy what they were looking for, precisely because, in Romualdi's words, "the teaching of Evola is also a philosophy of total war."[146] *Cavalcare la tigre* in particular, Romualdi noted, was "the breviary" for his generation of alienated right-wing intellectuals, a book to be placed alongside the works of Seneca, Marcus Aurelius, and Epictetus.[147]

Cavalcare la tigre also made a deep impression on the neofascist generation of 1977—those youths who believed that only a violent rejection of the status quo would enable Italy to escape a dual enslavement, to Marx and to Coca-Cola. For them Evola was a beacon in the long night of Italy's spiritual crisis, and they turned to him for instruction on how to validate themselves in a worthless age. What they learned, particularly from Evola's final homilies, was the paramount need to do battle against the forces of darkness, the Christian Democrats and Communists. "Nothing in this system deserves to be saved," Evola exhorted, and the implications of his exhortations were not very subtle. For example, in 1970 he wrote, "It is not a question of contesting and polemicizing, but of blowing up everything."[148] Three years later Evola was warning his followers about the imminent decisive hours as the Left, emboldened by the undoing of Italy's government, prepared to take power. Only armed resistance offered the Right any hope of victory, he counseled.

If Salierno's testimony is reliable, we can conclude that all along Evola, in his private audiences with right-wing youths, freely advocated violence without truce. Toward the end of his life, even in his published statements on the question of terrorism, Evola hardly bothered to conceal his true sentiment, that terrorism should be ruled out only when the odds against its success were overwhelming. He added, however, that if "the persons responsible for this contemporary subversion [could be kept] in a constant state of physical insecurity, that would be an excellent thing."[149] Evola's message here resembled Marx's view of terrorism in *The Civil War in France*: not to be employed indiscriminately, but only when the authentic revolutionary cause will be served effectively by it. As the German poet Gottfried Benn (1886–1956) had written more than thirty years earlier in an admiring review of *La rivolta contro il mondo moderno*, Evola appeals to those "black monks" who await the stroke of midnight; "when the time is full they will guide the forces of the resurrection."[150]

Evola's vision of "a formation of pure and decisive forces" could be and was interpreted as an appeal for a violent overthrow of the present order in favor of a "solar civilization." *Civiltà solare* was Evola's way of identifying a superior civilization, and his youthful disciples in Ordine Nuovo styled themselves "children of the sun." Such myth-making formed part of his larger argument, that an unprecedented degree of heroism would be required in the struggle against modernity, now grown to "monstrous dimensions": his followers would have to be spiritual warriors with "souls of steel," like the chivalrous Teutonic Knights, ready and eager for their "baptism by fire" in a holy war to establish "a metaphysical Regnum."[151] The disorders of the modern world had not happened spontaneously but had been produced by conscious planning and violent struggle; the conservative revolutionaries could succeed only if they developed and acted upon retaliatory tactics.

Georges Sorel's theories of violence held an irresistible fascination for Evola, and he completely agreed with the ethical assumption of *Reflections on Violence* that the highest good lay in the aggressive heroic action.[152] Violence always had been and always would be the hygiene of history. As he reminded Giorgio Almirante in an open letter published in *Noi Europa* in 1967, "one act of violence calls into existence and justifies another." Sometimes, he continued, violence alone can save the state, "as when in a cancerous organism the only recourse is surgical intervention."[153] This is precisely how *Quex*, a late 1970s gazette celebrating "armed spontaneity" and published by neofascist prisoners "for whomever wants to ride the tiger," understood Evola, as a call for a "purifying rite" of violence.[154] Their interpretation of Evola was common throughout the period, and such major terrorist groups as Costruiamo l'Azione, the Nuclei Armati Rivoluzionari, the Fronte Universitario di Azione Nazionale, and Terza Posizione found in his writings a philosophical justification for their violent campaigns. Different from Ordine Nuovo in their aggressive and specific appeal to alienated youth, they nevertheless belonged to the same ideological tradition in which Evola was the revered master.[155]

The right-wing strategy of tension has been a tragic fact of life in Italy since the end of World War II, and beginning with the Piazza Fontana explosion in Milan on 12 December 1969 this activity dramatically increased. In the years that followed, savage bombings and assassinations repeatedly brought home to the Italian people the extreme Right's power and will. Officially, the terror bombings have been crimes without authors. Although many neofascist terrorists are in jail for various offenses, prosecutors have not obtained convictions in the bombing cases, from Piazza Fontana to Bologna. While lamenting this lack, Judges Vito Zincani and Sergio Castaldo found on 14 June 1986 that the incontrovertible fact of the Bologna bombing—in their view a typical neofascist terrorist act in the pattern originating with the Piazza Fontana explosion—was this: "the tracing back of the massacre to the formations of the extreme Right [can be] in no way placed in doubt even if [it is] variously explained "[156]

They did not base this opinion on the public statements of the radical Right, for only in rare instances are such statements made, partly because the element of mystery reinforces public panic and disorientation and partly because the bombings are both the medium and the message. Other forms of evidence were not lacking, however. The judges made intelligent use of internal documents and the highly detailed testimony of numerous pentiti, most notably Paolo Aleandri, Sergio Calore, and Cristiano Fioravanti, who claimed that the surviving remnants of Ordine Nuovo helped form and guide the major neofascist violent groups of the late seventies.[157] Moreover, they did not ignore the cultural context of radical right-wing politics, characterized by a total contempt for the herd. In his courtroom testimony Mario Tuti, a neofascist *irriducibile*, allowed that, for the radical Right, mass bombings did not give rise to ethical perturbations.[158] A higher law called him and all other political soldiers to wage a war against the corrupt and corrupting system. In obedience to that law some innocent victims might have to be sacrificed, as in all wars. Finally, on one occasion police did capture a bomber at work, on 7 April 1973: Nico Azzi, then a *missino* who with other ordinovisti had recently reentered the party. Azzi's arrest possesses great historic value in linking Italy's distinctive form of right-wing terror with a particular ideological tradition.

Radical neofascist groups did not act alone, according to the Bologna judges. The terrorists had the support and protection of deviant elements in the secret services, of the criminal underworld, and of diverse conspiratorial groups.[159] The black bombings served a sinister political purpose for all these parties: the destabilization of Italian democracy so that a properly authoritarian government could get on with the necessary business of extirpating communism. At the same time the judges did not rule out the "existential" impulse as a factor in this terror; spectacular acts of violence doubtless would have an appeal to certain individuals suffering acute forms of alienation and anomie.

Evola's critique of democracy possessed a powerful appeal for many of the individuals and groups involved in the black terror. Examining the literature of radical neofascists, one judge found that Evola's name possessed an almost totemic power over them.[160] The parallel between Ordine Nuovo on the right and Autonomia Operaia on the left as transmitters of the Italian revolutionary traditions is striking; that so many alumni of these two organizations should have distinguished themselves as red and black terrorists cannot be ascribed to chance. As with Panzieri and Negri on the left, Evola on the right wrote about revolution. Not everybody who read him or came in contact with his argument adopted terrorism as a way of life, but some did, particularly those who coupled his critique of democracy with the practical revolutionary suggestions of Freda, Graziani, Delle Chiaie, and numerous other *cattivi maestri*. While philosophy does not explain everything about neofascist terrorism, it explains some things. The motivations of deviant secret service personnel, obsessed with a mortal vendetta against the Communists, or of power-seeking intriguers bear only a superficial and occasional resemblance to those of ordinovisti fanatics, who nevertheless remain a significant quantity in the black terror equation. No single explanation could encompass the variegated, multiform, and even contradictory subject of this terror. Nevertheless, as an antecedent in the history of contemporary Italy's radical Right, Evola performed the signal service of providing an ideological justification for the actions of some desperate reactionaries in an Italy overwhelmed by inflation, dispirited by unemployment, undermined by scandal, and traumatized by the Red Brigades.

EIGHT

The Crisis and Defeat of the Red Brigades

1980–1982

The summer roar of the radical Right in 1980 made a perfect contrast with the quiescence of the radical Left. The only sounds from the latter quarter well into the fall were the echoes of successful police raids on Red Brigade and Prima Linea hideouts. On 7 October alone the police arrested forty suspected terrorists in Piedmont, Lombardy, Emilia, and Tuscany. On the eighth, Paolo Zambianchi, one of Prima Linea's most notorious assassins, was captured, and the following day an organization founder and leader, Liviana Tosi, fell into a government dragnet. During the same period General Dalla Chiesa's men caught Walter Tobagi's killers, and at one stroke the XXVIII March Brigade was no more.

The Red Brigade response to the radical Left's reverses took both a theoretical and a practical shape. As for theory, the imprisoned historic nucleus of the Red Brigades still claimed to speak for the organization with an unimpeachable authority. In a document entitled "L'ape e il comunista: elementi per la critica marxista dell' economia politica e per la costruzione del programma di transizione al comunismo," they condemned the sectarianism that now afflicted Red Brigadism.[1] To Curcio, Franceschini, and the rest, all would be well if the comrades returned to the fundamentals of Marxism-Leninism. "Marx/Lenin repeatedly observed that . . ." remained a favorite introductory clause of these theorists. The misconceived departure from Marxism-Leninism, they averred, had led to disunity and crisis. "Back to Marx and Lenin" became their cry. The authors of "L'ape e il comunista" wanted to remind their followers of the communist vision with which they all had begun their battle against capitalism. Accordingly, in the first parts of their message they offered a refresher course on Marxist-Leninist terminology, complete with lengthy textual quotations. For Curcio, Franceschini, et al. the essential theoretical question for communists had to do with the meaning of Marxism-Leninism. That rightly understood, practical steps could be undertaken. They quoted Lenin himself on this point: "Without theory, no revolution."[2]

Far from containing anything theoretically new, "L'ape e il comunista" reflected Red Brigadism's traditional Marxist-Leninist point of view about revolutionary theory and practice. What the Red Brigadists had said before they now repeated, if with an unprecedented wealth of economic formulas, charts, graphs, and footnote references to the classic texts of Marxism-Leninism. Their justification for violence had always originated, they claimed, in Marx's words and Lenin's tactics. Marx himself, they reminded the world anew, had said repeatedly that capitalism would not fall easily, spontaneously, automatically, peacefully. Men would have to perform this operation in a necessarily violent manner. In the minds of the Red Brigadists, Marx pointed in the direction of what they as communists had to do. From Lenin they claimed to have received practical suggestions on how to wage a successful Marxist revolution—despite the ultimate degeneration of bolshevism into state capitalism.

The Red Brigades pictured the world as a victim of American and Soviet imperialism. These two camps had enslaved the proletariat. Because Italy lay in the American sphere of influence, however, NATO was the most available target for Italian anti-imperialist forces, of which the Red Brigades counted themselves the vanguard. This point, too, had been made in earlier Red Brigade documents, but in the fall of 1980 NATO received special mention and prolonged analysis, as a sign, events proved, of the new direction the movement would take. The Red Brigades continually searched for a popular issue that would serve as a basis of support for the Party of Combat they envisaged. Their search had resulted in repeated failures, and whatever else they had achieved a strong connection with the working class had eluded them. They now emphasized NATO's role as "the principal motor" of the imperialist system in the West. In their view that "supranational organization of military defense" for the multinationals had called upon the Italian government to create, at long last, some order in Italy. In concert these reactionary forces, led in Italy by the Christian Democrats ("this infamous race of pigs"), had devised the scandalous Piano Triennale for 1979–81 in an effort to impose neocorporativist restrictions on the workers.

A full-scale attack had to be mounted against this scheme, on the principle that every communist had the right to impose death on "the producers of death."[3] In practice that meant continued sabotage and guerrilla warfare in the factory. The capitalist state itself would be subjected to intensified pressure from the communist vanguards. In specific contradiction to the Italian Communist party, which had committed the unpardonable sin of yielding to the logic of democracy instead of Marxism, the Red Brigades proclaimed that the true cause of revolution could only be served by "encircling, neutralizing, and annihilating . . . imperialism."[4] In other words, the war against "the cliques of the state's imperialist bourgeoisie" would continue and expand.[5] In "Twenty Final Theses" they promised "one blow after another."[6] Their closing directions to the Red Brigades in the field were to destroy the Christian Democrats, resist the Piano Triennale, smash the capitalist command, strike the revisionists in the PCI, and eliminate NATO.

This call to arms signaled a new chapter in the revolutionary violence of the extreme Left. Attempting to thwart the state power that had pushed their fortunes to a dangerously low point, the Red Brigades and the remnants of Prima Linea joined forces in a jailbreak conspiracy at Nuoro on 27 October 1980. Nearly fifty terrorist convicts went on a rampage, hurling homemade bombs at security guards.

Despite the fury of their attack, they failed completely, and one terrorist, Roberto Ognibene, was badly wounded in the face and throat by a prematurely exploding bomb. At the same time Mafia or Camorra inmates took advantage of the confusion to murder two inmates with characteristic savagery.

Not every Red Brigade action in the fall of 1980 ended in failure. On 12 November, just as a colossal oil scandal was breaking—involving billions of lire and some of the highest officials in the Guardia di Finanza as well as prominent oil men and politicians—the Red Brigades effectively resumed the offensive. That morning a terrorist shot and killed Renato Briano, a forty-seven-year-old Milan personnel director, as he stood in the Metro on his way to work. The autumn offensive of the Red Brigades continued in Milan on 28 November when terrorists assassinated a fifty-four-year-old engineer, Manfredo Mazzanti. A Red Brigade caller exhorted: "Let us continue the campaign against the state and the bosses. Work less, everyone work, construct the organisms of mass revolution."[7]

Aided by the pentiti, General Dalla Chiesa reacted to this new terrorist onslaught with punishing blows. On the night and morning of 2–3 December 1980 anti-terrorist operations took place in nearly a dozen cities nationwide. In city after city terrorists were caught completely by surprise. The police made twenty-six arrests in all. Two exceedingly feared Prima Linea leaders, Susanna Ronconi and Roberto Rosso, surrendered. Hideouts were smashed, arsenals confiscated, and documents discovered in a series of raids described by authorities as the single most successful antiterrorist operation to date.

The tide of battle turned day by day now. Terrorists fought back on 11 December in Milan by kneecapping Maurizio Caramello, a fifty-three-year-old business executive, but that evening Red Brigade losses again heartened the nation. Carabinieri shot and killed Roberto Serafini, twenty-seven, and Walter Pezzoli, twenty-four, during a gun battle outside a Milan restaurant. Serafini had been a major figure in the Red Brigades, and a subsequent telephone call from the organization promised revenge for his death, at a rate of ten for one.

On the next night the Red Brigades kidnapped Judge Giovanni D'Urso, forty-eight, who was the director of Italy's penal institutions. Convinced that bulletproof cars and escorts were useless against terrorists, D'Urso traveled to and from work with no security arrangements of any kind. The Red Brigades took him easily on the streets of Rome. In exchange for "the executioner and jailer of thousands of proletarians, Giovanni D'Urso," they demanded that authorities shut down the special prison on the island of Asinara, off the Sardinian coast near Cagliari.[8] In the same document they called for the liberation of proletarian prisoners. Meanwhile, "the pig" D'Urso would undergo a proletarian trial.

Similar messages followed, and late in December government sources reported that even before D'Urso's kidnapping prison authorities had decided to close Asinara's nearly century-old facility, so isolated it was difficult to recruit guards for duty there. A political storm broke over this report, and the D'Urso case deeply divided the four parties supporting the government in power. To negotiate or not to negotiate; that was the question dividing Italy, as always when terrorist kidnappings occurred. Intransigents argued that to close Asinara now would make the government appear to be submitting to terrorist blackmail, whereas moderates countered that authorities had been handed a perfectly respectable solution to the dilemma posed by D'Urso's kidnapping. As this debate intensified the maximum security prison at Trani erupted in convict violence on the twenty-eighth. Imprisoned Red Brigadists led the revolt of some seventy inmates. Many guards were wounded and taken hostage before the Gruppi di Intervento Speciale (GIS) quelled the rising without further bloodshed.

Forty-eight hours after the Trani riots, on the last day of the year, the government formally announced the closing of Asinara. Nevertheless the Red Brigades continued to hold D'Urso. They threatened to continue doing so until the government met prior demands regarding the publication of their documents without excision, an end to the media blackout on the D'Urso case, and an assurance that there would be no reprisal against the rebel inmates at Trani.[9] Then in a document dated 14 January 1981 the Red Brigades declared that they had won "a great victory," which permitted them to grant "an act of magnanimity," the restoration of D'Urso to liberty.[10] In another demonstration of their uncanny ability to penetrate the tightest security arrangements and to embarrass the Italian police, the Red Brigades left D'Urso in an automobile nearly on the doorstep of the Ministry of Justice. His ordeal had lasted thirty-three days.

The D'Urso kidnapping was not the only year-end terrorist development in Italy. Despite the relentless pressure of Dalla Chiesa's antiterrorist offensive, the Red Brigades possessed sufficient power to execute major operations in addition to the D'Urso operation. While the judge's fate was still being weighed, the Red Brigades shocked Italy again with their daring. On the last day of the year two youths waited for over an hour in the Rome apartment building of a carabiniere general, Enrico Galvaligi, whom the Red Brigades described as Dalla Chiesa's "right arm" in the antiterrorist campaign.[11] They passed the time talking with the doorman, who later characterized his interlocutors as "very young, very normal."[12] When the general and his wife returned, having just come from mass and taken communion, the youths handed him a basket containing fruit, wine, and a *torrone*, presumably a holiday gift from a friend. The general reached into his pocket for a tip and produced a pair of one thousand lire bills. The youths had already drawn weapons and began firing, six shots in all. Two bullets hit him in the heart, and when doctors arrived they could do nothing but make a death pronouncement.

The fierce debate over the state's handling of the D'Urso kidnapping continued even after his release, but now the pace of events rushed with such speed that retrospective analysis gave way to the need of dealing with new developments. With the 5 February 1981 capture of Maurice Bignami, the last founding member of Prima Linea still at large, experts on terrorism certainly had something new of major significance to digest and analyze. Like Susanna Ronconi, Bignami was an alumnus of Autonomia Operaia who had gained notoriety as a terrorist. He had passed through the Potere Operaio experience as well and had been associated with Negri, Scalzone, and Piperno. On 21 March 1977 Bignami had been arrested in Negri's home in Milan but was later released for lack of evidence. The connection between Negri and Bignami lent added support to the *colpevolista* thesis in the 7 *aprile* controversy. In mid-February 1981 General Dalla Chiesa told a television interviewer that the difference between Curcio and Negri was that the Red Brigade chief went on terrorist missions whereas the professor sent terrorists on missions "and at the same time asked for financial support from the National Council for Research."[13]

The events of late 1980 and early 1981 drew attention to the continued strength of the Red Brigades in Milan and Rome. Indeed, they struck again in Milan on 17 February, killing forty-four-year-old Luigi Marangoni, medical director of the city's Policlinico.[14] Milan was also the scene of a 12 March kneecapping attack by the Red Brigades against Alberto Valenzasca, an executive. On the twenty-seventh, seven or eight brigatisti escaped with 130 million lire in a Rome robbery at the Banco Nazionale del Lavoro.

The success of the Red Brigades in Rome was offset by a stunning disaster for them in Milan on 4 April, when police captured the organization's military commander, Mario Moretti, and Enrico Fenzi, a literature professor and critically acclaimed Dante and Petrarch scholar who had become a terrorist leader. The capture of Moretti occasioned jubilation at General Dalla Chiesa's headquarters, but the relatively unimpaired Rome column continued to sow destruction. On the seventh the column killed Raffaele Cinotti, a twenty-eight-year-old prison guard at Rebibbia. This Red Brigade murder mingled in the public mind with other killings during the same period of convicts and prison personnel by the Mafia and the Camorra. Vendettas over drugs and extremist politics spread a pall of death over Italian prisons, and their wardens felt helpless.

The spring 1981 offensive of the Red Brigades began to assume its full force in late April when the organization successfully kidnapped four individuals. The cumulative impact of these kidnappings was enormous and left no doubt that the war against terrorism had taken a dramatic turn for the worse. The first one occurred in Naples on 27 April. Red Brigade terrorists kidnapped Ciro Cirillo, a regional assessor, and murdered his two bodyguards while kneecapping his secretary. This bloody abduction once again illustrated the ineffectiveness of bulletproof cars and escorts against terrorist attacks. The advantage of surprise was always overwhelming in these actions.

In Cirillo the Red Brigades hoped they had struck a symbolic target. Little known nationally, he long had been a prominent politician on his home ground. After the 23 November 1980 earthquake Cirillo had directed the relief operation but did not win the love of many Neapolitans when aid was slowed by the inevitable snags for which the southern bureaucracy in particular had a legendary reputation. Now, as part of the ransom for Cirillo, the Red Brigades demanded that housing be provided for earthquake survivors whose homes had been destroyed.[15] They thought of this demand as a Robin Hood gesture and hoped it would provide an opening for Red Brigadism in the south.

Another predictable development occurred immediately after the kidnapping and shootings: public disputes between rival Italian leaders over whether or not the government should negotiate with the terrorists. Strong precedents existed for both points of view. Those opposed to negotiations cited the Moro case, those in favor the recent D'Urso case. As usual the public airing of these viewpoints made the government look like what it was: deeply divided and totally incapable of even pretending that its actions proceeded from a coherent, carefully thought out, and prudently executed strategy.

The nation's daily regimen of front-page stories about Cirillo was interrupted on 12 May when Pope John Paul II fell with serious bullet wounds at the hands of a Turkish terrorist, Mehemet Ali Agca. Three days later, while the world held its breath in fright and shock over the spectacle of this assault on the vicar of Christ, the Red Brigades again attacked a leader of the Neapolitan Christian Democrats, Rosario Giovine. Four terrorists overpowered Giovine, placed a propaganda placard around his neck, photographed him, and shot him six times in the leg.

Then on 20 May the second kidnapping occurred. Five Red Brigadists appeared at the home of Giuseppe Taliercio, director of Montedison in Porto Marghera. His wife innocently let them in while the family was at its midday meal. Announcing their true identity, the terrorists tied and gagged Mrs. Taliercio and the two children. They spent forty-five minutes examining company documents and finally left, taking Taliercio with them. The Red Brigades subsequently justified his kidnapping by denouncing him as "a servant of the imperialist multinationals"; having mercilessly exploited the workers of Montedison for more than thirty years, he would now "have to face proletarian justice."[16]

In the midst of these multiple terrorist crises, just one day after a 350-million-lire Red Brigade robbery of a Rome supermarket, the Forlani government resigned on May 26. Government scandals arising out of the sensational mid-May disclosures about the Propaganda 2 (P2) Masonic Lodge of Licio Gelli, the so-called Venerable One, had been the last outrage—coming on top of ever-mounting financial improprieties, led by Roberto Calvi's Banco Ambrosiano debacle, and the more respectable but no less ruinous problem of inflation. All the suspicions about government-aided right-wing plots against the Italian republic now appeared to be confirmed.[17] Generals of the army and the carabinieri, political notables, journalists, editors, and magistrates had joined this mysterious Masonic organization, whose actual aims mattered less at this moment than its perceived aims. Even Gelli's enemies on the Left did not claim to have certain knowledge of a precise P2 attack on the government, and the newspapers were filled with mainly suppositious reports about the organization.[18]

It appeared that Gelli was building a *grande destra*, or conservative coalition, with the complicity of American supporters in and out of the United States government. A broadly based network of Italian members, perhaps unaware of any overall plan, were manipulated, insofar as possible in the given circumstances of a particular situation, into doing the Venerable One's will.[19] It would take years for Parliament and the courts to make even preliminary judgments about P2, but in the spring of 1981 the scandal had a profoundly debilitating effect on the Italian government, which in the wake of these revelations appeared more than ever to be constitutionally indisposed toward democratic practices. It remained to be seen how the radical Left would exploit the P2 windfall.

With the untimely demise of the Forlani government, a leaderless Italy faced the grim prospect of having to cope with rapidly proliferating political scandals, deepening financial crisis, and intensifying terrorist activity. Of these three Sisyphean tasks, terrorism provided the most brutal immediate challenge. Kneecappings in Rome and Naples preceded the third Red Brigade kidnapping of the spring. This one happened in Milan on 3 June, and it involved Renzo Sandrucci, an executive for Alfa Romeo. On the eleventh, Red Brigade kidnappers struck for the fourth time. Their victim was a twenty-five-year-old San Benedetto electrical worker whose relatively humble station in life normally would have excluded him from the plans or even the consciousness of the Red Brigades. However, he suffered from a singular misfortune. His name was Roberto Peci. He was the brother of Patrizio Peci, the great pentito, to whom the Red Brigades referred in a communication as an "infamous louse."[20]

With the Roberto Peci kidnapping the Red Brigades wanted to strike terror into the hearts of the pentiti, to silence them through fear for family and loved ones. At the same time the state demonstrated its commitment to encourage terrorist repentance. On 17 June a Turin court invoked the "Cossiga Law" and handed down extremely light sentences for the pentiti while condemning unrepentant terrorists to long prison terms. In this same courtroom Red Brigade *duri* threatened death for Roberto Peci, and three days later the organization warned "the traitors of yesterday, today [and] tomorrow" that to betray the revolution meant to be annihilated sooner or later by the revolution.[21] The Red Brigades claimed that Roberto, who had been arrested in December 1979, had given the police information leading to the arrest of Patrizio and to the worst disasters in their history.

Of the four abductions that spring, the first to be concluded was the Taliercio case. The Red Brigades murdered him on 5 July 1981. The police discovered his bullet-riddled body near the Montedison petrochemical factory he had directed. An autopsy revealed that someone first stunned Taliercio and then two gunmen emptied their pistols into him. Contrary to the expectations of the Red Brigades, this act of the people's justice provoked not a surge of revolutionary fervor and gratitude among the workers but a protest march of sixty thousand demonstrators in Mestre against "the Nazi Red Brigadists."

On 22 July 1981, the same day Ali Agca received a life sentence for his attempt to kill the pope, the Red Brigades announced that they would free two of the kidnap victims, Cirillo and Sandrucci. Held captive for fifty-five days, Alfa Romeo executive Sandrucci was the first to be released, on the twenty-third. Then the following day Cirillo went free after eighty-eight days in a people's prison, the longest kidnapping in the history of Italian terrorism. The Red Brigades bragged that they received an enormous ransom for Cirillo, later estimated to be as high as five billion lire. The Italian government heatedly denied that it had paid anything to the terrorists, calling their statement a grave provocation. Despite this denial Italy was thick with rumors about ransom money. The complete truth about the Cirillo case may never be known, any more than about the Moro case, but the Red Brigades—through negotiations with the underworld and the secret services—did receive a ransom.[22] The odor of the Cirillo scandal clung to Italian politics for months.

Now the Peci family began to hope that Roberto might be released soon. His mother publicly begged the Red Brigades to be merciful. His wife, five months pregnant, at last began to take heart after weeks of torment, intensified by her strong suspicion that the authorities had never given the Peci kidnapping serious attention. At the beginning of this ordeal a carabiniere officer, noting her swollen figure, had reacted to the hysterical woman's tears by saying, "But why are you crying! Your husband is probably enjoying himself with another woman."[23] The agony of weeks began to lift for her when Sandrucci and Cirillo returned to their families, and she refused to be discouraged by the continued threat of the Red Brigades to kill those who infiltrated the revolutionary movement.

Revolutionary vengeance proved mightier than the hope of the Peci women. "The Revolution is not to be tried, the proletariat tries the bourgeoisie," the Red Brigades had insisted; and by the bourgeoisie they meant as well its collaborators.[24] On 3 August the fifty-five-day Peci drama ended when, on instructions from the terrorists, the police found his body inside a building on the site of a garbage dump, seated on the floor and leaning against a wall. He had been shot eleven times, and his face had been disfigured beyond recognition. Before killing Peci the terrorists had blindfolded him, blocked up his ears, crossed his hands on his chest, and bound him—to make him think he was about to be freed. Peci probably did not realize what was happening until one of the killers put the barrel of a gun to his right ear. This official reconstruction of events proved to be essentially accurate when authorities later discovered, in a Red Brigade archive, a film, complete with explanatory voice-over, of Peci's execution.

His father identified the body. He broke into tears, embraced his dead son, and cried "Assassins, assassins. They have killed him for me. They killed a worker."[25] The Red Brigades had a different view of their conduct, expressed in a sign they left on the wall overlooking Peci's body: "Death to traitors." In a resolution they left near the corpse, the Red Brigades asserted that annihilation was the only way to intervene between the metropolitan proletariat and traitors. However, once again the Red Brigades misjudged the sentiments and values of the Italian people. Instead of being perceived as an act of the people's justice, the crime was widely condemned.

Although the newly installed government of Giovanni Spadolini vowed to devote all its energy and resources to the war on terrorism, autumn 1981 opened with a renewal of the terrorist offensive. Prison personnel and policemen remained preferred targets in diverse assassinations and assassination attempts. At the same time the arrest of Pietro Silvano Sorbi, an Italsider department head, as a Red Brigadist drew renewed attention to the presence of terrorists in the factories. Sorbi, who lived with his mother and brother in one of the best residential sections of Genoa, was the first white-collar worker to be connected directly with the Red Brigades. He had been completely above suspicion. It was utterly inconceivable to his colleagues that Sorbi had been involved with terrorism, let alone a leader of the so-called Italsider column, but the storm of pentiti confessions in these months had exposed a dense undergrowth of deep-cover operations. The police intensified their investigation of the great northern factories as nests of terrorist activity.

In November and December more policemen died in battles with terrorists of both the Left and the Right. The funeral for one of these victims, Elio Capobianco, on 7 December provided some nervous moments for government leaders. Coins and insults were hurled at President Sandro Pertini, President of the Senate Amintore Fanfani, President of the Chamber of Deputies Nilde Jotti, and Minister of the Interior Virginio Rognoni as they appeared at the church. A multitude of Capobianco's relatives from Naples was there, and his father turned to Pertini and said in an anguished voice, "Ciro, twenty-one years old, twenty-one years old. . . . "[26]

In his sermon Cardinal Poletti made an impassioned plea for an end to violence, but his words did not soothe those in the audience who wanted a restoration of the death penalty. Even the police took up the cry of "buffoni" as Italy's foremost political leaders filed out of the church. Bodyguards hurriedly escorted Fanfani, Jotti, and Rognoni to waiting cars, but Pertini refused to leave the funeral this way. He wanted to hear what the officers had to say. Those nearest Pertini applauded this gesture, but in the background other policemen continued to make abusive accusations about the cowardly and feeble manner in which the government was dealing with terrorism. Pertini answered, "I want to see the person who has the courage to say anything to me. I am always in the front line. I am sadder than you."[27] No one took up this challenge, but the public eruption at the Capobianco funeral demonstrated that if devastating lacerations now marked the face of terrorism the government itself was visibly in confusion and under growing pressure to win a decisive victory against its tormenting adversary.

On 14 December 1981 the Communist government in Poland suppressed the voice of the Polish workers, Solidarity. The Italian Communist leader Enrico Berlinguer appeared on television to declare that with these events in Poland the Revolution of 1917 had completely exhausted itself. *L'Unità* denounced the Polish government's martial law policies, and once again the official Left despaired of the Soviet model. While renewed leftist soul searching and predictable exultation of the Right commingled in Italy's densely ideological civic atmosphere, Red Brigade terrorists marshaled their dwindling though still sizable resources for what some of them hoped would be the breakthrough to revolution.

In "L'ape e il comunista" the Red Brigades had identified NATO as "the multinational army of the imperialist counterrevolution."[28] They had further observed, "We must begin to sabotage this machine of death, that for the metropolitan proletariat means internal preventive counterrevolution and external war of aggression."[29] "WAR ON NATO," they had concluded. Implementing this policy on 17 December, the Red Brigades kidnapped General James Lee Dozier, a fifty-year-old decorated Vietnam War veteran. At the time of his kidnapping in Verona he was deputy chief of staff for logistics and administration at NATO's headquarters in Southern Europe. Regarded by his superiors as a model officer in look and manner, he jogged every morning in a blue running suit before appearing punctually at work. His only limitation appeared to be that in a year and a half he had not succeeded in learning to understand or to speak Italian very well.

NATO had provided no security for him or his family. When four young men masquerading as plumbers appeared and announced that they had come to fix a water problem, Mrs. Dozier, who understood very little Italian, opened the door for them. Once inside they drew pistols. Dozier was subdued with a blow to the head from a pistol butt. The intruders placed him unconscious in a trunk, which they deposited in a van parked outside. They bound Mrs. Dozier hand and foot, covering her ears and mouth with adhesive tape. Almost four hours later, after banging her head against the wall and floor to attract the attention of neighbors, she was freed and alerted the police.

The next day authorities announced that the Red Brigades had claimed credit for the Dozier kidnapping, an action that involved the participation of columns from the Veneto, Milan, Naples, and Rome. The actual abduction was carried out by the Venice-based Anna Maria Ludmann-Cecilia brigade. The four kidnappers used walkie-talkies to communicate with as many as a dozen accomplices outside the building. An anonymous caller described the first American victim of the Red Brigades as "the hangman of NATO" and, without indicating conditions for Dozier's release, declared that the general was being held in a "people's prison where he will be judged by the proletariat."[30]

Experts voiced pessimism about Dozier's chances for survival. He would not be a submissive and compliant prisoner; the effect of his personality on the Red Brigades might be abrasive in the extreme, leading to an early execution. Moreover, in all the kidnappings of the Red Brigades only once had the police been able to help the victims in any way. The one exception had been the 1975 rescue of Vittorio Vallarino Gancia. In every other case the terrorists had overmatched the police. It was therefore not deeply reassuring when Prime Minister Spadolini promised the biggest manhunt since the search for Aldo Moro in 1978.

The first written Red Brigade communication in the Dozier case was a six-page leaflet found in a garbage can near Verona's railroad station on 19 December. This document spelled out the implications of principles set forth the previous year in "L'ape e il comunista" regarding the need for an international strategy against imperialism. Then on 27 December an anonymous caller directed the ANSA news agency to a trash can on a Milan street, where the Red Brigades had deposited an enlarged photograph of General Dozier, a sixteen-page leaflet announcing his proletarian trial, and a 188-page "Risoluzione della Direzione Strategica." Because the Red Brigades stated no demands or conditions for the general's release, Italian officials feared that he might already be dead or condemned to death.

The leaflet was a call to arms against "the domination of American imperialism" by attacking the structure of its military occupation in Italy: NATO.[31] The Red Brigades proposed a united revolutionary front against the repressive institutions, national and international, that threatened to turn Italy into an arsenal of U.S. nuclear weapons. The "executioner" and "swine" Dozier was an agent of this counterrevolutionary process, in their view. To them he was an "assassin" who had responded to the call of U.S. imperialism wherever its interests had been jeopardized by the legitimate revolutionary aspirations of the proletariat. Now this gendarme for the multinationals and symbol of NATO missiles would face the people's justice. The leaflet also contained a précis of points that were analyzed with unexampled attention to detail in the "Risoluzione della Direzione Strategica."

In the "Risoluzione," a nearly epic account of the prospects for revolution in 1981–82, the Red Brigades created the impression of having surveyed, in the company of Marx, the sad halls and circles of their personal Inferno, capitalism. In the final depths of the Land of the Dead, in the frozen lake of Cocytus, stood the three-mouthed Satan gorging on the Christian Democrats, the PCI, and the unions, and it was wearing an Uncle Sam suit with legions of Italian demon helpers from across the political spectrum scurrying about to do its bidding. The main theme of the document was "war to destroy the project, the men and the means of imperialist war."[32]

The Italian and United States governments agreed not to negotiate with the Red Brigades for Dozier's release, but behind this outward resolve the resurgence of terrorism could not be denied. Even with the help of experts from West Germany and the United States, the Italian authorities by year's end had turned up no clues in the case. Then, on 4 January 1982, the Red Brigades struck in Rovigo, where an assault team of twenty commandos freed Susanna Ronconi and three other female terrorists from prison. The escape of Ronconi, one of the renowned veterans of left-wing terrorism and a prototypal instance of how Autonomia Operaia had functioned in part as an annex for terrorism, had a desolating effect on the government.[33] President Pertini asked a reporter, "Would you please tell me why under fascism no one ever succeeded in escaping from prison? The truth is [with us] a surveillance system does not exist. You will see, now even Curcio will escape."[34] This outburst expressed the frustrations of many Italians at the beginning of 1982.

Then on 9 January the police captured Giovanni Senzani in his Rome hideout. This forty-two-year-old terrorist, named by numerous pentiti as the real leader of the Red Brigades since the period of Moro's kidnapping, had been a leading expert on Italian prisons and had written a well-known book, *Economia politica della criminalità*. A respected professor of criminology at the University of Florence, he also had been in residence at the University of California, Berkeley. Senzani's identity as a Red Brigadist had only been established in 1981 after he had gone underground. Prior to that time he had access to prisons and attended leading international conferences on criminality. At a 1975 conference in Lisbon, Judges Minervini and Tartaglione had been present; so had a medical doctor named Paolella. All three were later killed by the Red Brigades. The authorities claimed that Senzani had brought the three victims to the attention of the Red Brigades as inveterate foes of the revolutionary Left.

In Senzani's hideout the police found numerous weapons, including four ground-to-air missiles of exceptional power. Documents discovered there revealed that Senzani had been planning an attack—featuring missiles, machine guns, and bombs—on the next national council meeting of the Christian Democratic party, scheduled for 22 January. Senzani's plans called for as many as one hundred Christian Democratic delegates and policemen to be killed in this action. Also in preparation was a scheme to kidnap Cesare Romiti, the number two man at Fiat and a leading figure in the Italian Association of Industrialists. The terrorists had already built a prison for him. In addition Senzani had begun to make notations for an attack on one of the superprisons, probably the one at Trani. The police found notes for two other terrorist projects: attacks on the Rome police headquarters in Via Nazionale and a military barracks in the city. Finally, the extremely detailed archive in Senzani's apartment contained thick dossiers, including photographs, daily schedules, and personality profiles for six national union leaders who had been marked for kneecapping or death. In January 1982 Italy had been on the eve of a terror that would have been novel in its destructiveness and scope.

This staggering reverse for the Red Brigades was followed by an even worse disaster when an informer gave police the address of Dozier's prison. On the night of 27 January police surrounded an apartment house on Via Pindemonte in Padua, but a special NOCS (Nucleo Operativo Centrale di Sicurezza) team waited until morning to act so that their preliminary movements would go unnoticed in the hubbub of street life. Shortly before the assault, heavily armed officers cordoned off the neighborhood and turned on a bulldozer to cover the noise of the raid. The NOCS agents, masked and protected by bulletproof vests, burst through the apartment door. A terrorist jailer was pointing a gun at Dozier's head, but a member of the assault team swiftly disarmed him. Dozier had been kept in a pup tent that the terrorists had pitched in the apartment. The NOCS agents found him with his hands tied, dressed in a blue running suit, and barefoot. He was bearded and underweight but otherwise in apparent good health. The agents captured five terrorists on the spot, including two women: long-time fugitive Emilia Libera and Manuella Frascella, the daughter of a noted doctor, who served as an errand person for the kidnappers. The only other name released at the time was that of Antonio Savasta, twenty-six, the one-time leader of the Rome column.[35]

The Via Pindemonte prison of General Dozier yielded five machine pistols, seven hand grenades, six packages of plastic explosives, quantities of ammunition, about twenty thousand dollars in lire, false identity cards, and files of information on political leaders in the area as well as on other prominent individuals. The most notable discovery, however, was that the Red Brigades would choose not to fight when cornered. This humiliation had a blighting effect on the organization's élan and dramatically accelerated a decline that had been fully in evidence since the pentiti-inspired raids and arrests of the previous year. It proved to be a disaster from which they could not recover, and in the aftermath of Dozier's rescue pentiti came forward in greater numbers than ever. More raids and arrests followed as a gigantic wave of police power came crashing down on remaining terrorist structures.

The confessions of Savasta and dozens of other former terrorists at the Aldo Moro kidnapping trial, beginning on 14 April 1982, nearly completed the ruin of the Red Brigades and similar revolutionary organizations. The proceedings featured sixty-three defendants, nine of whom remained at large; 399 witnesses; more than a hundred lawyers; and 100,000 pages of testimony. Different cages were used for the pentiti, the *dissociati* (those who had abondoned terrorism, but would not name names), and the *irriducibili* (unreconstructed terrorists). Fifteen hundred policemen and carabinieri guarded the courtroom.

Red Brigade remnants tried to disrupt the trial. They continued to kill and maim people, but without accomplishing their main objective.[36] If the Red Brigades had not yet become a mere artifact of history, they could no longer pretend that revolution was in the offing. Mere survival and occasional forays into the field were all they could realistically manage.

The pentiti took the stand and told more or less similar "suburban dropout" stories, involving extraparliamentary Left movements in the area of Autonomia Operaia and Lotta Continua. It was not enough simply to want communism, which all of them had wanted; to become a Red Brigadist they had to pass an examination in Marxism-Leninism.[37] The successful recruit would then set out on the usual path for a regular brigatista rosso: torching cars, kneecapping the enemies of the people, and, finally, killing them. Recruits came primarily from the turbulent university world, most of the money from kidnappings and robberies—an assertion that undercut the theory of some experts that the Red Brigades were financed by the Soviet Union's KGB.[38] The Red Brigades and parallel terrorist organizations had come into existence because reformism's triumph had created a vacuum on the official Left, which a host of extraparliamentary Left organizations attempted to fill; in the process some of them had turned to violence according to precepts celebrated by Marx and put into practice by Lenin. At least that is what the pentiti thought they were doing. By following the premise of the revolutionary Left to its logical conclusion they reasoned that Red Brigadism was the only possible answer. They thought of this position as the translation of Marx and Lenin from universal theory to Italian political fact in the 1970s.

The 3 September 1982 Mafia murder of General Dalla Chiesa, who had been Italy's chief in the war on terrorism before being transferred to fight the Mafia, provoked a deafening cry of outrage and recrimination nationwide, but even this disheartening loss did nothing to retard the sharp decline of the Red Brigades.[39] Though fading rapidly, the Red Brigades still possessed enough resources to keep their revolutionary cause flickering. Intermittent terrorist acts continued to injure Italian public life. On 21 October 1982 Red Brigade terrorists held up a Turin bank and executed two guards, on the principle that servants of the bourgeoisie had to be taught a lesson. Mounting personnel and armaments losses did not prevent the Red Brigades from undertaking sporadic raids and acts of reprisal either, as on 3 December, when they critically wounded a Rebibbia prison doctor, Giuseppina Galfo.

On 24 January 1983 the court handed down its judgment in the Moro trial. The act of sentencing in Italy's most sensational trial within living memory took just sixteen minutes. Thirty-two life sentences and a total of 316 years of imprisonment were meted out to the sixty-three defendants.[40] The pentiti received minimal sentences.

Two days later Renato Curcio declared from his prison cell in Palmi that the war was over: "The armed struggle has been short-circuited, it did not succeed in making the great leap forward, it fell to the ground. Its protagonists can only mourn, liberating themselves from its ghost."[41] Scores of people had been killed or wounded and hundreds more were now in prison *per errore*—by error of Marxist diviners who misread the signs of the times. That is the epitaph of Red Brigadism, a movement that for several years convulsed the seventh largest industrial power in the world.

Curcio now learned that he did not have the power to stop the revolutionary movement he helped start. From the moment of conception in the Metropolitan

Collective of Milan the Red Brigades had risen to a position of power that enabled them to threaten the state as no revolutionary organization had done since the Fascist takeover in 1922. Now the Red Brigades had come tumbling down in ruinous defeat; they existed as leaderless fragments, each with its own independent will to survive as a nucleus for the communist revolution to come, each still capable of wounding Italian society though lacking the strength to implement a plan for revolution. The Red Brigades no longer existed as an organization; it was a scream of pain and rage resonating over the rubble of its own collapse.

For the next two years government experts, pentiti, and the Red Brigades themselves warned about the resurgence of terrorism in Italy, but terrorist acts of all kinds declined precipitately after 1982. After this date the Red Brigade tone was set by their murder of Germana Stefanini, an elderly woman who worked in Rebibbia prison, as part of a jailhouse vendetta. On 3 May 1983 they wounded University of Rome professor Gino Giugni, selected for revolutionary justice because this Socialist academic was one of the emblematic figures of reformism in the PSI. Imprisoned irriducibili terrorists hailed the attack on Giugni as the opening shot of a new Red Brigade campaign in the spring of 1983, but nothing of the kind occurred. A terrorist fiasco followed instead when on 17 May three Red Brigadists bungled a post-office robbery attempt. One of them escaped but later surrendered, telling authorities she had nowhere to go. The terror network had been largely dismantled.

The dark corners of leftist terrorism yielded some more of their secrets in the 7 aprile and Rosso-Tobagi trials that got under way in Rome and Milan during the late winter and spring of 1983. As these so-called maxi-trials moved ponderously toward their respective days of judgment, controversy was fueled by contradictory testimony regarding the central legal issues. For example, in the Negri trial neither the prosecutor nor the defense experienced any difficulty in finding cooperative witnesses. Numerous pentiti described Autonomia Operaia as a schoolroom for terrorism from which they themselves had graduated. For them Negri had been the arch cattivo maestro of Italy's lost terrorist generation. To be sure, the code language of radical Marxists, so rich in high-sounding euphemisms, made it unnecessary for Negri to use the word terrorism itself. Nevertheless, the awful reality of terrorism had received a powerful impetus from Negri's corrupting genius, these pentiti asserted.

Their argument against Negri was threefold: first, through his books and lectures he had cultivated the seed of violence in Italy; second, he had met with Curcio, and they had discussed a plan of attack on the capitalist state; third, he was guilty of planning numerous robberies as well as of involvement in the Saronio kidnapping and murder. Marco Barbone, one of Tobagi's assassins, was the most vindictive of Negri's former followers in Autonomia Operaia. He offered his own ideological itinerary as a typical example of how radical youths had been led astray by Negri. On the second point Mauro Borromeo, the former administrative director of Catholic University in Milan, made damaging charges. A long-time supporter of Autonomia Operaia, he had become one of Negri's sharpest critics. In the beginning, Borromeo explained, ideal motives, noble ends, and the tedium of modern life had led him into the world of left-wing political activism. Negri seemed to promise the glamor, risks, and fulfillment of partisan life. Under this spell Borromeo had allowed his villa to be used for a 1974 meeting between Negri and Curcio, two partisan chiefs discussing the revolution. As for the third part of the charge against Negri, Carlo Casirati, an underworld figure, testified that Autonomia Operaia had recruited him to perform kidnappings.

Following this testimony the prosecution explained that tactical differences alone separated Autonomia Operaia from the Red Brigades; their objectives had been identical. Apart from the matter of timing, the terrorists had attempted to bring about the revolution that Negri's journal, *Rosso*, had called for, and only a fool or a knave would claim otherwise. The violence of the autonomi came from somewhere, and Negri et al. were asking people to believe that the followers had acted against the express orders of the leaders. The independent testimony of so many former autonomi could not be nullified by Negri's wholly imaginary pacifism. The government's capital mistake, according to the prosecutor, lay in having allowed such an infamous antidemocratic threat to go unchecked for years. The state had been too passive in the face of repeated provocations from the radical Left, and only now, after the revolutionary project had been almost completely smashed, were some of its surviving proponents, such as Negri, arguing that they really had something other than revolution in mind all along.

Even before taking the witness stand, Negri pleaded his own case in a two-part article that he helped to write, "Do You Remember Revolution?"[42] He and his fellow authors conceded that they were part of the revolutionary movement, but this movement could not be equated with terrorism. On the contrary, only with a complete disregard for the facts could the movement be divorced from the country's history: if terrorism meant revolution, then tens of thousands of Italians were terrorists. Potere Operaio and Autonomia Operaia mirrored a genuine social upheaval but did not create it. Earlier Negri had insisted, "It seems to me erroneous to assert an unambiguous relationship between the generally developed anti-union polemic in the movement of the Marxist left and the military practice of the Red Brigades."[43] Negri did recognize that terrorist groups were "the tip of the iceberg of the Movement"—he even called them "a variable of the Movement gone crazy"—but:

> At the same time this does not mean that the Red Brigade comrades should not be respected. For it is necessary to have some respect for all those who are seeking proletarian communist goals, even as one deeply criticizes their "regicide" strategy, which is contrary to the premises of Marxism. Marx himself tipped his hat to Felice Orsini.[44]

In his courtroom testimony Negri continued to emphasize what he earlier had called the "huge and dramatic difference" between his position and that of the Red Brigades.[45] He did confess to moral responsibility for having written some "bad literature" in these years. Beyond this, Negri claimed to be guilty only of practicing his profession as a teacher and writer by reflecting on the problems of the day. In his mind and in the minds of many intellectuals, 7 *aprile* stood revealed as a gross attempt by the state to abrogate freedom of thought and expression.[46]

In June 1983 Negri benefited from the laws governing parliamentary immunity and went free. Elected as a Radical member of Parliament, he left prison while the court continued to hear his case. Italy's ninth Parliament—the most fragmented in the country's postwar history—opened on 11 July with a strong protest against Negri. The "pope of Autonomia" took his seat amid wild disorder. The dignity of Parliament, frequently compromised, disappeared entirely. Parliament immediately set up a commission to investigate his case. On 2 September, with Italy and much of the rest of the world in dismay over the Soviet Union's shooting down of a South Korean jumbo jet over Soviet territory the previous day, Negri reacted with disgust and impatience when this parliamentary commission recommended that he should be arrested again: "These people do not know what they are saying . . . they have not even read the court proceedings. These are the people who are governing us—and then they wonder when people come to shoot them."[47]

Some observers remained skeptical when Negri later claimed that he did not raise the specter of assassination as a threat, and controversy over the 7 *aprile* affair continued at white heat. By a vote of 300 to 293 the Chamber of Deputies decided, on 21 September, to have Negri arrested again, but he had already fled into Parisian exile. On 13 June 1984, the day following Enrico Berlinguer's death from an apoplectic stroke, Negri received a thirty-year sentence. Another court overturned this ruling and rejected, in effect, the so-called Calogero theorem, according to which Negri had been "the grand old man of the Red Brigades.[48] Appeals are still pending. No single trial could settle the many issues involved in Negri's case, least of all he vexing problem that Camus described as comfortable murder—the intellectual ensconced in his study, inciting others to make bloody sacrifices to the god of history.

Ambiguity pervaded the Rosso-Tobagi trial in Milan as well. Nowhere was the credibility of the pentiti more passionately negated than here. Ulderico Tobagi, Walter's father, struck the most telling blows. He could not overcome his grief. Later he would tell an interviewer that everyone had always envied him for having such a wonderful son. Even as a child Walter seemed too good to be true. Papa Tobagi never had to discipline him, and he was always a hard worker: "straightforward, good, kind, affectionate."[49] The professional success that came in such abundance so early was clearly the reward of a talent sedulously nurtured and a life virtuously lived. In court Walter's father attacked the *pentito* law. Barbone et al., so eloquent and even philosophical about their cruel action, merited no trust, Tobagi felt, in illuminating the tragedy of his son's murder. He reminded the court that these pentiti were assassins who could only demonstrate the authenticity of their repentance if they agreed to pay the consequences of their crimes without discount.

On 28 November 1983 a volley of whistles and shouts of "loathsome bastards" greeted the court's verdict that Barbone and the rest were free men, thanks to the pentito law. Ulderico Tobagi claimed that for him the sentence was tantamount to having his son killed a second time. No one could give him Walter back, but to have his son's murderers walking the streets was a gross miscarriage of justice. He declared, "I pray that God will pardon them, a father's heart cannot."[50]

The release of Tobagi's killers set off an explosive polemic in Italy over the moral character and practical utility of the pentito law. Defenders pointed out that Barbone alone had provided information leading to more than 150 arrests and that without the pentiti, terrorism might still be a scourge. On the other side of the argument critics bitterly asked how such a law could slake Ulderico Tobagi's thirst for justice. Moreover, his question about the character of the pentiti raised nagging doubts about how much reliance could be placed on their evidence. To be sure, the cumulative testimony of the pentiti has raised more questions about the major terrorist episodes than it has answered.

In the years to come there would be no dearth of legal action against terrorists, Left and Right, but the prospect for definitive answers in these cases remains dim. Most of the trials on the Right have ended in exoneration—for lack of evidence—of those charged. The thousands of pages generated by court proceedings dealing with left-wing terrorism present a dauntingly complex historical record that contains evidence to refute the comprehensive thesis of any researcher.[51] The time has not yet come for definitive judgments on Italy's age of lead. For some of the major terrorist episodes—the Moro affair, the Cirillo case, the Piazza Fontana bombing—it may never come. Moreover, on the Left small groups of Red Brigadists have stood their ground since 1983, stubbornly refusing to forgo the dream of a Marxist utopia. Though hardly more than a vestigial presence, they succeeded from 1984 to 1987 in revalidating their terrorist credentials with annual political murders: Leamon R. Hunt, the U.S. diplomat, on 15 February 1984; Professor Ezio Tarantelli on 27 March 1985; Lando Conti, the former mayor of Florence, on 10 February 1986; Giuseppe Scravaglieri and Rolando Lanari, policemen, on 14 February 1987; and General Licio Giorgieri on 20 March 1987. The state, proclaiming itself victorious on this front in the war against terrorism, must still deal with deadly if minuscule remnants of the most traumatic revolutionary challenge in the history of the republic.

At the same time only a rash prophet would predict that Italy has endured the last of its right-wing terror bombings, especially in view of what happened on Christmas eve 1984. At a site not far from the Italicus explosion of 4 August 1974 between Prato and Bologna, a train once again became the target of a terrorist attack. This time it was the 904 Naples-to-Milan run with fourteen densely crowded carriages. Many of the passengers had been forced to stand in the aisles. As it approached the Apennine tunnel, the longest in Europe, the train was only a minute or so behind schedule. A few minutes after seven in the evening, midway through the tunnel, seven to eight kilos of TNT exploded in the fifth car from the end. Windows were blown out and into the faces of many passengers. The force of the explosion propelled four bodies out of the train. One witness told a reporter that "whatever you write, it will not be enough. . . . you can write anything because there inside everything happened."[52] A railroad worker described what he saw in the fatal car: "It is a mass of backs, hands, pieces of people, slaughtered and quartered." Headlines proclaimed the "CHRISTMAS OF BLOOD." Fifteen people died and 117 were injured.

Although fifteen years had elapsed since the Piazza Fontana bombing, nothing fundamental had changed in the country's experience with terror by explosion. The wrathful condemnations emanating from high places of power had all been heard before. The usual ultra-Right organizations were vigorously denounced in the press again. Propaganda 2 and the secret service agencies came in for their predictable share of outraged criticism. Still, there was no concrete starting place for a serious criminal investigation, and an attitude of fatalistic bewilderment characterized the public mood, in large part a consequence of the archetypal Piazza Fontana case.

Conclusion

> The ultimate truth with respect to the character, the con-
> science, and the guilt of a people remains forever a se-
> cret; if only for the reason that its defects have another
> side, where they reappear as peculiarities or even as vir-
> tues—what follow are admittedly marginal notes.
>
> Jacob Burckhardt,
> *The Civilization of the Renaissance in Italy*

For about a decade and a half beginning in 1969, Italy endured systematic terrorist attacks from the Left and the Right, both of which continue to act intermittently against the country's political establishment. Statistically and psychologically terrorism in Italy far surpassed the political violence in other industrialized countries in the West. The paramount questions about this phenomenon are what caused it and where it came from. And how do we explain its unique force and staying power?

Conspiracy theories and socioeconomic theories—along with instinctual, psychoanalytic, and aggression-frustration theories—help us to see individual aspects of the problem, but they fail to explain why Italy has experienced terrorism in an unusually virulent form. Foreign conspiracies are afoot everywhere, not just in Italy. Moreover, it would be extremely surprising if Italy alone were plagued by deviant elements of domestic secret service agencies. *Emarginati*—unemployed workers and unemployable students—are not a uniquely Italian problem. Terrorism may be, as numerous experts have suggested, an animal compulsion or death wish or scream of the sexually impotent, the untalented ambitious, and the professionally hopeless who gravitate to revolutionary movements as an escape from their own wasted and sterile lives. But these points are equally valid or invalid for violent people in all societies. At the end of this list of theories we are still left asking: why should terrorism have been so much worse in Italy than in any other comparably developed European country?

Short of accepting genetic theories of terrorism and criminality, popularized a hundred years ago by Cesare Lombroso and now reappearing in the guise of sociobiology, it seems unreasonable to assume that Italy is naturally inhabited by more true believers and escapees from freedom than other countries. Italy, in fact, does produce a relatively large population of terrorists, but that is so because of complex historical and social reasons that draw politically activist individuals toward the utopian world of revolutionary mythology. For this reason the desolating events of

1969 and after would elude our understanding if we ignored the culture in which they occurred.

Historically, the Italian combination of population, land, and resources has not been a happy one. Despite the artistic and spiritual genius of the Italian people, centuries of miserable conditions in a land impoverished and degraded by the occupying armies of foreign countries did nothing to prepare Italy for a civic life of peaceful and orderly progress when unification came in the middle of the nineteenth century. Indeed, by then the logic of left-wing revolutionaries, who from Filippo Buonarroti's time on were collectively entranced by visions of a class war and a violent upheaval of the status quo, had led to a rejection of this kind of progress as class treason by another name. At the other end of the ideological spectrum, D'Annunzio's late nineteenth-century celebration of the Nietzschean superman gave a powerful boost to the traditional forces of Italian antiliberalism, increasingly unhappy for reasons of temperament with Catholic reaction, by providing an answer to Marx that was both reactionary and secular. In retrospect this cultural maneuver can be seen to have stimulated right-wing developments that eventually contributed to the Fascist destruction of the liberal state. Both revolutionary traditions, of the Right and the Left, survived the institutionalization and the fall of fascism. The starting point for an historical understanding of Italian terrorism must be an examination of these traditions.

Since World War II Italy has undergone a social and cultural crisis of astonishing force. The migration from countryside to city and from south to north continued at a prodigious rate, far faster than industrial growth.[1] The double effect of this epic migration, totaling 8.3 million in the two decades after 1951, was to injure Italian agriculture and to create an enormous lumpenproletariat in the cities. Italy eventually succeeded in creating the fifth largest economy in the world, but at the cost of serious social side effects.

Consumer society has made a shambles of the political parties and groups in Italy that claim inspiration from Marx, Nietzsche, and Christ. Marxist, Fascist, and Christian values were swamped during the postwar boom, and in a famous article Pier Paolo Pasolini described this process as an "anthropological mutation."[2] According to him, the whole country had gone the way of "borghesizzazione," leading to "the hedonistic ideology of consumerism and of the consequent modernist tolerance of the American type." Right-wing and left-wing terrorist groups have attempted to disrupt this process. Alberto Moravia offered a similar view, adding that twentieth-century terrorists have one thing, at least, in common with nineteenth-century terrorists: the fight for liberation—in the nineteenth century from tyranny, in the twentieth from fetishism, hedonism, corruption, alienation, and materialism.[3] Italian terrorism emerged in part as an extreme ideological reaction to society's post–World War II drift in a direction that was never prophesied by Marx and is equally remote from the prescriptions of Nietzsche or the preachments of Roman Catholic churchmen who speak in the name of Christ.

The religious crisis has been particularly acute. The church, while far from powerless, has suffered a notable loss of support among the young.[4] For the most ardent of the alienated Catholics it is a short psychological step from a spiritual

eschatology to an eschatology of social ideals, resulting in a Catholic-Marxist dialogue that neither group could ever have with people in the liberal Center. For
example, many Red Brigadists came to terrorism via an itinerary that began with
Catholicism.

Do these incontestable facts provide an adequate foundation for the widely
acclaimed *catto-comunismo* thesis regarding left-wing terrorism, that during the late
1960s the Catholic and Marxist traditions united at their fringes and produced the
monster Red Brigadism? Violence is certainly not missing from the Christian tradition, least of all from the annals of the Catholic Church. This Catholic violence
has taken an institutional and an intellectual form. Through the centuries of her
greatest power and influence the church employed force whenever necessary, as in
the cases of the Waldensians, the victims of the Inquisition, and, traditionally, the
non-Catholic minorities in Catholic lands as well as the Catholic dissenters in those
lands. Church teachers, including Thomas Aquinas, John of Salisbury, and Juan
de Mariana developed distinctively Catholic arguments in support of violence as a
legitimate moral response to certain unacceptable political and social conditions.[5]

The church's intellectual tradition of violent dissent has been reaffirmed periodically by leading Catholic thinkers and officials. For instance, in 1967 Pope
Paul VI wrote in *Populorum progressio* that "a revolutionary uprising" might be
defensible from a moral standpoint "where there is manifest long-standing tyranny
which would do great damage to fundamental personal rights and dangerous harm
to the common good of the country."[6] A Peruvian priest, Gustavo Gutierrez, based
his enormously influential *Theology of Liberation* (1970) on traditional Catholic
concepts of social justice together with Marxist theories of class struggle and revolution.

Certainly the catto-comunismo thesis is most appropriate as a means of explaining the theology of liberation, one of the signal political developments in Latin
America today. However, it is difficult with the naked eye to see how Catholicism
has any meaningful relationship with Red Brigadism and its like. In the documentary
history of left-wing terrorism, researchers are still looking for a single reference to
the New Testament, the church fathers, or any Christian thinker down to the present
day. Whatever the terrorists of the Left may have done objectively, they believed
that they were faithfully executing the timeless commands of Marx and Lenin.
Anyone who studies their propaganda statements cannot entertain an honest doubt
on this point. Rossana Rossanda, formerly of the PCI and now of Manifesto,
undertook such a study, and she had to admit that the ideas and vocabulary of the
Red Brigades were drawn from the Marxist Left. To read their statements, she
conceded in what has become a famous lament, was "like leafing through a family
album."

If the ideology of Red Brigadism bears no visible relationship to Catholicism,
it is nevertheless true that some of the most notorious Red Brigadists and their early
allies were Catholics. Renato Curcio, Mara Cagol, and Toni Negri—who shared
some of the prorevolutionary fervor of the early Red Brigades—are supremely representative of this Catholic-Marxist coupling in Italy's radical left-wing politics.
Without exception, though, in all of these "Catholic" terrorists or one-time apolo-

gists for revolutionary violence, the Catholic faith had vanished. This is very different from the theology-of-liberation experience in Latin America because Curcio, Cagol, and Negri did not attempt to unite two value systems; they emphatically abandoned Catholicism and either simultaneously or subsequently embraced revolutionary Marxism.

If former Catholics who become completely alienated from their faith are to be held responsible, as Catholics, for Red Brigadism, then logically this same argument should be applied to Catholics who become converts to yet other systems of thought and belief. But is it logical to conclude that Catholicism is in any meaningful way identifiable with Mormonism because former Catholics become Mormons, or with atheism because former Catholics become atheists, or with Islam because former Catholics become converted to the faith of Muhammad? The catto-comunismo line of reasoning requires us to make precisely this kind of association. Moreover, Italy's ubiquitous Catholic culture makes it highly likely that every Italian political movement will be influenced by individuals who have come into personal contact with the Catholic faith. In such an historical environment Catholicism can be reduced or exalted, depending on the motives of the researcher, to a deus ex machina. Therefore, the presence of ex-Catholics in the Red Brigades cannot be taken as a tell-tale sign of Catholicism's unusually severe psychological predisposition to heed the true believer's siren call, as the catto-comunismo school holds.

Even apart from the facts of this Italian case, there is something plainly unwarranted about the assumption that Catholics and Marxists have a special problem with the liberal values of tolerance, compromise, and pluralism—a problem that is said to incline the most radical members of these groups toward drastic solutions of their perceived problems. In fact, the Cromwells and the Robespierres of history serve to remind us that revolutionaries of other religious and ideological traditions are similarly intolerant of outside value systems and stand ready to implement their transcendental schemes with every weapon at hand. The only prudent way for the historian to proceed is on a case-by-case basis, and this approach subjects catto-communismo generalizations to unbearable stress.

The Red Brigadists and their fellow extremists came from backgrounds representing the gamut of religious and nonreligious possibilities in Italy: from devout Catholic families, from nonpracticing Catholic families, and from families with no religious identification at all. But to do the particular things that the terrorists did in Italy—for the reasons that they did—it was necessary for them to accept the distinctive world view of radical Marxism-Leninism. The key to the historical conundrum of Red Brigadism is to be found not in the repudiated religious background of some Red Brigadists but in the actual beliefs, hopes, and fears that inspired them all as they lived the *partito armato* experience. In these specific and concrete terms it requires an act of faith to find in Red Brigadism anything but the unexorcised ghosts of the revolutionary traditions in Marxism-Leninism.

No less than idealistic Catholics, idealistic Communists have watched the modern world pass them by as capitalism continues to mock all the Marxist reports of its impending demise. Trying to adapt to this evident reality, the PCI has shown a tolerant willingness to jettison Marx himself in all but name, and the party's historic ties to the revolutionary Bolshevik tradition have been covered over by the draperies of Eurocommunism. None of this has happened smoothly. Thousands of the party faithful have looked on in shock and dismay as the PCI has shifted toward new positions that only a short time before would have been unthinkable.

For example, in a September 1977 interview with American news correspondent Martin Agronsky, Giorgio Napolitano blithely revealed that the PCI saw nothing wrong with NATO.[7] Agronsky thought that the Communist leader had misspoken and asked for a clarification. Napolitano then added, "if there were an attack by the Warsaw Pact against NATO, naturally we would be obliged to defend our country against any external attack."[8] A perplexed Agronsky ventured to say, "The gentlemen in the Kremlin will be amazed when they hear this." Certainly, many Marxists in Italy were amazed. For decades the PCI had maintained its identity on the left as the upholder in Italy of the Soviet model, and *Rinascita's* hagiographic eulogy of Stalin in March 1953 documents the pervasive Soviet influence on the PCI until well into the postwar period. Only with Hungary, even more with Czechoslovakia, and then, in a coup de grâce, with Afghanistan was the old pro-Soviet faith completely overthrown in the name of polycentrism. As for Poland in late 1981 and early 1982, Washington could only have wished that the West German reaction and that of some of its other NATO allies had equaled the PCI's passionate condemnation of General Wojciech Jaruzelski's martial law regime. Moscow felt compelled to react to this condemnation with a shrill editorial in *Pravda*, denouncing the PCI for giving "direct aid to imperialism."[9]

Even apart from the extremely strained relationship with the Soviet Union, the PCI is now seen, correctly, as the heir of Turati, not of Bordiga or even of Gramsci. Surely Gramsci could not have abided pluralism as a permanent condition, which the PCI now claims it is willing and even eager to accept.[10] The need for the party to win new votes and to establish effective political alliances with other parties has overshadowed other considerations. It is this pragmatic attitude—once viewed by the PCI as a necessary evil, but now accepted as an intrinsic virtue—that has caused outrage among those Marxists for whom Marxism is still synonymous with the revolutionary project. In other words, the PCI has traveled in the direction of the major social democratic parties of Europe, but not without eliminating those fervent spirits among its former members and allies who only want to discard the parliamentary system, not to conquer it at the polls. It is at this point, in an extreme sector of the Italian Marxist tradition, that Red Brigadism and comparable left-wing terrorist movements have arisen.

For those right-wing zealots who view themselves in the self-congratulatory aura of Nietzsche's race of supermen, contemporary Italy has gone mad, her condition so desperate that only heroic measures will suffice. In the thinking of some of them the postwar reign of the errand boys for the United States in the Christian Democratic party—a collective Kerensky for Italy's Bolsheviks in the Communist party— made terrorism a duty. The obliterating failure of fascism in World War II condemned neofascism to play a marginal role in postwar Italy, and the MSI, with its 5 or 6 percent tally in the national elections, has been a movement tormented by dissension from the beginning. Like the PCI, the MSI has seen many of its most fanatical members secede and form sects of true believers where the mentality of direct action is supreme. From this ideological tradition come the fanatical bombers who seek to destroy democratic Italy.

Why do they blow up banks, trains, and train stations? Although the visible similarities between Fascist and neofascist violence are many, it is doubtful that the radical right-wing bombers of today amount to merely an imitative reincarnation of the first Fascist strategy. The genius of Fascist squadrism lay in its defensive image: it appeared to be only reacting to the menace of socialist revolution, whereas in fact the blackshirts authored much of the violence they purported to put down. In successfully presenting themselves as the only effective defenders of public order the Fascists also stripped the liberal government of its political prestige. The Reds were loose in the streets, it seemed, and if the government could not stop them, someone else would have to do the job; hence, the well-documented collective sigh of relief when Mussolini took charge in 1922.

Radical neofascists today go about their bombings in a public posture that is more complex than that adopted by Mussolini's *squadristi*. The Fascists, locked in a straightforward struggle with the Left and with part of the Center, developed a political strategy designed to achieve a government takeover in the near term. By comparison the neofascists are in an anterior revolutionary stage, still trying to cause enough confusion and anarchy to provoke a nationwide call for the radical right-wing dictatorship of their dreams. Political and economic chaos was endemic in the postwar Italian situation, which Mussolini effectively augmented and exploited for his own ends. The material conditions of Mussolini's success must be created anew, however, and it is this necessity that informs the political vision of today's neofascist strategists of tension. That preliminary stage of the revolutionary process completed, neofascism would then offer itself, in the manner of Mussolini, as the country's savior. Today the radical Right has replaced Italian nationalism, narrowly conceived, with a pan-European view of the world, and this ideological shift sharply differentiates neofascism from fascism. Nevertheless, neofascist extremists have perpetrated terrorist acts as the core of their *tanto peggio tanto meglio* strategy, linking up with criminal elements in a campaign to undermine the democratic government of Italy.[11] In this last neofascist objective the historical parallel with original fascism is striking.

Vast numbers of Marxists and neofascists alienated from their legally constituted parties existed as a potent disruptive force in an Italy painfully threading her way toward consumer society. Ideological traditions by themselves do not explain what went wrong in Italy. Deprived of a dysfunctional social situation, even the most gifted radical would languish in obscurity or at the very worst remain unthreatening to the power structure of his society. Social and political crises alone can create an effective constituency for ideologies of despair, and modern Italy is an object lesson of the truth that both failed and successful revolutions must be studied in the context of the social systems in which they occur. Revolutionary behavior cannot be studied apart from its social environment.[12]

To say this much is not to contradict an equally profound truth, that the contemporary social situation by itself fails to provide an adequate explanation for the country's problem with terrorism. The point here is a different one. Over the generations social problems and cultural responses to them have formed traditions of political anger that have made Italy unusually vulnerable to terrorism. Not the contemporary social situation alone but the social situation historically has created a culture in which radical revolutionary traditions, black and red, are part of the atmosphere in which every Italian lives and breathes. In such an atmosphere the unwanted freedom of capitalism is bound to produce disturbing effects of varying intensity in the minds of those individuals who have been shaped ideologically by the political values of the extreme Left and Right and who, consequently, want to see society reorganized in a revolutionary way. This is the point Patrizio Peci implicitly addressed in his memoir, *Io l'infame* (1983), when he wrote that had he been born in Australia or in almost any country but Italy he would not have become a terrorist.[13] On the other end of the ideological spectrum Roberto Chiarini and Paolo Corsini have shown in their meticulously detailed study of neofascism in Brescia how contemporary radical right-wing organizations in that city have roots in a historic reactionary culture, characterized for generations by active social, intellectual, and political forces.[14] In many cities, heavily politicized youth gangs dominate entire neighborhoods, and for the young this is the real hegemony of their most impressionable years.

Italy has never achieved social integration. This problem has been so severe during the past century that a conspicuous minority of intellectually vocal and politically active Italians in every generation has desired revolution. Such profound hostility to existing liberal institutions seems to be the fundamental explanation for the enormous popularity of socialism among Italian intellectuals almost from the movement's inception and the strong appeal now of Marxism to a broad cross section of the population, an appeal that must strike every foreign observer as one of the distinctive characteristics of Italian life."[15] As with every revolutionary movement in history, Marxism has attracted some cruel fanatics, ever inclined to give the dialectic a push with their rifle butts. The right-wing desire for an antiliberal revolution has complemented the agitation of the revolutionary Left. The result has been one of the most turbulent political traditions in the annals of Western Europe.

Society, ideology, and history are the elements that have created an environment for the Italian terror of our time, but they would remain mere abstractions if we failed to add the concrete presence of human actors, emphasizing how this particular terrorism came to be and how it unfolded in the specific ways it did. While all the citizens of a society victimized by a culture of political violence are subjected to the same forces, only some yield while others resist. The individual human factor is decisive. Without it no possibility exists for understanding how the historical process actually reveals itself in all of its multiformity.

The terrorists wanted revolution, and they believed that the Italian republic would fall before properly applied force. They perpetrated more than thirteen thousand acts of political violence over a fifteen-year period that resulted in death and injury to some twelve hundred people. The attempt to paint a composite portrait of the terrorists through statistical analysis has not been notably successful, for they came from all classes, regions, and age groups. For instance, to say that the left-wing terrorists tended to be young men and former university students who came from the higher strata of society is to point toward the common characteristics of many other elite political movements in the modern world.[16] Moreover, after being told that right-wing terrorists tended to come from lower middle-class backgrounds, we have not yet learned the most important things we need to know about these people.[17]

History is about tendencies, but it is also about particular men and women who command the interest of the historian precisely because they disrupt tendencies. The men and women who became terrorists were statistically insignificant exceptions in every class, regional, and generational category to which they belonged; therefore, the categories by themselves afford little insight into the historical character of Italian terrorism. What bound the terrorists together were not class, regional, or generational forces—important as these may have been to a certain extent—but shared visions of the world and history. They wanted society to reverse its present course. They believed this could be done. They were wrong, but in the light of their beliefs and values it is possible to see why, at the time, they thought they were right.

Soundings in the roily waters of Italy's radical politics enable us to understand what revolutionary visions motivated the terrorists. Evola, Panzieri, and Negri by no means exhaust the possibilities for this kind of research. Ten years before his death at the hands of terrorists, Walter Tobagi wrote a perceptive study that dealt with the revolutionary ferment of the far Left in Italy.[18] His book is an encyclopedia of the hundreds of revolutionary parties, newspapers, journals, committees, study groups, and personalities that followed in the wake of *Quaderni rossi*. It has been possible here to explore only a small portion of these materials in depth. Moreover, numerous other figures on the right were eligible for the kind of investigation to be found in the chapter on Julius Evola.[19] As it is, however, the present study contains some clear indications of how Italy's cultural and political traditions have exerted a powerful influence on the present. In Evola, Panzieri, and Negri, we have three intellectuals who inherited ways of radical thinking and acting that they then developed further along the lines of their own revolutionary aspirations.

In general both of these traditions in Italy are best understood in the light of an observation made by Ignazio Silone in his classic anti-Fascist novel, *Bread and Wine*:

> The race to which we belong is distinguished by the fact that it begins by taking seriously the principles taught us by our own educators and teachers. These principles are proclaimed to be the foundations of present-day society, but if one takes them seriously and uses them as a standard to test society as it is organized and as it functions today, it becomes evident that there is a radical contradiction between the two. Our society in practice ignores these principles altogether. It is this discovery that leads one to become a revolutionary.[20]

In other and poorer words Italy, a country of exalted ideals, faces a reality that extremists view as an insufferably degraded one. It is not difficult to understand how this disjunction between the ideal and the real would produce politically radical behavior, on the right as well as on the left, and this, in fact, has been the country's political destiny from the Carbonari to the present day. Negri himself commented on this point in his autobiographical *Pipe-line*, calling the Red Brigades a new edition of "the *carbonari* of an impossible revolution," the upholders of "a faithful and reassuring ideology" with deep roots in the Italian past.[21] The same point might just as easily be made about Negri's own Autonomia Operaia.

Nevertheless, the autobiographical publications of the terrorists themselves cast doubt on the argument that ideology was an unaided motivating force in their actions. The fascinating memoir of Giulio Salierno, *Autobiografia di un picchiatore fascista*, in which he depicts his adolescent experiences in Rome's neofascist Colle Oppio youth group, illustrates this point for the radical Right. Salierno admits that the sheer love of violence animated him and his friends, most of whom were the sons of fascist functionaries and on the radical fringes of the MSI.[22] What we find in this book are the reminiscences of a middle-aged Marxist who in his neofascist youth had been motivated by something as basic as human aggression and lust for violence. Salierno did emphasize Evola's intellectual importance for the postwar generation of Italian right-wing extremists; it was Evola's *La rivolta contro il mondo moderno* and related books that enabled them to identify themselves as Nietzsche's last good Europeans. Yet, Salierno concludes, not ideas and theories but "the machine gun had the effect on me of a drug."[23]

Since fascism and neofascism have always been ostentatiously anti-intellectual and action oriented, Salierno's revelations are not particularly remarkable. But even on the radical left, where the revolutionary word is venerated, Patrizio Peci's memoir, *Io l'infame*, illustrates in copious detail a psychological process that bears a close resemblance to the one briefly mentioned in Salierno's *Autobiografia di un picchiatore fascista*. Peci, too, began with a vision of the world, of history, and of man. He also acquired a tactic, from Lenin, with which to bring this vision to pass: "Strike one to educate a hundred."[24] We learn from his book where these values came from and the life stages at which he received them. The product of a normal apolitical family, Peci confides that at eighteen he became swept up in "the furious antifascism" of the early 1970s and began reading *Lotta continua*.[25] The obsessive nightmare of this newspaper was a right-wing coup, and it required only a short step for readers such as Peci to conclude that if such a coup were evil it would be correct to take preventive measures against the forces of reaction. This was the mentality that produced Red Brigadism, he assures us.

Peci's assertion on this point enables us to understand why the radical fringe of Italy's left-wing culture, pushed beyond the limits of equilibrium, erupted when it did. The Marxist radicals of Peci's generation were reacting to a perceived threat from the radical Right, which, according to Marxist theory, could always rely on the compliance of Italy's governing forces until the day of revolution when compliance would turn to active support. Their fears became ungovernable after the Piazza Fontana massacre of 1969. The Red Brigades intervened in a political dialectic that had already produced fascism once before in Italian history. The vivid memory of Italy's Fascist past created a mood of acute urgency about contemporary neofascism. For the Italians, unlike most peoples in the Western world, the domestic threat of neofascism conjured up harrowing images that were historic and not hypothetical.

To Peci the Red Brigades appeared to be the only dynamic component in the antifascist crusade. This impression became clearer under the influence of his increasingly radical reading matter: Marx, Mao, Lenin, Stalin, and *Potere operaio*.[26] He subsequently joined the Red Brigades because, in his judgment, the clandestine armed struggle was the best way to bring about the political victory of the proletariat, that is, "to install communism." According to Peci, belief in communism was the indispensable precondition of Red Brigadism: "It is obvious that one does not make such a choice if one does not believe completely in communism, if one does not believe in the armed struggle as the only way to bring it about, if one does not believe in victory."[27]

By joining the Red Brigades Peci thought that he was taking his place in "the vanguard of the proletariat"—the very place lately and formally abandoned by the PCI.[28] He and his fellow Red Brigadists saw themselves as the Italian version of Lenin's Bolshevik nucleus. Within five to ten years, they fondly believed, the masses would be with them. Only toward the end of his career as a terrorist did it begin to dawn on Peci that these assumptions might be based on nothing but dreams and myths. Then, following his arrest and repentance, Peci claimed to realize that as a Red Brigadist he had been a prisoner of the belief system engendered by the revolutionary Left. Into that mental universe was admitted nothing so coarse as a factual analysis of what the workers themselves earnestly desired, which by 1983 Peci understood to be higher pay, more free time, and better working conditions but not revolution in anything like the Marxist sense. He had come to understand the working-class truths that Berlinguer, as PCI chief, had understood all along. Education for Peci had come at a dreadful cost, but he did find some consolation in understanding the real historical significance of the Red Brigades: by attempting to translate the revolutionary myths of communist ideology into political reality they had only succeeded in ruining the mystique of revolution in Italy while simultaneously strengthening the establishment.

Ideas played a major role in Peci's evolution as a terrorist, but fortuitous quantities were part of the equation as well. He was bored with his small-town existence, and a poor academic record precluded any possibility of escape through an exciting and rewarding job. Eventually he did escape, to Milan, but his hatred of this city radicalized him still further. By contrast the extraparliamentary Left organizations offered a sense of hope and adventure. Thus Peci, motivated by a passionate commitment to revolutionary ideology and unrestrained by an opposing gravitational pull to the structure of Italian society, was drawn into the orbit of the Red Brigades, with results that he describes as completely tragic.

Nevertheless, when Peci recounts the six years that he lived as a terrorist, first as a subordinate and then as the leader of the Turin column, on balance he seems to have found fulfillment in this life. He lovingly details his passion for guns and the feeling of power they gave him. Although Peci claims to have vomited after every assassination, he never felt so alive as he did when on a mission. His ruling passion was a soldierly one, to cut a good figure in front of his comrades. As in Salierno's case, the terrorist life gradually assumed for Peci a reality of its own apart from ideological considerations.

There is a subtle and shifting line of analysis here that must not be made any more obscure than it already is. To put this complex point in the language of another memoirist of terror, a victim in this case, "The first time in violence is like the first time in love."[29] Jacobo Timerman's assertion in *Prisoner without a Name, Cell without a Number* regarding the Dionysian effects of violence echoes Dostoyevski's profound intuition about the tragic character of terror: after a time the philosophical ideas, the political goals, the human values, and the sense of historical mission, which to some degree at least influence the thinking of a terrorist, are compromised by violence as a way of life. Eventually violence ceases to be the means to an end and becomes the end itself. Both Salierno and Peci had ideological mentors. However, the literary confessions of these two ex-terrorists show how each confirmed the truth of Dostoyevski's principle, which as a tool of terrorist analysis is by no means obsolete.

In *The Possessed* Dostoyevski sought to depict the left-wing terrorists of his day, and what he claimed to be true about the psychological character of the *narodniki* applies to the Red Brigades as well as to the ordinovisti. The development of both left-wing and right-wing terrorism in Italy occurred along the lines of what Dostoyevski presciently said must befall movements based on the belief that an indescribably satisfying utopia can and will emerge from a revolutionary campaign of merciless extermination. The fanatics of both extremes have failed to see that the means they employ to reach their goal fatally contradict the formal ideal of a just society, variously defined. Dostoyevski was here addressing the problem of moral degeneration brought on by the philosophy of violence.

Of the thousands of violent images that crowd the history of Italian terrorism, the film sequence of Roberto Peci's execution at the hands of the Red Brigades remains the most vivid and shocking example of this moral degeneration. It is a scene that Dostoyevski could have written and, indeed, came close to writing in *The Possessed*. His moral, which amounts to a restatement of Thucydides's analysis of Athenian politics during the Peloponnesian War, is that while revolution appeals to the idealistic it is ever inclined to bring low human types—classically, the humorless megalomaniac—to the fore. The idealists are by nature unable to understand the demonic character of revolutionary political power that evolves in practical contradiction to programmatic ideals. Indeed, since 1789 successful revolutions have been followed not by a conspicuous increase in liberty, equality, and fraternity but by the radical augmentation of state power, culminating, as with the classic cases of France, Russia, and China, in varying degrees of state terrorism. With Robespierre, Stalin, and Mao revolution produced philosopher-executioners whose undeniable historic achievements must be balanced against acts of frightful inhumanity. In each case the moral economy of revolution was enormously complicated.[30]

While it would be historically simplistic to dismiss all revolutions as aberrant and nothing more, it requires an equally insensitive interpretation of history to overlook their horrors and calamities. These last led Raymond Aron to observe in *The Opium of the Intellectuals* that revolution is essentially a negative force: "It is wrong to expect salvation from triumphant catastrophe, wrong to despair of victory in peaceful struggle."[31] As for those intellectuals who are eager to promote the catastrophic resolution of political and social problems, Julien Benda's rancorous criticism of them in *The Treason of the Intellectuals* (1927) as romantics of harshness, contempt, and cruelty has lost none of its force. This was a passionate French intellectual's translation of the more sober academic language of Max Weber, who had condemned radical illusions in politics as the intoxication and the narcotic of a fool's paradise: "It is the stigma of our human dignity that the peace of our souls cannot be as great as the peace of one who dreams of such a paradise."[32]

In 1969 Hannah Arendt wrote that "The problem of violence still remains very obscure."[33] So it is in large part and will no doubt long remain with the violence that has afflicted Italy in our time. The tentative and partial conclusions here advanced concern the prehistory of contemporary Italian terrorism rather than its history. They are, first, that today's terrorism in Italy is linked to the country's revolutionary traditions. Second, present-day intellectuals have been prominently involved, directly or indirectly, in the process of interpreting those traditions to their contemporaries and of adapting them to the exigencies of political extremism. Third, Italy's hurried passage from a still largely intact traditional society to consumerism on the American model created an ideal social environment for revolutionary violence by alienated elites of the Right and the Left, who either believed that they had no place in the new order or did not want one in it.

To elucidate fully the spectacular explosion of contemporary Italian terrorism, the commanding instance of which was Moro's kidnapping and murder, requires knowledge that the historian cannot now or perhaps ever hope to possess. The documentation for crucial parts of this story is either nonexistent or unmanageable in its bulk. At every turn the historian risks a flagrant violation of his professional canons. Only a Dostoyevski, if such another could be found, might have the power, the vision, and the artistic license to do complete justice to these materials.

Moro, more than anyone, understood the problem of good and evil that lay at the heart of the terrorist darkness in Italy. He expressed this point in a photograph inscription to a young Sicilian admirer, Piersanti Mattarella, later murdered by Mafia gangsters: "This country will not save itself, the season of rights and liberties will prove ephemeral, if a new sense of duty is not born."[34] Out of the nightmare through which Italy has lived and suffered may come the wisdom beckoned by Moro. It would be a pearl acquired at an appalling price in blood if the terrorist illness that lurks in revolutionary ideology, black and red, might be seen by future generations of Italians in the light of lines written by the poet André de Chenier as he lay in the shadow of the guillotine nearly two hundred years ago: "Before the Terror worthy men retreat / Kindness dies, and virtues grow discreet."

Moro's cautionary inscription does not merely imply a concern with those men and women enchanted by the revolutionary mystique; it also calls attention to a need for all Italians to work at changing the moral climate in which the country's endemic political illnesses have taken hold. It is one thing to eradicate a group of these enchanted ones, as the tsarist government did with the *narodniki* after the terrorist murder of Tsar Alexander II in 1881. It is quite another to transform the conditions in which such groups take root and then sprout in a rank growth. The government of Alexander III succeeded brilliantly at the first task but failed altogether at the second, with results that eventually contributed to the revolutionary overthrow of the tsarist government.

In like manner, the government of Italy has succeeded in crushing or at least greatly diminishing the recent terrorist threats to the country's political institutions. Nevertheless, that left- and right-wing radicals could exist in such threatening numbers suggests, at the very least, some serious limitations in Italy's political structures. A major theme of Italian political life has been the divorce of the intellectuals from the Christian Democratic-run republic.[35] Both ideological extremes, fortified by powerful revolutionary traditions, were able to exploit an ominous mood of resentment against the government. Their recent reverses have eliminated neither the social factors that permitted terrorist groups to become a major force in Italian life nor the cultural legacy that has disposed Italian revolutionaries to embrace political violence in the ways they have. By surviving the revolutionary challenges of the Red Brigades and their counterparts on the radical Right, the Italian republic is stronger than it was before. Despite resorting to special antiterrorist laws and police procedures, it managed to protect itself without losing its democratic character. This was a heroic achievement, but Moro's admonition remains in effect.

Glossary

Autonomi: Members of Autonomia Operaia.

Autonomia Operaia (Worker Autonomy): Confederation of diverse extraparliamentary left-wing groups.

Avanguardia Nazionale (National Vanguard): Extraparliamentary right-wing group.

Avanguardia Operaia (Worker Vanguard): Extraparliamentary left-wing group.

Bierre: Members of the Red Brigades.

Brigata XXVIII Marzo (28 March Brigade): Revolutionary left-wing group.

Brigatisti rossi: Members of the Red Brigades.

Brigate Rosse (Red Brigades): Revolutionary left-wing group.

Carabinieri: A national police force under the Defense Ministry.

La Classe (Class): Extraparliamentary left-wing journal.

Classe operaia (Working Class): Extraparliamentary left-wing journal.

Collettivo Politico Metropolitano (Metropolitan Political Collective): Extraparliamentary left-wing organization from which the Red Brigades sprang.

Contropiano (Counterplan): Extraparliamentary left-wing journal.

Dissociati: Those who dissociate themselves from terrorism without divulging information about their former confederates.

Fasci di Azione Rivoluzionaria (FAR, Leagues of Revolutionary Action): Extreme right-wing group in post–World War II Italy.

Fronte Comunista Combattente (Fighting Communist Front): Revolutionary left-wing group.

Fronte Nazionale Rivoluzionario (National Revolutionary Front): Revolutionary right-wing group.

Gappisti: Members of the Gruppi di Azione Partigiana.

Gruppi di Azione Partigiana (GAP, Groups of Partisan Action): Revolutionary left-wing group.

Gruppi di Azione Rivoluzionaria (GAR, Groups of Revolutionary Action): Revolutionary right-wing group.

Irriducibili (the irreducible ones): Hard-core terrorists who remain unrepentant after capture.

Jeune Europe (Young Europe): International right-wing organization.

Lotta Continua (The Struggle Continues): Extraparliamentary left-wing group.

Lotta continua: Newspaper of Lotta Continua.

Manifesto: Extraparliamentary left-wing group.

Manifesto: Newspaper of Manifesto.

Metropoli: Extraparliamentary left-wing journal.

Militaristi: Faction of the Red Brigades.

Missini: Members of the Movimento Sociale Italiano.

Mondo Operaio (Working World): Pietro Nenni's Socialist journal.

Movimentisti: Faction of the Red Brigades.

Movimento di Resistenza Popolare (Movement of Popular Resistance): Extreme left-wing group in post–World War II Italy.

Movimento Sociale Italiano (MSI, Italian Social Movement): Neofascist party in Italy.

Nappisti: Members of the Armed Proletarian Nuclei (NAP).

Nouvel Ordre Européen (New European Order): International right-wing organization.

Nuclei Armati Proletari (NAP, Armed Proletarian Nuclei): Revolutionary left-wing group.

Nuclei Armati Rivoluzionari (NAR, Armed Revolutionary Nuclei): Revolutionary right-wing group.

Ordine Nero (Black Order): Extraparliamentary right-wing group.

Ordine Nuovo (New Order): Extraparliamentary right-wing group.

Ordinovisti: Members of Ordine Nuovo.
Partito armato (armed party): Generic term for left-wing terrorists.
Partito Comunista Italiano (PCI): Italian Communist party.
Partito Socialista Italiano (PSI): Italian Socialist party.
Pentiti (repentant ones): Those who repent of their past terrorist actions and cooperate with the authorities.
Piellini: Members of Prima Linea.
Potere Operaio (Worker Power): Extraparliamentary left-wing group.
Potere Operaio: Newspaper of Potere Operaio.
Potopisti: Members of Potere Operaio.
Prima Linea (Front Line): Revolutionary left-wing group.
Quaderni Rossi (Red Notebooks): Extraparliamentary left-wing group.
Quaderni rossi: Journal of Quaderni Rossi.
Rinascita: Journal of Italian communist party.
Rosso (Red): Extraparliamentary left-wing journal.
Sinistra Proletaria (Proletarian Left): Review of the Metropolitan Political Collective.
Stella Rossa (Red Star): Extreme left-wing group in post–World War II Italy.
L'Unità (Unity): Newspaper of Italian Communist party.

Notes

INTRODUCTION

1. Jean-Claude Chesnais, *Histoire de la violence en occident de 1800 à nos jours*, p. 41.
2. Franco Ferrarotti, Introduction to *Social Research*, vol. 48, no. 1, 1981, and "Riflessioni e dati su dodici anni di terrorismo in Italia (1969–1981)" in Mauro Galleni (ed.), *Rapporto sul terrorismo*.
3. Karl Mannheim, *Essays on the Sociology of Culture*, p. 84.
4. The legitimation of radical politics as an acceptable element of Italy's social character demonstrates in a concrete way the insight of a point adumbrated by Gramsci in "The Modern Prince," that "to write the history of a party means in fact to write the general history of a country from a monographic point of view." In Antonio Gramsci, *The Modern Prince and Other Writings*, p. 143.
5. Nando Dalla Chiesa, "Del sessantotto e del terrorismo: cultura e politica tra continuità e rottura," p. 72.
6. Giorgio Bocca, "Quelle br finite nelle mani di Cutolo . . . ," *La Repubblica*, 21 July 1982.
7. Michel Foucault, *The Archaeology of Knowledge*, esp. p. 144.
8. Ibid., p. 173.
9. Karl Marx, *The Civil War in France*, pp. 69 ff.
10. Alberto Franceschini, an architect of Red Brigadism, noted that in their analysis of the armed struggle he and his terrorist colleagues habitually observed to one another, "This we have read in *What Is to Be Done?* This we have found in *State and Revolution*: that the revolutionary party is created only in the struggle against the state." In Giorgio Bocca, *Noi terroristi*, p. 81.
11. For D'Annunzio's role as Nietzsche's popularizer in Italy, see Richard Drake, *Byzantium for Rome*, chap. 8.
12. Friedrich Nietzsche, *Beyond Good and Evil*.
13. Adriano Romualdi, *Nietzsche*.
14. In the wake of Giorgio Bocca's controversial best-seller, *Mussolini socialfascista* (1983), in which he accused Marx of being the *padre eterno* of Italy's revolutionary traditions—Left and Right—it seems especially important to insist on the fundamental differences between the black and the red. They are not, as Bocca suggested, the fraternal twins of Marx. There are some crossed bloodlines in these two, but their pedigrees are more complicated and less incestuous than readers of *Mussolini socialfascista* would be led to believe.
15. Gramsci, *Modern Prince*; see "Critical Notes on an Attempt at a Popular Presentation of Marxism by Bukharin" and "The Formation of the Intellectuals."
16. Alexis de Tocqueville, *The Old Régime and the French Revolution*, pt. 2.
17. Fernand Braudel, *The Mediterranean and the Mediterranean World in the Age of Philip II*, vol. 1, pp. 20–21.

1. THE TWO FACES OF ITALIAN TERRORISM

1. Arnaldo Giuliani, "Orrenda strage a Milano," *Corriere della sera*, 13 December 1969. Two bombs went off in Rome on 12 December: at the monument of the Unknown Soldier in Piazza Venezia and in an underground passage connecting the two buildings of the Banca Nazionale del Lavoro on Via Bissolati. In this last explosion sixteen people were wounded, though none seriously.
2. For an account of FAR by an active member, see Mario Tedeschi, *Fascisti dopo Mussolini*. Other violent right-wing groups of the period were Esercito Clandestino Anti-

comunista (ECA), Fronte Antibolscevico Italiano (FAI), and Squadre di Azione Mussolini (SAM). See Enzo Santarelli, "Cronologia sommaria dei movimenti neofascisti," in his *Fascismo e neofascismo.*

3. Jean-Marc Théolleyre, *Les Neo-Nazis*, p. 198.

4. Pino Rauti, "Dalle slogan al mito," *Ordine nuovo*, May 1958.

5. Rauti, "MSI: riprendiamo il discorso," ibid., February 1963.

6. Rauti, "Appuntamento alla storia," ibid., November 1960.

7. In 1972 the MSI garnered 2,894,789 votes (8.7% of the total), fifty-six Chamber seats, and twenty-six Senate seats.

8. Clemente Graziani, "La guerra rivoluzionaria," *Ordine nuovo*, April 1963.

9. The name of Graziani's group was Il Movimento Politico Ordine Nuovo; it published a journal, *Noi.*

10. Giampaolo Pansa, *Borghese mi ha detto*, pp. 157 ff. Giorgio Bocca pegged Avanguardia Nazionale's membership in 1970 at 1,500; in his *Il terrorismo italiano*, chap. 4, "Il terrorismo nero."

11. Petra Rosenbaum, *Il nuovo fascismo*, p. 84.

12. Pansa, *Borghese*, p. 44.

13. Camilla Cederna, "Infanzia di un uomo ricco che non poteva soffrire i ricchi," *L'Espresso*, 26 March 1972.

14. The PCI's Giorgio Amendola called these extraparliamentary Left critiques of his party "petulant and annoying, almost always calumnious . . . with extremely grave political damage" as their main result; in "Tre Domande Politiche," pt. 2, *Giovane Critica*, no. 30, 1972. For a comparative analysis of the new Left in Europe, see Massimo Teodori, *Storia delle nuove sinistre in Europa (1956–1976).*

15. See Palmiro Togliatti, *La politica di Salerno: Aprile–Dicembre 1944.* Also see Luigi Ganapini, "La 'svolta di Salerno' e la resistenza al Nord," in Il Manifesto (ed)., *Da Togliatti alla nuova sinistra*, and Paolo Spriano, *Storia del partito comunista italiano*, vol. 5, chaps. 11 and 12.

16. Nello Ajello, *Intellettuali e PCI: 1944–1958*, p. 46.

17. For example, see Fausto Lupetti et al., *La polemica Vittorini-Togliatti e la linea culturale del PCI nel 1945–1947*, and "Il caso Vittorini," in Ajello, *Intellettuali e PCI.*

18. Walter Tobagi, *Storia del movimento studentesco e dei marxisti-leninisti in Italia.*

19. Alessandro Silj, *Never Again without a Rifle*, pp. 212 ff.

20. "Applichiamo gli insegnamenti della grande rivoluzione culturale proletaria," *Lavoro politico*, no. 10, September 1968.

21. See Massimo Cavallini, *Il terrorismo in fabbrica*, for the workers' views of these study groups. His book is a compendium of worker interviews at four factories that were especially hard hit by terrorism.

22. "Lotta sociale e organizzazione nella metropoli," January 1970, in Soccorso Rosso, *Brigate rosse*, pp. 46–53.

23. *Foglio di lotta di sinistra proletaria*, 21 November 1970, in ibid., p. 66.

24. *Foglio di lotta di sinistra proletaria*, 20 October 1970, in ibid., p. 71.

25. A strong affinity existed between these two organizations. From the beginning the Red Brigades stressed the importance of the revolution's international context. The Baader-Meinhof Gang came to the admiring attention of the Red Brigades at about this time as well.

26. Red Brigade communication, no date, but late fall 1970, in Soccorso Rosso (eds.), *Brigate rosse*, p. 78.

27. Red Brigade communication, 1 December 1970, in ibid., p. 79.

28. Red Brigade communication, April 1971, in ibid., p. 84.

29. The Red Brigades also published two issues of a newspaper, *Nuova resistenza*, in 1971. Their first systematic theoretical statement appeared in September of that year; in ibid., pp. 103–8.

30. Red Brigade leaflet, 2 March 1972, in ibid., p. 111.

31. Red Brigade pamphlet, January 1973, in Soccorso Rosso (eds.), *Brigate rosse*, pp. 145–49.

32. Red Brigade leaflet, 10 December 1973, in ibid., pp. 167–68.

33. Red Brigade leaflet, 18 December 1973, in ibid., p. 175.

34. Norman Kogan, A *Political History of Italy*, p. 268.

35. Red Brigade communication no. 1, 19 April 1971, in Soccorso Rosso (eds.), *Brigate rosse*, pp. 193–95.

36. Giampaolo Pansa, "Il silenzio sul caso Sossi tradisce forti tensioni," *Corriere della sera*, 3 May 1974.

37. XXII Ottobre was organized on 22 October 1969 in Genoa's Piazzale Adriatico. About ten founding members pledged themselves to the destruction of the bourgeois state. The leader of the gang was Mario Rossi. In 1970–71 they perpetrated numerous terrorist actions, including attacks on the U.S. consulate and a carabiniere barracks. They also staged several holdups, which gang spokesmen glamorized, according to the extreme left-wing custom, as expropriations. On 26 March 1971 they killed a young worker, Alessandro Floris, during the last of these robberies, and the entire gang ended up in jail. Both Feltrinelli and Curcio paid tribute to Rossi et al. as "comrades."

38. Red Brigade communication no. 4, 5 May 1974, in Soccorso Rosso (eds.), *Brigate rosse*, pp. 207–8.

39. Mario Sossi, *Nella prigione delle Br*, p. 141.

40. Sossi to his wife, 30 April 1974, in Soccorso Rosso (eds.), *Brigate rosse*, p. 203.

41. Red Brigade communication no. 6, 18 May 1974, in ibid., pp. 231–32.

42. Antonio Padellaro, "Rumor alle Camere: 'Nessun patteggiamento con i criminali," *Corriere della sera*, 22 May 1974.

43. In his memoir, however, Sossi praised Coco for a "most exalted sense of the state." *Nella prigione delle Br*, p. 224.

44. Red Brigade communication no. 8, 23 May 1974, in Soccorso Rosso (eds.), *Brigate rosse*, pp. 238–39.

45. Enzo Passanisi, "Bomba contro un comizio anti fascista: sei morti e oltre novanta feriti a Brescia," *Corriere della sera*, 29 May 1974. In June two more of the victims died.

46. Arnaldo Giuliani, "La bomba sul treno ha fatto strage: sono dodici le vittime dell'attentato," ibid., 5 August 1974.

47. Antonio Padellaro, "Taviani afferma che fu un errore la teoria degli opposti estremismi," ibid., 29 August 1974.

48. Red Brigade communication, 18 June 1974, in Soccorso Rosso (eds.), *Brigate rosse*, pp. 253–54.

2. SURGING RED BRIGADISM

1. Giorgio Bocca, *Il terrorismo italiano*, "Il punto di svolta."

2. Gaetano Scardocchia, "Per l'assalto alle carceri di Casale scambio di accuse tra ministeri," *Corriere della sera*, 20 February 1975.

3. Red Brigade communication, 20 February 1975, in Soccorso Rosso (eds.), *Brigate Rosse*, p. 265.

4. See the following articles by Enrico Berlinguer in *Rinascita*: "Imperialismo e consistenza alla luce dei fatti cileni," 28 September 1973; "Riflessioni sull' Italia dopo i fatti di Cile: via democratica o violenza reazionaria," 5 October 1973; "Riflessioni sull' Italia dopo i fatti di Cile: alleanze sociali e schieramenti politici," 12 October 1973. See Peter Lange, "Crisis and Consent, Change and Compromise: Dilemmas of Italian Communism in the 1970s," in Lange and Sidney Tarrow (eds.), *Italy in Transition*, for an analysis of the PCI's "historic compromise" strategy.

5. Jane Kramer, *Unsettling Europe*, "The San Vincenzo Cell (1979)."

6. Sabino Acquaviva, *Il seme religioso della rivolta*, no. 40.

7. Umberto Terracini, *Intervista sul comunismo difficile*, p. 182.

8. Piero Agostini, *Mara Cagol,* "San Romedio: Margherita Cagol."

9. Ida Faré and Franca Spirito, *Mara e le altre,* p. 28.

10. Red Brigade communication, 5 June 1975, in Soccorso Rosso (eds.), *Brigate rosse,* p. 284.

11. Of these groups, 484 belonged to the Left and 113 to the Right. Most of the violence was the work of fifteen major groups, above all the Red Brigades, Prima Linea, the Nuclei Armati Proletari, and Proletari Comunisti Organizzati on the Left and Ordine Nuovo, Ordine Nero, the Nuclei Armati Rivoluzionari, and the Squadre d' Azione "Mussolini" on the Right. Mauro Galleni (ed.), *Rapporto sul terrorismo.*

12. Arnaldo Giuliani, "Canti, slogan e proclami in Corte d'assise," *Corriere della sera,* 18 May 1976.

13. Giampaolo Pansa, "Curcio alla sbarra a Torino e le Brigate Rosse confermano, "Ieri abbiamo giustiziato Coco nemico del proletariato," *Corriere della sera,* 10 June 1976.

14. Arnaldo Giuliani, "Tumultuosa scena nell' aula dell' assise, minacce ai giudici: 'Con Coco anche voi, egregie eccellenze, siete state giudicate'," *Corriere della sera,* 10 June 1976.

15. Luigi Irdi and Antonello Valentini, "L'uccisione del procuratore Occorsio a Roma, firmata dai fascisti fuori legge di Ordine Nuovo," *Corriere della sera,* 11 July 1976. Pierluigi Concutelli, the military leader of Ordine Nero, was charged with assassinating Occorsio.

16. Rodolfo Brancoli, *Spettatori interessati,* p. 99.

17. Giorgio Galli, *Storia del partito armato: 1968–1982,* p. 111.

18. Sabino Acquaviva and Mario Santuccio, *Social Structure in Italy,* p. 157.

19. Giorgio Manzini, *Indagine su un brigatista rosso,* p. 55.

20. Giampaola Pansa, "Mio figlio? Ora so che non lo conoscevo," *Corriere della sera,* 17 December 1976.

21. Kogan, *Political History of Italy,* chap. 19, "Economic Crises in the 1970s," and Michele Salvati, "Muddling Through: Economics and Politics in Italy, 1969–1979," in Lange and Tarrow (eds.), *Italy in Transition.*

22. Galli, *Storia del partito armato,* pp. 123ff.

23. Carlo Rivolta, "La rabbia studentesca esplode all' Università di Roma," *La Repubblica,* 19 February 1977.

24. For Lama's personal reflections on political violence in Italy, see "La sfida del terrorismo" in *Rinascita,* 15 February 1980. Here he called for a strengthening of the Italian police and a rejection of a typically Left response to the problem of terrorism during the early 1970s, "né con le Br né con lo Stato."

25. Felice Froio, "Scuola, laboratorio di violenza," *La Repubblica,* 5 December 1979.

26. Franco Foresta Martin, "Un alibi che si chiama università," *Corriere della sera,* 11 November 1977.

27. Alberto Ronchey, *Libro bianco sull' ultima generazione,* chap. 2, "S'avanza uno strano studente (Il parco antropologico)." For more on how Italian universities have been compromised since 1968, see the testimony of Professor Angelo Ventura in Giampaolo Pansa, *Storie italiane di violenza e terrorismo,* "Insegnare a Padova."

28. Giovanni Ceruti and Marco Marozzi, "Bologna sconvolta," *La Repubblica,* 12 March 1977.

29. Marco Marozzi, "In piazza, con i sindacati," *La Repubblica,* 13–14 March 1977.

30. Ulderico Munzi, "De Martino liberato indica un legame fra il terrorismo politico e la malavita," *Corriere della sera,* 16 May 1977.

31. Arnaldo Giuliani, "Rinviato a Torino il processo alle Brigate rosse, perchè i giudici popolari rifiutano l'incarico," *Corriere della sera,* 4 May 1977.

32. Antonio Ferrari, "I giurati raccontano la loro paura," *Corriere della sera,* 5 May 1977.

33. Roberto Ciuni, "Cominciò in un caffè del Vomero la sanguinosa avventura dei NAP," *Corriere della sera,* 3 July 1977.

34. Bocca, *Noi terroristi,* "La 'santa canaglia' dei NAP."

35. For a statistical breakdown of the NAP terrorist campaign, see Galleni (ed.), *Rapporto sul terrorismo*, pp. 188–90.

3. LIVING THE REVOLUTION

1. Arnaldo Giuliani, "Giornalista dell' Unità aggredita e ferita alle gambe da estremisti," *Corriere della sera*, 20 September 1977.

2. Tobagi, *Storia del movimento studentesco*, and "Dai gruppi organizzati ai 'cani sciolti,' la confusa mappa dell' ultra sinistra," *Corriere della sera*, 11 September 1977.

3. Giampaolo Pansa, "La nervosa vigilia a Bologna," *Corriere della sera*, 22 September 1977.

4. Giampaolo Pansa, "Giornata tranquilla nel centro di Bologna, aspri contatti fra gli ultri al Palasport," ibid., 24 September 1977.

5. For his earliest writings, see Raniero Panzieri, *L'alternativa socialista*.

6. See ibid. for the *testo ridotto* of Panzieri's thesis in which he argued that Morelly's *Code de la Nature* "is the ideological moment of *Babouvismo*," i.e., the 1796 Conspiracy of Equals.

7. Raniero Panzieri, "Osservazioni a un nuovo revisionismo," *Socialismo*, May 1946, reprinted in ibid. In "Il socialismo umanista in Francia," *Socialismo*, January–February 1947, reprinted in ibid., he denounced the entire reformist tradition from Jaurès and Blum to Saragat as "a radical deformation of Marxism," which really amounted to a counterrevolutionary rejection of Marx.

8. There is a vast bibliography on Morandi. Six volumes of *Opere di Rodolfo Morandi* were published by Einaudi, 1958–60. See also Aldo Agosti, *Rodolfo Morandi*; Stefano Merli, *Fronte antifascista e politica di classe*; and Pasquale Amato, *Il Psi tra frontismo e autonomia (1948–1954)*.

9. Giovanni Mottura, "Ricostruzione capitalistica e nuove istituzioni: in memoria di Raniero Panzieri," *Politica comunista*, no. 2, February 1975.

10. Raniero Panzieri, "Il piano socialista," *Bolletino dell'Istituto di Studi Socialisti*, 16–31 May 1947, reprinted in Panzieri, *L'alternativa socialista*.

11. Panzieri, "Per il piano socialista," ibid., 1–31 August 1947, reprinted in *L'alternativa socialista*.

12. Panzieri, "Rivoluzione catastrofica e rivoluzione permanente," in *L'alternativa socialista*.

13. For the relationship between Panzieri and Della Volpe, see Sandro Mancini, *Socialismo e democrazia diretta*, chap. 2, "L'interpretazione del Rapporto tra Politica e Cultura." See also John Fraser, *An Introduction to the Thought of Galvano Della Volpe*. Mariachiara Fugazza interprets *dellavolpismo* as "almost the theoretical prologue of all the successive experiences of the new heretics." See her "Dellavolpismo e nuova sinistra: sul rapporto tra i Quaderni rossi e il marxismo teorico," *Aut aut*, September–December 1975. On this theme, see also Mario Alcaro, *Dellavolpismo e nuova sinistra*.

14. In later years Panzieri became very critical of Della Volpe, especially when the latter entered the orbit of the PCI, becoming the official philosopher of the institutional Left. See Emilio Agazzi, Prefazione, in Alcari, *Dellavolpismo*, p. 14.

15. Panzieri also translated Engels's *La situazione della classe operaia in Inghilterra* and prepared a critical edition of Marx's *Critica del programma di Gotha*. Marx's early writings had a pervasive influence on Panzieri's views regarding worker alienation.

16. "Giant misery" is Aldous Huxley's phrase in his introduction to Danilo Dolci, *Report from Palermo*.

17: For example, after World War II the Mafia killed three of Sicily's most courageous peasant organizers: Placido Rizzotto, Accursio Miraglia, and Salvatore Carnevale. See Danilo Dolci, *Sicilian Lives*, p. 189 and pp. 239–49.

18. Panzieri, "L'occupazione delle terre (appunti inediti dal 1950)," in *L'alternativa socialista*.

19. Panzieri, "Vive la Sicilia," *Avanti!*, 6 June 1951, reprinted in *L'alternativa socialista*.
20. Stefano Merli, "Cronologia della vita di Raniero Panzieri," in *L'alternativa socialista*.
21. According to Luciano Della Mea, who was one of Panzieri's colleagues in those years, Mao Tse-tung was "discovered" for the Italian Left by Panzieri and Nenni. See "Una lettera su Raniero Panzieri (17 July 1969)" in Giampiero Mughini (ed.), *Il revisionismo socialista*, p. 234.
22. Panzieri, "Appunti di un viaggio in Cina," in *L'alternativa socialista*, pp. 166f.
23. Ibid.
24. In 1947 the Socialist party broke apart in the "Palazzo Barberini schism" over the issue of collaborating with the Communists. Giuseppe Saragat then formed the splinter PSDI. See Alberto Benzoni and Viva Tedesco, *Il movimento socialista nel dopoguerra*, pt. I, "Dalla ricostituzione alla scissione."
25. For the historical background of *Mondo operaio*, see the preface to Gaetano Arfé (ed.) *Mondo operaio: 1956–1965*.
26. Cited by Ajello, *Intellettuali e PCI*, p. 306.
27. See Anton Antonov-Ovseyenko, *The Time of Stalin*.
28. Pietro Nenni, Introduzione, Arfé (ed.), *Mondo operaio: 1956–1965*.
29. Nenni, "Luci e ombre del Congresso di Mosca," *Mondo operaio*, March 1956.
30. Nenni, "Primo bilancio sulla polemica del XX Congresso di Mosca," *Mondo operaio*, July 1956.
31. Panzieri, "Riesame del leninismo," *Opinione*, May 1956, reprinted in *L'alternativa socialista*.
32. Panzieri, "La crisi del comunismo," *Il punto* (Rome), 10 November 1956, reprinted in *L'alternativa socialista*.
33. Ibid.
34. According to Luciano Della Mea, a *Mondo operaio* contributor at the time, Panzieri was the de facto director of the journal from March 1957 to December 1958. See "Panzieri tra Mondo operaio e Quaderni rossi" in Della Mea, *Eppure si muove*.
35. Panzieri, "Appunti per un esame della situazione del movimento operaio," *Mondo operaio*, January 1957.
36. Ibid.
37. Neal Ascherson, *The Polish August*, pp. 66ff.
38. Ibid.
39. Ajello, *Intellettuali e Pci*, p. 415.
40. Panzieri, "La crisi del comunismo," *Il punto* (Rome), 10 November 1956.
41. Here again the influence of Morandi had been decisive in Panzieri's thinking. For Morandi's critique of Soviet Russia, see *Morandi e la democrazia del socialismo*, the published papers from a convention on Morandi called by Marsilio Editore of Venice, 7–8 January 1978. The book appeared that same year.
42. Agostino Novella, a member of the PCI Executive Committee, used this phrase in a roundtable discussion, "Twenty Years after Stalin." Republished in *The Italian Communists*, March–June 1973.
43. Ibid.
44. Ajello, *Intellettuali e Pci*, p. 359. Still, 1956 should be seen not as a beginning but as the culmination of a long-standing crisis within international Marxism that had begun during the Spanish Civil War and had worsened with the signing of the Nazi-Soviet Pact in August 1939. After World War II numerous leftist intellectuals, including Arthur Koestler and the other contributors to *The God That Failed*, steadily chipped away at the myth of Stalinist Russia.
45. For example, on 25 October 1958 Panzieri wrote to his friend Libero Lizzadri that "the only thing of which we have need is a return to Leninism." In Panzieri, *La crisi del movimento operaio*.
46. Panzieri, "Formule e sostanza della politica unitaria," *Mondo operaio*, September 1957.

47. Panzieri, "Appunti per un esame della situazione del movimento operaio," *Mondo operaio*, January 1957.

48. Ibid.

49. See especially Panzieri and Lucio Libertini, "Sette tesi sulla questione del controllo operaio," *Mondo operaio*, February 1958. Although Cesare Pianciola is right to insist that Panzieri's editorials in *Mondo operaio* had been characterized by this line of reasoning from the beginning of his association with the journal, it is still accurate to call "Seven Theses" the most systematic presentation of his ideas up to that point. See "Attualità di Panzieri," *Ombre rosse*, no. 5, 1974. Libertini later confirmed that the article had been written to confront the social democratic offensive within the PSI. See Introduzione to Lucio Libertini, *La sinistra e il controllo operaio*.

50. See "Un dibattito su *l'Unità*" and "La risposta de l'Unità" in Arfé (ed.), *Mondo operaio: 1956–1965*, pp. 880–90.

51. Spriano's criticism of Panzieri is reminiscent of what Georges Sorel had to say about Karl Kautsky: "he loves reasoning about abstractions and believes that he has brought a question nearer to solution when he manages to produce a phrase with a scientific appearance; the underlying reality interests him less than its academic presentment." Sorel, *Reflections on Violence*, p. 237.

52. Panzieri and Libertini wrote a long antireformist essay, "Tredici tesi sulla questione del partito di classe," for the November–December issue of *Mondo operaio* as a preliminary response to Spriano's challenging questions. It was Panzieri's swan song as the journal's editor.

53. Paolo Bufalini's insistence that the PCI "did not wait for Stalin's death and the Twentieth Congress to become a mass, national, and democratic party" is at least in part correct. See Bufalini, "The Party's Tasks in the Fight against Terrorism and for the Implementation of the Majority Program" (Report to the Central Committee, April 14, 1978), *The Italian Communists*, April–June 1978. Still, the events of 1956 did push the PCI farther and faster along a path it had been exploring since 1944.

54. Panzieri to Maria Adelaide Salvaco, 25 March 1960, in Panzieri, *La crisi del movimento operaio*.

55. Bufalini, "The Party's Tasks."

56. See the extremely apposite selections from the works of Bernstein and Lenin in Eugen Weber, *The Western Tradition*, pp. 760–68.

57. Panzieri to Salvaco, 1 August 1958, in Panzieri, *La crisi del movimento operaio*.

58. Panzieri (in collaboration with Lucio Libertini), "Conclusione al dibattito sul controllo operaio," *Mondo operaio*, March 1959.

59. Panzieri did make an exception of Lelio Basso's *Problemi del socialismo*, which was founded in 1958. See Panzieri to Salvaco, 25 March 1960.

60. Previously, Panzieri had worked as an editor for Edizioni Avanti. Publishing houses provide the same economic safety net for Italian intellectuals that the university system provides for American intellectuals, and for much of his life Panzieri earned his living as an editor.

61. For Panzieri alienation assumed painfully tangible forms in Turin. He frequently was at his wits' end about how to feed his three children and pay the rent. See Franco Fortini, "Per le origini di Quaderni rossi e Quaderni piacentini," *Aut aut*, July–October 1974.

62. Panzieri to Salvaco, 30 October 1959, in Panzieri, *La crisi del movimento operaio*.

63. Panzieri to Alberto Asor Rosa, 17 December 1959, in ibid.

64. Panzieri to Danilo Montaldi, 6 October 1959, in ibid. Montaldi played an important role in Italian Marxism during the 1950s by helping to introduce the ideas and works of the Frankfurt School into Italy. See Stefano Merli, *L'altra storia*, chap. 3, "Montaldi, la con-ricerca, il gruppo, la nuova sinistra." At this time Panzieri ceased to attend PSI congresses and was dropped from all party committees.

65. Panzieri to Montaldi, in Panzieri, *La crisi del movimento operaio*. In the previous

month Libertini, now the director of *Mondo nuovo*, had rejected an article by Panzieri while judging other proposals from his former collaborator as inopportune.

66. Panzieri to Montaldi, 24 September 1959, in ibid.

67. Panzieri to Asor Rosa, 17 December 1959, in ibid. Ingrao was the editor of *l'Unità* from 1947 to 1957.

68. Panzieri's principal new collaborators were Vittorio Foa, Mario Tronti, Alberto Asor Rosa, and Luciano Della Mea. See Dario Lanzardo, "Nota Biografica," in Panzieri, *La ripresa del marxismo leninismo in Italia*. For Della Mea's recollections of this period, see Della Mea, *La politica torna in fabbrica*.

69. Panzieri, "Intervento al Comitato Centrale del PSI," *Avanti!*, 1 October 1959, reprinted in *La crisi del movimento operaio*.

70. Rieser described the origin of Panzieri's movement as a "progressive gathering of groups of comrades" who sensed in the Italian economic boom, not "an ephemeral conjunctural fact," but a profound transformation of capitalist society, which, instead of the tepid reformist measures employed by the official Left, required a radical Marxist response. "I Quaderni rossi," *Rendiconti*, March 1965. Also see this article for a city-by-city analysis of Quaderni Rossi activities during 1960–61 in Turin, Milan, Genoa, Venice, Porto Marghera, Rome, and Florence.

71. Cited by Franco Livorsi, "Lenin in Italia," *Classe*, June 1971.

72. Panzieri to Asor Rosa, 17 December 1959, in *La crisi del movimento operaio*.

73. Some of Panzieri's collaborators had been initiated in the techniques of the *inchiesta* by no less a sociologist than Danilo Dolci, author of *Report from Palermo*. See Franco Fortini, "Per le origini di Quaderni rossi e Quaderni piacentini," *Aut aut*, July–October 1974.

74. Panzieri to Asor Rosa, 14 January 1960, in *La crisi del movimento operaio*.

75. Panzieri, "Nota redazionale per: Daniel Mothé, Diario di un operaio, 1956–1959," ibid.

76. Panzieri to Montaldi, 10 March 1960, ibid.

77. Panzieri to Salvaco, 25 March 1960, ibid.

78. For this reason Panzieri could not take heart from the formation of a radical Socialist splinter group, the Partito Socialista Italiano di Unità Proletaria (PSIUP), in 1963. This party came into existence as a reaction to the formation of the *centro-sinistra* government in which Nenni took part. PSIUP never attracted more than 4.5 percent of the vote (1968) in any national election before it disappeared in the early 1970s. See Teodori, *Storia delle nuove sinistre in Europa*, pt.II, chap. 7, "Italia: centro-sinistra e scissione nel partito socialista."

79. Rieser, "Panzieri e i Quaderni rossi," *Politica comunista*, 3, 1975.

80. Panzieri to Salvaco, 25 March 1960, in *La crisi del movimento operaio*.

81. Della Mea, *Eppure si muove*, Appendix 1.

82. Panzieri to Salvaco, 25 March 1960, in *La crisi del movimento operaio*.

83. *Quaderni rossi* was published irregularly for six issues from June 1961 to December 1965, the last two after Panzieri's death. In addition, a single issue of *Cronache dei Quaderni rossi* was published in September 1962. While *Quaderni rossi* fully deserves its place of eminence in the history of the extraparliamentary Left, it was not the only journal calling for an authentically Marxist attack on capitalism. In 1962–63, for example, a group of Paduan Communists published three numbers of *Viva il leninismo*, which adopted an ardently anti-Togliatti line. Togliatti responded by expelling four of these critics from the party. Mario Quaranta, "Storia dei tre numeri di Viva il leninismo," *Che fare*, no. 6–7, Spring 1970.

84. Panzieri to Asor Rosa, 26 October 1960, in *La crisi del movimento operaio*.

85. Untitled policy statement, *Quaderni rossi*, no. 4, 30 July 1964.

86. Panzieri to Salvaco, 12 December 1960, in *La crisi del movimento operaio*.

87. Panzieri to Mario Tronti, 12 December 1960, ibid. Approximately two thousand copies of the journal's first issue were sold and five thousand of the second issue. Giuseppe Vettori (ed.), *La sinistra extraparlamentare in Italia*, p. 20.

88. Panzieri's collaborators on *Quaderni rossi* were Emilio Agazzi, Romano Alquati,

176 | Notes to Pages 44–46

Alberto Asor Rosa, Giuliano Boaretto, Luciano Della Mea, Dino De Palma, Liliana Lanzardo, Mario Miegge, Giovanni Mottura, Giuseppe Muraro, Vittorio Rieser, Emilio Soave, and Mario Tronti. Antonio Negri was listed as a collaborator only on the third number, 30 June 1963.

89. For example, see Vittorio Foa, "Lotte operaie nello sviluppo capitalistico," and Panzieri, "Sull' uso capitalistico delle macchine nel neocapitalismo," *Quaderni rossi*, no. 1, June 1961. In November 1961 *Quaderni rossi* suffered the first of several schisms when Sergio Garavini and Emilio Pugno, collaborators on the journal's first issue, denounced the articles of Giovanni Mottura, Vittorio Rieser, Dino De Palma, and Romano Alquati for their schematic and simplistic character.

90. Panzieri's *Quaderni rossi* colleague Emilio Agazzi later described the extreme sympathy with which Panzieri spoke to him about Adorno. See Agazzi's Prefazione to Alcari, *Dellavolpismo*, p. 18.

91. See Maria Grazia Meriggi, "Raniero Panzieri e il 'francofortismo': il movimento operaio dall' apologia del piano 'socialista' all' analisi di classe," *Aut aut*, September–December 1975.

92. Ten years later Panzieri's friend and colleague Della Mea looked back and remembered that "we of *Quaderni rossi*" had given far too much credit to capitalism, thinking that a capitalist "global rationality" would be inevitable. In 1971 Della Mea asserted that no such rationalizing process had occurred. See "Tre Domande Politiche," *Giovane critica*, no. 29, Winter 1971. Giorgio Amendola, a moderate PCI voice, seized upon this theme of capitalist rationalization as Panzieri's primordial error, a legacy that *Quaderni rossi* passed on to the extraparliamentary Left. Amendola reasoned that no claim could be more anti-Marxist than one dismissing the inherent contradictions of capitalism. Moreover, he concluded that once the rationality of capitalism is conceded the Marxist revolutionary is left with no alternative but terror. In "Tre Domande Politiche," pt. 2, no. 30, Spring 1972.

93. Panzieri developed this point further in "Plusvalore e pianificazione: appunti di lettura del Capitale," *Quaderni rossi*, no. 4, July 1964.

94. Panzieri, "Sull'uso capitalistico delle macchine nel neocapitalismo," *Quaderni rossi*, no. 1, June 1961.

95. Giorgio Napolitano, "I Quaderni rossi e le lotte operaie nello sviluppo capitalistico," *Politica ed economia*, January–February 1962.

96. Paolo Santi, "Fabbrica e società nei Quaderni rossi," *Critica marxista*, January–February 1963.

97. Santi specifically called these arguments "the ultra-Left conception of *Quaderni rossi*." Ibid.

98. Cited by Giuseppe Vacca, "Il Marxismo come sociologia: analisi e proposte della rivista Quaderni rossi," *Il contemporaneo* (supplement to *Rinascita*), no. 4, 27 January 1967.

99. Panzieri, "Lotte operaie nello sviluppo capitalistico," in *La ripresa*. Despite his declining health, Panzieri undertook a tour of several Italian cities to promote *Quaderni rossi*: Milan (12 June), Venice (16 October), Padua (17 October), Rome (21 November), La Spezia (19 January 1962), Genoa (20 January 1962), and Siena (24 March 1962). On 10 May 1962 he wrote to Alberto Asor Rosa that he had been "in disastrous physical condition." *Aut aut*, September–December 1975.

100. Panzieri, "Lotte operaie."

101. For this image of Valletta in the Communist press, see Adalberto Minucci, "Storia del professor Valletta dal fascismo al centro-sinistra," *Rinascita*, 4 August 1962.

102. Valerio Castronovo, "Quel professore in Cinquecento che cambiò il volto della Fiat," *La Repubblica*, 9 July 1983.

103. Joanne Barkan, *Visions of Emancipation*, chap. 3, "The Reawakening of the Workers' Movement."

104. Vittorio Rieser, "I Quaderni rossi," *Rendiconti*, 10 March 1965.

105. Emilio Pugno and Sergio Garavini, *Gli anni duri alla Fiat*, pp. 3–4.

106. Vittorio Gorresio, "Alla Camera Domani Taviani indicherà i responsabili degli incidenti di Torino," *La Stampa*, 10 July 1962.

107. Palmiro Togliatti, "Vittoria alla Fiat," *Rinascita*, 14 July 1962.

108. Paolo Spriano, "Dalla sfida di Valletta ai fatti di Piazza Statuto," *Rinascita*, 14 July 1962.

109. Spriano, "Valore di uno sciopero," *Rinascita*, 28 July 1962. Panzieri sent a letter to *l'Unità*, protesting the newspaper's attempts to link him with "subproletarian anarchism." *L'Unità* did not print the letter, but *Avanti!* published a portion of it, which Spriano quoted in his article.

110. In "Dalla sfida di Valletta ai fatti di Piazza Statuto," Spriano averred that Turin, with its boom atmosphere and immigrant throngs, possessed certain aspects of a mining town in the old American west, especially "the same youthful taste of going wherever the action was."

111. Stefano Merli, "La provocazione di Raniero Panzieri," *Il manifesto*, 20 October 1974.

112. Alberto Asor Rosa, "Tre giorni a Torino (7, 8, e 9 luglio 1962)," *Cronache dei Quaderni rossi*, no. 1, September 1962.

113. "Agli operai della Fiat (volantino diffuso il 6 luglio)," ibid.

114. Ibid.

115. For a primary source account of the "shock" that Piazza Statuto provoked in the ranks of the Quaderni Rossi, see Antonio Negri, *Pipe-line*, "Lettera ottava, Piazza Statuto," pp. 87 ff.

116. Negri offers a similar interpretation, ibid.

117. Romano Alquati, Monica Brunatto, P. L. Gasparotto, and Romolo Gobbi, "Note sulle condizioni e lo svolgimento dello sciopero alla Fiat," *Cronache dei Quaderni rossi* no. 1, September 1962.

118. Dino De Palma and Gabriele Lolli, "Lo sviluppo della lotta dei metalmeccanici attraverso la stampa del movimento operaio," ibid.

119. Q R, "Alcuni osservazioni sui fatti di Piazza Statuto," ibid.

120. Panzieri, "Cosa ci insegna la lotta di metalmeccanici," *Progresso veneto*, November 1962, reprinted in Panzieri, *La ripresa*.

121. Panzieri, "Lotta sindacale e lotta politica," *Cronache operaie*, 15 July 1963, reprinted in *La ripresa*.

122. Ibid.

123. Ibid.

124. Panzieri to Asor Rosa, 10 May 1962, in "Materiali inediti" (ed. Dario Lanzardo), *Aut aut*, September–December 1975, a special issue entitled "Raniero Panzieri e i Quaderni Rossi." In this same letter he accused his young friend of "threatening to transform our Marxist renewal into a completely coherent and conceptually finished ideology." At this time Panzieri was suffering from increasing exasperation over the constant need "to clarify minutiae" in the Quaderni Rossi group.

125. According to Edoarda Masi, who began to collaborate on *Quaderni rossi* in the summer of 1964, Panzieri expressly proclaimed the "inadequacy" of the Leninist model for contemporary Italy. In "Panzieri e il movimento rivoluzionario," *Aut aut*, September–December 1975.

126. Panzieri stressed the dominance of Marxism in *Quaderni rossi*, "but in the research work that must bring new empirical results adequate to actual capitalist development it is possible and useful to use critically many other instruments of knowledge offered by recent developments in the social sciences." He further insisted that "bourgeois science" contained elements of value, in an untitled explanatory note concerning the the the ideological character of *Quaderni rossi*, July 1964. In a piece published after his death, Panzieri claimed that "the cultural history of the last twenty years presents us with a great development of a sociology outside Marxist thought" and that "Marxists would have to avail themselves of this contri-

bution." In "Uso socialista dell' inchiesta operaia; intervento di Raniero Panzieri," *Quaderni rossi*, March 1965.

127. Rieser, "Due inediti di Raniero Panzieri," *Quaderni piacentini*, no. 29, January 1967.

128. For a detailed analysis of this element in Panzieri's thinking, see Rieser, "Panzieri e i Quaderni rossi," *Politica comunista*, no. 3, March 1975, p. 37.

129. See Teodori, *Storia delle nuove sinistre in Europa*, pp. 439 ff., for an analysis of the clash between *Quaderni rossi* and *Classe operaia*. After the July 1964 issue, Negri, Tronti, Alquati, Asor Rosa, Di Leo, Gasparotto, Greppi, and Paci were no longer members of the *Quaderni rossi* staff.

130. Cited by Roberta Tomassini in "La ricomposizione di classe come nuovo partito operaio in Raniero Panzieri," *Aut aut*, September–December 1975.

131. Rieser, "I Quaderni rossi," *Rendiconti*, 10 March 1965.

132. Ibid.

133. See the Presentazione in *Lettere dei Quaderni rossi*, a spin-off publication of *Quaderni rossi* that lasted from November 1963 to January 1967; reprinted in 1971 by Sapere Edizioni (Varese-Milan). Earlier, beginning in September 1962, *Cronache dei Quaderni rossi* had undertaken the same task of group communication now essayed by *Lettere dei Quaderni rossi*.

134. Romano Luparini, "Saggio sulla sinistra rivoluzionaria da Quaderni rossi al Maggio 1969," *Che fare*, Spring 1970, no. 6–7.

135. For an assessment of this book's importance in the history of student radicalism during the late 1960s and early 1970s, see Angelo Ventura, "Il problema storico del terrorismo italiano," *Rivista storica italiana*, March 1980. Nicola Badaloni aptly described Tronti's position as "the inversion of the Togliattian [position]." In *Il marxismo italiano degli anni sessanta*, p. 54. Badaloni traces Tronti's ideological heritage to Lukacs through Galvano Della Volpe.

136. Mario Tronti, "La fabbrica e la società," *Quaderni rossi*, no. 2, June 1962. See also Tronti, "Il piano del capitale," ibid., no. 3, 30 June 1963, in which he analyzes in greater detail the need "to place the economic mechanism of the system in crisis, making it impossible for it to function."

137. Frantz Fanon, *The Wretched of the Earth*, p. 294.

138. For an analysis of the points that they shared at the outset of their association on *Quaderni rossi*, see "Introduzione alle 'Tesi Panzieri-Tronti," ed. Dario Lanzardo, *Aut aut*, September–December 1975. Panzieri later explained to Asor Rosa that he was "truly stunned and a little saddened" to learn that someone could think his opposition to Tronti arose from anything but a dispassionate political judgment. Panzieri to Asor Rosa, 10 May 1962, in *Aut aut*, ibid.

139. Panzieri, "Intervento alla riunione della redazione Quaderni rossi–Cronache operaie," in *La ripresa*.

140. Cited by Sandro Mancini, "Due puntualizzazioni sull' interpretazioni di Panzieri," *Aut aut*, September–December 1975.

141. Panzieri, "Intervento."

142. Panzieri to Asor Rosa, 10 May 1962, *Aut aut*, September–December 1975.

143. Ibid.

144. Cited by Roberto Massari, *Marxismo e critica del terrorismo*, p. 142.

145. Cited by E. P., "Toni Negri: I suoi docenti: 'è un genio'," *Il messaggero*, 9 April 1979. Norberto Bobbio described Negri as "a serious and profound scholar, among the most culturally prepared theorists of the new left." Ibid.

146. Guido Coppini, "Dietro quel filosofo c'è il profeta armato," *Gazzetta del Popolo*, 15 April 1979.

147. Cristina Mariotti, "Caso Negri, Scalzone, Piperno," *L'Espresso*, 22 April 1979.

148. Negri, *Pipe-line*, "Lettera terza: Souzy," 23 October 1981.

149. For Negri's own account of his passage from Catholicism to Marxism, see *Pipe-line*,

"Lettera prima: Veneto secco," 10 October 1981, and "Lettera seconda: movimento operaio," 15 October 1981.

150. Negri, "Ambiguità di Panzieri," *Aut aut*, September–December 1975. In *Dall' operaio massa all' operaio sociale*, Negri gave Panzieri credit for "an analytical deepening of Italian politics and, above all, of the new situation of capitalist development" from a Marxist perspective, p. 36.

151. This critique is a distinct echo of Georges Sorel, who in *Reflections on Violence* made the following observation about middle-class radicals; "They cannot apply to it [i.e., working-class violence] the commonplaces which generally serve them when they speak about force, and they look with terror on movements which may result in the ruin of the institutions by which they live," p. 40.

152. Negri, "Ambiguità di Panzieri."

153. Romano Alquati et al., *Terrorismo verso la seconda repubblica?*, p. 20.

154. Negri, *Pipe-line*, "Lettera settima, luglio '60," 8 December 1981.

155. Negri, "Ambiguità di Panzieri." Negri asserted flatly that "the break had been determined by different ways of conceiving the political struggle and [its] organization."

156. Massimo Cacciari, in "Note intorno a 'Sull'uso capitalistico delle macchine' di Raniero Panzieri," *Aut aut*, September–December 1975, argued that Panzieri's limitations on this very point inspired the *Quaderni rossi* radicals to strike out in a new theoretical direction. For the same viewpoint see R. Luparini, "Saggio sulla sinistra rivoluzionaria dai Quaderni rossi al maggio 1969," *Che fare*, no.6–7, Spring 1970.

157. It was Alberto Asor Rosa, however, who wrote a declaration of independence for the radicals, "Fine della battaglia culturale," *Classe operaia*, no. 2, 1964: "No longer the elaboration of (pseudo) alternative values, but a proposal of methods for struggle; no longer the battle of ideas and culture, but the search for adequate instruments of class struggle." Reprinted in Asor Rosa, *Intellettuali e classe operaia*, p. 48. This essay also appears in Giuseppe Vacca, *Politica e teoria nel marxismo italiano: 1959–1969*, pp. 221–33. Vacca's introduction, pp. 7–129, surveys the entire field of Italian Marxism in the 1960s.

158. Cited by Giorgio Bocca, *Il caso 7 aprile*, chap. 2, "Potere operaio."

159. Negri, *Pipe-line*, "Lettera ottava: piazza Statuto," 20 December 1981.

160. Ibid.

161. Cited by Paul Thomas, *Karl Marx and the Anarchists*, p. 285.

162. Rieser, Introduzione to "Due inediti di Raniero Panzieri," *Quaderni piacentini*, no. 29, January 1967.

163. For the origins of the Italian student movement, see Carlo Oliva and Aloisio Rendi, *Il movimento studentesco e le sue lotte*, and Tobagi, *Storia del movimento studentesco*. See also Luisa Cortese (ed.), *Il movimento studentesco*; and Gianfranco Camboni and Danilo Samsa, *PCI e movimento degli studenti (1968–1973)*. For a more specialized bibliography on the student movement and on university problems in Italy, see Mino Monicelli, *L'ultrasinistra in Italia, 1968–1978*.

164. As in so many other practical questions pertaining to revolution, Bakunin has proved to be a more prophetic thinker than his great rival in the First International, Marx. It was Bakunin who pointed out the fundamentally nonrevolutionary character of the working class and its inclination toward a reform mentality. Authentic revolution, he asserted, could only be made by the politicized criminal class—the bandits and brigands of the day—in alliance with disaffected students, marginal intellectuals, and peasants. Bakunin was drawn to this last group because of its marked penchant for violence. See Thomas, *Karl Marx and the Anarchists*, pp. 290ff. Even some Marxist thinkers have expressed disillusionment with the postindustrial working class; e.g., Herbert Marcuse, *One-Dimensional Man*.

165. Giorgio Amendola, a frequent contributor to *Rinascita*, noted that in the late 1960s fewer than 10 per cent of university students were from peasant or proletarian backgrounds, making the student movement, he concluded, "particularly susceptible to political and ideal oscillations"; in "The Lessons of a Decade," *The Italian Communists*, June–July 1972. For the last ten years of his life Amendola was one of the PCI's most searching critics of the

extraparliamentary Left, especially its "feverish search for and rapid wearing out of myths," including Castro, Che Guevara, the Black Panthers, the Fedayeen, the Chinese Cultural Revolution, and Lin Piao—"insubstantial revolutionary models" all; ibid.

166. Ida Regalia, Marino Regini, and Emilio Reyneri, "Labour Conflicts and Industrial Relations in Italy," in Colin Crouch and Alessandro Pizzorno (eds.), *The Resurgence of Class Conflict in Western Europe since 1968,* vol. 1, p. 129.

167. Panzieri to Luciano Della Mea, 18 August 1964, in "Materiali inediti" (ed. Lanzardo), *Aut aut* September–December 1975.

168. For the influence of Mao Tse-tung on Panzieri, see Della Mea, "Una lettera su Raniero Panzieri."

169. Panzieri and Libertini, "Tredici tesi sulla questione del partito di classe," *Mondo operaio,* November–December 1958.

170. Cited by Stefano Merli, "Cronologia della vita di Raniero Panzieri," in Panzieri, *L'alternativa socialista,* p. xlii.

171. *L'Unità,* 10 October 1964. On 2 October 1964 Nenni privately commented on Panzieri's death as follows: "Of the young men [who] came to the party and to its leadership during the past twenty years he was, from my point of view, the most peculiar but also the most honest and the most intelligent. His intellectual curiosity put new problems before him every day, which he attempted to resolve in close touch with the workers. He was unmanageable to the point that within a year he was outside every party and also from the Einaudi editorial house. . . . [He struggled] only for ideas and on the terrain of ideas. He deserved a much different fate." Nenni, *Gli anni del centro sinistra.*

172. Reprinted in Giovanni Bechelloni (ed.), *Cultura e ideologia nella nuova sinistra,* p. 14.

173. See esp. Panzieri, "Plusvalore e pianificazione: appunti di lettura di Capitale," *Quaderni rossi,* no. 4, 1964, which Giacomo Marramao, in "Teoria della crisi e problematica della costituzione," *Critica marxista,* March–June 1975, described as one of the major essays in the history of Italy's new Left. In his last piece Panzieri displayed the strengths for which his remaining supporters on *Quaderni rossi* admired him and the weaknesses for which the *Classe operaia* writers criticized him. Always forceful in denouncing capitalism as an inherently despotic system, he failed again—in the eyes of Tronti and Negri—to go beyond a rhetorical call for further study and analysis of the problem, i.e., he did not issue a call for revolution.

174. Negri, "Ambiguità di Panzieri," and *Pipe-line,* "Lettera settima, luglio '6o."

175. See the critique of Panzieri in Fugazza, "Dellavolpismo e nuova sinistra."

176. In "Plusvalore e pianificazione," Panzieri carefully distinguished between Marx's specific solutions, which were obsolete, and his analysis, which had lost none of its power and appeal.

177. Cited by Dario Lanzardo, "Appunti per una riconsiderazione del rapporto teoria-politica in Panzieri," in "Materiali inediti" (ed. Lanzardo), *Aut aut.*

178. For Tronti, see Franco Livorsi, "Lenin in Italia," *Classe,* June 1971. For Negri, see "Ambiguità di Panzieri," and *Pipe-line,* "Lettera settima: luglio '6o," and "Lettera ottava: piazza Statuto."

179. In "Tre Domande Politiche," *Giovane Critica,* no. 29, Winter 1971.

180. For more on the connections between extraparliamentary Left culture and terrorism, see Angelo Ventura, "Il problema storico del terrorismo italiano," *Rivista storica italiana,* March 1980.

181. Negri, "Ambiguità di Panzieri."

182. Maurice Merleau-Ponty, *Humanism and Terror,* p. xxxvi.

183. *Neue Frankfurter Zeitung,* 7 August 1969.

184. Panzieri, "Diario cinese (1955)," in *L'alternativa socialista,* p. 167.

185. Ibid.

4. ALDO MORO AND ITALY'S DIFFICULT DEMOCRACY

1. In a speech on 18 November 1977 Moro called Italy's problem with violence "the most grave sign of the political crisis the country is going through. . . . " Moro, *L'intelligenza e gli avvenimenti: testi 1959–1978.*

2. Cited by Giuseppe Zupo and Vincenzo Marini Recchia, *Operazione Moro*, p. 344.

3. Arnaldo Giuliani, "I giustizieri spiegano la sentenza della condanna a morte di Casalegno," *Corriere della sera,* 18 November 1977.

4. Pansa, *Storie italiane di violenza e terrorismo,* "Un berlingueriano."

5. Franco Di Bella, *Corriere segreto,* p. 410.

6. Aniello Coppola, *Moro,* chap. 1, "Che fatica entrare nella DC."

7. Moro, *L'intelligenza e gli avvenimenti,* Discorso, 16 September 1964.

8. Moro cited the encyclical in a 20 July 1961 speech, ibid.

9. Ibid., Discorso, 29 June 1969.

10. Giuseppe Di Palma, *Surviving without Governing,* pp. 237–39.

11. In *Diari 1976–1979,* Giulio Andreotti described Moro's conviction that after the 1975 election it was "indispensable . . . to involve the Communists in some manner," p. 19.

12. Moro, *L'intelligenza e gli avvenimenti,* Discorso, 18 July 1974.

13. Even in his last speech, on 28 February 1978, Moro emphasized Christian Democracy's unflagging opposition to Communist ideas. Ibid.

14. Henry Kissinger, *White House Years* pp. 920–21. Kissinger rated Moro as "the most formidable" Italian leader of the day: "He was as intelligent as he was taciturn; he had a reputation for superb intelligence," p. 100. However, the former secretary of state had "a soporific effect" on Moro: "more often than not he fell asleep in meetings with me; I considered it a success to keep him awake. International affairs clearly did not interest Moro," p. 101. According to Roberto Ducci, Italy's ambassador to the United States, Kissinger misinterpreted Moro's habit of closing his eyes while concentrating on the translation. In Mimmo Scarano and Maurizio De Luca, *Il mandarino è marcio,* chap. 1, "Minacce contro Aldo Moro."

15. CIA. *The Pike Report,* p. 193.

16. Moro, *L'intelligenza e gli avvenimenti,* chap. 3.

17. Andreotti, *Diari,* 14 March 1977.

18. Moro, *L'intelligenza e gli avvenimenti,* Discorso, 28 February 1978.

19. Ulderico Munzi, "Assassinato un dirigente Fiat a Casino, gli hanno sparato al volto con la pistola," *Corriere della sera,* 5 January 1978.

20. Munzi, "Il Procuratore di Casino dice con sicurezza 'La base degli assassini è dentro la fabbrica,' " ibid.

21. Andrea Purgatori, "Le Brigate Rosse a raffiche di mitra assassinano un magistrato a Roma," ibid., 15 February 1978.

22. Arnaldo Giuliani, "I brigatisti minacciano la giuria popolare a Torino," ibid., 10 March 1978.

23. Giuliani, "Le Brigate rosse uccidono un poliziotto, il processo di Torino rischia di saltare," ibid., 11 March 1978.

24. Robert Katz, *Days of Wrath,* provides a detailed account of the Via Fani attack (pp. 3–16), but six years later Giorgio Galli noted that one could write a series of books on the various aspects of "Operation Fritz," as the Red Brigades denominated the Moro kidnapping. This event has inspired thousands of pages of contradictory testimony and retains its aura of mystery. See Galli, *Storia del partito armato: 1968–1982,* chap. 8, "Moro."

25. "Rabbia e sgomento nel paese," *La Repubblica,* 16 March 1978.

26. Giorgio Bocca (ed.), *Moro,* p. 34.

27. Arnaldo Giuliani, "Curcio ha gridato in aula: 'Moro è in mano nostra,' " *Corriere della sera*, 21 March 1978.

28. Walter Tobagi, "I brigatisti in gabbia come in salotto," ibid.

29. Bocca (ed.), *Moro*, communication no. 2.

30. Ibid., Moro to Cossiga, 29 March 1978.

31. For this controversy, see Katz, *Days of Wrath*, esp. chap. 9, "Operation Moro Is Not Moro." The chapter title is a phrase used by Alessandro Silj in his *Brigate Rosse–Stato*. See also Robin Erica Wagner-Pacifici, *The Moro Morality Play*.

32. Sossi, *Nella prigione delle Br*, p. 123.

33. Ibid., p. 179.

34. Bocca (ed.), *Moro*, communication no. 3.

35. For Andreotti's account of the Moro affair, see his *Diari*, esp. 16 March–9 May 1978.

36. Wagner-Pacifici, *Moro Morality Play*, chap. 6, "Reconciliation or Schism: Theory."

37. Bocca (ed.), *Moro*, communication no. 4.

38. Ibid., Moro to Zaccagnini, 4 April 1978.

39. Ibid., communication no. 5.

40. Ibid., communication no. 6.

41. Ibid., communication no. 7.

42. Ibid., Moro to Zaccagnini, 21 April 1978.

43. Ibid., 22 April 1978.

44. Ibid., communication no. 8.

45. Ibid., Moro to Zaccagnini, 24 April 1978.

46. On the crisis of the ultra-Left during the Moro affair, see Wagner-Pacific, *Moro Morality Play*, pp. 149ff.

47. Bocca (ed.), *Moro*, "Lettera di Moro alla Famiglia," p. 137.

48. Luigi La Spina, "Saragat: 'Non si può rimproverare Moro la paura di morire per un motivo assurdo,' " *Corriere della sera*, 30 April 1978.

49. Bocca (ed.), *Moro*, "Appello della Famiglia Moro ai Dirigenti DC," 30 April 1978.

50. Katz, *Days of Wrath*, p. 214. Few people outside his own circle were willing to concede that Craxi's motives were entirely altruistic. For speculation on the Socialist leader's political designs during this period, particularly his hope of creating a split between the PCI and the Christian Democrats, see Galli, *Storia*, p. 169.

51. Antonio Padellaro, "Una vedova di via Fani: 'Se li liberate mi do fuoco!' " *Corriere della sera*, 4 May 1978. This appears to have been a story planted by the authorities.

52. See esp. Wagner-Pacifici, *Moro Morality Play*.

53. Andreotti, *Diari*. See esp. the entries for 30 April and 9 May.

54. Bocca (ed.), *Moro*, communication no. 9.

55. Renato Gaita, "Anche 'i duri' di Autonomia condannano l'assassinio: 'Sarebbe un grave errore politico,' " *Il Messaggero*, 7 May 1978.

56. Katz, *Days of Wrath*, pp. 239ff.

57. For a discussion of the highly controversial thesis that the Red Brigades could penetrate security around Via Caetani only with the help of individuals or groups within the secret services, see Galli, *Storia*, pp. 177–78.

58. Giuliani, "Il capo delle Br espulso per apologia di reato," *Corriere della sera*, 11 May 1978.

59. Bocca (ed.) *Moro*, "Comunicato della Famiglia Moro," 9 May 1978.

5. 7 APRILE 1979

1. Giancarlo Pertegato, "Così due killer hanno freddato in autobus il funzionario che indagò su Coco e Amerio," *Corriere della sera*, 22 June 1978.

2. Little was known about Prima Linea at this time. Its members described themselves as "the point of aggregation of guerrilla groups that until now have operated under different

insignia, with the intention of organizing armed political power." "Che cos'è 'Prima Linea,' " *Corriere della sera*, 27 December 1978.

3. Berardi hanged himself in prison on 24 October 1979. See "Cesare il postino," in Pansa, *Storie.*

4. The Red Brigades moved quickly to repair the damage. The target of their next attack was Italo Schettini, owner of some four hundred apartments in the poor Alessandrino quarter of Rome, who happened to be a provincial counselor of the Christian Democrats as well. These possessions marked him as "Jack the exploiter" and as an ideal villain for Red Brigade punishment. The Alessandrino neighborhood was spattered with antilandlord graffiti, e.g., "Let's hang Schettini," and a terrorist action against this man could only be interpreted as obedience to the will of the people. Accordingly, in the presence of his fourteen-year-old daughter, Schettini was shot down on 29 March with a bullet between the eyes. In a symbolic ritual borrowed from the Mafia, the killers then shot him twice more, once under each eye. Franco Magagnini, "Questi killer ora vogliono presentarsi come Robin Hood," *La Repubblica*, 30 March 1979.

5. Pansa, *Storie*, "L'orefice con la pistola".

6. Bocca, *Il caso 7 aprile*, chap. 1, "I professori in galera."

7. *Classe operaia* triumphantly noted the negative trend in worker affiliation with the PCI, e.g., in "Operai e P. C. I.," *Classe operaia*, September 1964, no. 8–9. Tronti especially attacked the PCI for its "openly social democratic positions" in "Classe e partito," ibid., December 1964, no. 10–12.

8. "Contro il padrone di stato," *Classe operaia*, July 1964, no. 7.

9. For Negri's recollections of his revolutionary activities during the mid-1960s, see Negri, *Pipe-line*, "Lettera nona: autonomia," 26 December 1981, in which he writes, for example: "enough with description, we only want deconstruction," p. 180.

10. Negri, "Operai senza alleati," *Classe operaia*, March 1964, no. 3.

11. Tronti later explained his change of mind. He claimed to have lost none of his passion regarding the evils of reformism and the blessings of revolution, but the extraparliamentary Left had become, in his judgment, a no-man's land of little and unconnected causes, with absolutely no chance of victory against the massive and constantly expanding capitalist hegemony. According to Tronti, party and class would have to be reunited, not driven further apart by petty ideological dissensions. In "Estremismo e riformismo," *Contropiano*, 1/1968.

12. "Primo bilancio," *Contropiano*, 2/1968.

13. Ibid.

14. Negri, "Marx sul ciclo e la crisi: Note," *Contropiano*, 2/68.

15. Announcement, *Contropiano*, 2/1968.

16. Negri's powerful lecture style is described by Mario Isnenghi, also a professor at the University of Padua, who helped to found *Progresso Veneto*. Marco Nozza, "I diavoli di Via del Santo," *Il Giorno*, March 1979.

17. *Potere operaio* provided a campus-by-campus analysis of student violence in the United States in "Verso il maggio rosso americano," *Potere operaio*, 16–23 May 1970, no. 22.

18. Negri was personally "most excited" about the ghetto revolts and confidently awaited "an American May." Bocca, *Noi terroristi*, pp. 71–72.

19. "Noi, i Vietcong," *Potere operaio*, 5–19 March 1971, no. 37.

20. "Il programma dei comunisti vince perchè i Vietcong sparano," ibid., 20 May–20 June 1972, no. 47–48.

21. "Noi, i Vietcong."

22. "Cominciamo a dire Lenin," ibid., 2–9 October 1969, no. 3.

23. "Offensiva operaia," ibid., 9–16 October 1969, no. 4.

24. "Noi e i marxisti-leninisti," ibid., 2–9 October 1969, no. 3.

25. "Crisi dello Stato-Piano, Comunismo e Organizzazione Rivoluzionaria," ibid., 25 September 1971, no. 43.

26. Ibid., 29 October–5 November 1969, no. 7.

27. Conference "Relazioni," ibid., 5–19 March 1971, no. 37.

28. "Mozione Conclusiva," ibid.

29. "3a Conferenza Nazionale d'organizzazione di Potere operaio," ibid., November 1971, no. 44. Persons who attended this conference testified during the 7 *aprile* trial that *potop* leaders created an "occult level"within the organization, i.e., a cadre of members, unknown to the majority, who had military responsibilities."Il Presidente interrompe il Pm del '7 aprile,' Sabato dovrà terminare," *La Repubblica*, 12 April 1984.

30. "Le lotte operaie hanno infranto il sogno emiliano della borghesia rossa," *Potere operaio*, 11–19 December 1969 no. 11, and "Operai e studenti contro l'ordine pubblico della 'città rossa,' " ibid., 16–23 May 1970, no. 22.

31. "PCI: zero in Marxismo," ibid., 17 April–1 May 1971, no. 38–39.

32. "Provocatori vecchi e nuovi e opportunisti," ibid., 16–22 October 1969, no. 5.

33. "Una lotta che costa tanto deve pagare molto di più," ibid., 23–29 October 1969, no. 6.

34. Cited by Guido Coppini, "Dietro quel 'filosofo' c'è il profeta armato," *Gazzetta del Popolo*, 15 April 1979.

35. "Il potere operaio nasce dalla Canna dei fucili," *Potere operaio*, November 1971, no. 44

36. "Proletari, è la guerra di classe," ibid., 20 May–20 June 1972, no. 47–48.

37. "Due documenti sulla militarizzazione del movimento," ibid., 17 April–1 May 1971, no. 38–39.

38. "I proletari seguono la regola: castiga uno educarne cento," ibid., 20 May–20 June 1972, no. 47–48.

39. Ibid.

40. Ibid.

41. Ibid.

42. "Proletari, è la guerra di classe."

43. Ibid.

44. "Epitaffio per Wasfi Tall," ibid., December 1971, no. 45.

45. "Avvertenza," ibid., November 1973, no. 50.

46. Fabio Isman, "Potop: una storia in 5 quadri dal 1969 a oggi," *Il Messaggero*, 9 April 1979.

47. Bocca described Autonomia Operaia not as an organized political party or military organization but as "a quarrelsome confederation of angry and marginalized people, of intellectuals in search of power, of last-gasp workerism (*operaismo*), and also of an obscure rabble (*oscura canaglia*)." In *Noi terroristi*, p. 173.

48. *Potere operaio*, November 1973, no. 50.

49. Negri, *Crisi dello stato-piano comunismo e organizzazione rivoluzionaria*, "Marx sul ciclo e la crisi: note."

50. Ibid., "Crisi dello stato-piano comunismo e organizzazione rivoluzionaria," pp. 169–70.

51. Negri went so far as to denounce reformists as "the diamond point of counter-revolution in Europe today." Ibid., "Lenin e i 'soviet,' " p. 124.

52. Ibid., "Crisi dello stato-piano comunismo e organizzazione rivoluzionaria," p. 147.

53. Ibid., "Marx sul ciclo e la crisi: note," pp. 80–81.

54. Ibid., "Crisi dello stato-piano comunismo e organizzazione rivoluzionaria," p. 168.

55. After thoroughly debunking the Communist parties of Russia and Italy, *Potere operaio* had attacked the New Left as an ideology of pre-Marxist utopian relics; e.g., in "No all'ideologia terzomondista," *Potere operaio*, 29 October–5 November 1969, no. 7. Here "all the hypotheses of the leftist sects"—save the most rigorously Marxist—were summarily dismissed.

56. "Referendum e famiglie," *Rosso*, February 1974.

57. "Liberazione, gioia, lotta di classe: quando il padrone piange l'operaio ride!!!" ibid., April 1976, no. 7 suppl.

58. Ibid.

59. "Il pluralismo. In fondo, a destra," ibid., 5 June 1976, no. 9.

60. "Ordine di cattura," ibid., 18 October 1975, no. 2.

61. "Il volantino delle Brigate Rosse," ibid., 12 November 1975, no. 3. See also "Continuano le provocazioni del nucleo antiterrorismo," ibid., 29 November 1975.

62. "Agnelli, Lama, Agnelli, Lama, Agnelli," ibid.

63. "Tre magistrati, un fraticello e il PCI: una lettera di Alberto Franceschini," ibid.

64. *Rosso* described Berlinguer's theory of Eurocommunism as "a flower of merde." In "Berlinguer, Marchais, Carillo," ibid.

65. "Processo Casselli-Franceschini," ibid.

66. "Onore alla campagna Ulrike Meinhof," ibid., 5 June 1976, no. 9.

67. "Contro le brigate il battaglione stampa," ibid., 14 February 1976, no. 6.

68. "Dichiarazione dei compagni davanti al Tribunale Speciale," ibid., 5 June 1976, no. 9.

69. "A noi non interessa più lo sviluppo del capitale, interessa solo lo sviluppo della forza produttiva del lavoro umano," ibid., June 1977, no. 19/20.

70. "Autonomia operaia: dalla lotta della classe il processo di organizzazione proletaria sul terreno della guerra civile," ibid., September 1977, special number.

71. "Autonomia operaia e il comunismo del proletariato multinazionale," ibid., March 1977, no. 17/18.

72. "Dal maccartismo al magistrismo: l'evoluzione di regime dell' Espresso," ibid., June 1977, no. 19/20.

73. "Non riuscirete a 'chiudere' il movimento," ibid., March 1977, no. 17/18.

74. "Primavera 1977: la repressione non è riuscita né riuscirà a fermare il processo rivoluzionario," ibid., June 1977, no. 19/20.

75. Ibid.

76. "Da nuovi ribelli a movimento politico contro lo Stato," ibid.

77. "Chi è Lenin oggi," ibid., 5 June 1976.

78. "L'attualità del compagno Panzieri," ibid.

79. Giuseppe Miccolis, "L'Università di Padova nel caos: 'peones' bloccano la didattica," *La Repubblica*, 9 February 1978, and Massimo Cavallini, "I veri amici della violenza rossa," *l'Unità*, 19 February 1978.

80. Cited by Cavallini, "I veri amici della violenza rossa." Professor Acquaviva also noted that Autonomia was strong in those departments where there was little hope for employment after graduation.

81. Valerio Di Donato, "Macchè inquieta! Questa Università in guerra," *7 Giorni Veneto*, May 1978.

82. Domenico Orati, "A Padova cento docenti contro il rettore," *La Repubblica*, 22 June 1978.

83. Pansa, *Storie*, "Il tam-tam di Autonomia."

84. Giovanni Belingardi, "Aggredito a colpi di spranga di ferro il preside (PCI) di lettere a Padova," *Corriere della sera*, 22 March 1979.

85. Sabino Acquaviva, "J'Accuse," *Il Mattino di Padova*, 11 July 1978.

86. "Autonomi aggrediscono due docenti: chiuso a Padova anche Magistero," *l'Unità* (Milan), 11 July 1978.

87. Michele Sartori, "Padova laboratorio della eversione," *l'Unità*, 5 April 1979.

88. "Padova: Università e lotte proletarie," *Rosso*, March 1978, no. 25/26.

89. "L'Autonomia organizzata di fronte al dopo Moro," ibid., May 1978.

90. Angelo Ventura, "Il problema storico del terrorismo italiano," *Rivista storica italiana*, March 1980, vol. 92, no. 1. After Moro's death Negri denounced the Red Brigades as "paranoid," "confused," and "stupid." In Negri, *Dall' operaio massa all' operaio sociale*, "Dall' eclisse dell' operaio massa alla centralità dell' operaio sociale."

91. Walter Tobagi, "Le Br: tornano a sparare a Milano e Genova," *Corriere della sera*, 5 May 1978.

92. These books were Negri, *Proletari e stato: per una discussione su autonomia operaia e compromesso storico, La fabbrica della strategia: 33 lezioni su Lenin, Il dominio e il sabotaggio: sul metodo marxista della trasformazione sociale, Marx oltre Marx: quaderno di lavoro sui Grundrisse,* and *Dall' operaio massa all' operaio sociale: intervista sull' operaismo.*

93. Negri, *Il dominio e il sabotaggio,* p. 12.

94. Ibid., p. 43.

95. Ibid., p. 45.

96. Negri, *Proletari e stato,* proposition 11, "Ora subito: appunti sul programma."

97. For more on the violence in Padua during this period, see Galli, *Storia,* pp. 201–2.

98. Piero Capella, "L'Università della Spranga," *Gente,* 20 April 1979.

99. Interview with Richard Drake, Padua, 4 July 1983. In 1984 Autonomia Operaia attempted to regain its influence among the students at the University of Padua, but little came of it. Professor Mario Isnenghi observed that levels of political violence were up from 1983, "but on the whole the climate here is tranquil." Roberto Bianchin, "A Padova ricompare Autonomia," *La Repubblica,* 19 April 1984.

100. Negri, *Pipe-line,* "Lettera decima: Capodanno '68," 7 January 1982, p. 111. However, in "Lettera sedicesima: scadenza '77," 3 March 1982, Negri still claimed that "the ski mask, the P38, and the raised Winchester were valid as elements of liberation," p. 182.

6. THE BLAST FURNACE OF TERRORISM

1. Brigate Rosse, "Risoluzione della Direzione Strategica, February 1978," *Controinformazione,* no. 11–12, July 1978.

2. Ibid.

3. Ibid.

4. Ibid.

5. Ibid.

6. *Lotta continua,* 25 July 1979.

7. For an analysis of the secessions and revolts that caused the Red Brigades to break up from within, see Gian Carlo Caselli and Donatella Della Porta, "La storia delle Brigate Rosse: Strutture organizzative e strategie d'azione, " in Della Porta (ed.), *Terrorismi in Italia,* pp. 206ff.

8. Guido Passalacqua, "Chi rinnega Curcio è nemico delle Br," *La Repubblica,* 22 September 1979.

9. For this argument, see Angelo Ventura, "Il problema storico del terrorismo italiano," *Rivista storica italiana,* March 1980.

10. Pansa, *Storie,* "Insegnare a Padova."

11. Passalacqua,, "Si ritorna a sparare nelle strade di Padova," *La Repubblica,* 27 September 1979.

12. Ibid.

13. "A sparare è Prima Linea," ibid., 6 October 1979.

14. Ibid.

15. The reference here was to Barbara Azzaroni and Matteo Caggegi, two piellini killed by police in a Turin bar on 28 February 1979.

16. Passalacqua, "Curcio promette guerra alla Fiat," *La Repubblica,* 17 October 1979.

17. Mauro Galleni noted that 597 groups claimed credit for violent acts in Italy; in Galleni (ed.), *Rapporto sul terrorismo,* p. 176.

18. Giovanni Cerruti, "E' la vendetta di Autonomia mettere Padova a ferro e a fuoco," *La Repubblica,* 5 December 1979.

19. For an analysis of guerrilla warfare, see Sabino Acquaviva, *Guerriglia e guerra rivoluzionaria in Italia.*

20. Passalacqua, "Hanno detto: chiudete gli occhi, hanno sparato, ho visto il sangue," *La Repubblica*, 12 December 1979.

21. For an analysis of how terrorism affected the Italian legal system, see Vittorio Grevi, "Sistema penale e leggi dell' emergenza: la risposta legislativa al terrorismo" in Gianfranco Pasquino (ed.), *La prova delle armi*.

22. Franco Vernice, "Questa notte ucciso un terrorista, per Torino un altro giorno di sangue," *La Repubblica*, 16–17 December 1979.

23. Franco Scottoni, "Fioroni ha raccontato tutto," ibid., 27 December 1979.

24. Pansa, *Storie*, "Il mito dell'insurrezione: una vita qualunque."

25. On 21 January 1980 Carlo Casirati, the common criminal convicted along with Fioroni in the Saronio kidnapping and slaying, added his voice to the chorus of accusations against Negri. Casirati supported Fioroni's contention that Negri had engineered the entire Saronio plot. According to him, the political science professor even attended a dinner with Saronio at the home of Mauro Borromeo on the night of the crime. Casirati also testified that Negri often used the services of underworld figures in other kidnappings and robberies.

26. Luigi Carracciolo, "Mafia e terrorismo alleati contro l'apertura ai comunisti," *La Repubblica*, 8 January 1980. La Torre himself was killed by the Mafia on 30 April 1982 in Palermo. As a result of testimony by Mafia pentito Tommaso Buscetta in 1984, Mattarella's murder was attributed to that criminal organization.

27. A. C. Jemolo, "Bachelet ucciso tra gli studenti da due br all' università di Roma," *La Stampa*, 13 February 1980.

28. This was a reference to Carducci's "Inno a Satana," first published in Bologna's *Il Popolo* on 8 December 1869 and later collected in *Edizione nazionale delle opere di Giosuè Carducci* (Bologna: Zanichelli, 1939).

29. Actually, Peci had been collaborating with the police since December 1979. Corrado Stajno, *L'Italia nichilista*, chap. 20.

30. Silvano Mazzocchi, "Magistrati chiedono 'misure eccezionali,' " *La Stampa*, 20 March 1980.

31. For the title of his autobiography Peci chose *Io l'infame* (I, the infamous one).

32. Ibid., "Grazie a Moro divenni famosissimo," pp. 16ff.

33. Ibid., "L'organigramma," pp. 56ff.

34. Luigi Bobbio, *Lotta continua*, "Lo 'Scontro Generale' (1971–1972)," in pt. 2, "L'estremismo."

35. "Ucciso Calabresi, il maggior responsabile dell'assassinio di Pinelli," *Lotta continua*, 18 May 1972.

36. Stajno, *L'Italia nichilista*, chap. 8.

37. See ibid., pp. 82ff. for an account of Giovanni Pesce's *Senza tregua: la guerra dei Gap*, about Partisan actions during World War II; this book inspired the piellini to deal with their adversaries in fundamentally the same way that Italian patriots had dealt with the Fascists and the Germans.

38. Ibid., p. 135.

39. Ibid., chap. 19.

40. Cited in Brigate Rosse, "Risoluzione della Direzione Strategica, February 1978."

41. For Tobagi's point of view about the radical Left in Italy, see Tobagi, *Storia del movimento studentesco*.

42. Piero V. Scorti discusses Tobagi's political outlook in *Il delitto paga? L'affare Tobagi*, Introduzione.

43. André Malraux, *Man's Fate*.

44. "Il testo del volantino di rivendicazione," in Scorti, *Il delitto paga?*, pt. 4, "I documenti."

45. Ibid.

46. Pier Paolo Benedetto, "Appello di un capo terrorista, 'Compagni deponete le armi,' " *La Stampa*, 30 May 1980.

7. THE CHILDREN OF THE SUN

1. G. Z., "Roma: due neofascisti dei Nar hanno ucciso il guidice Amato," *La Stampa*, 25 June 1980.

2. Galleni (ed.), *Rapporto sul terrorismo*.

3. Francesco Fornari, "Un medico, 'Per ore ho medicato gente che aveva perso le gambe e le braccia,'" *La Stampa*, 3 August 1980.

4. Giuseppe De Lutiis (ed.), *La strage*, pp. 189ff.

5. For a detailed analysis of the formative influences on Evola's thought, see Gian Franco Lami, *Introduzione a Evola*.

6. See esp. Alberto Cavaglion, *Otto Weininger in Italia*, "Julius Evola," pp. 114–121. Weininger's *Sesso e carattere* was a seminal book in Evola's mental development.

7. Adriano Romualdi, *Julius Evola: l'uomo e l'opera*, pp. 8ff. See also Lami, *Introduzione a Evola*, pp. 68ff. Lami notes that Evola fought without élan during World War I because he was more sympathetic to the cause of the Central Powers than to that of the Allies. For Evola's own analysis of his early years, see the autobiographical *Cammino del cinabro*, "Il fondo personale e le prime esperienze."

8. Evola wrote disapprovingly of Papini's postwar conversion to Catholicism and scarcely thought of him as a serious thinker after that. Nevertheless, Evola praised the "paradoxical, polemical, iconoclastic, anticonformist, revolutionary Papini" of the *Leonardo* and *Lacerba* prewar period, i.e., of the *prima maniera*. Evola, "Papini," *Ricognizioni: uomini e problemi*. Prezzolini, too, according to Evola, became a caricature of himself without ever possessing anything like Papini's intellectual power and originality. See "La Destra e la Cultura," ibid.

9. Evola, *Il cammino del cinabro*, p. 17.

10. Evola's poetry from the period 1916–22 was eventually collected in *Raâga blanda*. See also his "La parole obscure du paysage intérieur" (1920), republished by Scheiwiller in 1963. Many of Evola's poems were written in French. Before surrendering completely to the linguistic conceits of Dadaism, Evola wrote some excellent war poetry. See esp. "Baracca Alpina al Fronte" and "Reticolati" in *Raâga blanda*. One of the Dada paintings is still on display in Rome's Galleria Nazionale d'Arte Moderna, "Paesaggio interiore, ore 10,30."

11. Evola, *Il cammino del cinabro*, p. 26. In a 1964 essay, "Documenti del Dadaismo," Vittorio Orazi (Alessandro Prampolini) linked Evola's Dada past with the tradition by claiming that it was necessary to destroy the false "tradition" of art dating from the Renaissance. Gianfranco de Turris (ed.), *Omaggio a Julius Evola*.

12. Evola's hatred of the bourgeoisie remained at white heat as the years passed. In a November 1970 interview with Gianfranco de Turris he exclaimed that the central idea of his work was "to be completely and in every way antibourgeois, intolerant of every compromise and bourgeois conformism." De Turris (ed.), *Omaggio*.

13. Evola, *Il cammino del cinabro*, "L'arte astratta e il dadaismo," p. 23. This is exactly what he meant in *Fenomenologia dell'individuo assoluto* when he wrote that at a certain level of artistic consciousness "a tram ticket is as artistic as the Mona Lisa," p. 184.

14. Evola, *Teoria dell'individuo assoluto*, pp. 34 and 106.

15. For "the ways by which the complete determination of the self can be actuated," see Evola, *Fenomenologia*, esp. the Presentazione.

16. Ibid., pp. 277ff.

17. For the connection between Evola's art and poetry on the one hand and his philosophy on the other, see *Fenomenologia*, pp. 181ff.

18. Evola devoted an entire section of *Fenomenologia*, which was written in 1924, to an analysis of Eastern mysticism. See "Epoca della Dominazione."

19. Three volumes of their monographs, which appeared between 1927 and 1929, were republished in 1955 under the title *Introduzione alla magia*.

20. Evola translated Guénon's book as *La crisi del mondo moderno*. He wrote extensively on Guénon, but see esp. "René Guénon e il 'Tradizione Integrale,'" in *Ricognizioni*, and

the pamphlet "René Guénon." Although Guénon argued in *La crise* that Catholicism was the only proper vehicle for traditionalism in the West, he came to believe that Western civilization lacked the philosophical and religious insights necessary for true transcendence. He then converted to Islam and took the name Sheikh Abdel Wahîd Yasha.

21. Evola, "René Guénon," in *Ricognizioni*. See also "La Destra e la Tradizione," in ibid.

22. *La rivolta contro il mondo moderno* did meet with success in right-wing German circles, however. For example, see Gottfried Benn's March 1935 review of the book, reprinted in the appendix of Evola's *L'arco e la clava*. After reading *La rivolta* Benn wrote that "we feel ourselves transformed," p. 237.

23. Evola, *La rivolta*, Introduzione.

24. For example, in his view of history Calvin was "the pimp" who introduced the odious idea of money as a sign of man's worth in God's eyes. Ibid., p. 404.

25. With the Renaissance, Evola argued, Western civilization ceased to have a unitary axis: "The center no longer commands the individual parts, not only in political life, but in cultural life as well. A single organizing and animating force no longer exists." Ibid., pp. 377–78.

26. Ibid., p. 417.

27. A February 1970 interview of Evola by Enrico de Boccard in *Playmen* was entitled "Conversations without Complications with the 'Last Ghibelline.' " In De Turris (ed.), *Omaggio*.

28. Cited by Evola in *Gli uomini e le rovine*, p. 109. Evola held Sombart in great esteem. See "La potenza e l'infantilismo" in *Ricognizioni*.

29. Evola rarely missed an opportunity to attack the Catholic Church, and his own thought was the antithesis of "Semitic" Christianity. See his *Imperialismo pagano*, which was published on the eve of the Lateran Accords as a warning to Mussolini about the "Euro-Christian peril." In this book Evola claimed that neoguelfismo was "the principal danger [threatening] the resurrection of true *Romanità* in a regenerated Italy." See the Introduction. For a sample of his heated rhetoric against Catholicism in the Vatican II era, see his "Quo Vadis Ecclesia?" in *L'Italiano*, June–July 1963, 6–7. Reprinted in Dennis Eisenberg, *L'internazionale nera*, Appendix. He believed that the modernizing of Catholicism had brought about the triumph of the Protestant Reformation. See also "Il mito di Oriente e Occidente" and "L'incontro delle religioni" in Evola, *L'arco e la clava*. Here he scorns the "ecumenical euphoria" of the Vatican Council.

30. Evola, *La rivolta*, p. 83. See also his "Americanismo e Bolscevismo," in *Nuova antologia*, no. 1371, 1929. Later in life Evola found little to choose between the United States and the Soviet Union. He thought that the cold war was "devoid of every spiritual significance," i.e., the West was based on a negation of traditional values, and Marxism was a negation of the negation. Nevertheless, because of Italy's vulnerable political situation he argued that the Russians represented an even greater immediate danger than the Americans. Evola, *Cavalcare la tigre*, p. 249.

31. Evola, "Cose a Posto e Parole Chiare," *La torre*, 1 April 1930. The other principal contributors to *La torre* were Guido de Giorgio, Emilio Servadio, Leonardo Grassi, Guido Ferretti, Girolamo Comi, Roberto Pavese, and René Guénon. See Evola, *La torre*, Introduzione by Marco Tarchi. Evola had no compunction about challenging Mussolini on policy as well as on principle. For example, he criticized the duce's demographic campaign, arguing that "the maximum number of births" idea was inherently antielitist and demagogic. Italy needed quality, not quantity—"a handful of leaders and rulers" instead of a still larger mob than the one already in existence. "Le Razze Muoiono," *La torre*, 1 March 1930. The government reacted to Evola's article by sequestering this issue of the journal.

32. Evola contributed a number of articles to Preziosi's *Vita italiana*.

33. See Marco Tarchi (ed.), *Diorama*, vol. 1, 1934–35. In the early years of Evola's collaboration on *Regime fascista*, "Diorama" appeared biweekly and later on a monthly basis.

34. Roberto Farinacci, "Formare l'Italiano Nuovo," ibid.

35. Evola, "Metafisica della Guerra," I–IV, 25 May–12 August 1935, ibid.

36. Evola later admired Gentile's courage and fidelity in standing by Mussolini after 25 July 1943, an action that cost the philosopher his life. Nevertheless, Evola always criticized Gentile's ideas as essentially antitraditional and even implicitly Marxist. See "Il Caso di Giovanni Gentile," in Evola, *Ricognizioni*. For more on how intellectuals became objects of factional intrigue in Fascist Italy, see Alastair Hamilton, *The Appeal of Fascism*, pt. 1, "Italy."

37. For Bombacci's influence on the Salò regime, see F. W. Deakin, *The Brutal Friendship*, chap. 5, "The Congress of Verona."

38. Evola, *Il cammino del cinabro*, p. 162. Evola maintained that while the war was being fought the "institutional question" had to be suspended.

39. Ibid.

40. Evola, *Sintesi di dottrina della razza*, p. 224.

41. Tarchi (ed.), *Diorama*, Introduzione, p. lxxvii.

42. Evola, *Il cammino del cinabro*, p. 162.

43. Pino Rauti, "Evola una guida per domani," *Civiltà: rivista di dottrina politica e di cultura* (special number dedicated to Julius Evola), September–December 1974, p. 10.

44. Evola boasted that never in his life had he voted or joined any political party. *Il cammino del cinabro*, p. 72. He complained that all parties were "residues of democracy and of mass organizations." In "the antiparty and organic state" of his heart's desire there would be no room for such relics of the "modern past," and in the meantime he would only consider joining "orders," not parties. See De Turris (ed.), *Omaggio*, "Incontro con Julius Evola."

45. Evola, *Il fascismo*, also contains Evola's essay "Note sul Terzo Reich." Evola criticized Hitler's government, too, but he gave the Nazis credit for at least recognizing that the modern world was the enemy.

46. Evola, *Il fascismo*, pp. 17ff.

47. Ibid., chap. 6. In his memoirs Evola added this note about Mussolini: "Certainly, I could not fail to sympathize with someone who struggled against the forces of the Left and against the democratic regime." *Il cammino del cinabro*, p. 76.

48. Evola, *Il fascismo*, p. 76. See Evola, *Gli uomini e le rovine*, for an analysis of why Fascist corporativism failed, p. 114.

49. Evola, *Il fascismo*, p. 67.

50. Evola, *Sintesi*, p. 245. To the duce's delight, Evola celebrated "the race of Fascist man or the race of Mussolini's men," p. 266.

51. Evola, *Il fascismo*, pp. 76–77.

52. Giuseppe Gaddi observed that nearly all Italian neofascists attempt to put some distance between themselves and Mussolini's regime and thereby escape the onus of his debacle in World War II. See Gaddi, *Neofascismo in Europa*, Introduzione. Along the same line of argument, F. W. Deakin writes, "The collapse of the whole Party machinery throughout the morning of July 26, 1943 without a gesture in defense of the Duce and Fascism, had indeed been a decisive historic event." *Brutal Friendship*, p. 581. Evola—always the maverick—insisted that Mussolini was right to fight by Germany's side in World War II. Mussolini's mistake, in Evola's opinion, was to be timorous and vacillating at home.

53. In *Il fascismo* Evola theorized that had the king been strong "fascism would never have arisen," p. 49.

54. On this point Evola was as naive as Marx, who also thought that men of power, instead of always seeking to augment it, would freely give up their position under the right historical circumstances. The Fascist state was no more likely to wither away than its Communist counterpart.

55. Evola, *Imperialismo pagano*, pp. 17ff.

56. Ibid.

57. Evola, *Il fascismo*, p. 113.

58. Even so, Mussolini's Italy "was one of the most socially progressive and advanced

regimes of its time," Evola asserted. Ibid., p. 91. He always maintained that the ideas of fascism should be defended, though not necessarily Fascist practice. See Evola, *Gli uomini e le rovine*, p. 26

59. See Benito Mussolini, "Commento a Sintesi di dottrina della razza," in Giorgio Pini and Duilio Susmel, *Mussolini: l'uomo e l'opera*, vol. 4, p. 145. In the aftermath of this success Giuseppe Bottai, minister of national education, asked Evola to give a course of lectures at the universities of Milan and Florence on racial policy. For more on Mussolini's favorable reaction to this book, see Renzo De Felice, *Mussolini il duce II*, p. 316.

60. Earlier Evola had written that "an anti-Semitism is not out of the question," but anti-Semites were not yet in possession of a systematic and rational critique of Jewish culture. See Evola, *Tre aspetti del problema ebraico*. For a discussion of Evola's racial ideas, see Renzo De Felice, *Storia degli ebrei italiani sotto il fascismo*, and Giorgio Pisanò, *Mussolini e gli ebrei*.

61. *Tre aspetti del problema ebraico* fully reveals Evola's antipathy toward the Jews: "As the germinating force of a seed does not fully manifest itself until [its introduction into the soil] so Hebraism did not begin to universally manifest its destructive and ethically subversive power until its political fall and the dispersion into the world of the 'Chosen People,' " p. 33.

62. For Evola modernity meant, in part, "the hebraization of the economy." *Gli uomini e le rovine*, p. 164.

63. See esp. Evola, Introduzione, *I "Protocolli" dei "Savi Anziani" di Sion*, in which he adopted Henry Ford's line of reasoning about the Jews, i.e., whether or not the *Protocols* was an authentic historical document it did describe present reality. For Evola Judaism meant "a systematic and practical work of destruction" in the West. Even in his introduction to this notorious fabrication, however, Evola insisted that he "personally could not follow . . . a certain kind of anti-Semitism that sees the Jew everywhere as a deus ex machina. . . ," p. xiv. In addition, see Evola, Introduzione, *La guerra occulta*. Evola also translated this book, which purported to analyze Jewish subversion from 1848 down to the triumph of bolshevism.

64. In his earliest articles for "Diorama filosofico" Evola condemned Nazi race theory. See Evola and Roberto Pavese, "In margine al IX Congresso Filosofico," *Regime fascista*, 1 November–2 December 1934, in which they declared that "Racist and Nazi Germany gives us an instructive lesson regarding the dangers and the deviations . . . of biological materialism or nationalism more or less deified." Also see Evola's "Sorpassamento del Superuomo," 16 November 1934, and esp. his "Critica della Teoria dell' Eredità," 13 December 1934, for more on the "superbiological" character of Evolian race theory.

65. Evola, Introduzione, *I "Protocolli."* See also Evola, *Il mistero del Graal e la tradizione ghibellina dell'impero*, p. 185.

66. Evola, *Tre aspetti*, p. 43. He made the identical point in *Sintesi di dottrina della razza*, p. 118. In his Introduzione to *I "Protocolli"* he asserted that the Jew hates "as fire burns," p. xxvii.

67. Evola, *Tre aspetti*, p. 40.

68. Evola, *Sintesi*, p. 118. Evola was never prepared to discount the value of blood altogether, and he later wrote: "a certain balanced consciousness and dignity of race can be considered healthy, especially if one thinks where we are going in our time with the exaltation of the Negro and all the rest, with the anticolonialist psychosis, with the 'integrationist' fanaticism: all parallel phenomena in the decline of Europe and the West." Evola, *Il fascismo*, "Note sul Terzo Reich," p. 179.

69. For example, a beautiful Aryan woman could degenerate and become "full of bourgeois limitations." She would then belong to "another race," and, apart from romantic "adventures," a true Aryan male should have nothing to do with such a creature. Certainly, he should not have any children by her because they would be half-breeds. Evola, *Sintesi*, p. 240. Incidentally, Evola never married. He defined marriage as the surest means of forging iron links with bourgeois society. See "La gioventù, i Beats e gli anarchici di destra," in Evola, *L'arco e la clava*, p. 221.

70. For more on Mussolini's racial policy in Ethiopia, see Denis Mack Smith, *Mussolini's Roman Empire*, chap. 5, "The Ethiopian War." Angelo Del Bocca enumerates the Fascist government's racial atrocities in Africa, carried out by Mussolini's express command, in "Sterminateli tutti!" *Il messaggero*, 11 April 1983. See also E. M. Robertson, "Race as a Factor in Mussolini's Policy in Africa and Europe," *Journal of Contemporary History*, vol. 23, no. 1, January 1988, pp. 37–58.

71. Evola, *Sintesi*, p. 234.

72. Evola, *Il fascismo*, p. 110.

73. Cited by Deakin, *Brutal Friendship*, p. 557.

74. Evola, *Sintesi*, p. 237.

75. Evola, *Il fascismo*, p. 113. In *Gli uomini e le rovine* he added that "in spite of everything [fascism] remained bourgeois or became bourgeois by contagion. . . ," p. 155.

76. Evola, *Il cammino del cinabro*, "Ricerca di uomini fra le rovine."

77. Evola, *Il fascismo*, "Note sul Terzo Reich," p. 164. In *Gli uomini e le rovine* he severely criticized Italy's weak national character, symbolized by the image of "chiaro di luna in gondola"; since World War II, he asserted, the worst instincts of the Italians had been exaggerated, especially their "rather primitive sexuality," p. 212.

78. This is what "liberation" meant to Evola: "Italy has returned to itself, that is, to the little Italy of mandolins, of museums, of 'Sole mio,' and of the tourist industry, having been 'liberated'; liberated from the hard task of giving itself a form inspired by its highest [Roman] tradition. . . . " Evola, *Gli uomini e le rovine*, p. 206.

79. Tedeschi, *Fascisti dopo Mussolini*, p. 84.

80. Though destined to disappear from Italian politics by 1948, Giannini's conservative catchall party enjoyed a fantastic success in the immediate postwar period. In August 1945 his newspaper, *L'uomo qualunque*, was selling 850,000 copies per issue. See Petra Rosenbaum, *Il nuovo fascismo*, chap. 3.

81. Leonard B. Weinberg, *After Mussolini*, chap. 2, "Neofascism in Postwar Italy."

82. Cited by Galli, *La crisi italiana*, p. 20.

83. Pino Rauti, *Le idee che mossero il mondo*. See Thomas Sheehan, "Myth and Violence: The Fascism of Julius Evola and Alain de Benoist," *Social Research*, Spring 1981, for an analysis of Evola's impact on Rauti's book. Sheehan argues that this influence extended to wholesale plagiarism. Certainly, Rauti's view of the historical process is the same as the one we find in *La rivolta*. See Guilio Salierno, *Autobiografia di un picchiatore fascista*, chap. 4, in which Rauti is described as the chief of the *evoliani*.

84. Evola was not alone in wishing to purify fascism of all corrupt elements. For example, see Alberto Giovannini on "chilantismo," after Felice Chilanti, who fantasized about assassinating the major hierarchs of the regime, "liberating" Mussolini and obliging him to make a "total revolution." In the Prefazione, Tedeschi, *Fascisti dopo Mussolini*.

85. Evola, *Orientamenti*, p. 4.

86. Ibid., p. 6.

87. Ibid., p. 11.

88. Ibid., p. 13.

89. Ibid., p. 27.

90. Evola, "Autodifesa," *Quaderni di testi evoliani*, no. 2 (Rome: Fondazione Julius Evola, n.d.). For an account of FAR by an active member, see Tedeschi, *Fascisti dopo Mussolini*. According to him, factionalism between moderates and radicals had destroyed FAR by 1947.

91. Evola, "Autodifesa."

92. On this point one of Evola's most devoted followers, Pino Rauti, admitted that in the act of interpreting Evola's theories many of the young neofascists strayed from good sense: "there were acts of foolishness and ingenuousness, pointless crudities and mistaken references, as well as totally infantile or merely 'youthful' extreme acts that were, in substance, at the antipodes of a correct interpretation of those theses." in "Evola: una guida per domani," *Civiltà*, p. 14.

93. Pier Giuseppe Murgia, *Ritorneremo!*, pp. 129 ff.
94. Gaddi, *Neofascismo in Europa*, p. 35. Pansa noted in *Borghese mi ha detto* that Ordine Nuovo was founded after the tempestuous MSI congress of 1956 in which the radicals chanted, "Fewer double-breasted suits and more cudgels!" See the material on Ordine Nuovo in the section entitled "Documenti." For the historical background of the Nouvel Ordre Européen, see Théolleyre, *Les Neo-Nazis*.
95. Evola, *Il cammino del cinabro*, p. 212.
96. Fausto Gianfranceschini, "L'influenza di Evola sulla generazione che non ha fatto in tempo a perdere la guerra," in Gianfranco De Turris (ed.), *Testimonianze su Evola*.
97. Vintilă Horia, "I poeti e il simbolo della patria," ibid.
98. Silvano Panunzio, "Iniziati e metafisici della crisi," ibid.
99. For the impact of *Gli uomini e le rovine* on the radical Right, see Romualdi, *Julius Evola*, pp. 78ff.
100. Junio Valerio Borghese, Presentazione, in Evola, *Gli uomini e le rovine*, p. 7. For more on Borghese, see Pansa, *Borghese mi ha detto*. Borghese's Fronte Nazionale championed many of Evola's ideas. Deakin, *Brutal Friendship*, also contains useful information about Borghese's background, particularly during World War II, when he was the commander of the dreaded Decima Mas (Tenth Motor Torpedo Boat Flotilla); see pt. 3, "Salò: The Six Hundred Days." See also Borghese, *Decima flottiglia mas*, trans. into English by James Cleugh as *Sea Devils*.
101. Evola agreed with Joseph de Maistre that conservatives needed more than a counter-revolution; they needed "the contrary of a revolution," i.e., something positive with which to oppose revolution. *Gli uomini e le rovine*, p. 16.
102. Ibid., p. 218.
103. Evola argued that Italy had never succeeded in creating a conservative party "worthy of the name." Ibid., p. 22. For the same argument, see Evola, "La Destra e la Cultura," *Ricognizioni*.
104. Karl Mannheim, *Ideology and Utopia*, chap. 2, "Ideology and Utopia." Mannheim argued that Marx's greatest achievement lay in his recognition of political rhetoric as a cover for interest, but this discovery also applies to Marxists, whose interest, on the political level, is power.
105. Evola, *Gli uomini e le rovine*, p. 59. He believed that corporativism was the only way to control "the disorders and subversion of capitalism." Ibid., p. 161.
106. Ibid., p. 18.
107. In this book Evola employed many of Ernst Jünger's ideas about the modern world, particularly those found in *Der Arbeiter: Herrschaft und Gestalt* (1932) and *An der Zeitmauer* (1959). On the first, see Evola, *L' "Operaio" nel pensiero di Ernst Jünger*; on the second, see "Al Muro del Tempo" in *Ricognizioni*. Evola understood Jünger to be saying that only a new type of man could survive in the modern world, i.e., in past times men faced physical threats, but today men, though in some respects physically safer than their forbears, face a far more deadly peril, which is psychological and moral in nature. Evola's *Cavalcare la tigre* (To ride the tiger) was intended to be a survival manual for those among his contemporaries who had the wit to understand the evil character of the modern world.
108. Evola, *Cavalcare la tigre*, Introduzione. Most disappointing of all to him at the start of the 1960s was the rapid modernization of the East. See "Il Tramonto dell' Oriente" in *Ricognizioni* for a further elaboration of his argument that, by abandoning tradition, Oriental societies were setting the stage for their own Western-style decline. He was particularly bitter about the "tragic" Americanization of Japan. See "L'esempio giapponese," *Il conciliatore*, 15 August 1961.
109. Evola, *Cavalcare la tigre*, p. 292. See also his *Metafisica del sesso*. On the subject of women Evola gleefully quoted Joseph de Maistre: "Woman cannot be superior except as woman, but from the moment in which she desires to emulate man she is nothing but a monkey." Evola's comment on this observation was "Pure truth, whether or not it pleases the various contemporary 'feminist movements.' " Evola, "Joseph de Maistre," *Ricognizioni*.

110. For more on Evola and feminism, see the 23 August 1951 entry in Francesco Carnelutti, *Tempo perso*, a literary diary.

111. Evola, "Il fenomeno Henry Miller," *Ricognizioni*.

112. Evola, "La gioventù, i beat e gli anarchici di destra," *L'arco e la clava*, p. 225.

113. For Evola the very center of Western alienation was the United States. See esp. "America negrizzata" in *L'arco e la clava*, where he lamented the Americanization of the world. He trembled at the thought of "Negroid America" as the main line of defense against the powerful and disciplined governments of the Soviet Union and China. The only hope for the United States, Evola believed, was an apartheid policy. He recommended that one of the states be given to the blacks where they could "do whatever they want without annoying or contaminating anyone," p. 27.

114. Evola, "Civiltà dello spazio e civiltà del tempo," *L'arco e la clava*, p. 12.

115. Evola, *Cavalcare la tigre*, p. 247.

116. Ibid., pp. 248–49.

117. Romualdi pointed out that Evola regarded excessive nationalism as the worst failing of fascism. In *Julius Evola*, p. 60.

118. Evola, February 1970 *Playmen* interview with Enrico de Boccard, in De Turris (ed.), *Omaggio*. See also "Metternich" in Evola, *Ricognizioni*.

119. Evola also cited U. Varange's two-volume *Imperium* (London: Westropa Press, 1948) to support his cyclical interpretation of history, in *Gli uomini e le rovine*, p. 232. He made the same argument in *Cavalcare la tigre*, p. 19.

120. See Marc Augier (Saint Loup), *I volontari europei delle Waffen-SS*. Romualdi translated, edited, and introduced this Italian edition. Augier, a veteran of the Waffen-SS, described his basic training as a "novitiate," p. 14. For a detailed analysis of the impact of the SS on Evola's thinking, see Franco Ferraresi, "Da Evola a Freda: le dottrine della destra radicale fino al 1977," in Ferraresi (ed.), *La destra radicale*.

121. Angelo Del Boca and Mario Giovana, *Fascism Today: A World Survey*, p. 453.

122. Ibid.

123. Ibid. In all, thirty-two nationalities were represented in the Waffen-SS, with the Italians conspicuous by their absence. Deakin explains in *Brutal Friendship* how after 8 September 1943 the Germans, out of fear and suspicion over another Italian betrayal, completely took over the training and deployment of Italian troops until the end of the war. The main German concern in Italy during the last year and a half of the war was to build up an Italian force that at least could take over the police duties in northern Italy that were being performed by regular German troops. This objective was never achieved. See pt. 3, "Salò: The Six Hundred Days."

124. For Evola's views on the Order of Teutonic Knights as a splendid example of "the soldierly conception of life," see *Gli uomini e le rovine*, p. 123, and "La Destra e la Tradizione" in *Ricognizioni*, e.g., "Prussianism, with its ethic, was born as a secularization of the Order of Teutonic Knights," p. 241. He was even more enchanted by the SS because it was expressly neopagan. Incidentally, the motto of Ordine Nuovo was the same as that of the SS, "Our honor is called fidelity." Also see his study of chivalrous ideals in the Middle Ages, *Il mistero del Graal e la tradizione ghibellina dell'impero*. In his memoirs he called this study an apppendix to *La rivolta contro il mondo moderno*. Elsewhere he defined the Ghibelline ideal as "the reorganization and unification of the West under the sign of sacred imperialism." *Il cammino del cinabro*, p. 133.

125. Gaddi states that "the European idea" is the cornerstone of neofascism. Gaddi, *Neofascismo in Europa*, Introduzione. Evola's historical ideal was always "Roman and imperial supranationality." Evola, *Imperialismo pagano*, p. 36.

126. Ferraresi, "La destra eversiva," in Ferraresi (ed.), *La destra radicale*, p. 94.

127. Evola, *Gli uomini e le rovine*, p. 157.

128. Furio Jesi argues that neofascist culture possesses a coherent theory of man, of the world, of history, and of nature. See his *Cultura di destra*. For the last thirty years of his

life Evola was the major intellectual figure in this tradition. See also Ferraresi (ed.), *La destra radicale*, Presentazione.

129. Giulio Salierno, *Autobiografia di un picchiatore fascista*. For more on Salierno's testimony concerning the extreme Right during this period, see Murgia, *Ritorneremo*, pp. 119ff. Salierno claimed that he knew Evola's works by heart.

130. Salierno. *Autobiografia*, chap. 1, "L'allievo."

131. Ibid., p. 46.

132. Ibid., p. 137.

133. Ibid., p. 139. In answer to a question, Evola described Hitler as "a magister rationalis. . . . A genius," p. 142.

134. Ibid.

135. Ibid., p. 143. Pino Rauti, Evola's foremost admirer in the MSI, had said the same thing in a talk before the Colle Oppio youth section of the party: "We must be wolves and make ourselves known as such," p. 88. Mussolini had used identical language in describing his solution for the Partisans in 1944: "We must get rid of this odious plague with fire and steel." Cited by Deakin, *Brutal Friendship*, p. 723.

136. Salierno, *Autobiografia*, pp. 142–43.

137. Romano F. Cattaneo, "Significato e importanza di Julius Evola," *Il conciliatore*, no. 6, June 1974.

138. Pino Rauti, "Evola: una guida per domani," *Civiltà*, September–December 1974, p. 15.

139. Cited by Roberto Chiarini and Paolo Corsini, *Da Salò a piazza della Loggia*, p. 254.

140. Franco Freda, *La disintegrazione del sistema*, p. 58.

141. Ibid., p. 87.

142. Ferraresi, "La destra eversiva," in Ferraresi (ed.), *La destra radicale*, p. 69.

143. Clemente Graziani, *Processo a Ordine Nuovo, processo alle idee*, p. 27.

144. Ibid., p. 47.

145. Romualdi, *Julius Evola*, p. 7.

146. Ibid., p. 92.

147. Ibid., p. 87.

148. Evola, in a 15 January 1970 *Il conciliatore* interview with Gianfranco de Turris, in De Turris (ed.), *Omaggio*.

149. Evola, "La gioventù, i Beats e gli anarchici di destra," *L'arco e la clava*, p. 223.

150. Gottfried Benn, "Essere e Divenire," *Die Literatur*, March 1935. Republished in Evola, *L'arco e la clava*, p. 236. It is highly probable that Benn found this image in Evola's youthful poetry; in "Voyage Morbide" (1916) Evola conjured up a vision of "Black monks who will burn the city." Evola, *Raâga blanda*.

151. Evola, *Il mistero del Graal*, pt. 1, "Principii."

152. Evola, *Gli uomini e le rovine*. See also Evola, *Imperialismo pagano*, p. 41.

153. Evola to Almirante following the latter's 23 February 1967 appearance on a television program. The letter was originally published in *Noi Europa* and republished in *Heliodromos*, January–February 1982.

154. Ferraresi, "La Destra Eversiva," in Ferraresi (ed.), *La destra radicale*, p. 92.

155. De Lutiis (ed.), *La strage*, pt. 2, "Terrorismo Nero."

156. Ibid., p. 86.

157. Ibid., chap. 4, "Eversione, servizi segreti e P2."

158. Claudio Nunziata, "Dieci anni di processi alle trame nere," in Corsini and Novati (eds.), *L'eversione nera*, p. 263.

159. De Lutiis (ed.), *La strage*, pt. 2, "Terrorismo Nero," esp. chaps. 3–7.

160. Mario Battaglini, "Il movimento politico ordine nuovo. Il processo di Roma del 1973," in Vittorio Borraccetti (ed.), *Eversione di destra, terrorismo, stragi*, p. 30.

8. THE CRISIS AND DEFEAT OF THE RED BRIGADES

1. Collettivo prigionieri comunisti delle Brigate Rosse, "L'ape e il comunista: elementi per la critica marxista dell' economia politica e per la costruzione del programma di transizione al comunismo," *Corrispondenza internazionale*, October–December 1980, no. 16/17.

2. Ibid., p. 59.

3. Ibid., p. 187.

4. Ibid., p. 232.

5. Ibid., p. 248.

6. Ibid., p. 277.

7. Clemente Granata, "Milano, un direttore Falck ucciso dalle Br, in due gli sparano e fuggono in bicicletta," *La Stampa*, 29 November 1980.

8. Brigate Rosse, D'Urso communication no. 1, 13 December 1980 (mimeographed document in the author's possession).

9. Brigate Rosse, D'Urso communication no. 6, 29 December 1980, and no. 7, 1 January 1981 (mimeographed documents in the author's possession).

10. Brigate Rosse, D'Urso communication no. 10, 14 January 1981 (mimeographed document in the author's possession).

11. Brigate Rosse, D'Urso communication no. 7.

12. Sandra Bonsanti, "I brigatisti, 'Abbiamo ucciso Galvaligi,' " *La Stampa*, 2 January 1981.

13. Mario Fabbri, "Dalla Chiesa: il terrorismo fa gioco a potenze straniere," ibid., 13 February 1981.

14. The field of hospital work had been infiltrated by extremists in sympathy with terrorism, and Marangoni had received numerous death threats.

15. Brigate Rosse, "Autointervista del giugno 1981," in Luigi Manconi and Vittorio Dini, *Il discorso delle armi, Appendix-Documents, p.* 138.

16. Emanuela Monta, "Un volantino rivendica il rapimento di Mestre," *La Stampa*, 23 May 1981.

17. For a history of these plots, see Gianni Flamini, *Il partito del golpe*, vols. 1 and 2.

18. Alberto Cecchi, *Storia della P2.* This Communist analyst admitted that between Licio Gelli and terrorism "one cannot pretend to discover an absolute and rigid linearity. . . , " p. 136.

19. Cecchi, a PCI member of the Parliamentary commission investigating P2, objected to the Christian Democrats' majority report by Tina Anselmi because she hardly mentioned the American involvement in Gelli's operations. Ibid., p. 161.

20. Brigate Rosse, Peci communication no. 3, 20 June 1981, in Manconi and Dini, *Il discorso delle armi*, p. 148.

21. Ibid., p. 150.

22. Galli, *Storia del partito armato*, pp. 258–62.

23. Pietro Calderone, "Io Antonia Peci, ho fatto un sogno," *L'Espresso*, 9 August 1981.

24. Brigate Rosse, Peci communication no. 5, 10 July 1981, in Manconi and Dini, *Il discorso delle armi*, p. 154.

25. Claudio Cerasuolo, "Patrizio Peci: 'Sono belve, Roberto ha pagato per me,' " *La Stampa*, 5 August 1981.

26. Giuseppe Zaccaria, "Esplode la tensione degli agenti, Pertini 'chi può dirmi qualcosa?' " *La Stampa*, 10 December 1981.

27. Ibid.

28. Collettivo prigionieri comunisti delle Brigate Rosse, "L'ape e il comunista," p. 122.

29. Ibid., p. 123.

30. Henry Tanner, "Italians Find No Trace of U.S. General," *New York Times*, 19 December 1981.

31. Brigate Rosse, Dozier leaflet, 27 December 1981 (mimeographed document in the author's possession).

32. Brigate Rosse, "Risoluzione della Direzione Strategica," 27 December 1981 (mimeographed document in the author's possession).

33. Ronconi had studied political science at the University of Padua. She entered Prima Linea via the conduit of Autonomia Operaia.

34. Silvana Mazzocchi, "Fuga troppo facile: il carcere era insicuro," *La Repubblica*, 5 January 1982.

35. Rino Genova, *Missione antiterrorismo*, chap. 5, "La liberazione di Dozier." Genova was a police officer involved in numerous antiterrorist operations, including the liberation of Dozier. He strenuously objected to the charges of police brutality that were brought against him and his fellow officers by the Red Brigade captors of Dozier. See "Dalla gloria alla galera e di nuovo in prima linea." Elected to Parliament on the PSDI ticket, Genova did not have to accompany the other defendants to jail. On 26 March 1984 a higher court overturned these verdicts.

36. For example, on 28 April 1982 they killed Raffaele Delcogliano, the thirty-year-old regional assessor of the Christian Democratic party in Naples, and his driver. The assassinations occurred despite the protection afforded by an armor-plated car with bulletproof windows. The terrorists used diamond-tipped bullets that easily penetrated Delcogliano's vehicle.

37. Roberto Sandalo, a piellino who wanted to join the Red Brigades, described his examination to Rino Genova. To pass it, he had to study the classic texts of the Marxist-Leninist tradition. Genova, *Missione antiterrorismo*, p. 56.

38. Claire Sterling, *The Terror Network*, chap. 11.

39. As a sign that the government viewed the war against terrorism as virtually over, General Dalla Chiesa had been transferred to Sicily, where his military talents could be employed against the Mafia.

40. Franco Coppola, "Il carcere a vita per 32 terroristi," *La Repubblica*, 25 January 1983.

41. "Curcio dal carcere: 'La lotta armata è finita,' " ibid., 27 January 1983. Curcio thereafter developed a reputation for silence. In 1984 he published a hermetic memoir, *Wkhy*, that had more in common with Nietzsche than Marx. This book dealt with the cultural crisis of modern society, but Curcio did not attempt to elucidate "the divinity of the enigma" in Marxist terms. In *Gocce di sole nella città degli spettri*, which Curcio wrote with Alberto Franceschini and published in 1982, he still communicated in Marxist terms. Events of the following year plunged him into the existential confusion reflected in *Wkhy*.

42. Lucio Castellano, Arrigo Cavallina, Giustino Cortiana, Mario Dalmaviva, Luciano Ferrari Bravo, Chicco Funaro, Antonio Negri, Paolo Pozzi, Franco Tommei, Emilio Vesce, Paolo Virno, "Do You Remember Revolution? Proposta di lettura storico-politica per il movimento degli anni Settanta," *Il manifesto*, 20–22 February 1983. Prologo (no author) in *Metropoli: l'autonomia possibile*, no. 2, April 1980, contains an earlier and pithier version of this argument.

43. "Negri's Interrogation" in "Italy: Autonomia (Post-Political Politics)," *Semiotext(e)*, vol. 3, no. 3, 1980, p. 190.

44. Ibid., p. 194.

45. Ibid., p. 188.

46. This was especially true in France, where Negri's leftist allies took up his cause. See Gilles Deleuze, "Open Letter to Negri's Judges," in ibid.

47. "Ma ora il carcere non mi fa più paura,'" *La Repubblica*, 3 September 1983.

48. Pietro Calogero was the Padua prosecutor.

49. Osvaldo Orlandini in Scorti, *Il delitto paga? L'affare Tobagi*, pp. 222ff.

50. Ibid.

51. Galli, *Storia del partito armato*, p. 155.

52. Luca Savonuzzi, "E l'orrore sfila sul terzo binario," *La Repubblica*, 25 December 1984.

CONCLUSION

1. Alberto Ronchey, *Accade in Italia 1968–1977*, chap. 3, "Italinflazione."
2. Pier Paolo Pasolini, "Gli italiani non sono più quelli," *Il corriere della sera*, 10 June 1974.
3. Alberto Moravia, "Quel moralismo armato che non esita a uccidere," *Il corriere della sera*, 6 November 1977. In his novel *La vita interiore* (1978), Moravia presents an artistic vision of the terrorist "dream of a heroic community."
4. Acquaviva, *Il seme religioso della rivolta*.
5. Walter Laqueur (ed.), *The Terrorism Reader*. See the sections on John of Salisbury, pp. 19–24, Thomas Aquinas, pp. 24–26, and Juan de Mariana, pp. 30–35.
6. Pope Paul VI, "Populorum Progressio," 26 March 1967, in Claudia Carlen, *The Papal Encyclicals 1958–1981*.
7. In a 15 June 1976 interview with Giampaolo Pansa of the *Corriere della sera*, Enrico Berlinguer said that "the Italian way to socialism" was only possible because of NATO. Berlinguer was conscious of supervising a political experiment that could only occur in a climate of freedom. Without such a climate his hopes for the PCI would have been blasted by the chilling example of Czechoslovakia in 1968, an event the Communist leader had in mind when he made these remarks to Pansa. For a full analysis of this interview, see Alberto Ronchey, *Accade in Italia: 1968–1977*, "La questione dell'Est."
8. Cited by Rodolfo Brancoli, *Spettatori interessati*, p. 316.
9. John F. Burns, "Soviet Publishes Scathing Attack on Italian Party," *New York Times*, 25 January 1982.
10. For an analysis of Turati's enduring legacy on the left, see Spencer di Scala, *Dilemmas of Italian Socialism*.
11. For example, on the basis of confessions by right-wing pentiti, authorities now believe that the Camorra and radical neofascist elements perpetrated the Christmas 1984 railway massacre. Giuseppe D'Avanzo, "Ecco killer e mandanti della strage di Natale," *La Repubblica*, 20 December 1985.
12. Chalmers Johnson, *Revolutionary Change*, chap. 1, "Revolution: The Implication of a Political Concept."
13. Peci, *Io, l'infame*, p. 42.
14. Chiarini and Corsini, *Da Salò a Piazza della Loggia*, chap. 3, "Una politica coraggiosamente fascista."
15. Acquaviva describes Italian intellectual life as "culturally closed in a kind of orthodox Marxist ghetto." *Il seme religioso della rivolta*, no. 23.
16. Leonard Weinberg, *The Rise and Fall of Italian Terrorism*, chap. 5, "Who Were the Terrorists?"
17. Ibid.
18. Tobagi, *Storia del movimento studentesco*.
19. For an inventory of right-wing ideological extremism, see Ferraresi (ed.), *La destra radicale*.
20. Ignazio Silone, *Bread and Wine*, p. 157. The biography of the Red Brigadist Roberto Ognibene provides an apt illustration of this psychological process. According to one of his teachers, "Robert was, and still is, a young man who aims at the absolute. He is alien to half measures." Cited by Alessandro Silj, *Never Again without a Rifle*, pt. 2, "The Armed Proletarian Nuclei."
21. Negri, *Pipe-line*, "Lettera diciottesima: Moro," 15 March 1982, p. 201.
22. Salierno, *Autobiografia di un picchiatore fascista*. Ciancione, one of the thugs who trained Salierno, told him: "Often I did jobs just for the fun of doing them," p. 126. His

other mentor's name was Alvaro, and from the two he learned how to sabotage railroad trains and bridges, as well as methods for killing people.

23. Ibid., p. 55.
24. Peci, *Io, l'infame*, p. 15.
25. Ibid., p. 22.
26. Ibid., p. 38.
27. Ibid., p. 41.
28. Enrico Fenzi and Alberto Franceschini took a similar view of the PCI's role in the history of Red Brigadism. As the party moved toward a defense of existing institutions, those Marxists who still believed in revolution felt compelled to keep the Marxist-Leninist tradition alive. Red Brigadism was one possible form of political expression for these alienated Marxists. Bocca, *Noi terroristi*, "La lotta armata. Ma perché negli anni Settanta?"
29. Jacobo Timerman, *Prisoner without a Name, Cell without a Number*, chap. 2.
30. For a discussion of the moral economy of revolution, see D. W. Brogan, *The Price of Revolution*, esp. pp. 11ff.
31. Raymond Aron, *The Opium of the Intellectuals*, p. 95.
32. Cited by Guenther Roth and Wolfgang Schluchter, *Max Weber's Vision of History: Ethics and Methods*, frontispiece quotation.
33. Hannah Arendt, *On Violence*, pt. 2.
34. Alberto Stabile, "Ucciso anche in Sicilia l'uomo del dialogo col Pci," *La Repubblica*, 8 January 1980. Moro also used this sentence in a speech. See Moro, *L'intelligenza e gli avvenimenti*, Discorso, 20 March 1976, p. 337.
35. Angelo Ventura, "La responsabilità degli intellettuali e le radici culturali del terrorismo di sinistra."

Bibliography

Acquaviva Sabino S. *Guerriglia e guerra rivoluzionaria in Italia: ideologie, fatti, prospettive* (Milan: Rizzoli, 1979).
———. *Il seme religioso della rivolta* (Milan: Rusconi, 1979).
———, and Mario Santuccio. *Social Structure in Italy*, trans. Colin Hamer (London: Robertson, 1976).
Agosti, Aldo. *Rodolfo Morandi: il pensiero e l'azione politica* (Bari: Laterza, 1971).
Agostini, Piero. *Mara Cagol: una donna nelle prime brigate rosse* (Venice: Marsilio, 1980).
Ajello, Nello. *Intellettuali e Pci: 1944–1958* (Rome-Bari: Laterza, 1979).
Alcaro, Mario. *Dellavolpismo e nuova sinistra* (Bari: Dedalo, 1977).
Alexander, Yonah, and Kenneth A. Myers (eds.). *Terrorism in Europe* (London: Croom & Helm; New York: St Martin's Press, 1982).
Algardi, Zara. *Processi ai fascisti* (Florence: Editore, 1958).
Allum, P. A. *Italy—Republic without Government?* (London: Weidenfeld, 1973).
Almirante, Giorgio. *Autobiografia di un "fucilatore"* (Milan: Borghese, 1974).
Alquati, Romano, et al. *Terrorismo verso la seconda repubblica?* (Turin: Stampatori, 1980).
Amato, Pasquale. *Il Psi tra frontismo e autonomia (1948–1954)* (Cosenza: Lerice, 1978).
Andreotti, Giulio. *Diari 1976–1979: gli anni della solidarietà* (Milan: Rizzoli, 1981).
Antonov-Ovseyenko, Anton. *The Time of Stalin: Portrait of a Tyranny*, trans. George Saunders (New York: Harper and Row, 1981).
Arendt, Hannah. *On Violence* (New York: Harcourt, Brace and Jovanovich, 1969).
———. *The Origins of Totalitarianism* (New York: Harcourt, Brace, 1951).
Arfé, Gaetano (ed.). *Mondo operaio: 1956–1965*, 2 vols. (S. Giovanni Valdarno-Florence: Landi, 1966).
Aron, Raymond. *The Opium of the Intellectuals* (New York: Norton, 1955).
Ascherson, Neal. *The Polish August: The Self-Limiting Revolution* (Middlesex: Penguin, 1981).
Asor Rosa, Alberto. *Intellettuali e classe operaia: saggi sulle forme di uno storico conflitto e di una possibile alleanza* (Florence: La Nuova Italia, 1973).
Augier, Marc (Saint Loup). *I volontari Europei delle Waffen-SS* (Rome: Volpe, 1967 and 1971).
Aut aut (journal).
Avanti! (newspaper).
Badaloni, Nicola. *Il marxismo italiano degli anni sessanta* (Rome: Riuniti, 1971).
Barbieri, Daniele. *Agenda nera: trent'anni di neofascismo in Italia* (Rome: Coines, 1976).
Barkan, Joanne. *Visions of Emancipation: The Italian Workers' Movement since 1945* (New York: Praeger, 1984).
Bechelloni, Giovanni (ed.). *Cultura e ideologia nella nuova sinistra: materiali per un inventario della cultura politica delle riviste del dissenso marxista degli anni sessanta* (Milan: Edizioni di Comunità, 1973).
Bell, J. Bowyer. *A Time of Terror: How Democratic Societies Respond to Revolutionary Violence* (New York: Basic Books, 1979).
Benzoni, Alberto, and Viva Tedesco. *Il movimento socialista nel dopoguerra* (Padua: Marsilio, 1968).
Berlinguer, Enrico. "Imperialismo e consistenza alla luce dei fatti cileni," *Rinascita*, 28 September 1973.
———. "Riflessioni sull 'Italia dopo i fatti del Cile: Alleanze sociali e schieramenti politici," *Rinascita*, 12 October 1973.
———. "Riflessioni sull 'Italia dopo i fatti del Cile: Via democratica o violenza reazionaria," *Rinascita*, 5 October 1973.

Black, Cyril, and Thomas P. Thornton (eds.). *Communism and Revolution: The Strategic Uses of Political Violence* (Princeton: Princeton University Press, 1964).

Bobbio, Luigi. *Lotta continua: storia di una organizzazione rivoluzionaria* (Rome: Savelli, 1979).

Bocca, Giorgio. *Il caso 7 aprile: Toni Negri e la grande inquisizione* (Milan: Feltrinelli, 1980.

———. *Mussolini socialfascista: il socialismo reale non è fascismo ma come gli sommiglia* (Milan: Garzanti, 1983).

———. *Noi terroristi: 12 anni di lotta armata ricostruiti e discussi con i protagonisti* (Milan: Garzanti, 1985).

———. *Il terrorismo italiano: 1970–1980* (Milan: Rizzoli, 1981).

——— (ed.). *Moro: una trageda italiana (le lettere, i documenti, le polemiche)* (Milan: Bompiani, 1978).

Borghese, Junio Valerio. *Sea Devils [Decima flottiglia mas]*, trans. James Cleugh (Chicago: Henry Regnery, 1954).

———, et al. *La grande proletaria* (Rome: Centro Editoriale Nazionale, 1958).

Borraccetti, Vittorio (ed.). *Eversione di destra, terrorismo, stragi: i fatti e l'intervento giudiziario* (Milan: Angeli, 1986).

Bosio, Gianni. *Giornale di un organizzatore di cultura: 27 giugno 1955–27 dicembre 1955* (Milan: Edizioni Avanti!, 1962).

Brancoli, Rodolfo. *Spettatori interessati: gli Stati Uniti e la crisi italiana, 1975–1980* (Milan: Garzanti, 1980).

Braudel, Fernand. *The Mediterranean and the Mediterranean World in the Age of Philip II* (New York: Harper and Row, 1972).

Brigate Rosse. Dozier Leaflet (27 December 1981). Mimeographed document in the author's possession.

———. D'Urso Communications 1–10 (13 December–14 January 1981). Mimeographed documents in the author's possession.

———. "Risoluzione della Direzione Strategica" (February 1978), *Controinformazione*, no. 11–12, July 1978.

———. "Risoluzione della Direzione Strategica" (27 December 1981). Mimeographed document in the author's possession.

Brinton, Crane. *The Anatomy of Revolution* (New York: Random House, 1965 ed.)

Brogan, D. W. *The Price of Revolution* (New York: Harper, 1951).

Burke, John P., Lawrence Crocker, and Lyman H. Legters (eds.). *Marxism and the Good Society* (Cambridge: Cambridge University Press, 1981).

Camboni, Gianfranco, and Danilo Samsa. *PCI e movimento degli studenti (1968–1973): ceti medi e strategie delle riforme* (Bari: DeDonato, 1975).

Camus, Albert. *The Rebel: An Essay on Man in Revolt* (New York: Vintage, 1956).

Cantimori, Delio. *Utopisti e riformatori italiani: 1794–1847* (Florence: Sansoni, 1943).

——— (ed.). *Giacobini italiani* (Bari: Laterza, 1956).

Carlen, Claudia. *The Papal Encyclicals 1958–1981* (New York: McGrath, 1981).

Carnelutti, Francesco. *Tempo perso* (Bologna: Zuffi, 1952).

Castellano, Lucio (ed). *Autonomia operaia: la storia ed i documenti da Potere operaio all' autonomia organizzata* (Milan: Savelli, 1980).

Catelli, Giampaolo (ed). *La società marginale: contadini, sottoproletariato ed emarginati come società negativa* (Rome: Città Nuova, 1976).

Cavaglion, Alberto. *Otto Weininger in Italia* (Rome: Carucci, 1982).

Cavallini, Massimo. *Il terrorismo in fabbrica* (Rome: Riuniti, 1978).

Cecchi, Alberto. *Storia della P2* (Rome: Riuniti, 1985).

Ceolin, Carlo (ed.). *Università, cultura, terrorismo* (Milan: Franco Angeli, 1984).

Cerbone, Carlo (ed.). *L'antiparlamentarismo (1870–1919)* (Rome: Volpe, 1972).

Che fare (journal).

Chesnais, Jean-Claude. *Histoire de la violence en occident de 1800 à nos jours* (Paris: Editions Robert Laffont, 1981).

Chiarini, Roberto, and Paolo Corsini. *Da Salò a piazza della Loggia: blocco d'ordine, neo-fascismo, radicalismo di destra a Brescia (1945–1974)* (Milan: Angeli, 1983).

CIA. *The Pike Report* (Nottingham: Spokesman Books, 1977).

Classe (journal).

Classe operaia (journal).

Coi, Andrea, et al. *Politica e rivoluzione* (Milan: Giuseppe Mai Ed., 1983).

Collettivo prigionieri comunisti delle Brigate Rosse. "L'ape e il comunista: elementi per la critica marxista dell 'economia politica e per la costruzione del programma di transizione al comunismo," *Corrispondenza internazionale*, October–December 1980, no. 16/17.

Collin, Richard. *The De Lorenzo Gambit: The Italian Coup Manqué of 1964* (Beverly Hills: Sage, 1976).

Comitati autonomi operai di Roma (eds.). *Autonomia operaia* (Rome: Savelli, 1976).

Il conciliatore (journal).

Il contemporaneo (journal).

Controinformazione (journal).

Contropiano (journal).

Coppola, Aniello. *Moro* (Milan: Feltrinelli, 1976).

Corriere della sera (newspaper, Milan).

Corsini, Paolo, and Laura Novati (eds.). *L'eversione nera: cronache di un decennio (1974–1984)* (Milan: Angeli, 1985).

Cortese, Luisa (ed.) *Il movimento studentesco: storia e documenti (1968–1973)* (Milan: Bompiani, 1973).

Critica marxista (journal).

Cronache dei quaderni rossi (journal).

Crossman, Richard (ed.). *The God That Failed* (New York: Harper, 1950).

Crouch, Colin, and Alessandro Pizzorno (eds.). *The Resurgence of Class Conflict in Western Europe since 1968* (New York: Holmes and Meier, 1978).

Curcio, Renato. *Wkhy* (Rome: Fatamorgana, 1984).

——— and Alberto Franceschini. *Gocce di sole nella città degli spettri* (Rome: Corrispondenza Internazionale, 1982).

——— and Mauro Rostagno. *Fuori dai denti* (Milan: Gammalibri, 1980).

Dalla Chiesa, Nando. "Del sessantotto e del terrorismo: cultura e politica tra continuità e rottura," *Il Mulino* (January–February 1981).

Deakin, F. W. *The Brutal Friendship: Mussolini, Hitler, and the Fall of Fascism* (London: Weidenfeld and Nicolson, 1962).

De Felice, Renzo. *Mussolini il duce II: lo stato totalitario (1936–1940)* (Turin: Einaudi, 1972).

———. *Storia degli ebrei italiani sotto il fascismo* (Turin: Einaudi, 1972).

Del Boca, Angelo, and Mario Giovana. *Fascism Today: A World Survey* (New York: Pantheon, 1969).

Della Mea, Luciano. *Eppure si muove: rendiconto politico di un proletario rivoluzionario* (Milan: Jaca, 1970).

———. *La politica torna in fabbrica* (Milan: Jaca, 1973).

Della Porta, Donatella (ed.). *Terrorismi in Italia* (Bologna: Il Mulino, 1984).

Della Porta, Donatella, and Maurizio Rossi. "I terrorismi in Italia tra il 1969 e il 1982," *Cattaneo*, 1 March 1983.

De Lutiis, Giuseppe (ed.). *Attacco allo stato* (Rome: Napoleon, 1982).

———. *La strage: l'atto d'accusa dei giudici di Bologna* (Rome: Riuniti, 1986).

De Simone, Cesare. *La pista nera* (Rome: Riuniti, 1972).

La Destra (journal).

De Turris, Gianfranco (ed.). *Omaggio a Julius Evola* (Rome: Volpe, 1973).

———. *Testimonianze su Evola* (Rome: Edizioni Mediterranee, 1973).

Di Bella, Franco. *Corriere segreto* (Milan: Rizzoli, 1982).

Di Palma, Giuseppe. *Surviving without Governing: The Italian Parties in Parliament* (Berkeley: University of California Press, 1977).

Di Scala, Spencer. *Dilemmas of Italian Socialism: The Politics of Filippo Turati* (Amherst: University of Massachusetts Press, 1980).

Dizionario biografico degli italiani (Rome: Istituto della Enciclopedia Italiana, various dates).

Dolci, Danilo. *Report from Palermo* (New York: Viking, 1959).

———. *Sicilian Lives* (New York: Pantheon, 1981).

Dostoyevski, Fyodor. *The Possessed* (New York: Modern Library, 1936).

Drake, Richard. *Byzantium for Rome: The Politics of Nostalgia in Umbertian Italy (1878–1900)* (Chapel Hill: University of North Carolina Press, 1980).

Eco, Umberto. "Non soltanto il 7 aprile," *Alfabeta*, May 1983.

Eisenberg, Dennis. *L'internazionale nera: fascisti e nazisti oggi nel mondo* (Milan: Sugar, 1964).

L'Espresso (magazine).

Evola, Julius. "Americanismo e Bolscevismo," *Nuova Antologia*, no. 1371, 1929.

———. *L'arco e la clava* (Milan: Scheiwiller, 1968).

———. "Autodifesa," *Quaderni di testi Evoliani*, no. 2 (Rome: Fondazione Julius Evola, n.d.)

———. *Il cammino del cinabro* (Milan: Vanni Scheiwiller, 1972).

———. *Cavalcare la tigre* (Milan: Vanni Scheiwiller, 1961).

———. *Il fascismo: saggio di una analisi critica dal punto di vista della destra* (Rome: Volpe, 1970).

———. *Fenomenologia dell' individuo assoluto* (Rome: Edizioni Mediterranee, 1974 ed.)

———. *Imperialismo pagano: il fascismo dinnanzi al pericolo euro-cristiano* (Rome/Todi: Edizioni Atanor, 1928).

———. *L'individuo e il divenire del mondo* (Carmagnola: Arthos, 1976 ed.)

———. Introduzione, *La guerra occulta: armi e fasi dell' attacco ebraico-massonico alla tradizione europea*, by Emanuele Malinsky and Léon De Poncins (Milan: Hoepli, 1939).

———. Introduzione, *I "Protocolli" dei "Savi Anziani" di Sion* (Rome: La Vita Italiana, 1938).

———. *Maschera e volto dello spiritualismo contemporaneo: analisi critica delle principali correnti moderne verso il "sovrasensibile"* (Bari: Laterza, 1949).

———. *Metafisica del sesso* (Rome: Atanor, 1958).

———. *Il mistero del Graal e la tradizione ghibellina dell' impero* (Bari: Laterza, 1937).

———. *L' "Operaio" nel pensiero di Ernst Jünger* (Rome: Volpe, 1974 ed.)

———. *Orientamenti* (Rome: Libreria Editrice Europea, 1950).

———. *Raâga blanda (1916–1922)* (Milan: Vanni Scheiwiller, 1969 ed.)

———. "René Guénon" (pamphlet), ed. Aldo Perez (Rome: Le Arti Grafiche del Grosso, 1979).

———. *Ricognizioni: uomini e problemi* (Rome: Edizioni Mediterranee, 1974).

———. *La rivolta contro il mondo moderno* (Rome: Edizioni Mediterranee, 1969 ed.)

———. *Saggi di dottrina politica: crestomazia di saggi politici raccolti e curati da Renato del Ponte* (Sanremo: Edizioni Casabianca, 1979).

———. *Sintesi di dottrina della razza* (Padua: Edizioni di Ar, 1978).

———. *Teoria dell' individuo assoluto* (Rome: Edizioni Mediterranee, 1973 ed.)

———. *La torre* (Milan: Società Ed. Il Falco, 1977).

———. *Tre aspetti del problema ebraico* (Rome: Edizioni Mediterranee, 1936).

———. *Ultimi scritti* (Naples: Controcorrente, 1977).

———. *Gli uomini e le rovine* (Rome: Edizioni dell' Ascia, 1953).

Fanon, Frantz. *The Wretched of the Earth* (New York: Grove Press, 1963).

Fanti, Liano. *S'avanza uno strano soldato: genesi del brigatismo rosso reggiano* (Milan: Sugar, 1985).

Faré Ida, and Franca Spirito. *Mara e le altre: le donne e la lotta armata (storia, interviste, riflessioni)* (Milan: Feltrinelli, 1979).

Ferraresi, Franco (ed.) *La destra radicale* (Milan: Feltrinelli, 1984).

Ferrarotti, Franco. *Alle radici della violenza* (Milan: Rizzoli, 1979).

———. *L'ipnosi della violenza* (Milan: Rizzoli, 1980).

———. Introduction to "On Violence: Paradoxes and Antinomies," *Social Research*, vol. 48, no. 1, 1981.

Flamini, Gianni. *Il partito del golpe: le strategie della tensione e del terrore dal primo centrosinistra organico al sequestro Moro*, vol. 1, 1964–1968, vol. 2, 1968–1970 (Ferrara: Italo Bovolenta, 1981–82).

Foglio di lotta di sinistra proletaria (journal).

Foucault, Michel. *The Archaeology of Knowledge*, trans. A. M. Sheridan Smith (New York: Pantheon, 1972).

Fraser, John. *An Introduction to the Thought of Galvano Della Volpe* (London: Lawrence and Wisehart, 1977).

Freda, Franco (Giorgio). *La disintegrazione del sistema* (Padua: Edizioni di Ar, 1980 ed.)

Gaddi, Giuseppe. *Neofascismo in Europa* (Milan: La Pietra, 1974).

Galleni, Mauro (ed.) *Rapporto sul terrorismo: le stragi, gli agguati, i sequestri, le sigle 1969–1980* (Milan: Rizzoli, 1981).

Galli, Giorgio. *La crisi italiana e la destra internazionale* (Italy: Mondadori, 1974).

———. *L'Italia sotterranea: storia, politica e scandali* (Rome-Bari: Laterza, 1983).

———. *Storia del partito armato: 1968–1982* (Milan: Rizzoli, 1986).

———, and Paolo Facchi. *La sinistra democristiana: storia e ideologia* (Milan: Feltrinelli, 1962).

Garone, Alessandro Galante. *Filippo Buonarroti e i rivoluzionari dell' Ottocento: 1828–1837* (Turin: Einaudi, 1951).

Gaucher, Francois. *Il fascismo ed il mondo di oggi*, trans. Adriano Romualdi (Rome: Volpe, 1966).

Gazzetta del popolo (newspaper).

Genova, Rino. *Missione antiterrorismo* (Milan: Sugar, 1985).

Gente (magazine).

Il Giorno (newspaper).

Giovane Critica (journal).

Gorrieri, Ermanno. *La giungla retributiva* (Bologna: Il Mulino, 1972).

Gramsci, Antonio. *The Modern Prince and Other Writings*, trans. Louis Marks (New York: International Publishers, 1957).

Graziani, Clemente. *La guerra rivoluzionaria* (Rome: Quaderni di Ordine Nuovo, 1963).

———. *Processo a Ordine Nuovo, processo alle idee* (Rome: Ordine Nuovo, 1973).

Graziano, L., and S. Tarrow (eds.). *La crisi italiana*, 2 vols. (Turin: Einaudi, 1979).

Gregor, A. James. *The Ideology of Fascism: The Rationale of Totalitarianism* (New York: Free Press, 1969).

Guénon, René. *La crisi del mondo moderno*, trans. Julius Evola (Rome: Edizioni Mediteranee, 1972).

Günther, Hans F. K. *Religiosità indoeuropea*, trans. Adriano Romualdi and Carlo Minutoli (Padua: Edizioni di Ar, 1970).

Guzzanti, Paolo. *Il Neofascismo e le sue organizzazioni paramilitari* (Rome: Seti, 1972).

Hamilton, Alastair. *The Appeal of Fascism: A Study of Intellectuals and Fascism, 1919–1945* (New York: Macmillan, 1971).

Heliodromos (journal).

Hitler, Adolf. *La battaglia di Berlino*, ed. Adriano Romualdi (Padua: Edizioni di Ar, n.d.).

Hobsbawm, E. J. *Revolutionaries: Contemporary Essays* (New York: Pantheon, 1973).

Hoffer, Eric. *The True Believer* (New York: Harper, 1951).

The Italian Communists: Foreign Bulletin of the PCI (journal).

L'Italiano (journal).

Jesi, Furio. *Cultura di destra* (Milan: Garzanti, 1979).
Johnson, Chalmers. *Revolution and the Social System* (Stanford: Hoover Institution Press, 1964).
————. *Revolutionary Change* (Stanford: Stanford University Press, 1982).
Katz, Robert. *Days of Wrath: The Ordeal of Aldo Moro* (Garden City: Doubleday, 1980).
Kissinger, Henry. *White House Years* (Boston: Little, Brown, 1979).
Kogan, Norman. *A Political History of Italy: The Postwar Years* (New York: Praeger, 1983).
Kramer, Jane. *Unsettling Europe* (New York: Random House, 1980).
Lami, Gian Franco. *Introduzione a Evola* (Rome: Volpe, 1980).
Lange, Peter, and Sidney Tarrow (eds.). *Italy in Transition: Conflict and Consensus* (London: Frank Cass, 1980).
La Palombara, Joseph. *Democracy Italian Style* (New Haven: Yale University Press, 1987).
Laqueur, Walter. *Terrorism: A Study of National and International Political Violence* (Boston: Little, Brown, 1977).
———— (ed.) *The Terrorism Reader: A Historical Anthology* (New York: Meridian, 1978).
Lavoro politico (journal).
Lazagna, G. B., et al. *Antifascismo e partito armato* (Genoa: Angelo Ghiron, 1979).
Ledeen, Michael A. *Italy in Crisis* (Beverly Hills: Sage, 1977).
Lenin, V. I. *The Proletarian Revolution and Renegade Kautsky* (New York: International Publishers, 1934 ed.)
————. *State and Revolution* (New York: International Publishers, 1968).
Lettere dei Quaderni Rossi (journal)
Levi, Fabio, Umberto Levra, and Nicola Tranfaglia (eds.). *Storia d'Italia* (Florence: La Nuova Italia, 1978).
Libertini, Lucio. *La sinistra e il controllo operaio* (Milan: Feltrinelli, 1969).
Lotta continua (newspaper).
Lupetti, Fausto, et al. *La polemica Vittorini-Togliatti e la linea culturale del PCI nel 1945–1947: testi con interventi e studi* (Milan: Lavoro Liberato, 1974).
Mack Smith, Denis. *Mussolini's Roman Empire* (New York: Viking, 1976).
Maffi, Mario. *Le origini della sinistra extraparlamentare* (Milan: Mondadori, 1976).
Malraux, Andrè. *Man's Fate* (New York: Random House, 1968).
Mammarella, Giuseppe. *L'Italia dopo il fascismo: 1943–1973* (Bologna: Il Mulino, 1974).
Mancini, Sandro. *Socialismo e democrazia diretta: introduzione a Raniero Panzieri* (Bari: Dedalo, 1977).
Manconi, Luigi, and Vittorio Dini. *Il discorso delle armi: l'ideologia terroristica nel linguaggio delle Brigate Rosse e di Prima Linea* (Milan: Savelli, 1981).
Il Manifesto (newspaper).
Il Manifesto (ed.). *Da Togliatti alla nuova sinistra* (Rome: Alfani, 1976).
Mannheim, Karl. *Essays on the Sociology of Culture* (London: Routledge, 1956).
————. *Ideology and Utopia: An Introduction to the Sociology of Knowledge* (New York: Harcourt, Brace and World, 1936).
Manzini, Giorgio. *Indagine su un brigatista rosso: la storia di Walter Alasia* (Turin: Einaudi, 1978).
Marcuse, Herbert. *One-Dimensional Man* (Boston: Beacon, 1964).
Marx, Karl. *The Civil War in France: The Paris Commune* (New York: International Publishers, 1968).
Massari, Roberto. *Marxismo e critica del terrorismo* (Rome: Newton Compton, 1979).
Il Mattino di Padova (newspaper).
Mazzetti, Roberto. *Genesi e sviluppo del terrorismo in Italia: il maggio troppo lungo* (Rome: Armando, 1979).
Merkl, Peter H. (ed.). *Political Violence and Terror: Motifs and Motivations* (Berkeley: University of California Press, 1986).
Merleau-Ponty, Maurice. *Humanism and Terror: An Essay on the Communist Problem*, trans. John O'Neill (Boston: Beacon, 1969).

Merli, Stefano. *L'altra storia: Bosio, Montaldi e le origini della nuova sinistra* (Milan: Feltrinelli, 1977).

———. *Fronte antifascista e politica di classe: socialisti e comunisti in Italia (1923–1939)* (Beri: De Donato, 1975).

———. "La provocazione di Raniero Panzieri," *Il Manifesto*, 20 October 1974.

Il messaggero (newspaper).

Metropoli: l'autonomia possibile (journal).

Monicelli, Mino. *L'ultrasinistra in Italia, 1968–1978* (Rome-Bari: Laterza, 1978).

Montanelli, Indro. "Italians Have Lost All Faith in Democracy," *New York Times*, 21 April 1978.

Morandi e la democrazia del socialismo: problemi dell'autonomia e dell'unità nel dibattito della sinistra italiana. (Venice: Marsilio, 1978).

Morandi, Rodolfo. *Opere di Rodolfo Morandi*, 6 vol. (Turin: Einaudi, 1958–60).

Moravia, Alberto. "Quel moralismo armato che non esita a uccidere," *Corriere della sera*, 6 November 1977.

———. *Time of Desecration [La vita interiore]*, trans. Angus Davidson (New York: Farrar, Straus & Giroux, 1980).

———. "Un terrorismo vecchio da secoli," *Corriere della sera*, 13 November 1977.

Moro, Aldo. *L'intelligenza e gli avvenimenti: testi 1959–1978* (Italy: Garzanti, 1979).

Mughini, Giampiero (ed.). *Il revisionismo socialista: antologia di testi 1955–1962* (Rome: Nuova serie di Quaderni di Mondo operaio, 1975).

Murgia, Pier Giuseppe. *Ritorneremo!: storia e cronaca del fascismo dopo la Resistenza (1950–1953)* (Milan, Sugar, 1976).

Mussi, R. "Chi è responsabile della violenza politica: intervista a Giorgio Amendola," *Rinascita*, 7 April 1978.

Negri, Antonio. *Alcune riflessioni sullo "stato dei partiti"* (Padua: Tipografia Poligrafica Moderna, 1963).

———. *Crisi dello stato-piano comunismo e organizzazione revoluzionaria* (Florence: CLUSF, 1972).

———. *Il dominio e il sabotaggio: sul metodo marxista della trasformazione sociale* (Milan: Feltrinelli, 1978).

———. *La fabbrica della strategia: 33 lezioni su Lenin* (Padua: CLEUP, 1976).

———. *Marx oltre Marx: quaderno di lavoro sui Grundrisse* (Milan: Feltrinelli, 1979).

———. "Il memoriale difensivo di Toni Negri," I–II, *Lotta continua*, 19–21, January 1980.

———. *Dall' operaio massa all' operaio sociale: intervista sull' operaismo*, ed. Paolo Pozzi and Roberta Tommasini (Milan: Multhipia, 1979).

———. *Pipe-line: lettere da Rebibbia* (Turin: Einaudi, 1983).

———. *Proletari e stato: per una discussione su autonomia operaia e compromesso storico* (Milan: Feltrinelli, 1976).

———, et al. "Do You Remember Revolution? Proposta di lettura storico-politica per il movimento degli anni Settanta," *Il Manifesto*, 20–22, February 1983.

"Negri's Interrogation" in "Italy: Autonomia (Post-Political Politics)," *Semiotext(e)*, vol. 3, no. 3, 1980.

Nenni, Pietro. *Gli anni del centro sinistra: diari 1957–1966* (Turin: Sugar, 1982).

———. *Tempo di guerra fredda: diari 1943–1956*, ed. Guiliana Nenni and Domenico Zucaro (Milan: Sugar, 1981).

Neue Frankfurter Zeitung (newspaper).

New York Times (newspaper).

Nietzsche, Friedrich. *Beyond Good and Evil: Prelude to a Philosophy of the Future* (Middlesex: Penguin, 1973).

Noi Europa (journal).

Notarnicola, Sante. *L'evasione impossibile* (Milan: Feltrinelli, 1972).

Oliva, Carlo, and Aloisio Rendi. *Il movimento studentesco e le sue lotte* (Milan: Feltrinelli, 1969).

Ombre rosse (journal).

Ordine Nuovo (journal, Rome).

Orlando, Federico. *P 38 il medioevo di una nazione drogata dalle ideologie e nel baratro della crisi* (Milan: Editoriale Nuova, 1978).

————. *Siamo in guerra: documenti per la storia dell' Italia d' oggi* (Rome: Armando, 1980).

Pansa, Giampaolo. *Borghese mi ha detto* (Milan: Palazzi, 1971).

————. *Ottobre addio: viaggio fra i comunisti italiani* (Milan: Mondadori, 1982).

————. *Storie italiane di violenza e terrorismo* (Rome-Bari: Laterza, 1980).

Panzieri, Raniero. *L'alternativa socialista: scritti scelti 1944–1956*, ed. Stefano Merli (Turin: Einaudi, 1982).

————. *La crisi del movimento operaio: scritti, interventi, lettere (1956–1960)*, ed. Dario Lanzardo and Giovanni Pirelli (Milan: Lampugnani Nigri, 1973).

————. *Lotte operaie nello sviluppo capitalistico*, ed. Sandro Mancini (Turin: Einaudi, 1976).

————. *La ripresa del marxismo leninismo in Italia*, ed. Dario Lanzardo (Milan-Rome: Sapere, 1975).

Papa, Emilio R. *Il processo alle Brigate rosse (Torino, 17 maggio 1976–23 giugno 1978)* (Turin: G. Giappichelli Editore, 1979).

Pasolini, Pier Paolo. "Gli italiani non sono più quelli," *Corriere della sera*, 10 June 1974.

Pasquino, Gianfranco (ed.). *La prova delle armi* (Bologna: Il Mulino, 1984).

Peci, Patrizio. *Io l'infame*, ed. Giordano Bruno Guerri (Milan: Mondadori, 1983).

Pedió, Tommaso. *Giacobini e Sanfedisti in Italia Meridionale*, 2 vols. (Bari: Adriatica Editrice, 1974).

Pesce, Giovanni. *Senza tregua: la guerra dei Gap* (Milan: Feltrinelli, 1967).

Piazzesi, Gianfranco. *Gelli: la carriera di un eroe di questa Italia* (Italy: Garzanti, 1983).

Pini, Giorgio, and Duilio Susmel. *Mussolini: l'uomo e l'opera* (Florence: La Fenice, 1958).

Pisanò, Giorgio. *Mussolini e gli ebrei* (Milan: FPE, 1967).

Pisano, Vittorfranco S. *Contemporary Italian Terrorism* (Washington, D. C.: Library of Congress, 1979).

Politica comunista (journal).

Potere operaio (journal).

Preprint: L'autonomia possibile (journal).

Progresso Veneto (newspaper).

Pugno, Emilio, and Sergio Garavini. *Gli anni duri alla Fiat: la resistenza sindacale e la ripresa* (Turin: Einaudi, 1974).

Il punto (journal).

Quaderni piacentini (journal).

Quaderni rossi (journal).

Quaderni rossi—cronache operaie (journal).

Rauti, Pino. "Evola una guida per domani," *Civiltà: rivista di dottrina politica e di cultura* (special number dedicated to Julius Evola), September–December 1974.

————. *Le idee che mossero il mondo* (Rome: Centro Editoriale Nazionale, 1965).

————. *L'immane conflitto* (Rome: Centro Editoriale Nazionale, 1965).

————. *Storia d'Italia nei discorsi di Mussolini: 1915–1945*, 2 vols. (Rome: Centro Editoriale Nazionale, 1965).

Rendiconti (journal).

La Repubblica (newspaper, Rome).

Rieser, Vittorio. "Due inediti di Raniero Panzieri," *Quaderni piacentini*, no. 29, January 1967.

————. "Panzieri e i Quaderni rossi," *Politica comunista*, no. 3, March 1975.

————. "I Quaderni rossi," *Rendiconti*, 10 March 1965.

Rinascita (journal).

Romeo, Rosario, and George Urban. "Troubled Italy," *New York Times*, 2 January 1978.

Romualdi, Adriano. *Correnti politiche ed ideologiche della destra tedesca dal 1918 al 1932* (Italy: L'Italiano-Edizioni, 1981).

————. *Julius Evola: l'uomo e l'opera* (Rome: Volpe, 1971).

————. *Nietzsche* (Padua: Edizioni di Ar, n.d.).

————. *Platone* (Rome: Volpe, 1965).

————. *Le ultime ore dell' Europa* (Rome: Ciarrapico, 1976).

————. (ed.). *Drieu La Rochelle: il mito dell' Europa* (Rome: Edizioni del Solstizio, 1965).

Romualdi, Pino (ed.). *Ricordo di Adriano (fuori commercio)* (Cassino: Saipem, June 1974).

Ronchey, Alberto. *Accade in Italia: 1968–1977* (Milan: Garzanti, 1977).

————. *Atlante ideologico: programmi e utopie degli anni settanta alla prova dei fatti* (Milan: Garzanti, 1973).

————. "Guns and Grey Matter: Terrorism in Italy," *Foreign Affairs*, Spring 1979.

————. *Libro bianco sull' ultima generazione: tra candore e terrore* (Milan: Garzanti, 1978).

————. "Terrorism in Italy: Between Red and Black." *Dissent*, Spring 1978.

Rosenbaum, Petra. *Il nuovo fascismo: da Salò ad Almirante. Storia del MSI* (Milan: Feltrinelli, 1975).

Rosso (journal).

Roth, Guenther, and Wolfgang Schluchter. *Max Weber's Vision of History: Ethics and Methods* (Berkeley: University of California Press, 1979).

Saitta, Armando. "Il Roberspierrismo di Filippo Buonarroti e le premesse dell' unità," *Belfagor*, 31 May 1955.

Salierno, Giulio. *Autobiografia di un picchiatore fascista* (Turin: Einaudi, 1976).

Sani, Giacomo. "Mass Constraints on Political Realignments: Perceptions of Anti-System Parties in Italy," *British Journal of Political Science*, vol. 6, pt. 1, January 1976.

Santarelli, Enzo. *Fascismo e neofascismo* (Rome: Riuniti, 1974).

Scarano, Mimmo, and Maurizio De Luca. *Il mandarino è marcio: terrorismo e cospirazione nel caso Moro* (Rome: Riuniti, 1985).

Sciascia, Leonardo. *L'affare Moro* (Palermo: Sellerio, 1978).

Scorti, Piero V. *Il delitto paga? L'affare Tobagi* (Milan: Sugar, 1985).

Semiotext(e) (journal).

7 Giorni Veneto (newspaper).

Sheehan, Thomas. "Italy behind the Ski Mask," *New York Review of Books*, 16 August 1979.

————. "Italy: Terror on the Right," *New York Review of Books*, 22 January 1981.

————. "Myth and Violence: The Fascism of Julius Evola and Alain de Benoist," *Social Research*, vol. 48, no. 1, Spring 1981.

Silj, Alessandro. *Brigate Rosse–Stato: lo scontro spettacolo nella regia della stampa quotidiana* (Florence: Vallecchi, 1978).

————. *Never Again without a Rifle: The Origins of Italian Terrorism*, trans. Salvatore Attanasio (New York: Karz, 1979).

Silone, Ignazio. *Bread and Wine* (New York: Harper, 1937).

Soccorso Rosso (eds.). *Brigate rosse: che cosa hanno fatto, che cosa hanno detto, che cosa se ne è detto* (Milan: Feltrinelli, 1976).

Soccorso Rosso Napoletano (eds.). *I NAP: storia dei nuclei armati proletari* (Milan: Collettivo Editoriale Libri Rossi, 1976).

Sorel, Georges. *Reflections on Violence* (New York: Collier, 1950).

Sossi, Mario. *Nella prigione delle Br* (Milan: Editoriale Nuova, 1979).

Spengler, Oswald, *Ombre sull' occidente*, ed. Adriano Romualdi (Rome: Volpe, 1973).

Spriano, Paolo. *Storia del partito comunista italiano*, 5 vols. (Turin: Einaudi, 1967–75).

Stajno, Corrado. *L'Italia nichilista: il caso di Marco Donat Cattin, la rivolta, il potere* (Milan: Mondadori, 1982).

La Stampa (newspaper).

Sterling, Claire. *The Terror Network: The Secret War of International Terrorism* (New York: Holt, Rinehart and Winston, 1981).

Tarchi, Marco (ed.) *Diorama: problemi dello spirito nell'etica fascista (Antologia della pagina speciale di "Regime fascista" diretta da Julius Evola)* (Rome: Ed. Europa, 1974).
Tedeschi, Mario. *Fascisti dopo Mussolini* (Rome: Arnia, 1950).
Teodori, Massimo. *P2: la controstoria* (Milan, Sugar, 1986).
———. *Storia delle nuove sinistre in Europa (1956–1976)* (Bologna: Il Mulino, 1976).
Terracini, Umberto. *Intervista sul comunismo difficile*, ed. Arturo Gismondi (Bari: Laterza, 1978).
Tessandori, Vincenzo. *Br Imputazione: banda armata (cronaca e documenti delle Brigate rosse)* (Milan: Garzanti, 1977).
Théolleyre, Jean-Marc. *Les Neo-Nazis* (Paris: Temps Actuels, 1982).
Thomas, Paul. *Karl Marx and the Anarchists* (London: Routledge & Kegan Paul, 1980).
Timerman, Jacobo. *Prisoner without a Name, Cell without a Number (New York: Knopf, 1981).
Tobagi, Walter. *Storia del movimento studentesco e dei marxisti-leninisti in Italia* (Milan: Sugar, 1970).
Tocqueville, Alexis de. *The Old Régime and the French Revolution* (Garden City: Doubleday, 1955).
Togliatti, Palmiro. *La politica di Salerno: Aprile–Dicembre 1944* (Rome: Riuniti, 1969).
Tronti, Mario. *Operai e capitale* (Turin: Einaudi, 1966).
———. *Il tempo della politica* (Rome: Riuniti, 1980).
Trotsky, Leon. *Terrorism and Communism: A Reply to Karl Kautsky* (Ann Arbor: University of Michigan Press, 1961).
Turone, Sergio. *Corrotti e corruttori dall' Unità d' Italia alla P2* (Bari: Laterza, 1984).
Ulam, Adam B. *The Bolsheviks: The Intellectual, Personal, and Political History of the Triumph of Communism in Russia* (Toronto: Collier, 1965).
L' Unità (newspaper).
Urban, Joan Barth. *Moscow and the Italian Communist Party: From Togliatti to Berlinguer* (Ithaca: Cornell University Press, 1986).
Vacca, Giuseppe. *Politica e teoria nel marxismo italiano: 1959–1969* (Bari: De Donato, 1972).
Vasale, Claudio. *Terrorismo e ideologia in Italia: metamorfosi della rivoluzione* (Rome: Armando Armando, 1980).
Ventura, Angelo. "Il problema storico del terrorismo italiano," *Rivista storica italiana*, March 1980, vol. 92, no. 1, pp. 125–151.
———. "La responsabilità degli intellettuali e le radici culturali del terrorismo di sinistra," in Ceolin, Carlo (ed.), *Università, cultura, terrorismo* (Milan, Franco Angeli, 1984), pp. 43ff.
Vettori, Guiseppe (ed.) *La sinistra extraparlamentare in Italia* (Rome: Newton Compton, 1974).
Violi, Patrizia. *I giornali dell' estrema sinistra* (Milan: Garzanti, 1977).
Wagner-Pacifici, Robin Erica. *The Moro Morality Play: Terrorism as Social Drama* (Chicago: University of Chicago Press, 1986).
Weber, Eugen. *The Western Tradition* (Lexington, Mass.: Heath, 1972).
Weber, Max. *The Protestant Ethic and the Spirit of Capitalism* (New York: Scribner, 1958).
Weinberg, Leonard B. *After Mussolini: Italian Neofascism and the Nature of Fascism* (Washington, D. C.: University Press of America, 1979).
———, and William Lee Eubank. *The Rise and Fall of Italian Terrorism* (Boulder: Westview Press, 1987).
West, Morris. "Terror as an Historical Inheritance," *Esquire*, 25 April 1978.
Wilkinson, Paul. *The New Fascists* (London: Pan Books, 1983).
———. *Terrorism and the Liberal State* (London: Macmillan, 1977; rev. ed. 1986).
Zupo, Giuseppe, and Vincenzo Marini Recchia. *Operazione Moro: i fili ancora coperti di una trama politica criminale* (Milan: Angeli, 1984).

Index

RICHARD DRAKE is the Lucile Speer Research Professor in Politics and History at the University of Montana. His other book publications are *Byzantium for Rome: The Politics of Nostalgia in Umbertian Italy, 1878–1900* (1980), *The Aldo Moro Murder Case* (1995), *Apostles and Agitators: Italy's Marxist Revolutionary Tradition* (2003), *The Education of an Anti-Imperialist: Robert La Follette and U. S. Expansion* (2013), and *Charles Austin Beard: The Return of the Master Historian of American Imperialism* (2018).